When Display Becomes Art

# When Display Becomes Art

## Living in Exhibition Design

Mathilde Roman

HATJE
CANTZ

# Contents

**Interviews**

To Philippe Duboÿ (1942–2024),
for his generous passion for the work of Carlo Scarpa
and the Italian rationalists

# When Display Becomes Art

> "I am desperately in need of the bricks ... All we need is bricks, PLEASE."
>
> Barbara Hepworth, 1968

Mentioning exhibition design in the contemporary art world often elicits dismissive reactions and bursts of laughter. For many curators and artists, the design of the exhibition lies outside the scope of their specific creative practice and instead belongs to the world of history museums. Declarations such as "a good artist doesn't need an exhibition designer" or "a curator considers the hanging without the exhibition scenography" can still be heard here and there. They are revealing because they express a distrust of approaches to exhibition-making that place too much emphasis on concepts seen as preceding or taking precedence over the artistic act rather than emerging directly from it: the choice of supports for a work—the frame, the pedestal, the picture rail—the space that contains it—the room, the space, the floor, the ceiling—what renders it visible—the lighting, the atmosphere, or visitor itinerary. Yet to assert that display can itself constitute a work of art is to immediately challenge these reservations: first by recognizing exhibition design as an artistic act, one that is too often reduced to its technical aspects, and second, by including it in the creative process. The title of this book evokes the disruption that occurs when the technical elements of an exhibition become embodied within the artistic process and inseparable from the aesthetic experience, a phenomenon that encourages a broader rewriting of art history. *When Display Becomes Art* seeks to confront such hasty judgments and contribute to a wider revaluation of designing an exhibition as an artistic act, one that is informed both by the little-known history of exhibition design and by the practices of contemporary artists who are reappropriating its mechanisms and tools, thereby foregrounding its conceptual implications. The interviews that follow the historical introduction reveal the extent to which many artists have integrated exhibition design into their practice.

The vocabulary of exhibition design first emerged in the European art world in the 1920s. In France, the term *scénographie* referred both to the technical and conceptual arrangement of works within space and to the visitor's movement through an exhibition; the notion that scenography therefore shaped not only exhibition and museum practices but also the general philosophy of exhibitions. In the English-speaking world, the terms "display" and "exhibition design" were preferred, which established links with architecture and interior design. The term "scenography," meanwhile, is more closely associated with theater history, stage design, and the central, fixed viewpoint of the stage-audience relationship. These associations have contributed to the term being rejected by many artists, who fear its distancing effect and its tendency to overwhelm the polysemy of artworks. Institutions also bear responsibility for this unease, as demonstrated by the recent participation of Grace Ndiritu in the 17th edition of the Lyon Biennale, *Crossing the Water*.[1] She created a richly designed exhibition at the MAC Lyon contemporary art museum entitled *The Blue Room*, which was structured around works from public collections. Inspired by a modernist vocabulary as well as regular spiritual retreats, visions from her shamanic experiences, and sojourns at her grandmother's hut in Kenya, Grace Ndiritu develops work situated at the intersection of multiple disciplines and frequently incorporates living elements such as plants. In *The Blue Room*, the floor, walls, ceiling, and lighting all contributed to an exhibition design that invited visitors to expand their perspective, linger in the space, and combine an aesthetic experience with a spiritual journey. Visitors were asked to remove their shoes, immersing them in a colorful environment that conveyed a meditative energy and emphasized a visual shock meant to be felt directly by the body; the artist also urged visitors to sit, lie on the floor, close their220 eyes, and then reopen them. *The Blue Room* functioned as an exhibition display that was itself a work of art, attempting to resist the consumerist appropriation of art by offering an experience that unfolded over an extended duration. The traditional museum labels accompanying individual works were deliberately omitted in favor of emotional and sensory impact, although viewers could deepen the experience by reading a beautifully designed booklet. There was an introduction displayed beside the entrance to the exhibition, and the English version stated, "Exhibition curated and designed by the artist"; however, the French text read "Exposition conçue et réalisée par l'artiste" [Exhibition conceived and produced by the artist], which changed the meaning by significantly downplaying Grace Ndiritu's curatorial and

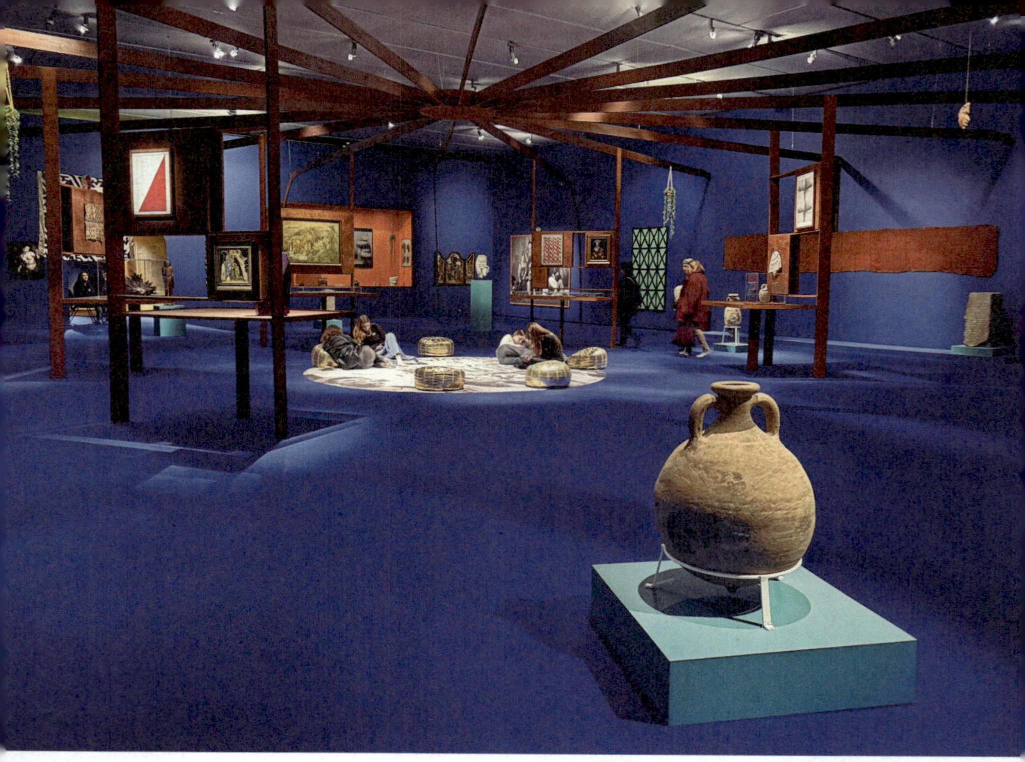

Fig. 1 *The Blue Room*, Grace Ndiritu, Lyon Biennale, Musée d'art contemporain, 2024

exhibition design work.[2] The errant translation, even if unintentional, contributed to a devaluation of this aspect of the work, which was too central to the overall project for such consequences not to have been considered. For several years now, I have been vigilant on this point while visiting galleries and museums, and have repeatedly encountered similar forms of disregard toward exhibition design, the artistic value of which remains largely unrecognized.

This was not always the case. When André Malraux republished *Le Musée Imaginaire* [Museum Without Walls] in 1965, he included a photograph of Carlo Scarpa's exhibition design for the Museo Correr in Venice on the first page of the introduction, opposite a painting depicting a salon-style hanging (*Archduke Leopold Wilhelm in his Painting Gallery in Brussels* by David Teniers the Younger, 1647). Although Malraux does not comment on Scarpa's exhibition design, this iconographic choice nevertheless testifies to the attention he paid to the contribution of modern notions of exhibition scenography to the history of museography. *The New Museum: Architecture and Display* by Michael Brawne, published by Praeger in 1965, catalogued modern museums built in different parts of the world and offered a valuable analysis of their exhibition-design ambitions on both a conceptual and technical level. During the 1960s, questions associated with exhibition display were rapidly incorporated into architectural history and permeated theoretical research; it is therefore surprising that more than seventy years later they continue to encounter such reluctance.

"Living in exhibition design" is a concept that draws its strength from the tension inherent in its impossibility: one cannot literally live in the design of an exhibition any more than one can truly live in the exhibition itself. The linking of these two terms serves to blur the semantic discord, encouraging artists to become an integral part of exhibition design and creating a place for the question of display in the history of exhibitions. The idea of display becoming art is the idea of an invitation to extend the perimeter of an artwork by including the technical and architectural aspects of its environment. The title of this book is also the legacy of *Live in your Head: When Attitudes Become Form*, a show curated by Harald Szeemann at the Kunsthalle Bern in 1969 which helped to broaden the vision of art. Since the beginning of the twentieth century, artists, architects, exhibition designers, historians, and philosophers have been encouraging museums to rethink their architecture, atmospheres, and visitor itineraries, all with the goal of reconfiguring interior spaces so they reflect bodies, emotions, and sensations, thereby transforming ways of seeing and perceiving while connecting exhibition spaces to broader histories of art and thought. This book is based on a genealogy of exhibition design and artistic practices drawn from the long history of museums and temporary exhibitions. It focuses on the years 1930 to 1960 and serves as a continuation of the first part of my research, which was published in French by Manuella Éditions in 2020: *Habiter l'exposition. L'artiste et la scénographie* [Living in Exhibition: The Artist and Exhibition Design]. Taking a historical perspective provides inspiration for thinking about contemporary productions, but also for engaging with them by reconnecting them to a still little-known part of art history. This research examines moments in which the picture rail, the plinth, the museum label, the visitor itinerary, and the lighting have been employed as tools for transformation, reappropriation, and, at times, emancipation—both of the museum and of aesthetic experience itself—by asserting their central role within exhibition design.

In 2022, Tacita Dean dedicated a large part of her exhibition at the Mudam (Luxembourg) to the works she created for the scenography of the ballet *The Dante Project* (choreography by Wayne McGregor and music by Thomas Adès for the Royal Ballet & Opera House in London). Presented without documentation or contextualization in relation to the ballet, these stage backdrops, which were created for each act using a different medium—drawing, photography, film—were displayed alone, thus achieving an aesthetic and conceptual impact that was enhanced because the exhibition setting afforded the opportunity for a more comprehensive viewing of them. Later, when I saw them again on stage at the Paris Opera,[3] the experience was completely different, with the works creating powerful and highly specific atmospheres for each act as they became inseparable from the choreography, the bodies of the dancers, the costumes designed by the artist, the lighting, and the musical score. During my visit to the Mudam with the exhibition curator, Christophe Gallois, I understood how important it was for Tacita Dean to detach her works from their status as scenography and thus affirm the fuller role they played in her own artistic journey, as they were merely one phase of an extended creative project. There is a long history of artists collaborating on set design or scenography for performances, one that dates back to the early twentieth century, so she was following in the footsteps of many other artists. However, by exhibiting her works in a disconnected manner, she affirmed their primary autonomy from the ballet scenography. Nevertheless, as I left the exhibition and absentmindedly read the exhibition credits on the wall, I was surprised to see that the artist was credited for the exhibition design in collaboration with Polaris Architects. Through the exhibition, the work lost its dimension as scenography, yet Tacita Dean nonetheless asserted that she had designed the exhibition, a practice often neglected by artists. While these were not works of traditional scenography, even though they were able to fulfill that function for the ballet, from the French perspective, the artist had still carried out the action of "scenographing" the exhibition, and the shift from the passive noun "scenography" to the active verb "scenographing" is significant. It is a question of naming an artistic dynamic whereby the design of the display contributes to the enhancement of the spatial and temporal aspect of the exhibition within the broader creative process, including considerations that have often been overlooked, such as the visitor's itinerary, lighting, seating, wall texts and museum labels, exhibition maps, and, of course, the picture rail in a larger sense. When creating an exhibition design, the artist sometimes consults with scenographers, and always works with production managers, technicians, and the entire on-site team in order to produce artistic elements in a format suitable for exhibition.

Since the beginning of the twentieth century, museums have attracted considerable criticism. One especially virulent example was that leveled by members of the Futurist movement, who notably rejected bourgeois archetypes arising from the cabinet of curiosities and the religious temple, which led to exhibition formats that distanced the viewer from the emotions aroused by the artistic experience and reinforced the notion that art should be disconnected from everyday life. However, as Pamela Bianchi points out in *The Origins of Exhibition Space*,[4] along with being displayed in curiosity cabinets, private collections in Venice and the Netherlands were also hung in corridors, staircases, and entrance halls, and the choice of paintings and sculptures was part of a scripted social journey for guests through the domestic space and served as a form of self-representation for the hosts. By placing art in conjunction with the specific uses of a space, the arrangements explored the idea of living with the exhibition and took into account the body of the observer. Pamela Bianchi quotes William Sanderson (1586–1676), who gave advice to his contemporaries on how to choose paintings to hang in the entrance hall or on the staircase, as "the grace of the Painting invites your guest to breathe, and stop at the ease-pease" before allowing them to continue onward to other states of aesthetic pleasure that will mark their progress through the home.[5] The description of the physical and emotional journey of works hung in different spaces of the collector's house broadens the cabinet-of-curiosities approach, revealing similarities between this historical context and a contemporary vision concerned with creating open relationships between works, bodies, and places that are permeable to the realities of everyday life. Museums have never stopped trying to reinvent themselves by reflecting on their role and status in society, their capacity to contextualize social upheavals, and, according to Michel Foucault's analysis, their ability to produce heterotopias linked to the accumulation of time as well as the accumulation of spaces and bodies.[6]

In a museum, we are multiple bodies, engaging with sixteenth-century artworks in a wholly different manner from contemporary environments and installations;[7] museums, however, have long forgotten they are dealing with human bodies and have given these bodies little consideration in the design of their spaces. As a repository of memory, the museum is first and foremost a place of refuge, a space designed to welcome and collect, preserve and research, but it is also supposed to accomplish a monumental and Sisyphean task of curation in the face of the immense volume of artistic production. Reflecting on this produces the same feelings of anxiety that assail the viewer when watching Alain Resnais's *All the Memory in the World* (1956). This film plays with the conventions of documentary filmmaking to present the work of the French national library, exposing its dystopian dimensions: the corridors, elevators, the aisles of shelves, and the acts of sorting, preserving, and consulting are imbued with an overwhelming sense of responsibility that evokes nightmares and prisons rather than the peaceful haven dedicated to study and knowledge. Also divided into sections and periods, the museum is a segmented space that can be traversed room by room, in a journey punctuated by passageways, corridors, stairways, and elevators. Its carefully controlled organization of spaces open to the public attempts to distract from the invisibility of the works kept in the darkness of the museum's storage rooms, some of which have not seen the light of day since their acquisition.

In *The Hidden Conference* (2023), Rosa Barba creates a dialogue between three installations that she filmed in the storage rooms of different museums: the Neue Nationalgalerie in Berlin, the Tate Modern in London, and the Musei Capitolini in Rome. The camera slips into the basements, pausing on works hung on racks or placed on shelves, regardless of whether they are immediately recognizable masterpieces or little-known paintings; these works become characters and the film becomes a receptacle for their conversations in the darkness of the storage rooms. The multiple viewpoints enabled by the projections and the complex editing, which integrates the museum architecture, create a contemplative, somewhat melancholic atmosphere, reinforced by the brutalist Tanks exhibition space within the Tate Modern (former oil storage tanks dating to when the building was a power station) where the film installation was presented in 2023. This work powerfully evokes the ambiguity of preservation, which renders the majority of conserved works invisible. The museum is a protective space, ensuring a constant temperature and moderate light, but these preventive conservation strategies also impose constraints that limit the movement of works and undermine atypical exhibition scenarios that are unable to ensure atmospheric stability. The intense summer heat, which is becoming more pronounced every year in Europe, further complicates exhibition projects outside major museums, despite the fact these spaces often have architectural qualities and decentralized locations that make them ideal venues for presenting art from the past.

Cyprien Gaillard's work[8] is permeated by a similar reflection on the conflicting desires to preserve artworks and preserve humanity, with the fates of both directly impacted by the permanent air conditioning used in museum spaces. In 2022, the artist was offered a major carte blanche exhibition at the Palais de Tokyo in Paris. He chose to create a dialogue between his own pieces and the works of historical figures. From the outset, he sought to include a painting by Giorgio de Chirico, but the display conditions imposed by the potential lenders were clearly not possible given the exposed architecture of the Palais de Tokyo, which regularly struggles with leaks and cannot guarantee a stable environment. For another work by Giorgio de Chirico, the 1928 charcoal drawing *Oreste e Pilade*, which depicts two human figures merging with architectural structures, Cyprien Gaillard devised his own solution. In collaboration with the technical teams at the Palais de Tokyo, he transformed a glass display case from the reserves of a Parisian museum into a customized display unit to exhibit the climate control equipment necessary for the proper conservation of the drawing. The display functions as a work of art by creating a potent ensemble that both provides the necessary quality of atmosphere and questions its necessity. The museum label ironically points out that the drawing had to be placed "on life support," referring both to the artist's conceptual and political gesture and to the work's very human fragility, as well as our inability to come to terms with this reality; we prefer to transform a drawing into a sculpture, and thus undermine its visual presence, rather

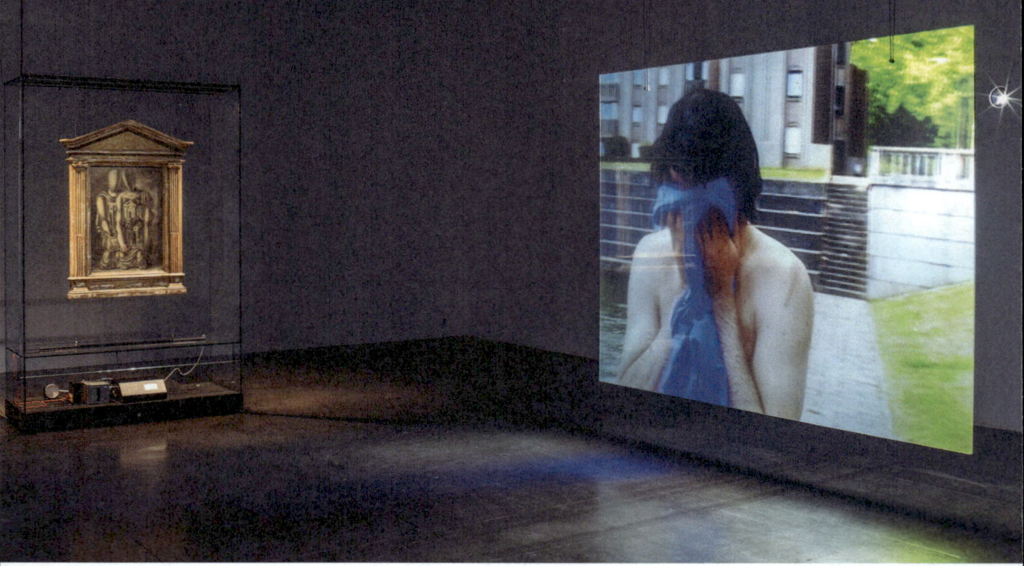

Fig. 2 *Oreste e Pilade*, Giorgio de Chirico, 1928, exhibition view *HUMPTY | DUMPTY*
Cyprien Gaillard, Palais de Tokyo, Paris, 2022

than expose it to an uncontrolled atmosphere. Museums are places of conservation that, due to increasingly demanding protective measures, also risk preventing the free circulation of the works in their collections. By inventing a specific device for the exhibition design, Cyprien Gaillard produced a visual effect with powerful narrative force.

This work by Cyprien Gaillard ironically evoked the question of the display case and the pedestal, two central elements of exhibition design conceived as tools for presenting and protecting works of art. Most often integrated into the aesthetics of the white cube, they reinforce the aura of the museum and contribute to distancing the work through a uniform visitor itinerary created by an overall exhibition design plan. However, many artists prefer to integrate pedestals and display cases into their work as a way to intimately link form and support. Constantin Brancusi's explorations into the relationships between the pedestal and the sculpture and the interplay of stacking and assembling different support materials continue to inform this approach, and the artist's process is still very visible today thanks to the preservation of his studio, which was bequeathed to the Centre Pompidou.[9] Brancusi devoted the last years of his life to completely rethinking and analyzing his sculptures as they existed in space. During this period, he no longer produced new pieces and created plaster casts of sculptures that had been sold. His work as an artist then focused on the arrangement of his works in relation to each other, on the creation of compositions, and on the observation of the effects of natural light. The wooden pedestals could become stools for guests, but they could also be combined with stone pedestals in stacks that did not seek any type of uniformity to hold a sculpture. In the photographs and films he made in his studio, Brancusi also interspersed tools and workbenches with sculptures, choreographing their presence. Far from the dominant viewpoint offered by museums, he revealed the full potential of using the design of the display to connect works with elements from a life devoted to art. When he sold a sculpture, he also sold the pedestal, which was often composed of several pieces and combined different materials. While the sculpture maintained its own unified identity that was clearly distinct from the vocabulary of the pedestal, the pedestal was treated as a sculptural element in its own right.

The pedestal has always been an important consideration for sculptors, whether they decide to include it in their work, as Germaine Richier did by treating it as a sculptural element, or to dispense with it altogether by placing the work directly on the floor, as Eva Hesse did.

Germaine Richier often extended human or animal figures with frames that connected them directly to the bronze or stone pedestal, such as with *La Mante, grande* (1946), where the pedestal accentuates the earthy strength of this insect-like woman. Germaine Richier also played with elements of the exhibition design, including for the work *Torse II (Torse de femme Muhlethaler)* from 1941, where the figure, suspended on metal frames, clung to a picture rail to avoid falling. This arrangement creates a fascinating narrative tension between the work and its display, in a dialogue that is often found in contemporary sculpture. Barbara Hepworth made this a subject of creative experimentation in the 1960s as she reflected on ways to reproduce the poignant relationships her sculptures had in gardens within the spaces provided by museums. In 1965, the Kröller-Müller Museum in the Netherlands dedicated a retrospective to her work, displaying her pieces in the pavilion designed by Gerrit Rietveld, which has a broad opening onto the garden. The pavilion was built with concrete blocks arranged to create a visual rhythm in the space that played with the full and empty spaces of the raw materials, thus creating a powerful environment for the artworks. Barbara Hepworth drew inspiration from this experience, as well as from Aldo van Eyck's sculpture pavilion for Sonsbeek Park (1966), also built with concrete blocks but left open to the landscape—a creation we will return to in the discussion with Berger&Berger—to conceptualize her retrospective at the Tate Gallery in 1968. She designed it in collaboration with the scenographer Michael Brawne, a professor and architect who was an important figure in the United Kingdom, and whose seminal book, *The New Museum: Architecture and Display*,[10] she had read. Eleanor Clayton[11] recounts the importance Barbara Hepworth attached to the creation of pedestals and how the artist strongly defended her choice to use bricks as a base for some of her sculptures, despite the difficulties this posed for the institution, going so far as to write in a letter to Michael Brawne: "I am desperately in need of the bricks ... All we need is bricks, PLEASE."[12] Barbara Hepworth thus created a striking display system that she would later reuse, which was not a reflection on the creation of the sculpture itself, but rather on the exhibition. She made another strong gesture in the exhibition design by asking for plants to be brought into the gallery in order to recreate a garden atmosphere, which she considered the ideal setting for her works.

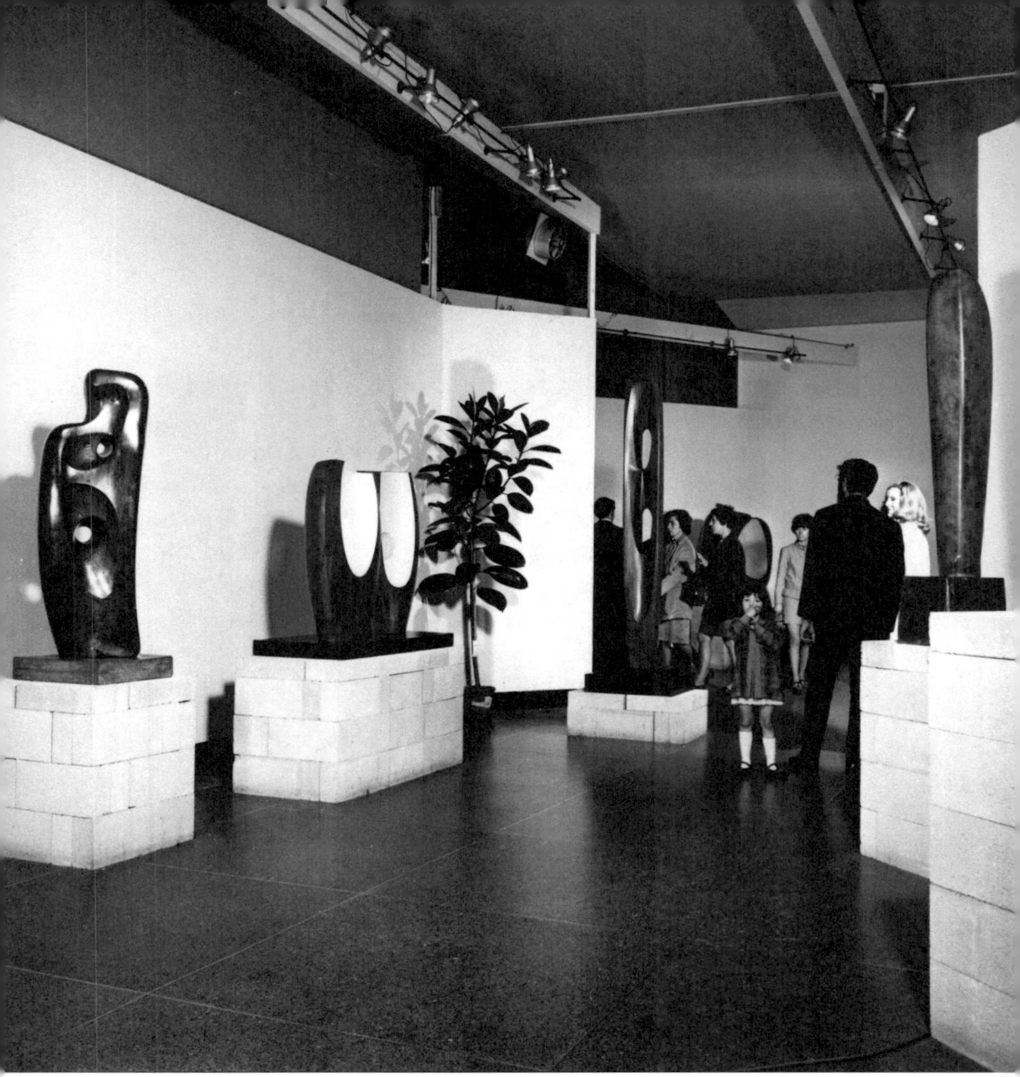

Fig. 3 *Barbara Hepworth*, Tate, Duveen Gallery, London, 1968

## A display, a display, a display![13]

> "Clifford was really clever at that slightly humorous analysis of people and motives which leaves everything in bits at the end. But it was rather like puppies tearing the sofa cushions to bits; except that it was not young and playful, but curiously old, and rather obstinately conceited. It was weird and it was nothing. This was the feeling that echoed and re-echoed at the bottom of Connie's soul: it was all flag, a wonderful display of nothingness; At the same time a display. A display! a display! a display!"[14]

In this excerpt from *Lady Chatterley's Lover*, D. H. Lawrence describes Lady Chatterley's husband as an intelligent and witty man, respected for his writings and his clever remarks in society, wielding language with skill and elegance. And yet all this seems futile in the eyes of his wife, amounting to nothing more than superficial effects and strategies for organizing emptiness, and above all, serving as a tool for domination by a man who is certainly physically diminished—having returned from the battlefield an invalid—but who remains entrenched in his position of superiority due to his status as a member of the English aristocracy. The phrase "A display, a display, a display!" is a cry of contempt thrown in the face of a social class locked in its prejudices, incapable of living in reality because it is entangled in structures of representation that dominate the world by keeping it at a distance. D. H. Lawrence uses the term "display" in its everyday sense, describing strategies of presentation and effects of staging, of which language, as a tool for orchestrating and manipulating reality, is an integral part. *Lady Chatterley's Lover* is a story of feminist emancipation, of the discovery and appropriation of desire, of the adventure of a blossoming romantic and sexual sensitivity that unfolds in the undergrowth, in the humidity, amid that which escapes and overflows. The display is positioned on the same side as the oppressive and frigid patriarchal system, participating in a heavy and futile organization of the world that keeps emotions at bay and that must be escaped. Lady Chatterley frees herself by embracing the intensity of the sensations coursing through her body as she walks in the forest, dances naked in a heavy rainstorm, and discovers the intensity of erotic exploration. This book on exhibition design will steadfastly examine the ideological tension of display by taking a step back from its effects of domination and questioning its mechanisms from the perspective of an art history informed by feminist methodology.

Although "display" is a common term in English, it has a specific meaning that cannot be translated into French, which explains its use in the field of art, even if its meaning is often rather vague. In his lecture "To display or not to display? That is the question,"[15] Chris Dercon pointed out that the term itself comes from the Latin *displicare*, meaning "to unfold, to spread out" (*aufliegen* in German). These translations clearly convey the idea of opening up, creating dialogues between the works and the space, but also of an expansion. Unfolding a work through display is also a way of stretching its meaning, of multiplying the way it echoes through our senses. As Emma Barker points out in the introduction of the book *Contemporary Cultures of Display*, "However, display itself is just as much an issue here as art. We can put this in focus by noting that display is a verb as well as a noun, active as well as passive: the point being that display is always produced by curators, designers, etc. As such, it is necessarily informed by definite aims and assumptions and evokes some larger meaning or deeper reality beyond the individual works in the display. In short, it is a form of representation as well as a mode of presentation."[16] Display thus describes a conceptual and technical act of exhibition that consists of placing an object or work in a space to make it visible, to make it accessible to the public while managing its effects on the experience. It is an undertaking that combines a theoretical and practical approach and requires an understanding of the aesthetic issues as well as the technical constraints and specificities of the works and spaces. In English, the term also has the advantage of being able to be broadened by combining it with other terms: "display narrative" thus expresses the idea of writing art history through hanging, as the curator Alexander Dorner did at the Landesmuseum in Hanover in the 1930s.[17]

## Machine Art

Inspired by his conversations with philosopher John Dewey, who published *Art as Experience* in 1934, as well as by his travels in Europe and visits to Bauhaus exhibitions, the architect Philip Johnson came to understand the impact of museography and exhibition design. Using what he learned, he embraced an exploration of the possibilities of display in 1934 at MoMA with the *Machine Art* exhibition that was dedicated to the aesthetic value of industrial materials. This project was also informed by Johnson's discussions with Alfred H. Barr Jr. (the founding director of MoMA), Henry-Russell Hitchcock (an architectural historian), and Alan R. Blackburn Jr. (executive director of MoMA). These conversations centered on the men's observations on societal changes that were setting aside traditional artisan work in favor of industrial production. *Machine Art* sought to showcase the aesthetic value of industrial objects, sharing the experience of their natural beauty by enhancing them with the display techniques of museography. The displays and lighting were meticulously designed, with the objects presented on pedestals or hung on the walls to emphasize their formal power. The molded walls and ceilings of the building that housed MoMA at the time were covered with white fabric. In one room, a false ceiling made of muslin fabric covered the lighting system, creating a powerful visual impression that enhanced the aesthetic impact of the industrial objects. The hanging reproduced the rhythm and repetition of mechanical movement, but by installing the objects in a state of rest and silence, it removed the pieces from the context of their functionality. Most of the objects chosen—propellers, springs, sets of pans, and glass utensils—were not conceived by designers, and their beauty was therefore unintentional, a product of the needs of the machine, which reinforced their ideological power. Alfred H. Barr's text in the exhibition catalogue highlights a quote from Plato on the absolute beauty of simple forms not related to representations of living beings, such as lines or circles, and suggests looking at industrial objects through this prism: as extensions of mathematical forms produced by the machine. A jury consisting of aviator Amelia Earhart and professors John Dewey and Charles R. Richards awarded prizes to three objects after visiting the exhibition, and the MoMA press release reflects the educational significance of the exhibition. The choice of Amelia Earhart, the first woman to fly solo non-stop across the Atlantic and a prominent figure at the time, shows how important it was to MoMA to reach an audience outside the art world. The aviator was quoted in the press release as saying: "I think the exhibition as a whole is a great step forward in that I believe people may see the beauty in a machine which so often we think of as only crude or lacking individuality, which isn't the case at all for anyone who has eyes to see."[18] Many of these objects were loaned by stores, and the list in the catalogue even mentions their provenance and retail price (starting at $1), allowing visitors to easily acquire the objects whose beauty they have come to appreciate. But without the aura of the white cube, do these objects retain their aesthetic value? Can the artistic dimension be separated from the scenography?

## an Exhibit

In 1957, the artists Richard Hamilton and Victor Pasmore and the critic Lawrence Alloway, who had formed the International Group and shared their creative research as part of their teaching at King's College (University of Durham), created *an Exhibit* in the university's Hatton Gallery, and then reproduced it at the Institute of Contemporary Arts (ICA) in London. This project explored the mechanisms of exhibition-making, focusing on certain principles of scenography. Richard Hamilton began his career by collaborating with Reimann Studios, a German design studio that moved to London in 1935 and was close to the Bauhaus spirit but with a more commercial approach. He then went on to make models and he continued to attach great importance to exhibition design in his work. In 1951 and 1955, he organized two important group exhibitions at the ICA, *Growth and Form* and *Man, Machine and Motion*, where the curatorial approach was combined with a highly specific exhibition design that incorporated the understanding that the challenge of an exhibition lay in the path the visitor took through it, as opposed to the static position of the reader or filmgoer. When Victor Pasmore visited *Man, Machine and Motion*, he was enchanted by the exhibition design but less so by the photographs on display, which documented human attempts to overcome their physical limitations by inventing machines to improve their ability to move around. He then suggested to Hamilton that they embrace a self-referential approach and create an exhibition where the design itself would be the work of art. They installed a plexiglass display in the space, which they presented in the invitation card in the following manner:

> "a game / an artwork / an environment
> pre-planned / individuated / verbalized
> by
> RICHARD HAMILTON / VICTOR PASMORE / LAWRENCE ALLOWAY to be
> played / viewed / populated"[19]

Richard Hamilton later recalled in a conversation with Hans Ulrich Obrist that this experimental design arrangement could be deployed in any space but it could not be constructed in advance with blueprints and elevations: "Once the first mark was made, by putting a plane in that space, it led to the consequence of placing a second plane, and so on. The whole thing had to develop organically."[20]

As Elena Crippa explains,[21] it was essential for the three artists to give an active role to the viewer in the post-war context of a British society dominated by trauma and deprivation as it sought to rebuild itself by affirming the capacity of each individual for agency. She also addresses Pasmore's approach and his way of thinking about the viewer within a common vision of art, design, and architecture, noting that "as early as 1951, Pasmore asserted that the work was an object that acted on and infected the viewer like nature." While teaching at the university in Newcastle upon Tyne, they used the Hatton Gallery as a place for experimentation. For his part, Richard Hamilton continued Marcel Duchamp's conceptual approach, giving a central place to the viewer and their position as an observer, as deployed in his project *The Large Glass*, also called *The Bride Stripped Bare by Her Bachelors, Even* (1915–23), which Hamilton studied by creating a diagram analyzing the mental and intellectual participation of the viewer that is brought into play by this work. Duchamp also paved the way for the artist's position as a "generator-arbiter," transforming the exhibition into an irreverent event with his "mile-of-string" installation that stretched highly intrusive threads throughout the space where the *First Papers of Surrealism* exhibition was organized by André Breton in New York in 1942. Duchamp had a strong influence on Hamilton, particularly on the *an Exhibit* project, which was constructed as a connection between plexiglass panels of different colors that were suspended in the gallery space to create a multiplicity of viewpoints, strata, and visual labyrinths without resorting to any pre-existing

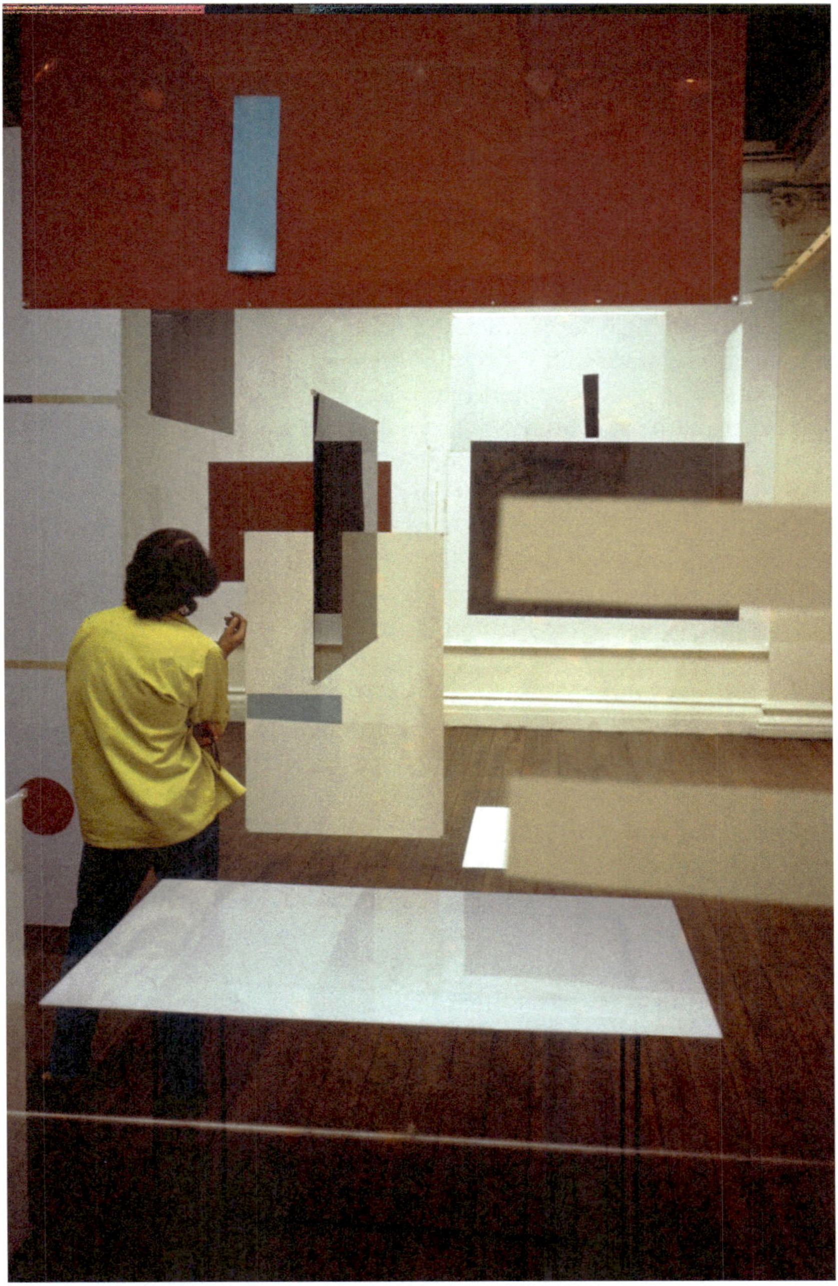

Fig. 4 *an Exhibit*, Richard Hamilton, Victor Pasmore, Lawrence Alloway, Hatton Gallery, Newcastle upon Tyne, 1957

work. The pictorial forms deployed by Pasmore within this installation served as a continuation of these effects without overwhelming them. The gallery visitors were also actively integrated into the installation as the bodies of people, whether static or moving, strongly impacted the aesthetic experience, and numerous exhibition views document this. Hamilton's drawings and paintings from the 1950s onwards reflect this interest in the movement of the gaze in space. The title, *an Exhibit*, evokes the construction of the exhibition and the inherent conventions and functions associated with these undertakings, all while questioning whether the exhibition could become autonomous from works of art or to truly expose its tools.

As Elena Crippa also points out, the years 1945 to 1955 saw numerous experiments in exhibition design for political or commercial propaganda purposes that highlighted the power of display and encouraged artists to question its perceptual and ideological mechanisms. While still a student, Richard Hamilton created exhibition models and worked on the installation and scenography of exhibitions at the ICA, developing an interest and expertise he would later apply to his own projects, such as the highly architectural metal installation *Man, Machine and Motion*. Partly suspended and partly placed on the floor, the installation played with reproductions, projections, and lighting effects while incorporating movements that break through the viewer's gaze. For this project, which was linked to his teaching, he gathered a wealth of resources on exhibition scenography, identifying experimental proposals from different countries in the context of commercial and industrial exhibitions and sharing them with students during screenings. He was thus highly knowledgeable about what design work had already been done in Germany, Italy, and the United States, and could both draw inspiration from these past projects and develop a critical analysis of their manipulative effects on perception.

The participatory aspect of *an Exhibit* attempted to remedy the overly prescriptive nature of conventional exhibitions, which developed strategies for telling stories without allowing the viewer to take an active part in them. An illustrated, fold-out poster-pamphlet available to visitors to the gallery explained the process behind the project, the ideas put forward by the authors, and the technical protocol for setting up the panels in accordance with a conceptual approach (without denying its aesthetic effects), with the actual exhibition just one possible activation among others. Viewers had different ways of participating, either by becoming players or by watching others take part in the game. The pamphlet features highly accomplished graphics and confidently states:

"Visitors are invited not to look for separate works of art or symbols, but to inhabit a real environment for the duration of the game. The meaning of *an Exhibit* now depends on the decisions of the visitor, just as, in a previous stage, it depended on the artists who were the players."[22] On the evening of the opening, the George Brown choir came to sing in the exhibition space, performing a text written by Richard Hamilton in a detached and joyful manner, reminiscent of how Marcel Duchamp had invited a group of children to come and play ball games at the opening of the *First Papers of Surrealism* exhibition. The chorus of the song, which was titled "An Exhibit Calypso,"[23] combines detachment and a touch of irony toward the enthusiasm of the project's authors, repeating the sentence that Lawrence Alloway had been asked to remove from the pamphlet: "*An Exhibit* is a test and an entertainment; are you maze-bright or maze-dim?"

> "So everybody's wondering if it's right,
> To be maze-dim or to be maze-bright,
> But we're sure you'll say this is it
> When you see this amazing exhibit."

The *an Exhibit* project is similar to the experimental work Allan Kaprow was conducting at the same time in the United States, where he was constructing his first "environments," vast assemblages of found materials, texts, and instructions given to the viewer: "Each person must enter the environment, must push their way through, literally, in order to 'see'."[24] In an environment, seeing depends on an action, physical immersion, and penetration into a space, because the image alone is not enough to produce a vision. The participatory challenge is political: it is about freeing the viewer from their submission to the media and encouraging them to be active in their perception, but also in their relationship to knowledge. Kaprow's *18 Happenings in 6 Parts*, which he produced in October 1959 at the Reuben Gallery in New York, combines one of his environments with a happening in a staging orchestrated in space and time, while also being open to the interventions of the spectators. The precise instructions sent to participants and distributed to the public create a participatory framework, as do the semi-transparent structures that divide the gallery. The exhibition design is crucial here, as it allows for the creation of a path through the space interspersed with different lighting atmospheres, while also providing supports for the hanging of paintings, words, and objects, thus producing sensations of space as well as settings for the actions. In art historical accounts of this event, great emphasis has been placed on the rules of the game given to the spectator to take part in the happening. It seems equally essential, however, to point out how the structuring of space, the confusion produced between space and work, and the integration of scenography tools into the artistic conception constituted a central aspect of this project, as they did in *an Exhibit*.

# Conversations with historical figures

In *Support Structures*,[25] the artist Céline Condorelli creates a manual devoted to things that support, an idea that Derrida analyzed through the semiotic lens of the parergon in *The Truth in Painting* (1978), following Kant's idea in the *Critique of Judgment* (1790). The premise is that something supplementary was necessitated by a lack in the work, in the color, but also in the frame of the painting, which remains external to it and yet "speaks from within the work, in and to its very core, through the work's inherent, unspoken, lack-of-being."[26] Noting the lack of publications exploring the format of the exhibition,[27] Condorelli conducts collaborative research on exhibition scenography as it is conceived as a friendly, social, and political gesture. It forms a consideration on the act of support that becomes one with a work and gives it a place in space, in a physical proximity that can only occur in a relationship of friendship and attention. Exhibition design, which is generally conceived as a temporary arrangement, is first and foremost thought of as a one-off support for a painting or sculpture, as a formal and technical production aimed at establishing the work in a space, giving it a place. Céline Condorelli is particularly compelling in the way she explores history by replaying it and, by sharing her admiration for certain developments, resuscitates them. It is in this spirit that we propose to explore several major figures of modern scenography.

## Lilly Reich (1885–1947)

While exhibition design was initially conceived as the arrangement of a flat surface—picture rails, walls, but also panels and floors—and as a visitor's pathway through the works, as El Lissitzky and Herbert Bayer experimented so brilliantly with in the 1920s and 1930s, another approach emerged in parallel, one that sought to empower the objects and works on display. The German designer Lilly Reich (1885–1947) is an iconic historical figure associated with this second approach.

She began her career in interior design, a field that women could easily enter because it had long been considered part of the domestic space and was not highly regarded. She then moved on to designing shop windows for fabric and fashion stores, gradually progressing to designing structures and visitor pathways for exhibitions. Lilly Reich thus transitioned from textiles to exhibitions. She first made a name for herself with displays favoring transparent materials such as glass, where she "consistently applied avant-garde, objective aesthetics to the design of exhibitions,"[28] and then through her long period of collaboration with Ludwig Mies van der Rohe, which lasted from 1925 until his departure for the United States in 1938.

Linked to the Werkbund, a German association of artisans facilitating collaboration between design, architecture, and industry, she created several shop windows, such as for the *Elefanten-Apotheke pharmacy* (Berlin, 1913), where she broke with the romantic vision developed in the nineteenth century, which displayed objects within a narrative structure that often included mannequins. Instead, Lilly Reich detached the object from its production and consumption cycle and displayed it for its own intrinsic qualities. Her installations were also very different from the window displays created by the Surrealists in the 1930s, which incorporated industrial objects into a *mise-en-scène* of the body as a place of desire and unconscious impulses. Using modern industrial materials (metal, glass) and orchestrating spaces through the repetition of identical objects, Lilly Reich created abstract visual landscapes that distanced themselves from specific individual characteristics. The photographs from this period are striking in their installation-like quality, closer to the artistic concerns of the 1960s than to the industrial fairs of the time. She met Mies van der Rohe through the Werkbund, of which they were both members. They were both involved in the major four-part exhibition *Die Wohnung* [The Dwelling] at the Weissenhof Estate in Stuttgart in 1926 and became responsible for most of the various spaces presenting industrial products, kitchen models, textiles, curtains, and Bauhaus productions. Lilly Reich placed the objects at the center of light-filled settings, playing with the transparency of glass *(The Plate-Glass Hall)* and the colors of linoleum, creating trajectories for the eye to follow and spaces linked by a common atmosphere. The sculptural force she gave to objects and industrial materials foreshadowed what Philip Johnson would achieve with the 1934 *Machine Art* exhibition cited above. Lilly Reich explored the possibility of glass and curtains to stand independently, structuring space while also exhibiting, creating

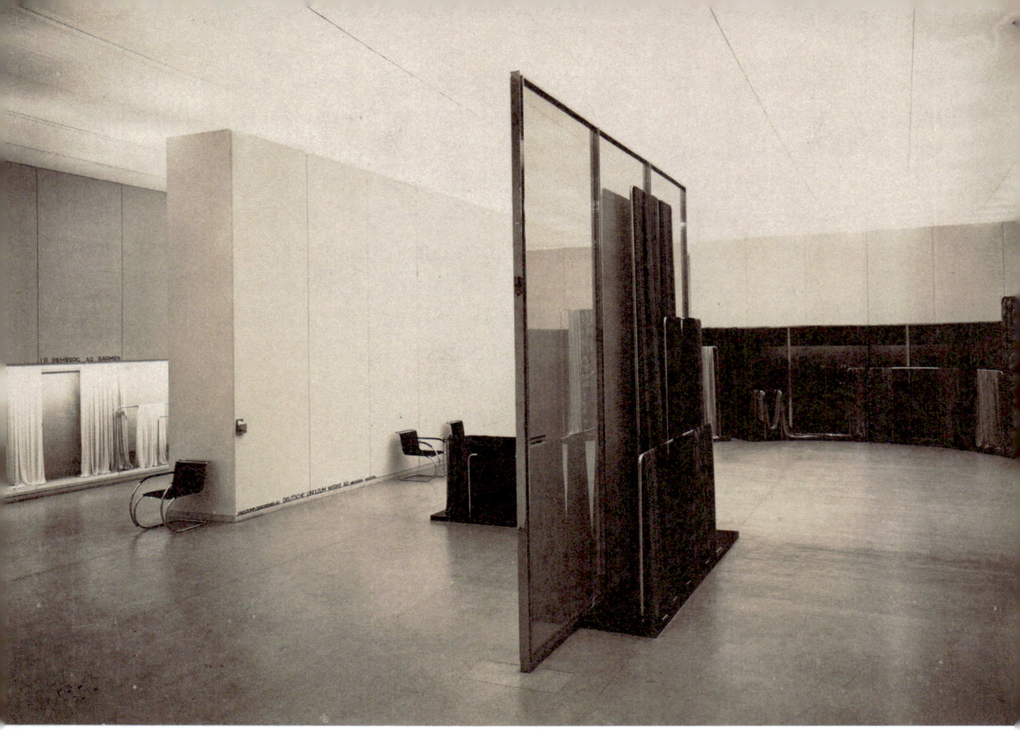


Fig. 5 *Barcelona Exhibition*, Spain, 1929. German Section, view of the I.G. Farben exhibit.
Lilly Reich (with Mies van der Rohe)

scenography tools from the very objects that were being displayed. In this way, she greatly simplified the formal vocabulary and produced a sense of lightness and visual efficiency emblematic of a modern vision. Esther da Costa Meyer uses powerful terms to describe the way Lilly Reich works with space, asserting that she "galvanizes" it, "elevating consumer objects to the status of museum pieces."[29] The materials created effects through juxtaposition and layering, establishing an imagery disconnected from functionality, where "the emphasis is not on the objects: it is the display itself that becomes endowed with an aura."[30] This is precisely the ambiguity of the display, which is the support for an object or a work that can be transformed into a work of art itself when it participates in a spatial construction that seeks to produce an aesthetic effect. Although Lilly Reich rarely asserted this position for her work, and often placed herself at the service of large-scale projects in which she played only a small part—her collaborations with Mies van der Rohe, for example—the experience we have of her installations today through their photographic documentation invites this interpretation. Displayed on freestanding racks and steel tubes, the fabrics Lilly Reich exhibited blend their colorful patterns with the bouquets of flowers arranged on the floor. The feminine interior design embodied by the arrangements of flowers—the task of the eponymous protagonist in Virginia Woolf's 1925 novel *Mrs. Dalloway*, who spends the morning preparing for the evening's reception—is here associated with the power of textiles to take erect forms, to establish their own innate qualities, thus prompting a feminist reinterpretation. One wishes it were possible to see bodies moving about in these settings, but unfortunately the photographs do not provide such views. I therefore like to imagine these arrangements based on the model of the composed social arrangements known as "Occasions," created by the artist Isabel Lewis, and recall the tango dancers, electronic music, and diffuse movements of visitors mingling with plants and plant sculptures that I discovered during her installation for the Dia Art Foundation in New York in 2016. Lilly Reich's displays were made for industrial fairs with large crowds of people whose wandering gaze was shaped by productivist and patriarchal ideology, and viewers may well have been struck by her installations that distanced themselves from such frameworks.

Lilly Reich's collaboration with Mies van der Rohe continued for many years, and their landmark achievement was the creation of the *Café Samt & Seide* [Velvet Silk Café] in 1927 for the *Die Mode der Dame* [Women's Fashion] exhibition in Berlin. This design project was again structured without walls or picture rails, using curtains of different materials and colors suspended from tubular steel systems to create a space. Matilda McQuaid, curator of the first exhibition devoted to Lilly Reich at MoMA in 1996, pointed out that "In both displays the flexible or floating wall was the great innovation, an idea Mies used to brilliant advantage in his architecture, notably in his next and possibly most famous work, the German Pavilion at the International Exposition in Barcelona."[31] It was only later that Lilly Reich was credited for her contribution to the pavilion in Barcelona, which was designed in 1929 and has since been reconstructed identically.[32] However, she played an important role in its interior design and the creation of the furniture; her contribution is also evident in the use of colored marble walls as decorative elements as well as in the orchestration of light and reflections through transparent walls and openings. The similarity to her use of glass and curtains on self-supporting structures for her displays at industrial fairs is obvious. Furthermore, it should not be forgotten that the German Pavilion in Barcelona was only part of the collaboration between Reich and Mies van der Rohe, as they were also responsible for the scenography of the entire German section of the industrial part of the exposition, which comprised more than 16,000 square meters of exhibition space.[33] The images that have been preserved show a modern setting, with self-supporting structures arranged within the neoclassical building. The German Pavilion in Barcelona was intended as a venue for the official opening ceremonies, and to receive the royal family, but Mies van der Rohe and Lilly Reich designed it as an element in the longer sequence in the industrial section. There are many similarities in the treatment of materials, spatial compositions, and interplay of layers offered to the eye.

In 1930, Mies van der Rohe took over as director of the Bauhaus school and invited Lilly Reich to teach there, first in Dessau and later in Berlin, fostering connections and collaborations between the various workshops and the field of interior design. Their personal and professional lives became closely intertwined. The images that today convey the memory of Lilly Reich's projects —many of which unfortunately went undocumented—testify to her interest in transparency and the penetration of natural light, but also in the use of colored backgrounds, elements that clearly do not belong to Mies van der Rohe's vocabulary. Displaying glass panels provided the framework for a formidable formal and conceptual interaction, offering numerous repetitions, multiplications, and dispersions of figures. Above all, the absence of restrictions on the conservation standards of the objects on display allowed her to fully utilize the natural light coming in through the large windows and glass roofs. When Mies van der Rohe left Nazi Germany for the United States, where he was offered a teaching position, Lilly Reich visited him but decided not to stay, for reasons that remain unclear (material difficulties for a woman whose professional reputation was unknown on the other side of the Atlantic? Romantic disappointment? Ideological neutrality toward National Socialism?). All of these theories, debated by historians, likely contain some truth. By remaining in Germany, she deprived herself of international recognition and ended her career largely forgotten, while continuing to manage Mies van der Rohe's affairs in the country until his death in 1947. She also ensured the preservation of his archives, more than two thousand drawings that are now part of the MoMA collection. Her role remained largely unknown for a long time, overshadowed by the widespread recognition of Mies van der Rohe, but also by the ephemeral nature of many of her projects.

## The Italian rationalists

> "Architecture must mediate between the public and the exhibits; it must enhance the environment as a source of inspiration for visitors. To achieve this, I believe we must resort to spatial rather than physical solutions: we must create architectural spaces or enhance existing ones, linking them in perfect harmony with the exhibits. I believe that it is precisely the empty spaces that need to be constructed, with air and light as the building materials. The atmosphere should not be static or stagnant, but vibrant, and the public should find themselves immersed and stimulated without even realizing it."
>
> Franco Albini, lecture at the University Institute of Architecture in Venice, 1954. Translated from the Italian[34]

For the 1936 Triennale di Milano, Edoardo Persico[35] worked with Marcello Nizzoli, Giancarlo Palanti, and Franco Albini to design a striking creation: the *Sala della Vittoria* or Victory Salon, an architectural installation featuring a sculpture by Lucio Fontana. They produced an immersive, rhythmic scenography in a vast hall where panels seemed to detach themselves from the walls, allowing air and the echoes of an invisible crowd to infiltrate as visitors made their way toward Lucio Fontana's statue placed in the center of the room. The attention paid to the lighting

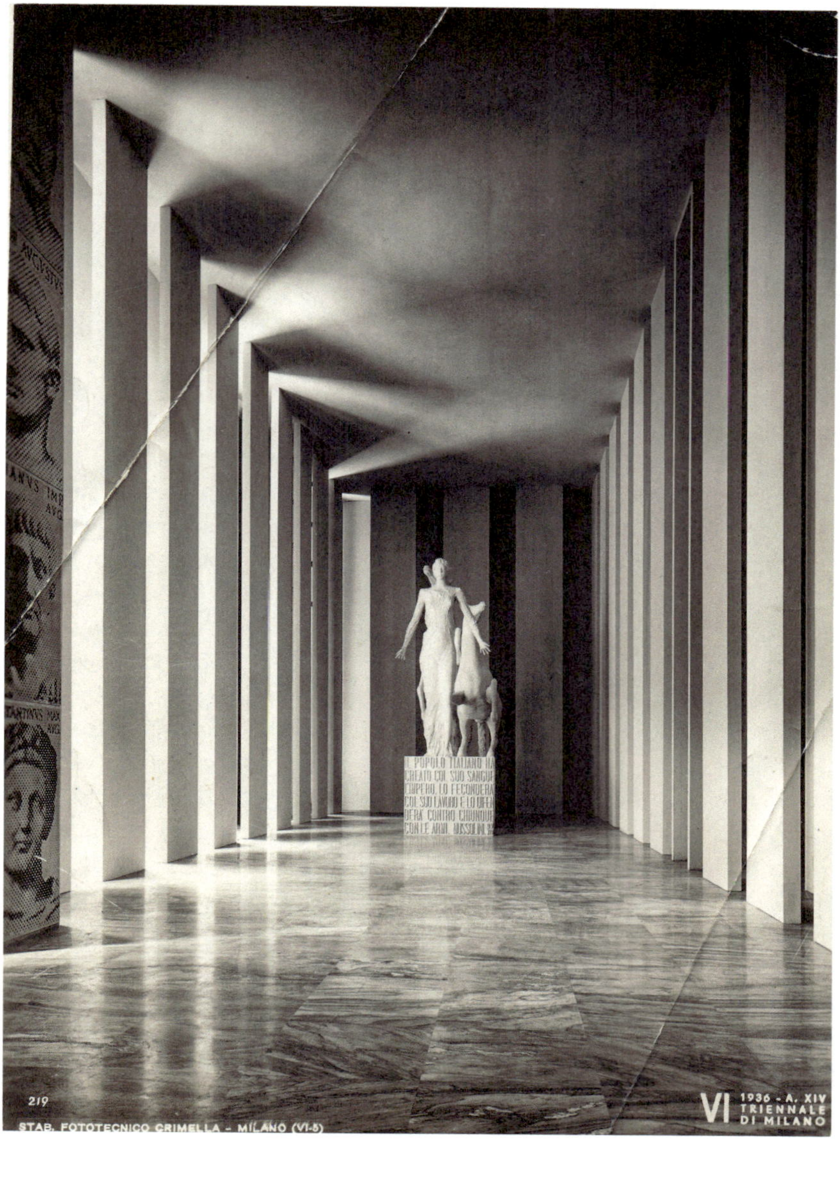


Fig. 6 View of the *Salone d'onore*, by Edoardo Persico, Marcello Nizzoli, and Giancarlo Palanti, at the 1936 VI Milan Triennale. In the background is the *Athena Nike* by Lucio Fontana.

and the sensorial journey accompanying the visual experience of the sculpture left a deep impression on those who experienced it, describing it as an "orgy of white, of absolute white,"[36] a perceptual flickering. The images documenting the exhibition testify to the dramatic impact of the exhibition display, its proximity to a composition by Giorgio de Chirico, and the manner in which the atmosphere surrounding a sculpture was utterly inseparable from the work itself. Edoardo Persico had a major influence on the design because he was well versed in the exhibition display experiments carried out in Germany by El Lissitzky and Alexander Dorner with the *Abstract Cabinet* room to display paintings (1927). He was also familiar with Frederick Kiesler's *City of Space* project (1925) and the exhibitions organized by the Bauhaus. Persico was also a graphic designer—he did the layout for the journal *Casabella*, edited by Persico and Giuseppe Pagano, and dedicated to promoting architectural modernism—which gave him a keen understanding of how to stage photographs and design documents on architectural displays, playing with framing, rhythm, and superimposition effects. Persico, Nizzoli, and Palanti had already created the *Sala delle Medaglie d'Oro* (Gold Medals Room)[37] at the Palazzo dell'Arte for the *Esposizione dell'Aeronautica Italiana* exhibition in Milan in 1934, a design in which the space was conceived as an environment pierced by corridors of vision, with images and objects suspended through a system of grids in a deliberate detachment from the walls. In both cases, the exhibition design was concerned less with making objects or works available for viewing through modules and fittings than with making the viewer physically and mentally available to the work through the creation of a specific atmosphere, or a genuine tool for mediation, as Franco Albini put it. The focus therefore lay in how to make an impression on the observer, to attract attention in a space designed as an environment where relationships emerge through expanded and open conditions of perception.

Through the graphic exhibition display choices that relied on an interplay between absence and presence, the *Sala della Vittoria* strove to create positive perceptual conditions. The scenography acted on the space and the atmosphere to facilitate viewing by fostering a quality of attention. It is not neutrality and emptiness that usher in the aesthetic experience, but an environment already charged with a relationship to the works that activates something in the space, that brings the works to life and engages the viewer. Echoing the words of Raffaello Giolli, an anti-fascist journalist and contributor to *Casabella*, Ross Jenner describes the *Sala della Vittoria* as a journey through a space that mobilizes the body and mind and transforms the gaze:

Filtering through the "constant frenetic appearing of these excited white screens," Giolli sought "breathing space and peace," finding it only when "suddenly two large horizontal planes appear, one down low, the other high up; matching, parallel, gliding, launched as if in flight": the floor and ceiling. The full volume of the interior is now gained. One has moved from the trembling rhythmic verticality of the periphery to the gliding central space, where the screens now appear to hold the dark planes of floor and ceiling together. Giolli found this counterpoint even more subtle and daring than that between black and white: the two planes "overturn the first pattern: where before black was associated with the perpendicular, now airy planes come alive suspended in the light."[38]

The attention Raffaello Giolli paid to the way space affected his perception and constructed an experience that unfolded as he immersed himself within it and evoked physiological and psychological reactions provides us with an exceptionally accurate description of the *Sala della Vittoria*. Another analysis, by Renato Luiz Sobral Anelli, of Persico's contributions to the work affirms that he was already establishing what would become a major feature of the work later carried out by Italian exhibition designers:

"Both [*Sala delle Medaglie d'Oro* and the *Sala della Vittoria*] share the goal of prioritizing the visitor's spatial and visual experience, thereby helping to shape and disseminate modern taste. The use of graphic techniques and images interacting with spaces was merely a by-product of these objectives. Suspended images seemingly floating in the air became a recurring feature, as this relatively simple solution allowed objects of diverse nature and from different historical periods to coexist in the same space."[39]

### *Franco Albini (1905–1977) and Franca Helg (1920–1989)*

Franco Albini graduated with a degree in architecture from the Politecnico di Milano in 1929, which was still a fairly traditional university at the time and its architecture school was dominated by the Neoclassic and Novecento Italiano styles of the period. He began his career working for Gio Ponti, who took him along to the 1929 Barcelona International Exposition, where Ponti was curator of the Italian Pavilion, an excursion that introduced Albini to the work of Mies van der Rohe and Lilly Reich. Ponti also encouraged him to meet

Le Corbusier in Paris. Shortly afterwards, Albini opened his own studio, sharing a workshop and collaborating with Giancarlo Palanti and Renato Camus, whom he had graduated with. He continued to enjoy the support of Gio Ponti and his sister, Carla Albini, whom he was particularly close to. She supported his graphic design and interior design work and wrote articles about his work in magazines and newspapers such as *Domus*, *Casabella*, and *Cellini*. Through her, he met Italian avant-garde figures who were linked to international rationalism, such as Edoardo Persico. They shared a revolutionary vision of architecture that was debated in the pages of *Casabella*, which was edited by Persico and Giuseppe Pagano. Franco Albini then continued his research into creating atmospheres through light and modern forms, paying great attention to the artisanship of the productions. Along with Edoardo Persico and Marcello Nizzoli, in 1935 he took part in the competition for the design of the hall of honor for the 1936 Triennale di Milano, which has been previously discussed, and became responsible for the project after Persico's death in 1936.

During this period, the industrial sector began producing structural glass panels, which Albini often used in his architecture to open up buildings to the outside and allow natural light to enter. His first exhibition designs for the Triennale di Milano helped promote national identity in a fascist context, but he enjoyed considerable freedom to experiment. At the 1936 Triennale, he designed the exhibition of ancient Italian goldsmithing (with Giovanni Romano), conceiving geometrical, open display cases that included industrial lighting fixtures with a sculptural presence that was deliberately emphasized. The uprights were made of white-painted iron and the pillars and ceiling were painted black, creating a striking visual environment. Albini always sought to achieve an airiness in his designs and invented principles of suspended modules that allowed volumes to interpenetrate visually. For the exhibition of work by Scipione and selected contemporary drawings at the Pinacoteca di Brera in Milan in 1941, he exhibited the unframed works by arranging them on transparent panels fixed with metal cables so they weren't stuck to the walls or ceiling and seemingly floated in space, creating a genuine unity in the display and an overall impression that is well captured in the photographs. The exhibition also included several paintings, detached from the walls and hung on poles and secured by metal cables, with some works displayed in a brick semicircle niche built at the back. This was a bold design statement: these brick elements served no technical purpose and were clearly the result of a formal approach to the space

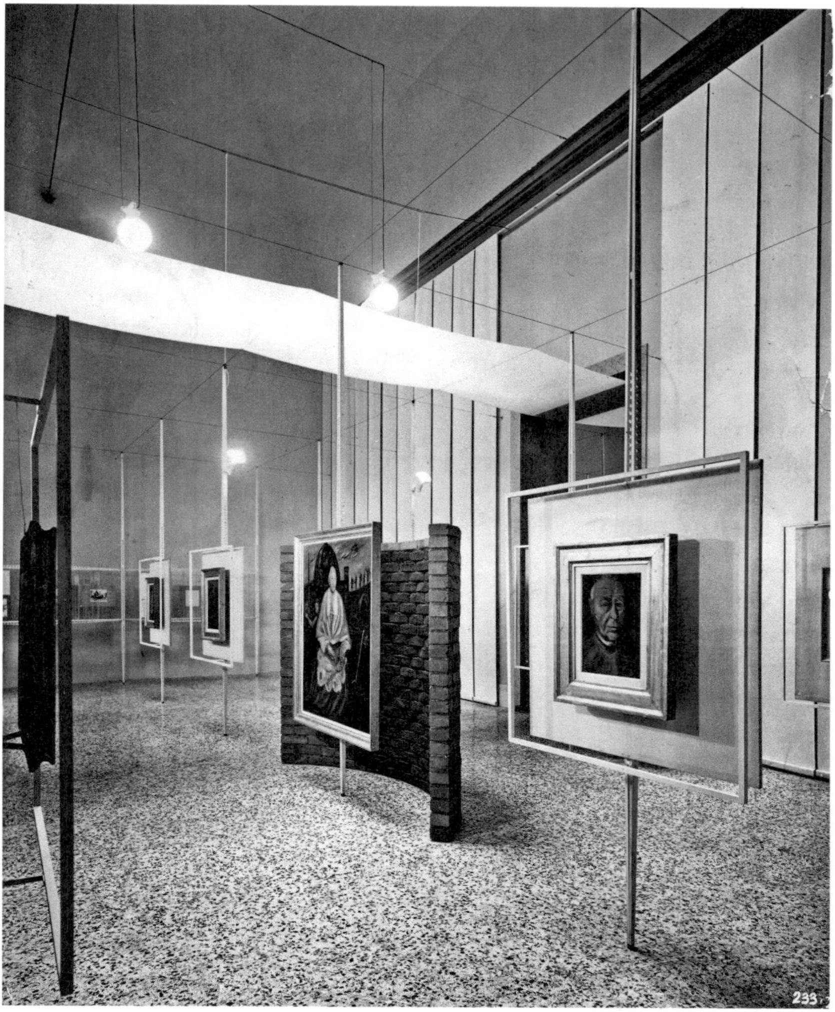

Fig. 7 Franco Albini, Pinacoteca di Brera (Brera Art Gallery). *Mostra Scipione e del Bianco e Nero* (Scipione & Black and White Exhibition), Milan, 1941

aimed at empowering the work and creating dramatic tension through-out the exhibition. Visual pathways were also implied in the space through strips of white paper hung from the ceiling. The diagrams for the scenography clearly illustrate Albini's concept, which involved using metal wires to draw a grid in the space in which he placed the installations, carefully considering the effects of rhythm and creating different ensembles in each room. The lighting attached to the poles was directed toward the top of the ceilings, once again favoring the creation of an overall luminous atmosphere. Chairs were also specifically positioned in front of certain works (classic chairs that were undoubtedly borrowed from the museum). The architect Franca Helg, who became Albini's collaborator in 1951, described the shock she felt during her visit: "[...] these were extraordinary arrangements for the time, and they thrilled me with their sober yet magical character: they gave me a profound impression of surreal lightness. [...] This is, I believe, the first example of Franco Albini developing the characteristics that became his trademark: the rhythmic scanning of space through light elements and the technical and constructive support for expressive experimentation. The very thin uprights (one of Albini's 'obsessions', as he himself called them), which were easy to assemble and offered flexible solutions, were thinned at the ends and thickened in the middle, according to the calculations to avoid buckling."[40]

Caterina Marcenaro, art historian, took over as director of Genoa's network of fine arts museums in 1948, and she embarked on a vast renovation project following the destruction of World War II. She was close to the rationalist architects in Milan thanks to architect Mario Labò, based also in Genoa, and decided to rebuild and reorganize the museography of the Palazzo Bianco and Palazzo Rosso with Franco Albini, who, although he had not yet designed any museum displays at the time, had already made a name for himself with his scenography for temporary exhibitions. He had also designed a showroom for the Olivetti company in Genoa. He and Caterina Marcenaro shared the conviction that the museum's redevelopment should enable it to reach a wider audience by transforming the aristocratic and bourgeois heritage into a platform for education and democratization. This was, as Patricia Falguières points out, a conviction shared by many people in Italy in the 1950s, a time when "exhibitions were imbued with ethical and political issues and became a central part of the most heated public debates."[41] Caterina Marcenaro decided to exhibit a much smaller number of works than before and to remove the frames from paintings if they were not original in order to defuse their dominance over the viewer.[42] The two

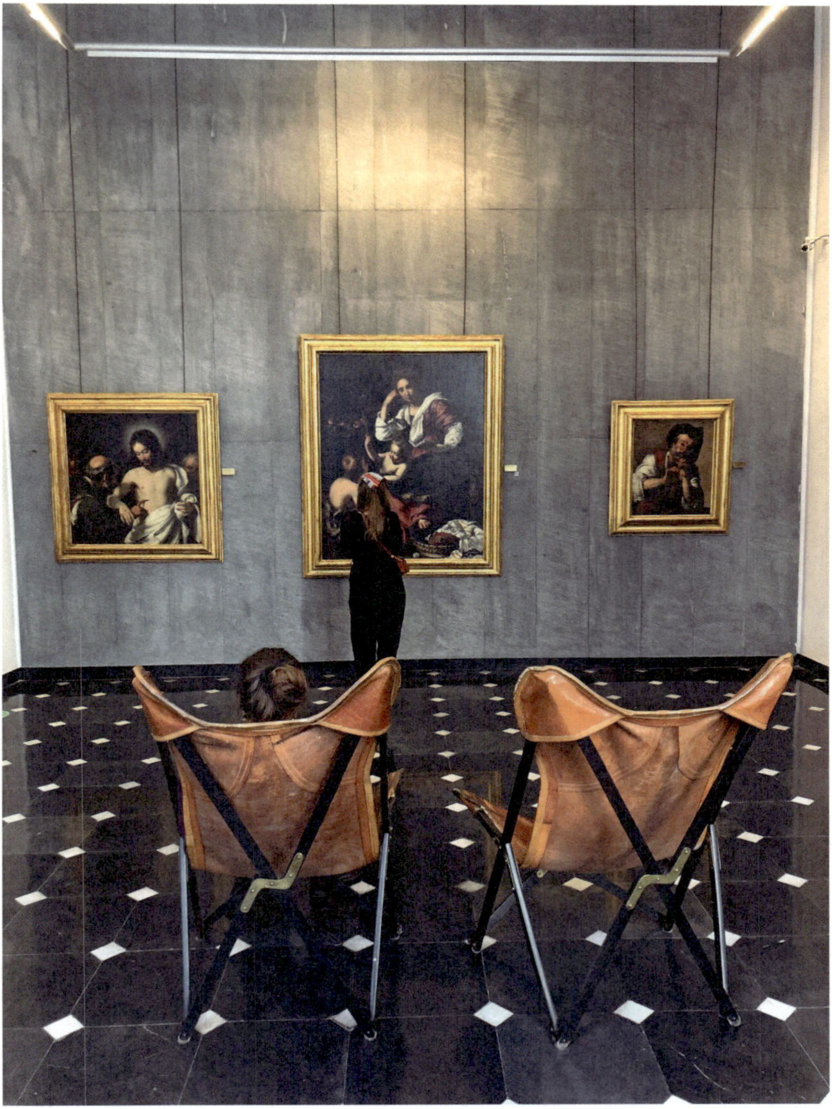

Fig. 8 View of the Palazzo Bianco in 2023, exhibition design by Franco Albini and Franca Helg, Genoa, with paintings by Bernardo Strozzi

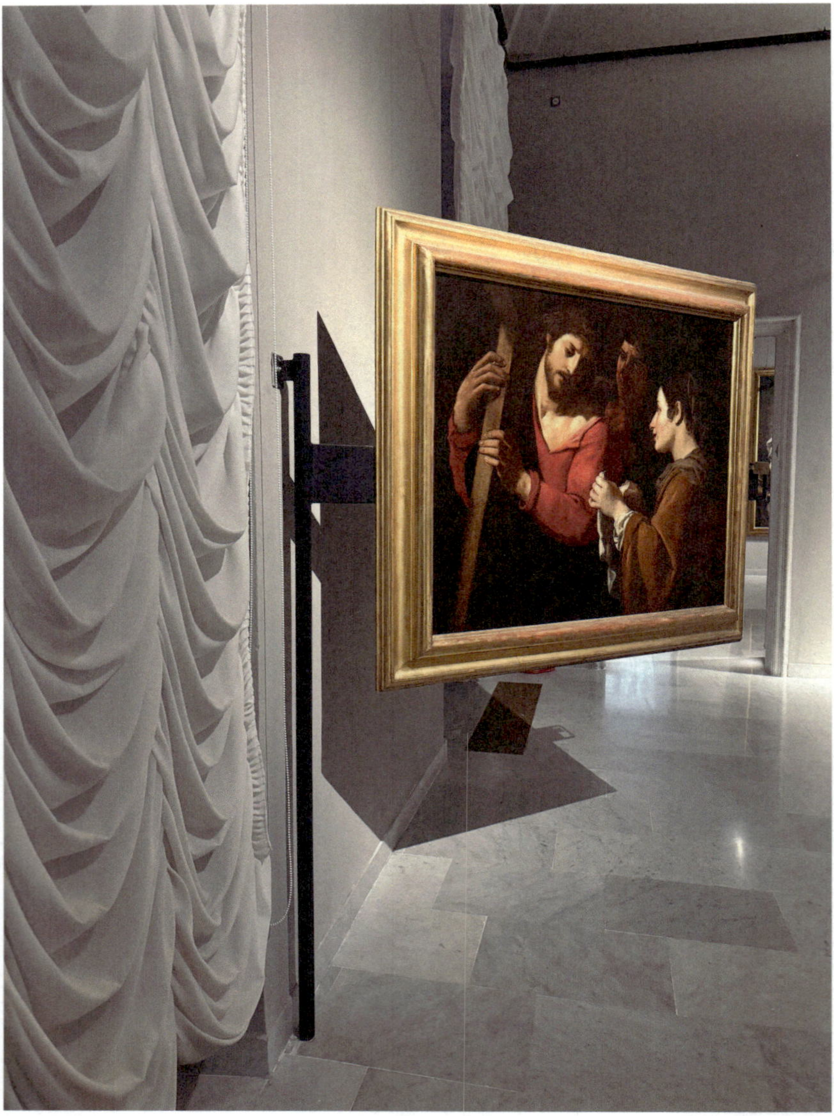

Fig. 9 View of the Palazzo Bianco in 2023, exhibition design by Franco Albini and Franca Helg, Genoa, with a movable display supporting a painting by Michele Taddeo di Giovanni Bono, c. 1400–62

museums each benefited from a specific approach to their scenography but shared many common features: the design focuses on individual relationships with paintings and sculptures, without giving historical context or a clear narrative path, seeking above all to create a dialogue between the ancient and the contemporary. Marcenaro noted this in her statement on museography that she published in 1954 in the UNESCO magazine *Museum* to answer her critics: "No art, science or historical document has any life if it does not have contemporary significance."[43] The Palazzo Bianco, largely destroyed during the bombings, was the first to reopen in 1951, but today's historical tour invites visitors to start at the Palazzo Rosso, which includes the reconstruction of the apartment they had created on the top floor for Caterina Marcenaro, which had been destroyed after she left the museum's management.

For both museums, Albini and Helg designed suspended supports for height-adjustable paintings, using a system of flat raw steel rails that followed and defined the lines of the architectural volumes. The same style of supports was used for the paintings, lifting them slightly off the walls to create a somewhat floating effect, and for the modern industrial lighting, which was also suspended. Albini and Helg isolated the architecture of the building with glass walls, integrating the corridors leading to the patios into the exhibition spaces, taking care never to enclose the works and inviting natural light to flood the rooms. In one of these corridors, they designed highly sculptural pedestals in black metal that linked the floor to the wall through geometric shapes. Candlesticks featuring cherubs were installed on these pedestals and were accentuated by the aesthetic power of the light-bathed space, which intimately linked the marble floor with the design elements. Curtains were installed on the windows when the paintings needed to be protected, but each time the material, color, and hanging system were very carefully selected, such as the use of Venetian blinds. Meanwhile, the lighting fixtures borrowed from a modern industrial rationale that was rarely used in museums, which contributed to the variety of ambiences throughout the visit. As Orietta Lanzarini points out in *The Living Museums*,[44] Franco Albini and Franca Helg likely saw the paintings for the first time after they had been hung, meaning, unlike Carlo Scarpa, they did not produce hanging devices for specific works. Similarly, Caterina Marcenaro was not considered a highly rigorous art historian, which undoubtedly contributed to the sense of freedom with which the works were presented and the lack of historical contextualization that favored visual effects over precise knowledge.[45] Nevertheless, some rooms were

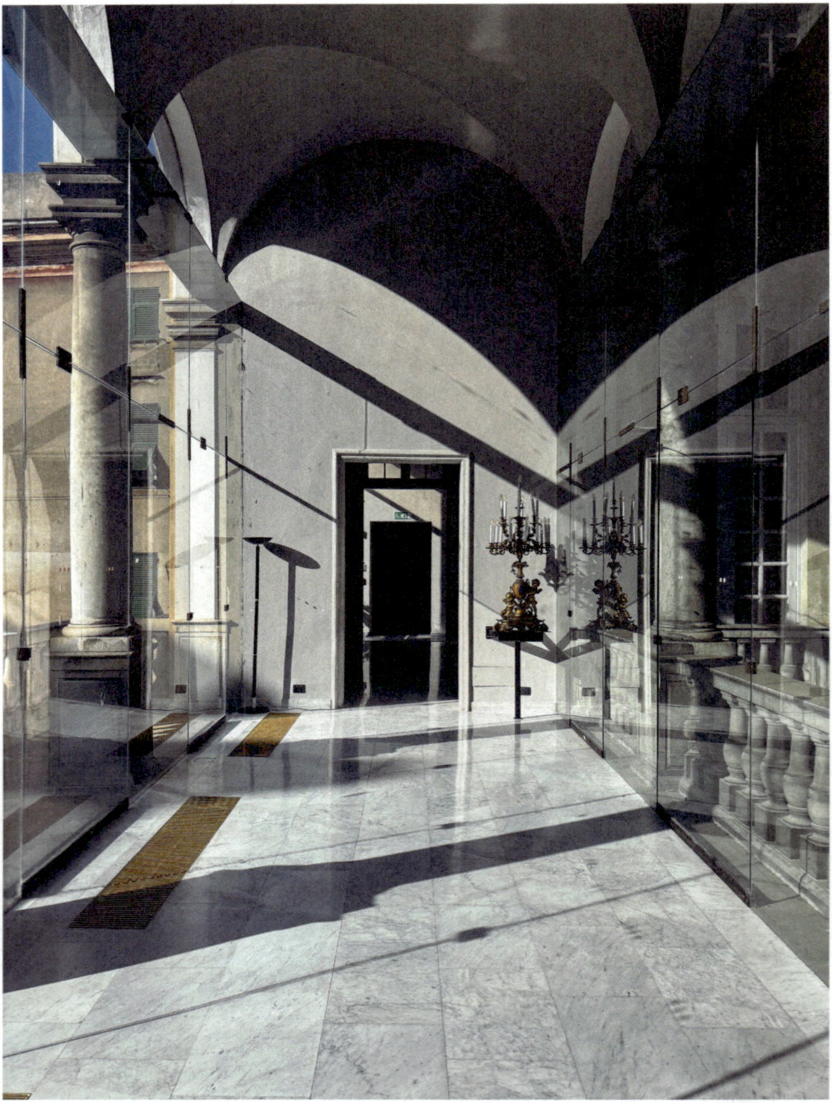

Fig. 10 View of the Palazzo Bianco in 2023, exhibition design by Franco Albini and Franca Helg, Genoa

organized around certain important figures in the collection, such as Bernardo Strozzi. However, Caterina Marcenaro was a forward-thinking museographer; like Albini and Helg, she believed it was important for the hanging systems to be modular so the works on display could be easily rotated and contribute to a broader social project of making art history accessible. With these devices, visitors could use the metal handle attached to certain paintings and turn them to discover the rich detail of the backs of the frames, including abandoned paintings, old half-torn labels, scribbled or typed notes on conservation labels, pictorial forms created from assemblages of wood, and traces of colored backgrounds. It was a powerful act to allow such direct contact and manipulation of ancient works, without frames or glass, and it created a very intimate relationship that shattered the usual distance between observer and artwork. This also allowed the viewer to create different perspectives between the works in the space and to integrate the variations in light. The viewer was thus placed at the center of the installation through their choices, as in El Lissitzky's *Abstract Cabinet* created at the Landesmuseum in Hanover in 1927, where visitors could manipulate wooden panels to reveal and conceal the paintings hanging on the wall, an exhibition that Albini and Helg were probably familiar with. One famous gesture has been the mechanical display designed for the *Elevatio animae di Margherita di Brabate* (Pisano, 1313), placed on a mobile stand connected to a pump and motor concealed in the wall (the mechanism was inspired by the car industry). The visitor could activate it freely and move it up and down. The display was dismantled when Marcenaro decided to move the sculpture collection to Museo di Sant'Agostino.

As for the museum labels, they were engraved metal plates attached directly to the side of the paintings, fixed in place in a light and elegant manner. This choice further accentuated the sculptural presence of the paintings. Albini and Helg also created black steel easels that allowed the paintings to be placed in the space of the rooms and easily turned. Their most ambitious display was probably the one in which paintings were attached to metal tubes mounted on stones recovered from Romanesque or Gothic column capitals, creating a highly modern ensemble. The viewer's gaze moves from the painting to the base, in a gentle trajectory prompted by the curve of the metal bar. Archive photographs show that these paintings were arranged in different places in a room, creating a sculptural journey, but today only two remain, placed near the wall between three imposing windows that, even when closed, allow light to enter through the shutters, producing reflections on the dark floor. Their modest size contrasted with the space of the room and the paintings on the walls. However, when visitors weave through the Tripolina chairs arranged in the center of the room—when the museum opened, these chairs were also scattered throughout the space—and approach this strange, light combination of shapes and materials, they exude such powerful visual poetry that they leave a lasting impression. The balance between the chairs and the works also impressed Orietta Lanzarini: "The design of the Tripolina chairs evokes a comfortable and protective envelope that viewers can literally sink into; the high, curved backrest also provides a slight soundproofing effect. There, isolated from their surroundings and having chosen the work they prefer to observe, their 'visual education' can begin."[46] Permitted to move the chairs to create a special relationship with selected works, people can comfortably immerse themselves and take the time to engage with the space while bathed in the smells and sounds of aged, slightly brittle leather and enjoying the chair whose deep seat remains as comfortable as ever.[47] Albini, Helg, and Marcenaro chose all the seats arranged throughout the museum, which are numerous and have a greater presence in the rooms than we are accustomed to seeing in museums. Although they vary in age, the antique chairs are nevertheless reupholstered with a neutral, uniform fabric, and modern seats are favored, in particular several Barcelona chairs by Mies van der Rohe and Lilly Reich, which Albini was able to experience in 1929 during his visit to the German Pavilion in Barcelona. The ensembles of high-backed antique chairs, epitomized by the Barcelona and Tripolina chairs, make a strong impression as soon as one enters the rooms, while also encouraging viewers to settle into a contemplative position.

The exhibition layout designed by Caterina Marcenaro is spacious, allowing for specific groupings of works to be considered and an aesthetic balance to be achieved in each room. The walls of some rooms are covered with slate cladding, creating a backdrop that accentuates the paintings on display, partly through the effect of renewing the viewer's perspective. Franco Albini and Franca Helg designed the rooms as a whole, and the ensemble contributes to the atmosphere: the colorful patterns of the marble floor covering, which evolve as the visit progresses, script the sensory experience with stages marked by doorways, which are also enhanced by stone frames. At the Palazzo Bianco, visitors begin their tour on the first floor. After a slow climb up the stairs, they arrive on a large balcony enclosed by glass walls where a soft, fragrant leather Tripolina chair awaits them, inviting them to sit comfortably opposite Filippino Lippi's painted altarpiece *Saint Sebastian with Madonna and Child* (1502).[48] Originally designed for a church, and thus a religious setting with a rather somber atmosphere, the altarpiece occupies a white wall bathed in bright natural light. The arrangement creates a sense of proximity between the viewer seated on the chair and the figure of Saint Sebastian, who takes on a human dimension because the work is hung much lower than it would be in a church. This sense of proximity is also accentuated by the resonance between the columns depicted in the painting and those of the Palazzo Bianco. We then move into a room where the wall facing the entrance is entirely covered with a layer of slate, contrasting with the white-painted walls throughout the palace, which majestically frame Bernardo Strozzi's *Saint Teresa in Glory* (seventeenth century). The large-format painting is accompanied by two smaller works by the same painter, accentuating their religious power while placing them in a modern context.

In the 1950s, Tripolina chairs were also placed inside the Galleria d'Arte Moderna in Milan. This building was designed by Ignazio Gardella and constructed at the site of the former stables of the Villa Reale, which had been damaged by bombing in 1943. Born into a family of Milanese architects, Gardella was a leading figure in Italian rationalism and devoted little attention to museum design outside of this project. The trapezoidal building was organized around a glass-fronted area on the ground floor, creating a connection with the park outside and its mature trees. Gardella also designed mobile easels for individual paintings that were positioned at angles, as can be seen in photographs from the period, so that they were visible from both inside and outside. The ground floor was nevertheless mainly devoted to the sculpture collection, with the idea of integrating natural light into their presentation by approximating outdoor conditions. The first floor houses the paintings with a system of mobile picture rails and is also infused with natural light from the roof, with intensities that could be controlled by means of a system of filters in the ceiling. The decorative and aesthetic value of plants is fully embraced; the greenery offers a rhythm to the spaces, including the painting galleries, where the plants are arranged in front of white picture rails installed in a highly sculptural manner. Finally, several photographs offer glimpses of two Tripolina chairs in the space, while others, such as the one reproduced here, show Campanino chairs produced by Azucena in 1952. Together, they testify to Gardella's attention to the visual impact of these seats, which placed viewers in a different relationship with the

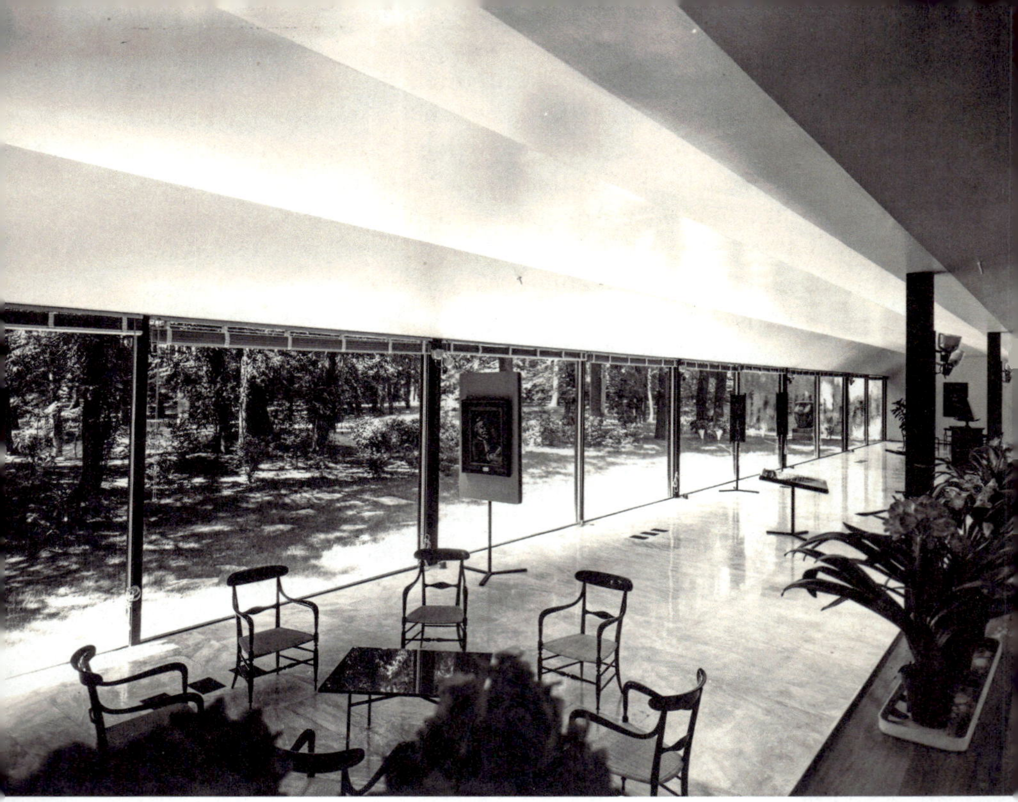

Fig. 11 Padiglione d'Arte Contemporanea, Ignazio Gardella, Milan, 1947–54

works while contributing to an overall decor characterized by modernity. Other chairs from earlier periods, or with less distinctive designs, are distributed throughout the various spaces. While the choice of these mobile seats instead of the usual uniform benches reflects a bourgeois vision that Gardella was criticized for, it also reflects a concern for providing conditions for an individual experience with artworks. Destroyed in 1993 by a mafia bomb, the building was reconstructed by Gardella according to the original plans but with technical improvements, and it remains an important contemporary art venue in Milan. Gardella subsequently designed new exhibition rooms for the Uffizi Galleries in Florence (1956) in collaboration with Carlo Scarpa and Giovanni Michelucci. Carlo Scarpa's influence was notable, especially in the decision to create an arrangement for a crucifix on an unbalanced display inspired by Giotto's frescoes at the Basilica of Saint Francis of Assisi. There were numerous collaborations and discussions among Italian rationalists, as these projects demonstrate.

In the museums designed by Albini and Helg, visitors experience highly distinctive vibrational atmospheres. Each room has its own specific tone and rhythm that encourages the movement of bodies and gazes. Kay Bea Jones refers to Albini's modernism as "situated," pointing to the consideration of context and commissions in his work, which does not always make it easy to identify.[49] The place and role of the viewer are activated by movable systems that allow them to discover the backs of certain paintings and, more broadly, by the impact of the aesthetic shock. Federico Bucci explains that Albini aimed to intensify aesthetic emotions to "enable the public to express an opinion on the reasons behind past or present creations in order to take action for the future."[50] In an article devoted to the work of Franco Albini, Edoardo Persico referred to "artistic rationalism,"[51] asserting the importance of creating an effect through a spatial composition while also evoking a moral and ethical undertaking where the work of art is presented as inseparable from the present time. It is therefore decontextualized from the era in which it was created and staged in such a way as to produce an intense formal effect, particularly through the attention paid to the detail and the design of the space. Door handles, ventilation systems, and signage indicating room numbers were all treated with the same concern for their visual effect.

Later, Albini and Helg were once again invited to Genoa to design the Museo di Sant'Agostino on the site of a former museum of Ligurian architecture and sculpture that opened in 1939 but was almost completely destroyed during the World War II bombings.

The collections had been preserved, and in the late 1960s, Caterina Marcenaro arranged for a large museum dedicated to architecture to open on the site of the ruins, and she reimagined the layout of the Palazzo Bianco in order to move the sculpture part of its collections to this new museum. She asked Albini and Helg to design a building that included a contemporary cloister echoing the ancient triangular cloister dating from the eighteenth century, which was the only remaining element of the old monastery. The highly ambitious project (8,000 square meters) was not completed during the lifetime of the project's initiators, as Caterina Marcenaro died in 1976 and Franco Albini in 1977, so the work was carried out from 1977 to 1984 by Franca Helg and the Albini studio. While the museum building was designed by Franco Albini, he did not have time to consider the layout. Franca Helg also did not have the opportunity to do so, except for some big slate displays, due to a lack of funding at the time. In terms of the building, Albini designed a masterful welcome for visitors with a wide staircase leading to exhibition rooms on a gentle slope and ending with a large fresco depicting an angel. The staircase creates the sensation of aerial movement that continues in the sweeping, floating perspective offered by an exhibition space with vast windows and no pillars or picture rails to obstruct the eye. The architectural structures are incorporated into the roof, and the presence of large steel beams evokes the inside of an upturned boat hull. The atmosphere is further enhanced by trees and vegetation in the raised rectangular patio, a contemporary interpretation of the monastery's former cloister. Albini and Helg took specific measures to produce strong visual effects and an ethereal atmosphere that creates an immersive experience of the City of Genoa's collection of sculptures. Presented on pedestals and museum displays that Albini did not have time to design before his death, the sculptures face outward and are placed at different levels, inviting visitors to wander freely, without a set route, once again favoring emotional encounters over contextual explanations. Unfortunately, the museum built by Albini and Helg is now closed because the structural glass façade system could not withstand the weight of the green terraces—the plants and shrubs having grown into trees with deep roots—combined with water infiltration and oxidation of the metal structures, leaving the building in danger of collapse.[52] It would appear that there was a problem with the structural weight of the glass walls from the outset, a technique that Albini and Helg had already experimented with at the Palazzo Bianco and Palazzo Rosso to integrate the walkways into the exhibition routes, but they were a load-bearing structure at the Museo di Sant'Agostino. Work is now planned to allow the museum to reopen and meet safety and public access standards.

*BBPR*

The Milanese group BBPR (Gian Luigi Banfi, Lodovico Barbiano di Belgiojoso, Enrico Peressutti, and Ernesto Nathan Rogers) also contributed to the exceptional vitality of exhibition design in post-war Italy. They were entrusted with major reconstruction projects, the most notable of which is the Museo d'Arte Antica in the Castello Sforzesco in Milan, which was designed by Barbiano di Belgiojoso, Peressutti, and Nathan Rogers. As with the Palazzo Bianco and Palazzo Rosso in Genoa, the museum was in ruins and its renovation was part of a social transformation and arts education project led by its director Costantino Baroni. However, the methodology was different because BBPR did not undertake the project alone—they only designed certain sections of the museum—and the work was implemented over a long period of time due to financial difficulties: the project began in 1948 and was completed in 1963. The architects experimented with different alternatives using 1:1 scale models that they brought to the site, and they included the various authorities in the decision-making process. Their long-term involvement enabled them to gradually convince Baroni and the city's politicians of the benefits of embracing modernity and opting for flexible exhibition facilities, which Baroni expressed in a 1954 statement to the mayor, explaining that BBPR "is now seeking to create a museum that does not embody an individual interpretation, but an abstract museum, capable of withstanding the test of time and changing tastes."[53] The layout begins with the ground floor galleries. BBPR did not divide this space, in order to create a visual dialogue around the idea of depth that unfolds to a rhythm produced by variations in the hanging systems and the positioning of the antique sculptures between the floor and the walls. Wooden plinths of varying heights support the column fragments, integrating them into an overall design. BBPR paid particular attention to the treatment of the floor, which consists of large paving stones, the level of which varies throughout the visit, and in places it is covered with metal grilles or calade (cobblestones), discreetly and effectively marking out areas where a distance should be kept. Some of the picture rails are made from the same stones used for the floor; they are raised, placed at an angle and face each other while being held in place by a wooden

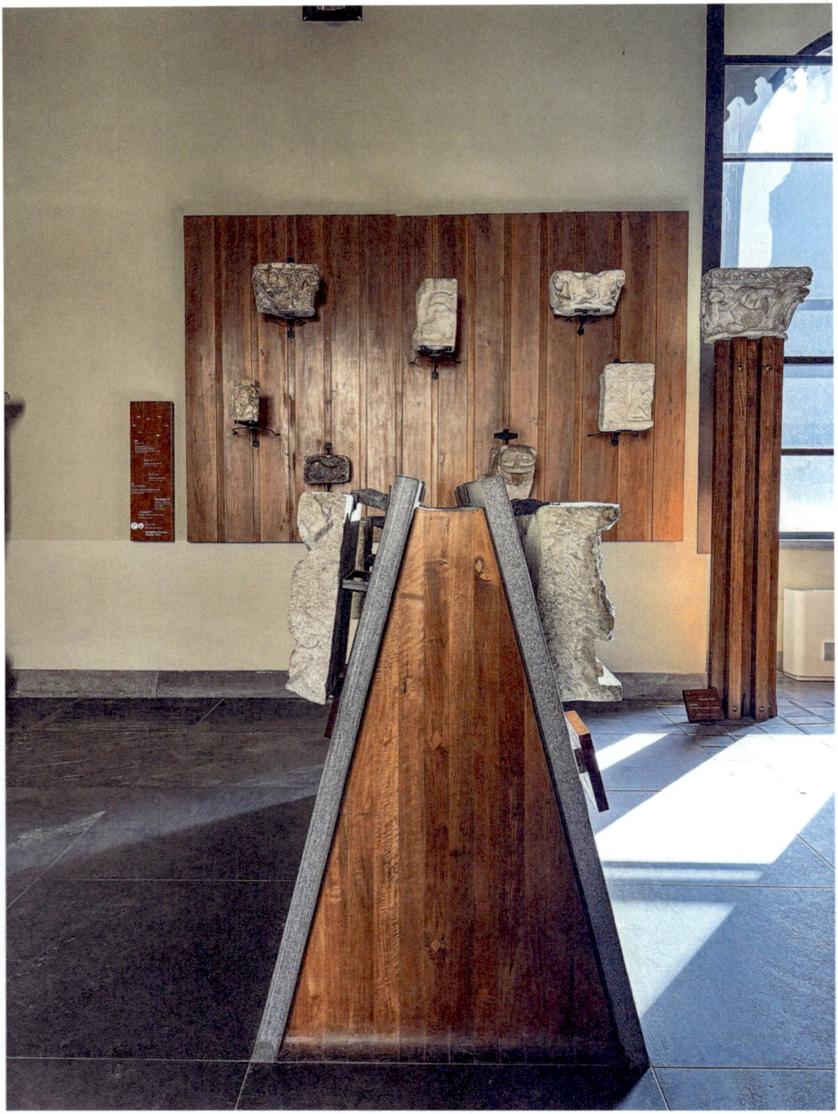

Fig. 12 View of the Castello Sforzesco in 2023, Museum of Ancient Art, exhibition design by BBPR, Lodovico Barbiano di Belgiojoso, Enrico Peressutti and Ernesto Nathan Rogers, Milan, 1948–63

piece. They thus form a highly sculptural and dynamic display for sculptures. In other places, the floor has been lowered to isolate and protect certain works in the exhibition (although, unfortunately, distancing measures have now been added) and to give a sense of volume to the exhibition space. Numerous shelves, display cases, and pedestals are also made of wood and steel, playing on the visual encounter between these materials and the stone of the sculptures, with the wood bringing a genuine warmth and softness to the galleries. The benches have also been given a very specific look: made of solid wood battens held in place by two embedded steel tubes, they offer a wide seat with a fold suggesting a backrest. Placed near the windows, they provide stopping points along the route and allow visitors to fully immerse themselves in the atmosphere. Sculptural compositions are also placed on high shelves against blue backgrounds, extending the effects of the original ceiling paintings in this room, but with a more modern interpretation.
The hanging system consists of steel elements inserted into the walls. The mounting systems vary throughout the spaces and are partially movable: these areas can be identified by the presence of unused metal rings forming geometric compositions. Every technical detail is treated with aesthetic ambition and constantly invites a dual gaze from the work to the display.

The masterpiece of the collection is Michelangelo's *Rondanini Pietà*, a sculpture acquired by the City of Milan in 1952. BBPR designed a dedicated room for the work called the Sala degli Scarlioni, which was reached at the end of the visitor's path through the museum. Unfortunately, the dramatic effect of the museography designed to lead visitors to this climax was lost in 2015 when the *Rondanini Pietà* was moved and installed in a new setting designed by Michele De Lucchi, in another dedicated space within the Castello Sforzesco. As they are caught up in the movement of a floor descending in three levels, people still see the sandstone niche at the end of the visit that promises a unique emotional experience. However, instead of the *Rondanini Pietà*, there is unfortunately just a video screen showing a television report on the museum. It is only through archival documents that we can imagine the aesthetic amazement produced by this carefully designed route with the niche concealing the work from view until the last minute, creating a sense of suspense and surprise. With the inside covered in wooden panels, the small space of the niche invited a personal, meditative relationship with Michelangelo's masterpiece, as the archive photographs clearly show.

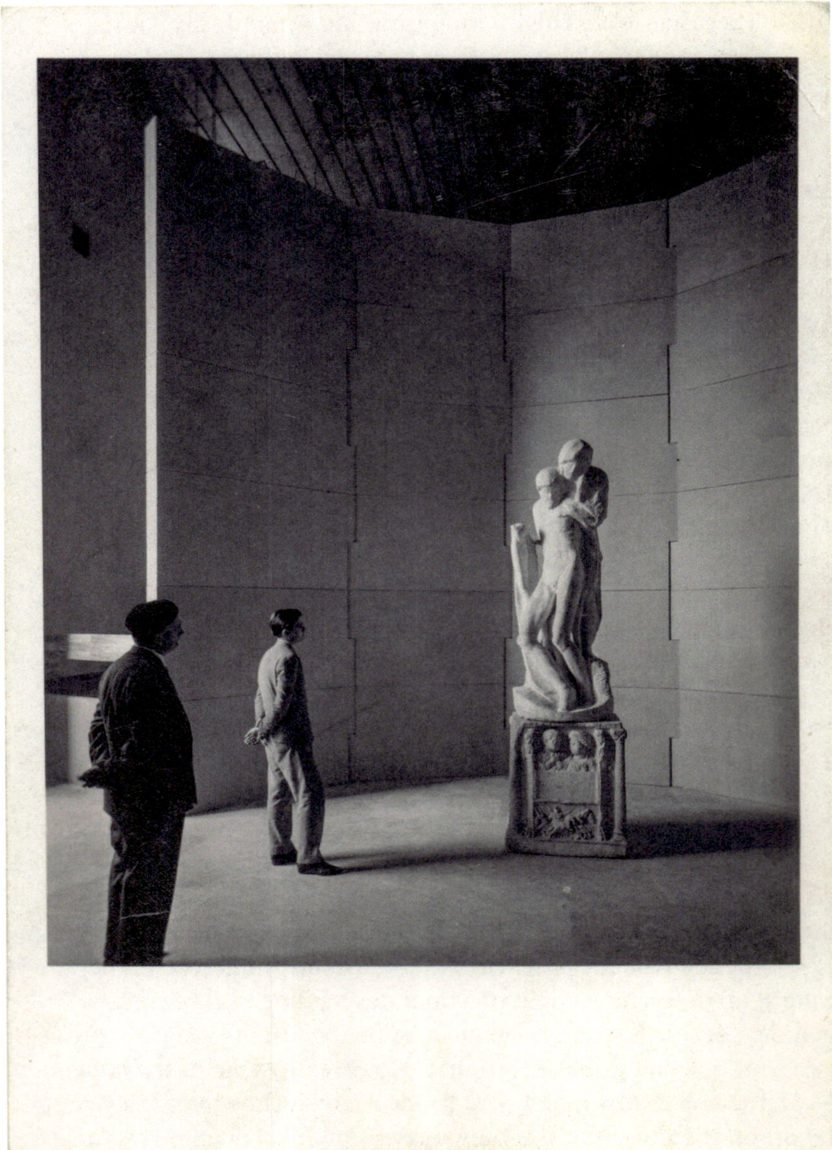

Fig. 13 *Rondanini Pietà*, Michelangelo, Castello Sforzesco in 2023, Museum of Ancient Art, exhibition design by BBPR, Lodovico Barbiano di Belgiojoso, Enrico Peressutti and Ernesto Nathan Rogers, Milan, 1948–63

The reasons for moving the sculpture are difficult to understand given that its current location is a dedicated room in another building of the castle that is generally disappointing (the city was expecting a large influx of visitors in 2015 for the World Expo). In addition, the museum emphasizes the story of the *Rondanini Pietà* in various installations throughout its history with photographs and texts recounting its journey from the quarry in Carrara to the present-day location. Three very surprising pedestals are also displayed in small adjacent rooms: the first, an ancient funerary urn, is the one on which the sculpture was displayed from 1911 to 2015. The second, designed and built by BBPR, is a two-part wooden pedestal with a rotating upper section, which would have allowed the viewing angle of the work to be constantly changed, but which was never installed due to the fierce criticism received by the museum upon its delivery. Finally, the third and last pedestal was created for the first temporary exhibition of the *Rondanini Pietà* at the Palazzo Reale Milano after its acquisition by the city in 1952. Although there are no wall texts presenting BBPR's overall museography project at the museum entrance, and a central aspect of the layout has been removed, thus greatly spoiling the intended effect, it is interesting to note the accent placed on the relationship between the work, its plinth, and its exhibition space through the historical narrative that is presented as well as through the preservation of the layout of the museum space and the enhancement of the space where the work once sat. We can only hope that one day the management will decide to reverse this decision to move the sculptures, since all the elements are still available to do so.

## *Carlo Scarpa (1906–1978)*

Carlo Scarpa was a major figure in exhibition design and museography in Italy and is probably the best-known designer in this field today. In the context of this research, it is difficult to discuss his work without devoting an entire book to it, but fortunately other writers have already done so. Many of Scarpa's creations can still be admired in cities frequented by contemporary art lovers: in Venice, visitors can see his designs for the Gallerie dell'Accademia, the Museo Correr, the Olivetti showroom, the Fondazione Querini Stampalia, the sculpture garden of the central pavilion in the Giardini, and the Venezuelan Pavilion;[54] in Verona, the Castelvecchio Museum; in Palermo, the

Palazzo Abatellis and its Galleria Regionale della Sicilia; in Possagno, his extension to the Museo Canova; and in San Vito d'Altivole, the Brion Cemetery. A "grand tour" of Italy in the footsteps of Scarpa's creations reveals the capacity of exhibition design to produce a sculptural and architectural force, to create atmospheres, to give a central place to both natural light and to everything that surrounds the artwork through a linking of the interior and the exterior. Carlo Scarpa was close to the artists of his time, but also to those of earlier periods; he never ceased to initiate dialogues, drawing heavily on the work of Piet Mondrian, for example, for whom he designed an exhibition in Rome in 1956. Mondrian remained a major influence throughout his career, though Scarpa also drew inspiration from earlier painters, such as Lorenzo Lotto, whose window depicting *Christ Taking Leave of his Mother* (1521) he reproduced in the architecture of the central pavilion of the Venice Biennale. He was also greatly inspired by Adolphe Appia's rejection of naturalism and his stage sets with sculptural effects that embrace a formalist approach, in which light took on a central role. Adolphe Appia remains a central figure for many artists and scenographers today, such as Ulla von Brandenburg (see the interview pp. 176–188) Carlo Scarpa's projects were always inspired by the artworks he staged, which he studied as a historian and envisaged in space as a curator, with a view to creating continuity between the work and its location. He made extensive drawings that enabled him to pay close attention to the works he was to exhibit and to the spaces themselves, which he meticulously surveyed. In 1948, his scenography for the Paul Klee exhibition at the first post-war Venice Biennale was a great success. Its poignancy arose from his close relationship with the artist's work, which he studied in depth and considered a source of profound inspiration, but also from his transformation of a narrow room with a high ceiling, which he "halved in height with a white velum stretched with *cencio di nonna* fabric, which filters the natural light,"[55] thereby avoiding the use of artificial lighting. He also introduced false walls, a device he would go on to use multiple times, enabling him to break free from the existing walls and create designs in the space by multiplying the viewpoints. The geometric spatial structure he developed was made up of lines, planes, and curves that echoed Klee's paintings. As Philippe Duboÿ notes, one important innovation was "the picture rails [which] frame the skillfully assembled paintings so that the glass protecting them is at the same level as the fustian (called *pelle del diavolo*) covering them."[56]
A study by Giacomo Ontano[57] shows how decisive Scarpa's exposure to

Klee's work was in his subsequent exhibition designs, which gave rhythm to the space by playing with planes, lines, and colors, with remarkable freedom in relation to objects and an attention to composition deeply informed by Klee's approach to geometric abstraction.

Scarpa continued to collaborate with the Venice Biennale throughout his career, working on international exhibitions as well as individual pavilions. As noted above, he left a particularly visible mark on the Giardini: in 1952 he designed the ticket booth at the entrance and the sculpture garden of the Central Pavilion; in 1968 he added a mezzanine to the pavilion's central hall, effectively doubling the exhibition space, together with a new upper-level window. Beyond these interventions, he also designed the Venezuelan Pavilion (1954). He carried out numerous projects with very tight deadlines, collaborating with artists, curators, and museum directors to develop designs that reflected shared visions. While his aesthetic style is recognizable, it remains at the service of projects and he never sought to assert himself as the sole author and, unlike star architects, he never prioritized architectural expression over the museum layout. He invented specific displays for each work and space, considering the movement of people and the path of natural light to enhance the experience. His designs are therefore not modular: each room, painting, and statue is considered in its singularity and treated with such precise consideration of the form and aesthetic effect that using different iterations was impossible. Carlo Scarpa trained from a young age in art and craftsmanship and was an excellent draftsman; he was initially destined to become a master glassmaker before pursuing architecture. As a result of this background, he attached great importance to the technical quality of his scenography. With the Venice area being a renowned bastion for talented artisans, he built long-lasting collaborative relationships with ironworkers and carpenters, who helped create powerful museum displays that have remained vital to this day. As Philippe Duboÿ points out, Le Corbusier also had a significant influence on Scarpa, while he also took inspiration from the Bauhaus movement and had a special affinity for the vision of Willem Sandberg, the graphic designer, typographer, and founding director of the Van Abbemuseum in Amsterdam. Nevertheless, graphic design was not a central part of his practice, which distinguishes his work from that of Herbert Bayer, for example. Here we will discuss two of his most ambitious projects, which can still be visited today: the Palazzo Abatellis Palace in Palermo and the Museo Canova in Possagno.

In 1953, Carlo Scarpa designed the scenography for the exhibition *Antonello da Messina* with the curator Giorgio Vigni, who subsequently hired him to renovate the Galleria Regionale della Sicilia at the Palazzo Abatellis, where he served as the director. The dialogue between them was pivotal, and Giorgio Vigni considered this an important aspect of good exhibition design practice: "Fraternal and benevolent criticism will help us better achieve our common goal and, where necessary, prevent overzealousness from giving the installation of art objects more importance than the objects themselves."[58] The Palazzo Abatellis offers visitors a modest welcome without any overt reverence for Scarpa's work. But a visit to the premises quickly reveals its presence: in the first room, a raised picture rail with three colored panels makes a bold statement in the space, further highlighting a wooden virgin placed on a sculptural pedestal. The wall texts are held by wooden hooks, which separate them from the panels and give them their own presence. Every technical detail is treated with the same rigor, encouraging visitors to crouch down to observe the systems and combinations of materials (marble/concrete/metal) or to linger with their eyes and hands on the door handles and their magnificent leather loops. Scarpa's exhibition designs feature compositions that often lean toward verticality, freeing up space through superimpositions in height. An angel is thus isolated in an off-center position on a white panel that serves as a pedestal for two virgins with child, themselves placed in front of two painted vertical panels. The ensemble produces an impression of a pictorial composition on the scale of the space. The most striking effect occurs a little further on, where the architect dedicates large, colored panels to fragments of sculptures delicately inserted into a wooden assembly. This time, the composition plays with depth, maintaining the autonomy of the fragment while simultaneously magnifying it. Further on, pedestals display marble busts and integrate them into a set of green panels. Each pedestal has different aspects, one metal and the other in wood, yet together they generate an atmosphere of exquisite precision within the room. Carlo Scarpa also drew inspiration from a painting by Giovanni Bellini, *Madonna of the Small Trees* (1487), which he knew well through his work on the installation of the collection at the Gallerie dell'Accademia in Venice. In the painting, the Virgin and Child are set apart from the outdoor landscape by a rectangular background painted green and framed by a wooden strip; the echo with the picture rails installed at the Palazzo Abatellis is obvious. The construction of the viewpoint is also a central aspect of Scarpa's museography, which artfully combines wide shots and close-ups, regularly encouraging the viewer to turn around before leaving a room. Sometimes it is even the back of a painting that greets

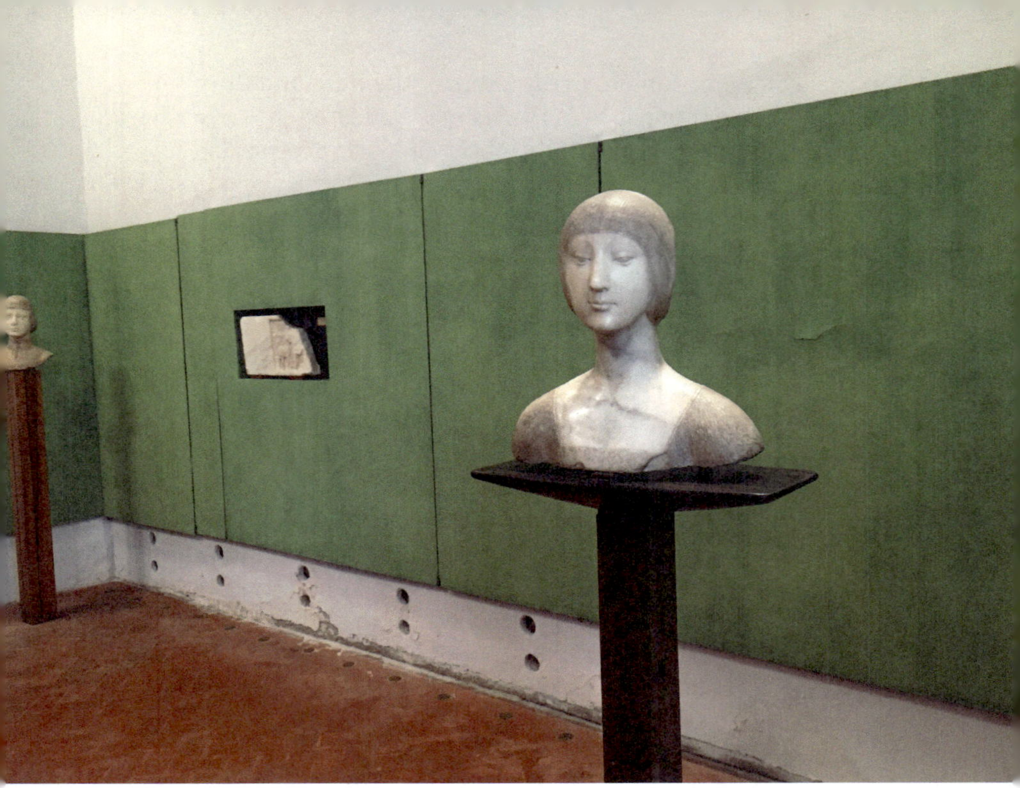

Fig. 14 View of the Palazzo Abatellis in 2023, exhibition design by Carlo Scarpa, Palermo, 1953

visitors, delaying the moment of discovery of the work and thus generating a moment of pause in the visit, as well as a sense of anticipation that motivates the gaze of the observer. Carlo Scarpa also invented numerous technical support structures for the works, which create depth of field and produce gaps. At the Palazzo Abatellis, for example, he placed pieces of fresco into a colored wall that is a few centimeters deeper than the frescoes, creating a layered composition. A little further on, he placed a Christ on the cross painted on wood on a metal frame-shaped structure in the corner of a room. The base becomes a pictorial composition and the fact that it is attached to the walls and floor provides a full integration into the architecture of the space. Scarpa also created numerous anachronistic effects by combining modern concrete elements with classical works. The entire journey exudes a musicality linked to the rhythm and flow of moving through the spaces, playing on variations and peaks of intensity of attention.

His extension of the Museo Gypsotheca Antonio Canova in Possagno, which was a family home that became a museum for the artist's plaster casts, is also well worth the trip. To reach it by public transport, you have to take the train and then the bus, which leaves you time to get into a specific frame of mind, as you would for works of land art. Scarpa's contribution to the museum, implemented between 1955 and 1957, is completely unexpected in the context of a small provincial museum: he truly transformed the experience of Canova's sculptures by removing them from the domestic and somber scale of the rooms of the family home and installing them in an open space built on a small plot of land. He created a building with multiple openings, placing rectangular windows high up and even embedded in the roof, a system he had already experimented with for the Venezuelan Pavilion in the Giardini of the Venice Biennale. Carlo Scarpa paid great attention to natural light. The rectangular extension contrasts with the house's colorful tiling and ornate walls. It evoke san ethereal atmosphere from the outset and features a floor of concrete slabs of varying heights. The different open spaces create a unified whole while offering specific atmospheres that are intensely experienced at each change of level. The installation of the base of the sculpture of a sleeping nymph straddling two heights creates a striking effect that is not without humor.

The overall view offered by the design reveals an extremely open layout, with a dynamic flow of the gaze establishing a constant dialogue between the upper and lower levels. Each plaster cast has its own display, designed with great precision and bold combinations of

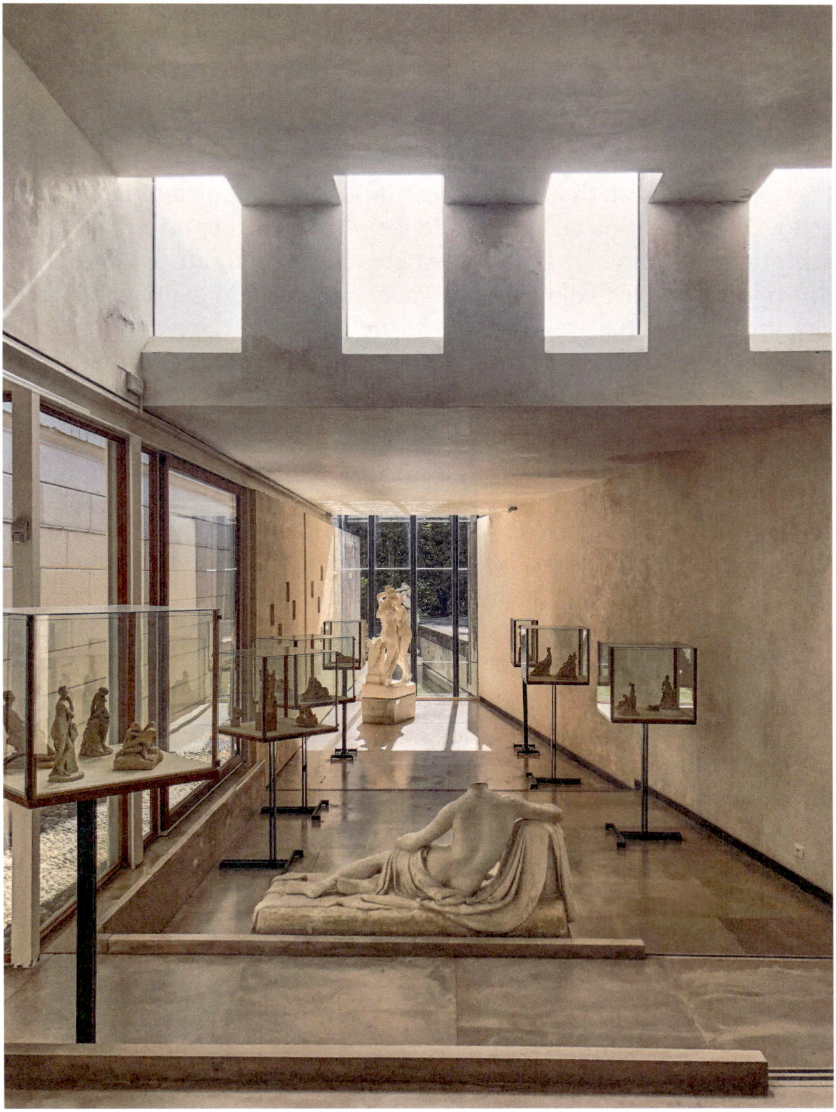

Fig. 15 View of the Museum Gypsotheca Antonio Canova in 2023, exhibition design by Carlo Scarpa, Possagno, 1955–57

materials such as stone, wood, metal, and glass. The eye moves constantly between the work and its support. Some casts are housed in individual display cases placed on metal easels that define the space in resonance with the suspended pedestals. There is an admirable balance between solids and voids, while certain stones have even been removed from the façade, creating an enthralling ambience that echoes the sensation visitors would feel when walking through the sculpture galleries of the Louvre, where the originals are exhibited. The openings bring color into the galleries thanks to the blue of the sky, the green of the grass and trees, and the red of the neighboring façade, all of which create backgrounds for the sculptures. Light penetrates the space and interacts directly with the plaster casts, transforming their presence throughout the day and opening new possibilities of interpretation when a ray of sunlight gently falls across the buttocks of the sleeping nymph. The experience is stimulating on every level and even manages to give models, such as the one for the *Monument to Pope Clement XIV* (1783), installed on a light pedestal floating on a wall, a rare sculptural presence. The pedestal, composed of a double layer of wood, one layer of concrete, and one layer of metal, is a modern touch that brings the plaster into a vibrant contemporary setting, giving full power to the striking gesture of the pope's outstretched hand.

In his museum designs, Scarpa integrates seating into the overall layout, blending it harmoniously with the pedestals, as Frederick Kiesler did in his design for the Surrealist section of Peggy Guggenheim's Art of This Century gallery in 1942, where the same modules could serve as seats or pedestals depending on their arrangement. Scarpa also created benches that extended directly from the walls, forming folds and creases in the architecture to accommodate bodies, and perhaps also to make them disappear: a body that merges into the architecture is less conspicuous than a body sitting on a bench placed in the space or in a Tripolina chair. The viewer takes a seat on the ledges without being able to change their position, and they are thus integrated into the narrative scheme conceived by the exhibition designer. This is the case in a room at Castelvecchio in Verona, where the concrete plinth extends into a staircase composition that offers different seating levels. This is a far cry from the comfort of the Tripolina and the proximity it allowed so viewers could have face-to-face interactions with artworks, but here again Scarpa favored a refined spatial composition of the room to capture a modern vision. The shape also echoes the steel staircase found in a room upstairs,

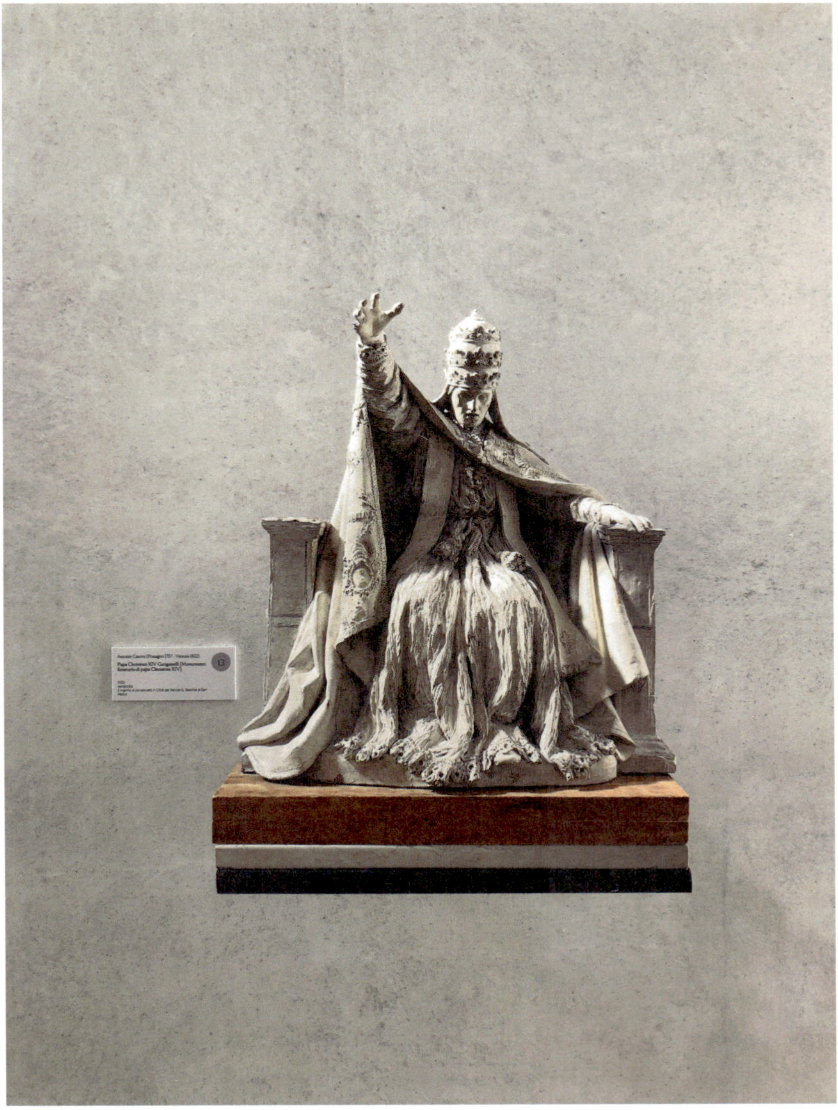

Fig. 16 *Monument to Pope Clement XIV*, Antonio Canova. View of the Museum Gypsotheca Antonio Canova in 2023, exhibition design by Carlo Scarpa, Possagno, 1955–57

an architectural feature that creates a suspended partition with a masterful aesthetic effect.

After the Galleria Regionale della Sicilia at the Palazzo Abatellis and the Museo Gypsotheca Antonio Canova in Possagno, the Castelvecchio, which Scarpa designed between 1957 and 1974, is his most ambitious project in terms of the scale of renovation. It is also the museum where his work is most celebrated, with a tribute as soon as you enter Castelvecchio, and a slideshow recounting the renovation.[59] This is in contrast to the Accademia in Venice or the Palazzo Abatellis in Palermo, where his exhibition display installations are not even mentioned and therefore remain unnoticed by the vast majority of visitors. The scenography principles he previously explored are also evident here, deployed with masterful skill and great freedom in the choice of the exposed elements. His displays are veritable stage sets integrated into the architecture with great precision in terms of perspective and constant formal invention in the combination of materials. From the outside, a sculptural effect is produced by the layout of the entrance with stone slabs, flower beds, and fragments of columns that blend perfectly with the refined, renovated architecture. The sequence of rooms offers a wide variety of displays, each as striking as the next, combining colorful panels on which a small number of works from the collection are staged, in generous dialogue with natural light and with meticulous attention to the finishing touches of the technical elements. Visiting Castelvecchio is a moment of great aesthetic emotion, where even the smallest fragment of an ancient sculpture is transformed by a gem of exhibition display. Yet the effect is always in the service of the work, as evidenced by the sculpture of Christ on the cross attributed to the Maestro di Sant'Anastasia, staged in a highly theatrical manner: the work is placed on a dark panel in the shape of a Tau cross, while the Virgin and Saint John stand on either side on hollowed-out blocks with modernist forms. The ensemble creates a visual shock, capable of sustaining a spiritual and religious experience. Scarpa also produced numerous points of rupture with the architecture, in perspectives that play with gaps and reversals, exemplifying the idea of a museum that is not only a place for the preservation and exhibition of a collection but also a staged visual object. The Museo di Castelvecchio was originally a medieval castle, and Scarpa also had to integrate the constraints of exhibiting parts of the historical monument alongside the collections. This is a rare occurrence, which can be linked to the work carried out by Peter Zumthor between 1997 and 2017, when he built and designed the

Kolumba Museum in Cologne on the ruins of an old Gothic church that was destroyed, like most of the city's churches, during the bombings of World War II. The building connects the ruins to an imposing modern structure whose identity is linked to the use of "Kolumba" bricks. As it was adapted to the Gothic bricks, this choice allowed Zumthor to produce variations in materials throughout the visit using a meticulous technique that immersed visitors in the history of the place and its destruction while exhibiting the collections. The result is a highly expressive dramaturgy with a deep significance as visitors move between outside and inside spaces. The Kolumba Museum houses a collection of religious art presented amid an exhibition design of great visual poetry and with a sense of spiritual elevation. The link between Zumthor's work and Carlo Scarpa's design at Castelvecchio is obvious.

## Lina Bo Bardi (1914–1992)

> "New museums should open their doors and let in fresh air and new light. [...] The purpose of a museum is to create an atmosphere, a behavior that encourages visitors to be open to understanding the work of art, and in this sense no distinction is made between an ancient work of art and a modern work of art."
>
> Lina Bo Bardi, São Paulo Art Museum, 1957–1968,
> Instituto Lina Bo e Pietro Maria Bardi, Blau Portfolio Series

Although the Italian rationalist movement consisted overwhelmingly of men, its legacy also includes the contributions of Lina Bo Bardi, an Italian who became a naturalized Brazilian and whose profoundly modern work invented its own language. She trained at Sapienza University of Rome's Faculty of Architecture, where the teaching was dominated by proponents of the Novecento style and promoted a vision of architecture in the service of Mussolini's fascism. After graduating, she moved to Milan and Genoa, where she discovered a much more avant-garde vision of the field with the rationalists and collaborated with Gio Ponti on the magazine *Domus*. Amid the morose political and economic climate, she emigrated to Brazil in 1946 with her husband Pietro Maria Bardi, an intellectual and gallery owner who had invaluable connections in the country who had been invited to present an exhibition of Italian paintings in Rio de Janeiro.

There they met Brazilian industrialist Assis Chateaubriand, who invited them to exhibit Pietro Maria Bardi's collection of European art to Brazilian audiences and then to design and build a museum of modern art. Alongside her husband's activities, which brought them into contact with Brazil's most privileged circles, Lina Bo Bardi was deeply influenced by her encounters with Brazilian popular culture, particularly during her long stays in Bahia in the northeast of the country between 1959 and 1964. It was there that she befriended the theater director and set designer Martim Gonçalves, who would work with her on several museum projects. She also joined groups of intellectuals campaigning for the emancipation of the people through access to education and culture, and for the recognition of the importance of popular cultures. Quickly naturalized as a Brazilian citizen, she settled in São Paulo, where she built the Casa di Vidro or Glass House, where she lived until her death. Typical of the modern European sensibility, this house was constructed around a tree in the Morumbi garden district and maintains an intimate and exuberant relationship with the plant world, allowing wildlife to enter through its multiple openings to the outside. Now home to the Instituto Bo Bardi, which manages the archives of Lina Bo and Pietro Maria Bardi, it is open to visitors. It embodies a porous and vibrant relationship between the interior and exterior, with an elegant balance between the architecture, furniture, indoor plants, and the exuberant vitality of the garden's vegetation. For Lina Bo Bardi, each project was an opportunity to create new ways of blending energies and invent ways of intertwining the inside and the outside so people were permeated by the effervescence of life. The drawings and sketches for projects are of a high artistic quality. Lina Bo Bardi created shapes and combinations of materials with precise lines, imagined different atmospheres, delineated different levels with colors, and annotated the works with texts, and these archives deserve to be exhibited more widely today.[60] The house is also filled with objects she brought back from her travels throughout Brazil. They serve as a celebration of the inventiveness of the indigenous and Afro-Brazilian populations, who often lived in difficult conditions and whose cause Lina Bo Bardi tirelessly championed. Although her creative perspective was initially linked to the modern architecture movement, it matured through her contact with these populations, who produced high-quality handcrafted objects from discarded materials. She was fascinated by their ingenuity in designing everyday spaces and reappropriating and transforming unwanted items into furniture. Her architectural projects were also

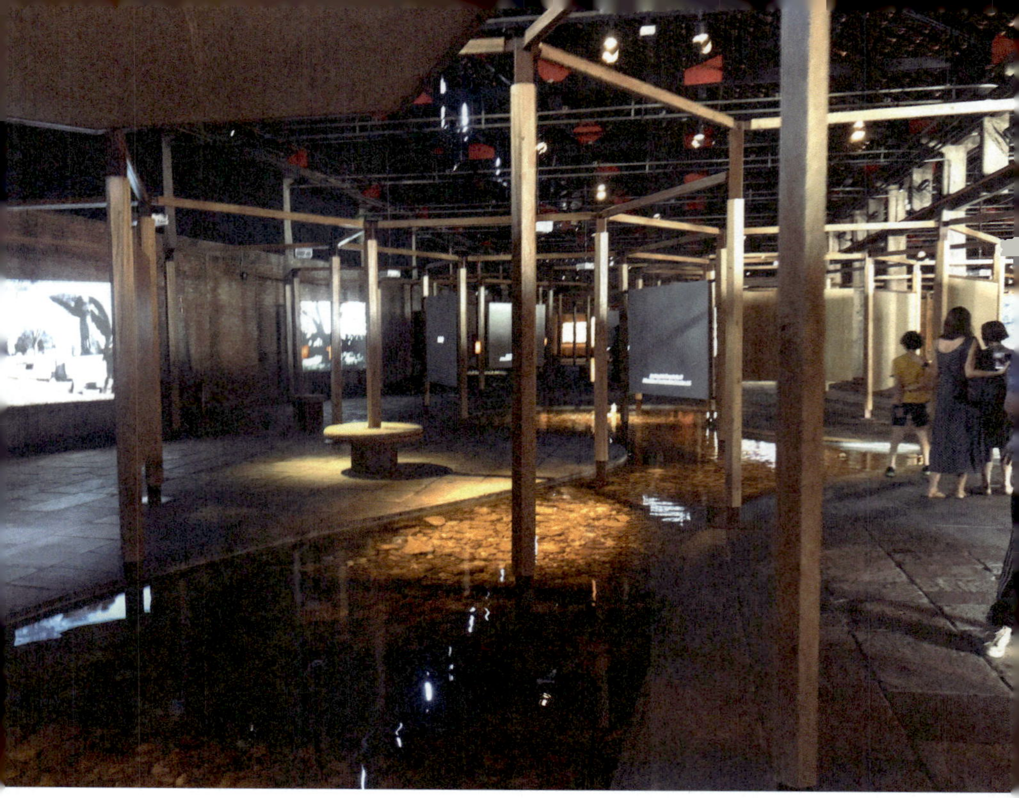

Fig. 17 View of the SESC Pompeia in 2023, exhibition design by Lina Bo Bardi, São Paulo, 1977–82

marked by her appreciation for the vitality of bodies and their uninhibited relationship with an environment that combined built spaces with lush nature, a phenomenon that also unfolded in city centers of the country. This interest could be seen in her earliest preparatory drawings, which gave a central place to trees, plants, and water, such as the one she did for the SESC Pompeia. The SESCs are community structures located in various neighborhoods of São Paulo that offer free access to facilities for relaxation, sports, and cultural activities. The one in Pompeia is located on the site of a former drum factory, whose structure Lina Bo Bardi preserved and transformed, creating emblematic openings such as those in the towers, which resemble drawings on the façades. Meanwhile, pathways bring color, water and vegetation into this vast concrete complex. The exhibition rooms are thus traversed by a stream and pebbles that draw lines between the spaces and the picture rails, becoming an integral part of the visitor experience. In 2023, the retrospective dedicated to Ana Mendieta at SESC Pompeia benefited from this beautiful meditative atmosphere, with suspended screens interacting directly with the movement of the water, echoing the artist's performances.

Lina Bo Bardi was also extremely interested in the theater and on several occasions collaborated with live performances. In 1984, she designed the Teatro Oficina on a very narrow site in São Paulo as a street-stage that the audience can walk through like the actors and watch the performance from the scaffold seating that rises on either side. The building has a large modular glass wall penetrated by a majestic tree, providing multiple ways to use it as a dramatic device. In September 2023, the Rasga Coração company created a musical show inspired by the work of the composer Heitor Villa-Lobos. It was driven by the revolutionary energy of Oswald de Andrade's *Manifesto Antropófago* and the Tropicália movement, and it was in full resonance with the indigenous movement's victories in securing recognition of their rights. The entire building vibrated with dancing, singing, playing bodies in close dialogue with the tree and the moon (the removable glass roof allows the theater to be opened up to the skies). It was an embodiment of the wild freedom of this space that invites spectators to take part in collective actions. The grassroots dimension of Lina Bo Bardi's projects was essential, and it is wonderful to see that this continues today in the theater, as well as in the exhibitions held at SESC Pompeia and the Museu de Arte de São Paulo (MASP). Lina Bo Bardi reflected on museum projects on numerous occasions, thinking of their architecture as a tool for education and inclusion.

Her ambition was to bring a wide audience through the doors of these spaces, and therefore to link them as closely as possible with the city and nature in order to make them vibrant and non-dominating places. Her preparatory sketches and drawings reveal her emphasis on integrating plants, water, and color while also accounting for the moving bodies of people through the spaces. It is striking to note the number of visitors visible in the archive documents, and the attention paid to the way their gazes and body positions interact with the works and with each other. In both the drawings and the photographs, visitors circulate, discuss, pause for contemplative moments, sometimes sit down, and create an intimate relationship to the space. Lina Bo Bardi always sought to create flexibility, never immobilizing bodies or spaces, allowing for a modularity in the exhibition layout that gave viewers freedom in their interpretation. The museum labels are there to provide information to accompany reflection, not to impose an aesthetic judgment;[61] the works do not force themselves upon the viewer but allow themselves to be discovered as the visit progresses.

Lina Bo Bardi's profound interest in popular and folk works in Brazil led her to devote several exhibitions to them. In 1959, she organized the exhibition *Bahia no Ibirapuera* in collaboration with the scenographer Martim Gonçalves, whom she had met in Bahia. The exhibition included photographs by Pierre Verger and Marcel Gautherot, two French artists living in Brazil who were dedicated to using an ethnographic approach to document local traditions as well as modern architecture. Lina Bo Bardi remained close to Pierre Verger throughout her life, sharing his passion for traditional rituals and local culture, as well as a strong political commitment to marginalized indigenous and Afro-Brazilian communities, which led both of them to campaign for universal access to culture. *Bahia no Ibirapuera* was presented as part of the fifth edition of the Bienal de São Paulo, an event notable for being the first major international art gathering to take place in the Southern Hemisphere, though it nonetheless reproduced Western models by literally copying the structure of the Venice Biennale. By inviting different Western countries to propose their national representatives, it prolonged colonial influences and reinforced the cultural domination of Europe and the United States over the South American art scene. In response, Lina Bo Bardi and Martim Gonçalves decided to showcase handicrafts and pay tribute to the vitality of traditional music by designing an exhibit based on their research in Salvador de Bahia on local customs, everyday objects, religious symbols, and costumes. The musical performances and scenography blended everything together without hierarchy and integrated images through slide carousels. In her preparatory watercolor drawings, Lina Bo Bardi constructed a highly dynamic layout with a blue curtain that interacted with picture rails and created a formal structure combining linear, circular, and rectangular spaces installed on one side of the building. A tree stood proudly in the center, while the floor was covered with eucalyptus leaves collected each day from the park, referencing places of worship associated with Candomblé, a religion derived from African traditions that played a central role in Salvador de Bahia. In addition to transporting these objects from Bahia to the capital São Paulo, the designers sought to convey an intangible heritage through an exhibition atmosphere that reflected the spirit of these objects. Recordings of Afro-Brazilian songs and percussion were played throughout the space, creating a "global, immersive and ritualistic synesthetic experience."[62] The exhibition was scheduled to travel to Rome, Lina Bo Bardi's hometown, but was abruptly cancelled before the opening, despite having already been installed, because Brazilian officials did not want their country to be represented internationally through these objects that stood in stark contrast to the modern image of Brazil that they wished to project abroad.

Lina Bo Bardi also designed the architecture for the Museu de Arte de São Paulo (MASP) in consultation with her husband Pietro Maria Bardi, who was its director (this project, which began in 1957, was only inaugurated in 1968 due to delays in funding). It was essential for them that this museum be a tool for education and emancipation, a place that reached out to the overwhelming mega-city but was adapted to the scale of individual bodies. Seen from the outside, it is a glass structure built on São Paulo's main avenue, Avenida Paulista, and supported by a red exposed concrete structure on stilts, while the urban environment can be viewed through the space below the building. The architect followed the modernist principles laid down by Le Corbusier, whose work and philosophy she admired, yet she also placed the rear of the building on the natural slope and designed terrace systems with rich vegetation. The MASP therefore has two faces, one sober, made of glass and concrete, and the other green and lush. Lina Bo Bardi, who learned the importance of expressing a political vision of architecture through writing from her experience at *Domus* magazine in Milan, always took the time to put her intentions into words. She explained the challenge of the MASP as follows: "To remove from the museum the air of churches that excludes

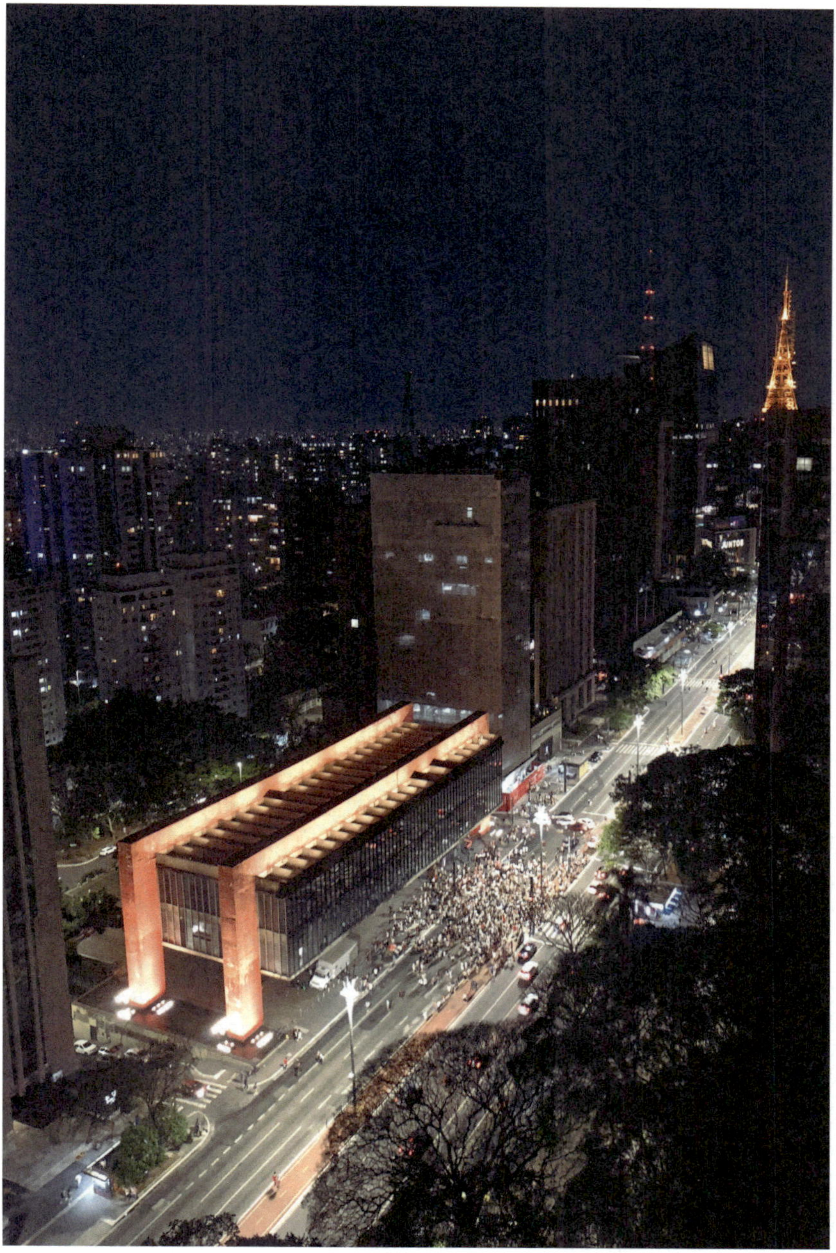

Fig. 18 Exterior view of MASP with crowd gathered after a soccer victory in 2023, São Paulo

newcomers, to remove the 'aura' from paintings in order to present the artwork as 'work', highly skilled, but work nonetheless; presenting it in such a way that it can be understood by unqualified people, by the senhores of Guarulhos, so different from the visitors to large traditional museums, whose 'aura' persists, even in modern settings. Seeing hundreds of people walking among the paintings in an almost familiar, non-auratic atmosphere ... is disturbing, like a prophecy of fundamental change. The São Paulo art museum is popular."[63]

Lina Bo Bardi made a radical statement with her choice of exhibition design at the MASP by arranging the main gallery with glass easels placed on concrete and wooden bases. The layout is similar to that created by Franco Albini at the Palazzo Bianco in Genoa, but here it was extended to the entire gallery, which has no picture rails. The effect is immediately striking: all the works are separated from the walls and integrated into an overall view, like an assembly of bodies without hierarchy or sequence. Visitors face the paintings in a frontal relationship that tends toward horizontality and the museum labels are located on the backs of the works, which encourages the visitors to move around them. The most frequently shown photographs of the gallery favor a central, overall view devoid of spectators, which I believe creates a misleading perception. In reality, the experience of the MASP plays out step by step in an intimate dance between the works and bodies, mixing them with the gazes of other spectators, so that the entire ensemble creates a powerful image. The photograph reproduced here comes from a series of images published in 1997 in a beautiful volume on the MASP edited by the Instituto Bo Bardi with a text by Aldo van Eyck.[64] In this book, the photographs emphasize the intimate and personal relationships between the visitors and the works, the presence of racialized bodies, and the viewers' own positions as they themselves become part of the gaze. Through this exhibition design, Lina Bo Bardi dissociates herself from the complicity and excesses of a visual regime tied to distant, disembodied perspectives inherited from a dominant colonial society. When the museum is open, the gallery is never empty of bodies, and Lina Bo Bardi's glass easels give them a genuine place in the space, de-hierarchizing aesthetic relationships and incorporating each person into the whole.

These iconic MASP easels were unfortunately destroyed in the 1990s, but research conducted by the Instituto Bo Bardi together with the current director of MASP, Adriano Pedrosa, has made it possible to reproduce and reinstall them. It is particularly interesting to observe the diversity of audiences at different times of day.[65] People make slow

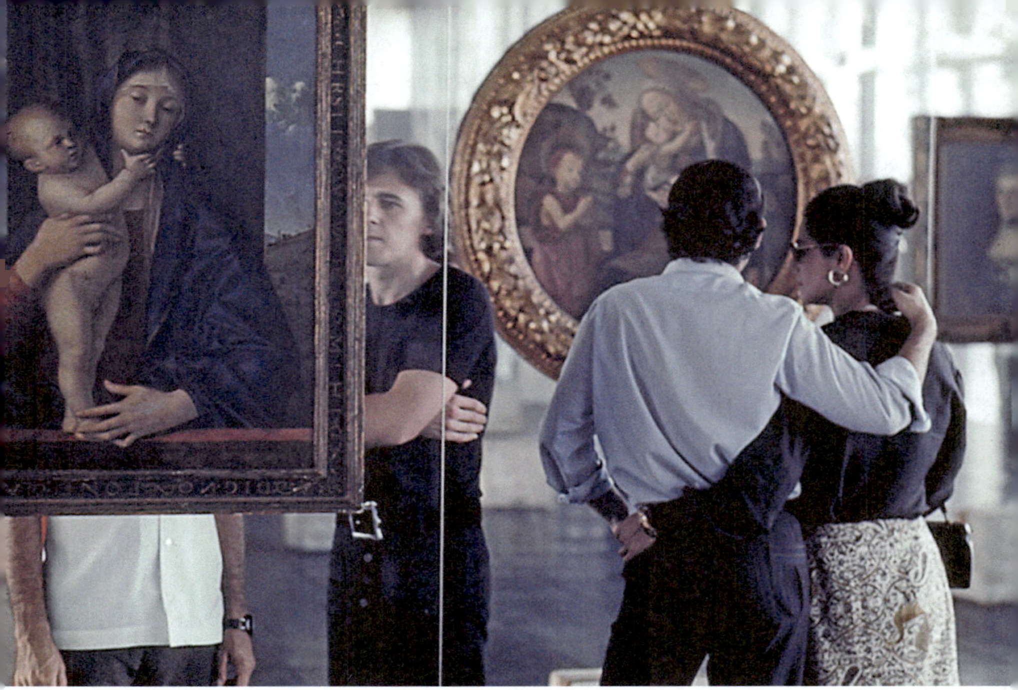

Fig. 19 View of the Picture Gallery in 1997, MASP, exhibition design by Lina Bo Bardi, São Paulo, 1957–68. Archive Instituto Lina Bo e P. M. Bardi

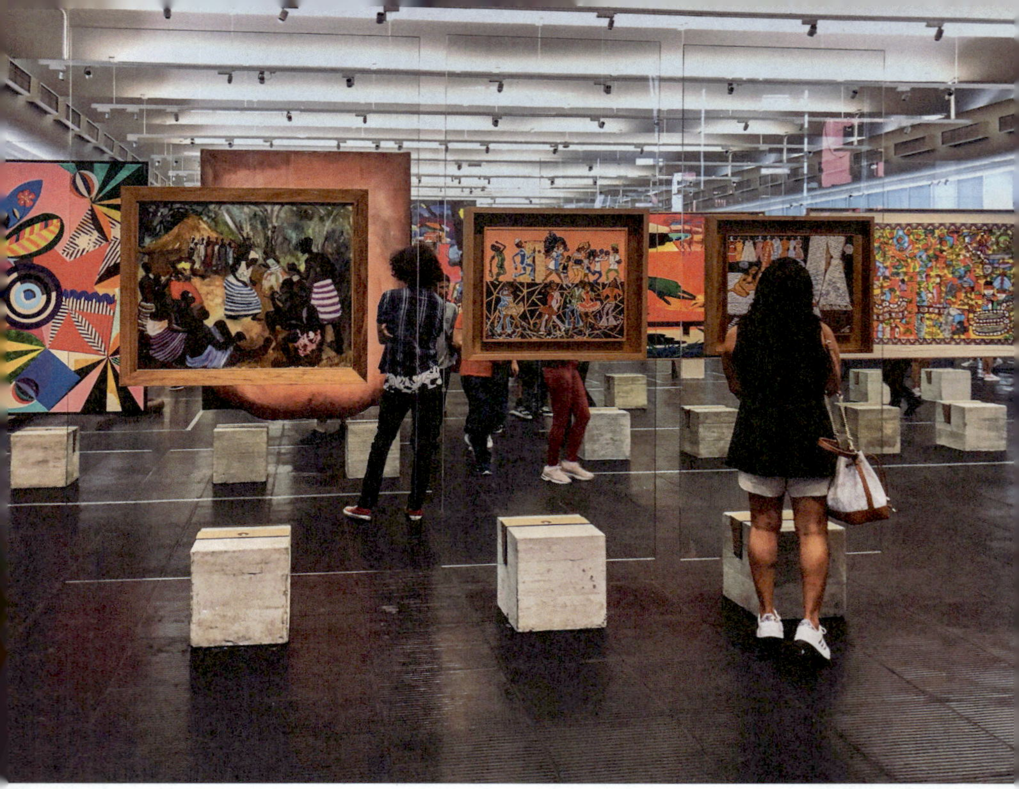

Fig. 20 View of the Picture Gallery in 2023, MASP, exhibition design by Lina Bo Bardi, São Paulo, 1957–68

progress through the space; they take numerous pauses, and the routes, which are different each time, often revolve around the works, creating loops and counter-movements between bodies. The audiences reflect the diversity of the Brazilian population, although South American tourists outnumber São Paulo residents and the poorest populations remain largely under-represented. The time each person spends looking at the paintings is quite long, much longer than in a room at the Louvre, although the fact that the collection is limited to a single gallery naturally contributes to this. The long-term exhibition *Picture Gallery in Transformation* is semi-permanent, organized chronologically beginning with the most recent works while incorporating occasional contemporary insertions throughout the layout. It explores the capacity of this exhibition model to reinvent the conventions of art history, for example by integrating photographs by the Guerrilla Girls at the entrance and highlighting artists from under-represented communities: women, Black people, indigenous people, trans people, and so on. Further into the gallery, visitors encounter major works from European art history that were added to the MASP's collections when it first opened, thanks to Pietro Maria Bardi's relationships with European artists and dealers, as well as with the industrialists and wealthy figures of the time. The feminist and decolonial perspective established at the beginning of the exhibition continues with juxtapositions between historical and contemporary works, maintaining a conceptual framework that, without preventing visitors from experiencing the aesthetic force of these major works, challenges them to deconstruct the cultural and political model on which Brazil—and Western art history in general—were built. Lina Bo Bardi believed in exhibition strategies motivated not by a chronological perspective but by a desire to "produce a shock, arouse reactions of curiosity and research,"[66] which closely aligns with what Adriano Pedrosa proposes today.

In 1969, Lina Bo and Pietro Maria Bardi opted to inaugurate the MASP with the exhibition *A mão do povo brasileiro* [The Hand of the Brazilian People] in the temporary gallery space on the lower floor, which was a continuation of the exhibition *Bahia no Ibirapuera*, whose presentation in Italy had been censored. It was a powerful political gesture, asserting a vision of Brazil that extended beyond its European history, bringing together artisanal and religious works as well as "primitive" sculptures created by Afro-Brazilian communities. The extensive collection was grouped by function and context, presented on wooden pedestals where necessary, creating an overall impression of great density far removed from the effect produced by the

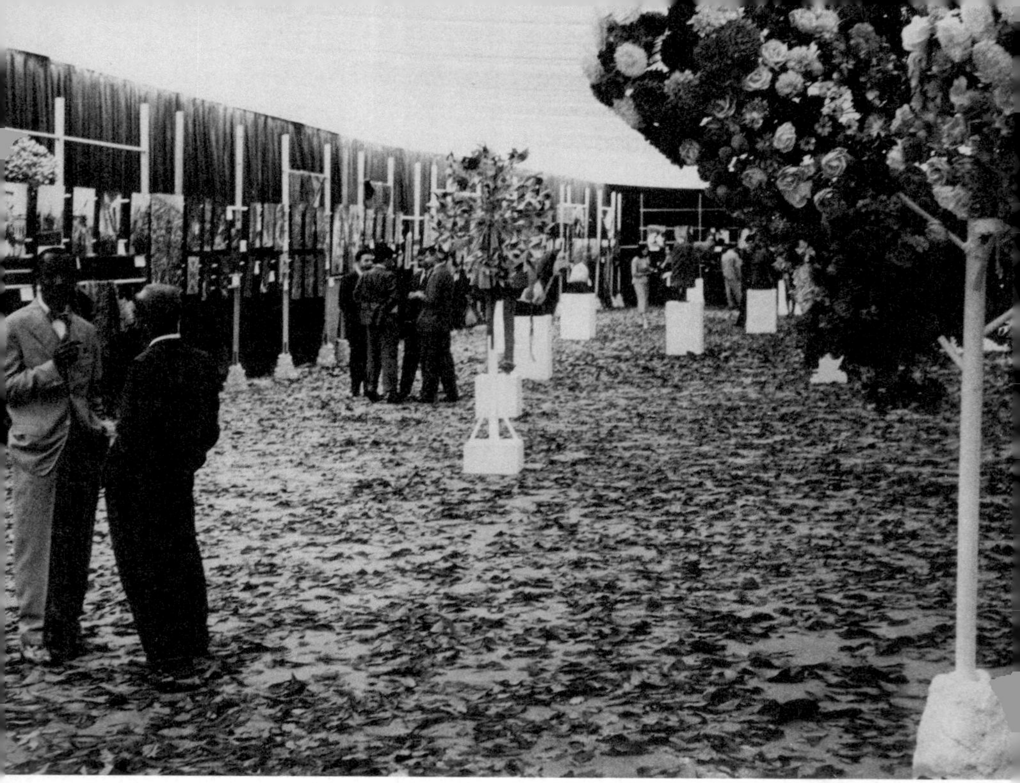

Fig. 21 *Bahia no Ibirapuera*, exhibition for the 5th São Paulo Biennial, exhibition design by Lina Bo Bardi and Martim Gonçalves, 1959. The floor is covered with eucalyptus leaves.

transparent, airy easels in the main gallery upstairs. Some displays had a more sculptural effect, such as the pyramidal pedestal that concluded the presentation with a group of statues. This exhibition was reconstructed by the MASP in 2016; the project provided an opportunity to initiate a research project (a catalogue was published, although unfortunately only in Portuguese) and to place the non-hierarchical inclusion of all forms of human production at the center of the museum's mission.

As Pedrosa points out, the separation of the two exhibitions on two floors of the museum, and the difference in approach to the exhibition design, are important issues to be considered. Nevertheless, Lina Bo and Pietro Maria Bardi's decision to borrow objects from the museum devoted to popular arts and combine them with objects from indigenous populations was a powerful political gesture within a conservative and racially prejudiced Brazilian society entirely focused on European modernity. Like most of Lina Bo Bardi's museum projects, the MASP also features an auditorium, a restaurant, a bookshop, and a space dedicated to artistic workshops, as well as a patio under the building, at street level, which she imagined as a space for games, sports, and concerts. Even today, it remains a popular gathering place for spontaneous celebrations of football victories or election victories (the crowd that gathered around the MASP to celebrate Lula's election in 2022 was impressive), making this museum a powerful symbolic location, even for those who do not visit the collections.

Lina Bo Bardi's last museum project was the renovation of the Museu de Arte Moderna de São Paulo (the MAM), transforming the triangular building in Ibirapuera Park opposite the facilities where the biennale was held, where she had presented the 1959 exhibition. Lina Bo Bardi opened the building onto the park by modifying the façade with glass walls. She also proposed reversing the entrance to face the biennale facilities and painting the opposite walls in shades of blue, but this was not carried out. There were several designs for the scenography, the first of which, dating from 1982, was based on the idea of an exhibition design conceived as a labyrinth, where a long picture rail with a fairly low height of two meters maximum created a lighter atmosphere. In this project, she paid particular attention to the architectural layout, and in another drawing from 1982, she refined the scenography by proposing wooden displays for one or two works embedded in stones placed directly on the floor, which could be easily repositioned. They also interact directly with the exterior, which Lina Bo Bardi proposed to redesign as a sculpture park, which was later done in 1991 by Roberto Burle Marx. As she emphasized in her drawings, these displays would have allowed hanging on both sides and offered the modularity necessary for a temporary exhibition space. However, the dialogue with the MAM team proved difficult[67] and she abandoned this idea, proposing instead a layout rediscovered in a drawing updated in 2023 by the MAM documentation department. In it, Lina Bo Bardi proposed a light wooden structure crossing the space parallel to the glass façade, allowing paintings and sculptures to be hung without installing panels. As in her project for the MASP, the system would have allowed the gaze to traverse the space, bodies to connect with the works, and multiple points of view to be created. The bird's-eye view drawing also reveals the idea of a structure playing on different heights, in an urban dynamic. The non-modularity of this system, which was certainly too restrictive for the museum, once again led to the abandonment of this idea, and the conflict that subsequently arose with the MAM unfortunately prevented the architect from producing an exhibition system.

Lina Bo Bardi's figure and legacy are now widely recognized outside Brazil, and the interviews published below testify to her importance for many artists. Isaac Julien created a multi-screen video installation dedicated to her, entitled *Lina Bo Bardi. A Marvellous Entanglement* (2019), which presents a choreographed portrait of her, where her body and voice intertwine with her architecture and assert a non-linear conception of time. Julien immerses us in her shared vision with Pierre Verger, explores the graphic dimension of constructed forms, films concrete floors covered with leaves and dust, and façades pierced with organic cut-outs, creating a sensory portrait of an architect who was able to distance herself from the ideology of modernity. In 2024, as curator of the 60th Venice Biennale, Adriano Pedrosa installed Lina Bo Bardi's glass easels in a section of the Arsenale entitled *Nucleo Storico* that was dedicated to twentieth-century Italian artists who traveled and developed their careers abroad. This was an opportunity for a wide audience to discover and experience these easels as part of their tour of the Arsenale, but it also dissociated them from the context of her architectural project.

## Gae Aulenti (1927–2012)

Based in Milan, Gae Aulenti had links with the radical architecture movement through Ernesto Nathan Rogers (BBPR) from her student days, when she was his student at the Politecnico di Milano. She also gained design insights through her visits and collaborations with the Triennale di Milano, as well as through her involvement with the journal *Casabella*. A turning point for her was a meeting with Germano Celant, which was probably facilitated by Marcello Nizzoli, a designer at Olivetti with whom she worked on several occasions, notably on the layout of the company's store in Buenos Aires in 1968. Through this connection, she went on to design a large number of his exhibitions in Italy and abroad. Their first collaboration dates to 1973, with the Christo *Valley Curtain* (1970–72) exhibition in the Rotonda della Besana in Milan, where she designed a white geometric space completely isolated from the rotunda, with a low ceiling allowing light to filter through. The visitor route, however, began and ended in one of the four naves left open, offering a view of the impressive vaults and columns. Christo's work was thus isolated from the rotonda to better fit in with the Baroque architecture, in a postmodern interpretation characteristic of Gae Aulenti's aesthetic philosophy, which was similar to the vision of her friend Aldo Rossi.

In her historical analysis of museums where the exhibition display was the subject of specific attention and notable experimentation, the historian Emma Barker[68] mentions the Musée d'Orsay (1986), Gae Aulenti's most well-known work. Her project was to integrate the museum layout into the architecture of the former train station without erasing the building's history so that visitors remain travelers while becoming spectators, thus creating a blended experience. By occupying the station, which was built for the 1900 Exposition Universelle with an architecture that was emblematic of the modern movement, the Musée d'Orsay reinvented the museum experience by creating gaps and discomforts, encouraging the public to diversify their perspective without impacting the care taken in the presentation of the works. While a train station is representative of the acceleration of human and material flows and produces a state of constant alertness, the museum exudes a state of quiet contemplation of major works from the nineteenth and early twentieth centuries. The layout of the works alternates perspectives and creates a sense of disorientation and complexity in the central hall, "giving the viewer the feeling of being in a mental labyrinth."[69] In this way, Gae Aulenti counters the idea of a museum layout designed to guide the viewer and facilitate their relationship with the works. The display is charged with tension, becoming a tool for connecting the spatial-temporal experience and the conceptual relationship, creating colorful and open geometric compositions. The architect includes the viewer's body in her design for the central span of the museum: this structure creates both pedestals for the sculptures and long benches for visitors, thereby creating a sharing of space with the works, a symbolically powerful statement. The movement of the visitor is also at the heart of this central layout, which is constructed on several levels connected by steps, in a dramaturgy of movement embraced by Gae Aulenti in her design of the project: "Working in the theater, I realized the importance of action in architecture, and this concept of action plays a role in the layout of the Musée d'Orsay, in the routes, in the passages from one space to another, in the wide aisles. An idea of time as much as of space."[70]

Gae Aulenti was involved in the period when picture rails returned to museum architecture, as she was the one who responded to the request to reintroduce them to the Pompidou Centre in 1985, after the radical opening proposed by Renzo Piano and Richard Rogers, where wall-less galleries favored modularity in layout that facilitated a play of echoes between the works and a dialogue with the city that was visible through the glass walls. Gae Aulenti designed the layout of the spaces dedicated to the collections, conceiving high picture rails that define a path to the rooms served by a wide central corridor. She was long accused of having disfigured Piano and Rogers's project with these picture rails, which closed off the spaces, but this is now common practice, with semi-permanent scenography also responding to the economic and ecological challenges of exhibition production.

In 1986, Gae Aulenti designed the interior of the Palazzo Grassi in Venice. The eighteenth-century palace, which is now owned by François Pinault, had been acquired by Fiat, which wanted to use it for exhibitions. The architect designed the entire project, including the picture rails, lighting, and highly sculptural sofas arranged throughout the rooms, and went on to create the scenography for close to two dozen temporary exhibitions. In the exhibition dedicated to her in 2024 by the Triennale di Milano, which took the approach of reconstructing elements of her design and architectural projects on a scale of 1:1, visitors could discover a room from the inaugural exhibition at Palazzo Grassi, *Futurismo & Futurismi*, curated by Pontus Hultén. Although the walls were covered with white picture rails, Gae Aulenti chose to leave the architecture of the palace exposed by maintaining a gap between the plasterboard and the walls, in a gesture not unlike that made much later by Rem Koolhaas and Thomas Demand for the scenography of the exhibition they designed in concert with the curator Germano Celant, *When Attitudes Become*

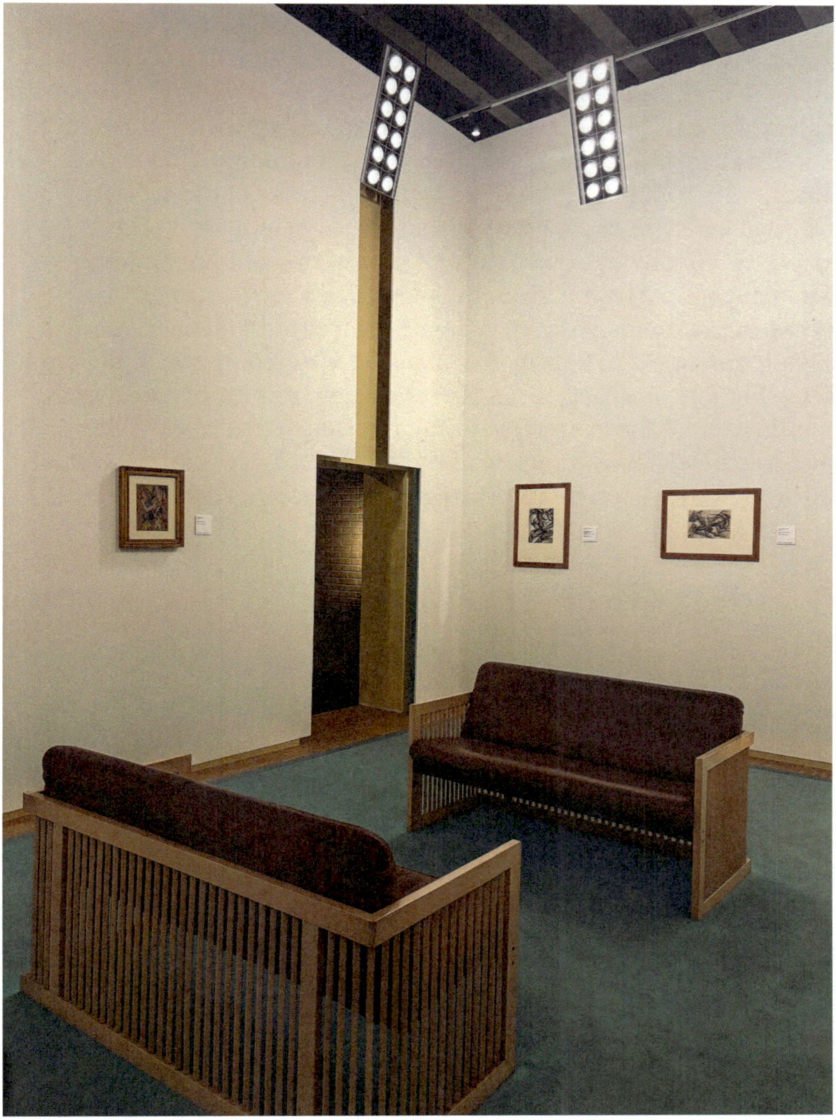

Fig. 22 View of the reconstruction of the Palazzo Grassi exhibition design in the exhibition *Gae Aulenti (1927–2012)*, curated by G. Agosti, Milan Triennale, 2024–25

*Form: Berne 1969/Venice 2013*. To maintain a dialogue between the Palazzo Corner della Regina in Venice and the Kunsthalle in Bern, the architectural plan of the Kunsthalle was implemented in the Venetian palace through picture rails cut flush with the palace's architecture but installed with a visual gap, creating an oxymoronic and dialectical effect.[71] Gae Aulenti also designed cut-outs in the corridors that blended with the existing architecture without erasing it and extended directly into the lighting fixtures. In addition, painted wooden pegs protruded from the picture rail above the passages between the rooms, fully asserting these technical elements as an artistic gesture. The lighting consisted of industrial-style light panels hung high up, creating atmospheres without pointing to the works, reminiscent of those used by Albini and Helg. Finally, the white picture rails gave prominence to the richly decorated ceilings, which integrated the vision by embracing the historical break.

# Exhibition design as an artistic gesture

## Revealing the modernist heritage of the exhibition

Over the past decade, the contemporary art world has paid increasing attention to the history of exhibition design through both acts of reappropriation and homage, although many of these have been focused on the work of Carlo Scarpa and Lina Bo Bardi. One example is Pierre Huyghe's *Untilled* (2013) at documenta 13. For this in situ creation in a park in Kassel, Germany, Pierre Huyghe chose to carry out his interventions at a vegetable compost site, including a work that was a direct reference to the Brion tomb designed and built by Carlo Scarpa between 1968 and 1978, where he himself was buried following his accidental death in 1978. The reference to this site is noted in the plans Pierre Huyghe drew for *Untilled* and is accompanied by other tributes to Joseph Beuys and Dominique Gonzalez-Foerster in a section entitled "cemetery of culture." The evocation of the Brion tomb is particularly noticeable in the concrete basin and its powerful association with vegetation, creating a Brutalist atmosphere connected to living things. As part of the seminar "Something you should know" in 2015, Philippe Duboÿ organized a study day devoted to "Carlo Scarpa and his friends: The art of exhibiting," and welcomed Scarpa's collaborators and specialists as well as artists strongly inspired by his work, such as Dominique Gonzalez-Foerster and Danh Vo.

Danh Vo's work is linked to his personal history as the child of Vietnamese boat people immigrants who were welcomed into Denmark. He assembles fragments, samples layers of historical realities, and creates poetic gestures that engage in dialogue with the locations. In 2023, under the rotunda of the Bourse de Commerce exhibition space in Paris, and in 2018 in the main nave of the CAPC contemporary art museum in Bordeaux, he created monumental installations designed as distinctive exhibition devices. At the CAPC, he installed large blocks of Carrara marble, a set of shelves, and a mirrored structure. The museum's great nave was also filled with photographs, sculptures, and words. Like Carlo Scarpa, Danh Vo likes to take

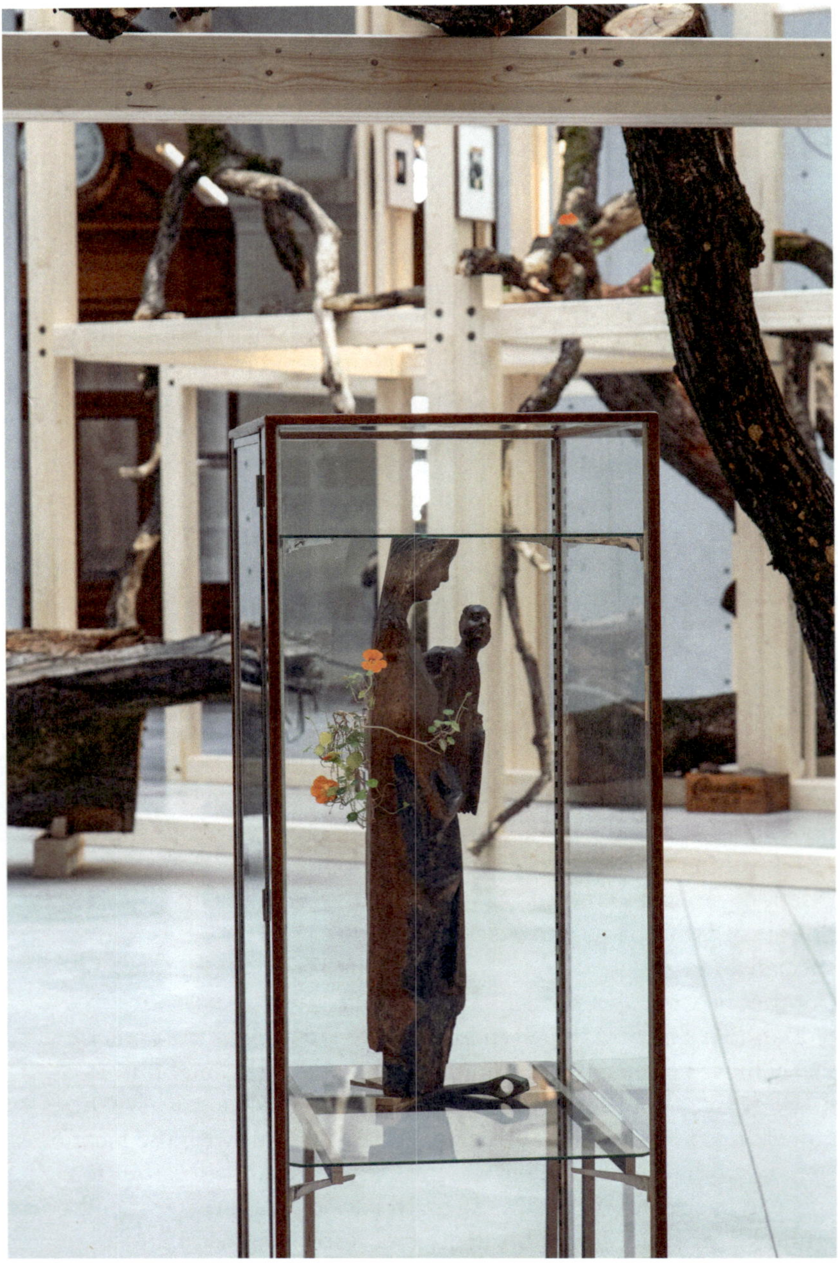

Fig. 23 Exhibition view *Before the storm*, Danh Vo, *Untitled*, Bourse de Commerce, Paris, 2023

fragments of ancient sculptures and create specific displays for them, combining the melancholy of ruins with the sculptural force of an act rooted in a specific place. His fragments of sculptures, placed off-center on ledges, created an intense visual atmosphere and a sense of general instability. The dialogue with tree branches collected in the forest also contributes to a perspective imbued with the fragility of the world. For the Bourse de Commerce, he conceived his project as a pavilion, a setting for his sculptures, that "allows him to free himself as a creator of objects"[72] to focus more on developing relationships and tensions between the sculptures and the structures. The installation brought together ancient sculptures, tree branches from French forests uprooted during storms, and photographs of cut flowers taken in the shop of an immigrant florist family who survive by responding to the desire for beauty in the daily lives of a privileged population that now includes the artist himself. His exhibitions and pieces are assemblages that borrow from the art of the base, a questioning of what connects, what supports, what brings together, and what repairs. The precision of the hangings and viewing paths and the play of imbalance with sculptures frozen in an off-center position evokes Scarpa's work, in particular the place he gave to the equestrian statue representing *Cangrande I della Scala* (1340) in the Museo di Castelvecchio in Verona. Placed on an off-center pedestal that protrudes from the building in a radical geometric composition, the statue can be seen from a multitude of angles and even takes on an aerial dimension when seen from below. This perspective of Danh Vo's work invites reflection on Scarpa's design and dialogues between the two that testify to the meticulous attention given to these fragments of history that have come down to us and that must be cared for in order to allow them to properly encounter the present moment. At the Bourse de Commerce, Danh Vo displayed part of a wooden statue of Mary and Jesus in a glass case; however, far from being a bubble of preservation, the structure also housed a nasturtium plant that climbed up the wood, mingling its cheerful orange flowers with the sculpture. This non-aggressive plant did not endanger the sculpture, but it does challenge the reflexes of museum conservation, which fears possible contamination from living plants. Danh Vo also played with the vocabulary of support here, balancing the sculpture on two wooden wedges and the blade of an axe, in a logic of reappropriating materials and playing with their meanings. Finally, the display case itself is a true sculptural composition, articulating emptiness and fullness through a succession of levels and spaces. As a whole, the work had an immensely powerful sculptural presence that was reinforced by the rotunda's enveloping concrete designed by Tadao Ando, which provokes multiple dialogues with the exhibition display analyzed above.

## Leaning toward the floor

The shift away from the white cube model and, more broadly, the primacy of the wall as a display space, led to an ideological shift toward the floor and ceiling, which are now considered for their architectural qualities and no longer merely as technical surfaces. Carlo Scarpa, Franco Albini, and Franca Helg often installed fabrics on ceilings; Lina Bo Bardi transformed the floor into a garden strewn with leaves, and all of them created atmospheres that demonstrated exhibitions are not limited to hanging works on walls. In the white cube model, the floor is often neutralized and overlooked in favor of picture rails, pedestals, or sculptural elements which, even when placed directly on the floor, often seem to be there only by accident. There is thus a veritable shift in focus for the viewer when the exhibition directs them toward the floor rather than the walls, as in Tatiana Trouvé's exhibition in the Galerie Sud at the Centre Pompidou in 2022. Here, the entire floor was covered with multiple paths inspired by Aboriginal songlines and lines representing the autistic spectrum designed by Fernand Deligny,[73] and everything intermingled with the shadows of suspended picture rails and the movement of natural light. The floor immediately asserted itself as a place charged with poetic intensity and personal variations. In this floating yet anchored space that combined drawings on the front pages of international newspapers published during the Covid pandemic and voices echoing amid the abstraction of the floors, the meticulously staged exhibition brought into play the complexity of meaning and the ambiguity of presences. We discussed some of these ideas in an interview that can be found later in this book.

Another striking example of this shift toward the floor is Guillaume Leblon's exhibition *Parade*, which was held at the Palais de Tokyo in 2022. It featured the installation *Faces contre terre* [Faces against the ground], which was created in Saint-Nazaire in 2010. As a sculptor, Guillaume Leblon always starts with the space when designing his exhibitions, and he requested to use a specific gallery at the Palais de Tokyo, one with high ceilings and large bay windows overlooking the forecourt. As the Palais de Tokyo is built on uneven ground, this

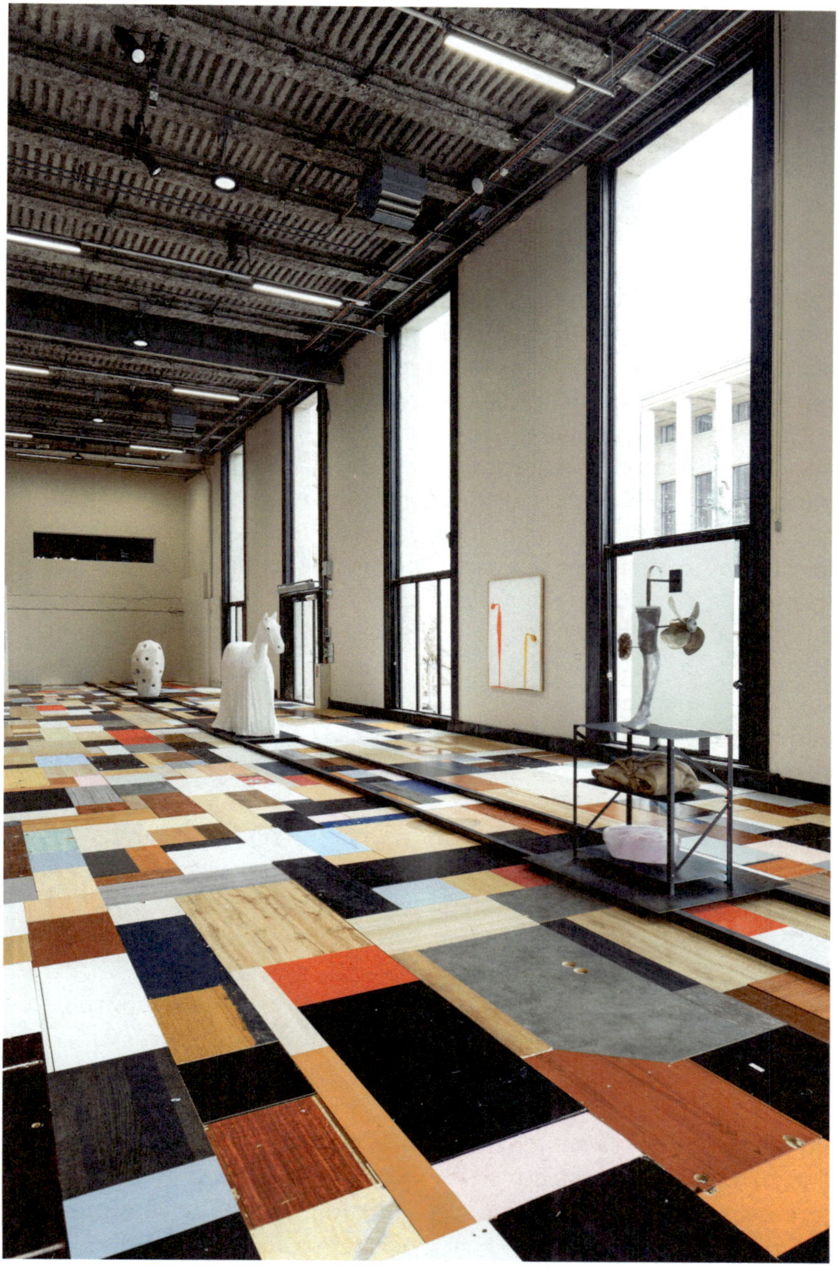

Fig. 24 Exhibition view *Parade*, Guillaume Leblon, Palais de Tokyo, Paris, 2022

gallery is accessed from a floor that first reveals the exhibition from above, accentuating the visual dimension of *Faces contre terre*, which covers the gallery floor with an assemblage of planks of various colors and materials, without walls or picture rails. This installation was created after collecting furniture from waste disposal sites and extracting panels to compose a floor that serves as a reflection of an era. The combination of colors and materials does not seek to produce an aesthetic effect but rather a textured landscape, which Guillaume Leblon invites us to explore as walkers rather than observers, instilling a sense of inclusion and changing our usual viewing position. The work, raised above the floor of the building, is also a pedestal structure that can accommodate sculptures above and below the wooden surfaces in a complex balance of presence on a structure that itself becomes a sculpture. Walking through the space takes us onto a plinth and establishes a powerful and intimate relationship with the architecture, its details, its marked surfaces, its vanishing points, and its viewpoints that draw our gaze outside, toward the esplanade and its pools, where the artist has continued the exhibition. The horse positioned on stationary rails that cross the floor of the installation also questions our viewpoints when looking at things, returning the visitor to their central place within a system activated by their physical and intellectual journey. *Faces contre terre* is a way of appropriating a space and renewing the artistic experience, a central issue in any exhibition design.

The *Parade* exhibition emphasized what lies on the ground, what is abandoned, neglected, invisible. *The Death of Mary* (2022), a cast-iron jacket placed face down on a concrete floor, protected by a display case, is imbued with this meaning. Inspired by an image that has stayed with Guillaume Leblon, "that of bodies on the ground in Harlem, where I live, wrapped in their jackets, struck down by the opioid addiction that is ravaging certain populations in New York, particularly since the lockdowns and massive job losses during the Covid-19 pandemic."[74] *The Death of Mary* installation and the journey through the *Faces contre terre* structure convey a critical message about everything that anchors our steps: the exploitation of humans and resources, structural violence, and addiction. By shifting attention from walls to floor and from inside to exterior, by foregrounding what lies on the ground and transforming street debris and wind-bent umbrellas into sculpture, Guillaume Leblon reverses positions in an artistic and political gesture. This transfer into the sculptural, a sometimes minimal endeavor in its appropriation of elements from

the surrounding world, does away with the museum setting.
The Palais de Tokyo is already an art center far removed from the traditional museum model, thanks to the choice made by architects Anne Lacaton and Jean-Philippe Vassal to leave the structural elements of the building exposed and not to homogenize and neutralize the entirety of the space with white picture rails. While the venue thus has a distinct aura, it is not always the most suitable for showcasing the works on display, encouraging artists to make significant decisions when it comes to the scenography of their exhibitions, even if it is not always easy to describe them as such. Guillaume Leblon prefers to use the image of the coffee table in the living room[75] to describe this creative act, a place for displaying and exhibiting objects and books on two levels, playing as much on what we want to show as on what we prefer to hide from outside view.

## The seating for artworks

> "Places to rest are what is most lacking in contemporary exhibitions and museums."[76]
>
> Franz West

We imagine exhibition visitors standing still and absorbed in contemplation. However, since the earliest museums, the sheer scale of their architecture (The Hermitage in Saint Petersburg, which opened in 1854, has more than a thousand rooms) has also made it necessary to take the physical needs of visitors into account when designing routes through the exhibition spaces. Benches or chairs were therefore placed in the galleries and corridors, chosen more for their discretion than for their comfort, and limited in number so as not to encourage visitors to prolong their breaks. Little attention was generally paid to this furniture, even though it is present in nearly every exhibition space, nor was much thought given to what happens aesthetically at this junction between the viewer's body and the experience of the works. In November 2021, while browsing the exhibition at the Musée des Beaux-Arts in Rennes, I discovered a sculptural type of bench in the seventeenth-and eighteenth-century altarpiece room, which I initially struggled to identify. It was thanks to the postcards sold in the bookshop that I realized that this series of wooden elements serving as seats for admiring the altarpieces was a contemporary work by a sculptor, John Cornu,

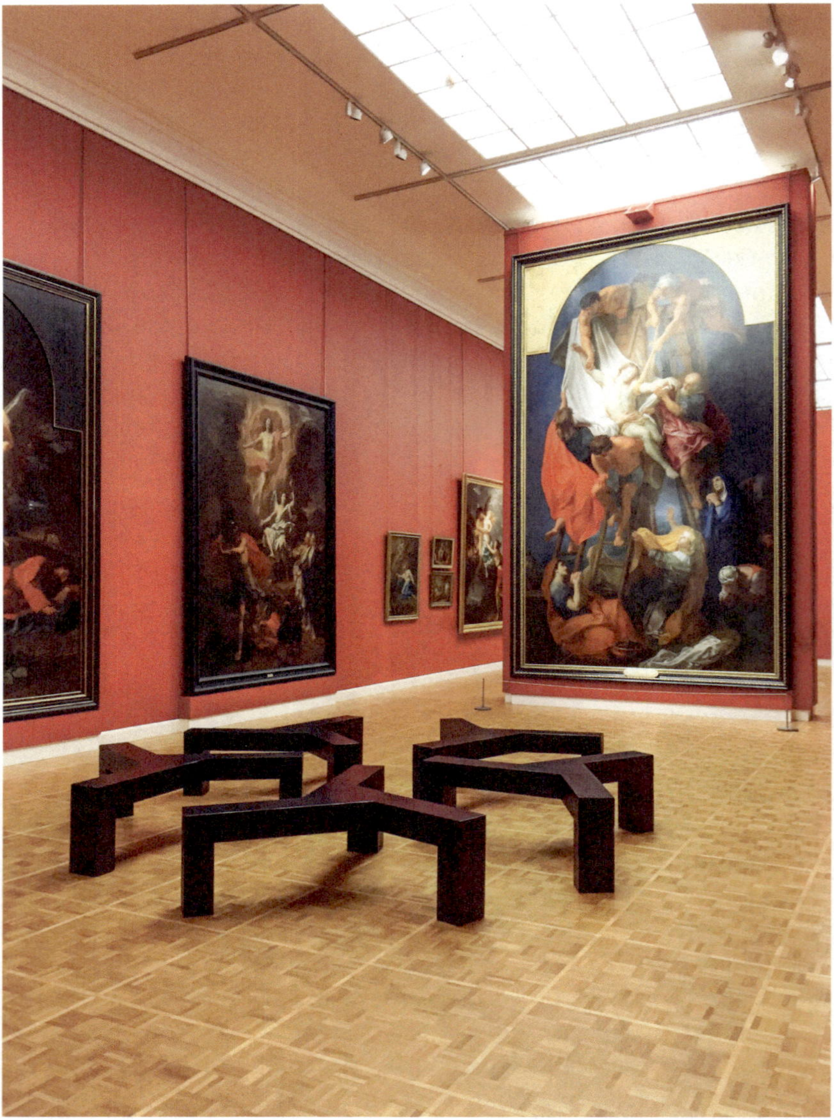

Fig. 25 *Sans titre (Fleury-Mérogis)*, John Cornu, Musée des Beaux-Arts, Rennes, 2012

and that it was entitled *Sans titre (Fleury-Mérogis).*[77] Part of the museum's collection and on permanent display, this sculpture, according to Anne Dary's text, which I was able to consult afterwards, "allows visitors to pause in meditation and creates a hiatus between mediums, eras, and the purposes of art."[78] These benches thus responded both to a desire for transhistorical dialogue and to the need for a pause in a museum tour. What they offer is not only a position from which to observe works, but also, through the "hiatus" in the tour, a moment of pause and a distancing of the gaze, which then detaches itself from the works to take in the room as a whole, a phenomenon also prompted by Gae Aulenti's design for the Musée d'Orsay. All the different elements present on the floor and ceiling, as well as the overhead lighting system, are chosen for the effects they produce: a contemplative atmosphere bordering on the meditative and spiritual, which evokes the architectural context of the churches from which these altarpieces originate. Cornu's seats therefore represent a break but also a connection, allowing for the symbolic projection between distinct temporalities and contexts. However, these sculptures were not produced specifically for this room, they come from a series inspired by the modernist architecture of the Fleury-Mérogis prison in France, and form a reappropriation of Michel Foucault's reflections on architectural surveillance devices. The work was conceived from the outset as something practical and invites the body to test this coercive structure that has become a support and a form of welcome. Built on the scale of a bench, the characteristic three-wing form of the Fleury-Mérogis prison buildings allows three bodies to be seated and connected, in an overall arrangement that echoes the layout of the prison: five of the bench-sculptures are presented together, while the sixth, referring to the women's wing, is placed apart. It was Anne Dary, then director of the Musée des Beaux-Arts in Rennes, who came up with the bold proposal to install this series of sculptures within the narrative framework of seventeenth- and eighteenth-century altarpieces, with the collaboration of the curator in charge of the collection and, of course, the artist's agreement. While looking at Charles Le Brun's *La Descente de Croix* (c. 1679), the viewer is immersed in the gentle sensation of the Douglas fir wood that the benches have been handcrafted from. The unease we feel when confronted with the formal seduction of the modernist architecture of Fleury-Mérogis prison, so out of step with the daily reality of those incarcerated there in far too great numbers, echoes the history of religious painting, where the depiction of a crucified body can create a gentle aesthetic emotion. In the words of the American painter

Ad Reinhardt as quoted by John Cornu, within this ambiguous context, the sculpture asserts itself for what it is: "what you bump into when you back up to look at a painting."[79]

Franz West gave the viewer's body a central place in the experience and interaction with his works, particularly in his *Passstücke* series that consisted of plaster sculptures designed to be worn on the body, which created unusual postures. He also used sculptures to explore the question of sitting with works such as *Eo Ipso* (1987), which allows two people to sit on an elongated rounded structure that partly envelops their bodies. The photographs of *Eo Ipso* taken in Franz West's studio show two people sitting comfortably in the sculpture, immersed in their thoughts, taking time to reflect (or rest?). However, although they are part of a sculptural installation that creates a space, they are not in an active state of involvement. Later reproduced in the public space as part of the *Skulptur Projekte* in Münster in 1987, *Eo Ipso* once again affirmed its duality between a sculptural work and a device for waiting and resting, while becoming a tool for interaction between people who, without necessarily knowing each other, merge together like a stretched-out limb, articulated in a common structure that nonetheless respects the need for personal space. Franz West defined the *Passstücke* series as "a coat hanger or a chair; it is what connects objects to each other."[80] The idea of relationship is central, envisaging the chair as a link between a body and a space. In 1989, a large number of these styles of seats were installed in Franz West's exhibition at the Kunsthistorisches Museum in Vienna, permeating the museum and its historical collections by inviting the public to lie down on a sofa in front of a painting by a great master, for example. The iconoclastic, even provocative dimension toward the institution of the museum and the academic relationship to art provoked diverse reactions.[81]

In 1992, Franz West presented *Auditorium* at documenta 9 in Kassel: an installation of 72 couches covered with rugs and cushions that were offered to visitors as places to sit, lie down, and take a break. The installation was located in a vast, powerful space and the aesthetic impact was as central for visitors as the time for rest. Upon entering, as the title suggests, the viewer took their place within a collective space and became part of a shared situation that could drift toward playful or intimate moments, as certain photographs suggest. Two years earlier in 1990, Franz West had created an installation with an iron sculpture in the shape of a conversation chair (two seats linked together) facing a relief painting in papier mâché hung on the wall; he continued this avenue of artistic experimentation in 1995 with *Plural*, an installation in which he positioned two iron-sculpted seats on a linoleum floor facing four monochrome plaster paintings. The linoleum flooring delimited a space in the gallery that connected the seats to the paintings and cast the visitor in the role of an actor wandering or sitting in a space with theatrical qualities. In other exhibitions, the chairs were simply placed facing the paintings, but always in specific positions, whether they were connected to each other or had a specific seat/backrest relationship, and assert their sculptural dimension. These original pieces were made in the artist's studio, using his expertise as a sculptor (cutting, bending and welding metal, plastering, and sewing fabric, in a deliberately DIY, rough and dirty aesthetic). There are numerous creations of this kind and the plurality of projects that arise from these seating areas is highly inspiring.

Physical comfort and the immersive qualities of seating are rarely prioritized when considering museum displays, with chairs generally offering very limited comfort so as not to encourage visitors to linger and are positioned out of the way to avoid the type of overcrowding that was staged intentionally by Franz West. The presence of a Tripolina chair in a museum is surprising in that it provides genuine comfort, but also because it is a visually striking piece of design that transforms the seated viewer into an important presence when other people enter the room. This contrasts sharply with the emptiness usually preferred in front of works of art, as evidenced by the absence of bodies in most photographs of exhibition views. Sometimes, however, designers are asked to create or install modules that allow visitors to rest, often in intermediate spaces, between two galleries or at the end of a museum visit. These benches or seats meet the need for a break for visitors who are forced to stand for long periods of time to visit certain museums, but also encourage them to take the time to look around. In the early 1980s, Dominique Bozo, the first director of the Musée Picasso in Paris, began the transformation of the Hôtel Salé to house the museum. He had the idea of commissioning the sculptor Diego Giacometti, brother of Alberto Giacometti, who had already designed benches, chairs and lighting for the exhibition spaces and bar of the Fondation Maeght in Saint-Paul-de-Vence (1964), to create chandeliers, chairs for staff, benches for the public, and coffee tables. Diego Giacometti created bronze seats inspired by plant motifs and designed each piece according to its intended use—photographs show him present during the staging of the plaster models. Now inseparable from the Musée Picasso, as well as the Fondation Maeght and the

Musée Chagall in Nice, where they were also installed when the museum opened in 1973, they remain inconspicuous to most visitors, but become striking in their sculptural dimension as soon as one pays attention to them. Museums that choose to invite designers or incorporate signature chairs or benches in their spaces create different relationships between the body and the works on display. This is the case in Copenhagen, where the SMK, Statens Museum for Kunst, has structured a series of rooms dedicated to Danish art from the late-nineteenth to the early-twentieth century around a set of CH24 chairs by designer Hans Wegner that date from 1949 and have a strong sculptural effect that shapes the positions of the body as it rests in close proximity to the paintings. The chair invites visitors to immerse themselves in solitary contemplation, mirroring certain characters depicted in the paintings, whereas the benches usually favored in museums offer the possibility of sharing in discussion. These chairs are particularly slender and airy, with curved, open backs through which the gaze can pass. Hans Wegner's understated design characterizes this section of the museum, yet remains invisible to many visitors who do not notice these chairs, which are famous but lack museum labels.

The Louvre recently commissioned Martin Szekely to create chairs for security guards and benches for the public, which have been added to designer seating areas already in place in various sections of the museum: Pierre Paulin's Bornes, Charlotte Perriand's Tokyo benches,[82] and Jean-Michel Wilmotte's chairs. The collection, which has been assembled over the years, is mismatched, and it was this observation, combined with the need to take greater account of the visitor experience and the working conditions of the staff in the galleries, that led Jean-Luc Martinez, then President-Director of the Louvre, to commission Martin Szekely to design three types of seating, totaling almost four hundred pieces of furniture, that "combine ergonomics, comfort, simplicity, and elegance" while fitting "harmoniously into the museum's rooms without competing with the architecture of the Palace and the works on display."[83] The three items developed—the seat for the guards, the sit-stand stool, and the bench—reflect Martin Szekely's belief that "the original purpose of furniture is to support or contain, not to be displayed."[84] They therefore discreetly integrate into the museum's layout, offering moments of respite without altering the quality of the spaces. Martin Szekely was inspired by the elegance and verticality of a sculpture of King Khafre seated on his throne dating from around

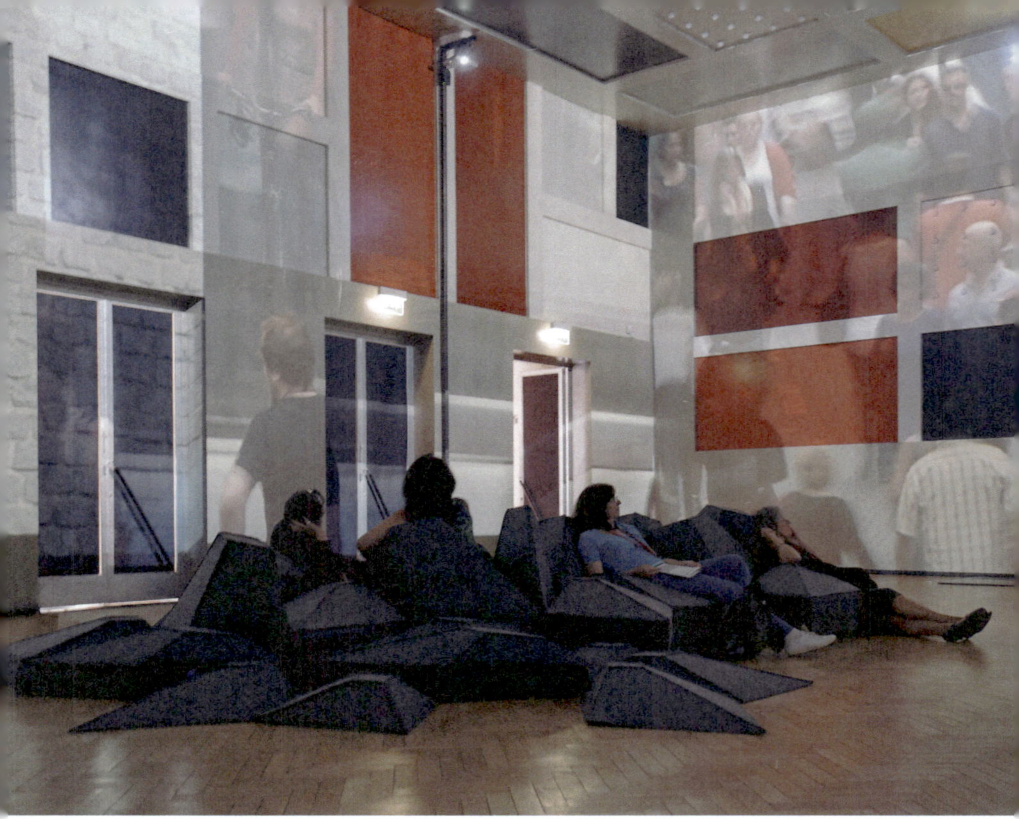

Fig. 26 *Les Angles*, installation designed by Smarin for the exhibition *Vidéodrones* by Céleste Boursier-Mougenot at l'Aubette (1928, Strasbourg)

2500 BCE, now on display at the Egyptian Museum in Cairo. As a result, in these seats at the Louvre, the body is invited to rest without slouching. Among the twenty or so photographs by Fabrice Gousset documenting the project in the book *S'asseoir au Louvre* [Sitting in the Louvre], only one includes the presence of a body on a guard's chair, in a concentrated and serene pose. Apart from this image, the leather-covered benches and wooden standing chairs, all very elegant, are photographed only in dialogue with the artworks and architecture, in the bare state of their materials. The highly aesthetic approach is surprising for a project that claims to highlight the visitor experience: we are far from the everyday reality of the Louvre with the masses of visitors wandering through the rooms seeking to relax on the seats, stretching out their legs, bending their necks, and letting their arms fall, in attitudes that were much better documented by Thomas Struth in 1989 in his photographic series on the Louvre. The *S'asseoir au Louvre* project is probably driven by a desire to provide the viewer with a certain aesthetic education by inviting them to sit like a king, in a dignified and proud posture, as evidenced by this single photograph of a visitor, and thus encouraging them to change their attitude when encountering works of art, rather than simply alleviating physical fatigue during a museum visit.

The designer Stéphanie Marin, from the smarin studio, has carried out several seating projects in close collaboration with artists. In 2014, when Céleste Boursier-Mougenot was invited to exhibit in the Aubette 1928 space in Strasbourg (a rare "total art" project created by Sophie Taeuber-Arp, Jean Arp, and Theo van Doesburg), he asked Marin to design a seating area. The installation *Les Angles*, a modular geometric structure that offered visitors a chance to sit or lie down, was subsequently acquired by the Musées de Strasbourg. It is now on permanent display, and its pieces can be maneuvered into new configurations in one of the rooms at the Aubette 1928. Although there is no museum label providing a precise identification, it fits the philosophy of the Aubette 1928 project, which crosses the fields of painting, sculpture, and architecture. The dialogue between Céleste Boursier-Mougenot and the smarin studio continued in 2015 with *Les Marches*, a set of elements evoking the concrete blocks of seafronts created for the French pavilion at the Venice Biennale. Their smooth, firm finish provides comfortable seating and ideal conditions for listening to the artist's sonic works, inviting visitors to engage more intimately with an architecture renowned for its stark nature. Their presence has a strong sculptural dimension and thus contributes to the experience of the works, giving visibility to the bodies that spontaneously stretch out and recline on the pieces. The porosity between art and design was fully embraced, as the installation was co-signed by the artist and the designer, but this shared authorship remains a rare practice. Stéphanie Marin was then invited to design and manufacture an installation for Narimane Mari's film *Le Fort des fous* [The Fort of Fools] exhibited at the Ballhaus in Kassel as part of documenta 14 (2017). This museum is the former residence of Jérôme Bonaparte, Napoleon's brother, and the installation breaks with an architecture emblematic of the violent power relations that structure societies, which is also the subject of Narimane Mari's film. A barricade of cushions divided the room in two, and viewers could climb inside this vast pile to seek a space of their own among the other visitors. There were many positions to choose from, all of which created a comfortable acoustic isolation within a sensory form of cohabitation. The initial image of the structure evokes the revolutionary barricade, hastily constructed in the urgency and energy of the struggle; visitors lean on it to project themselves into a film that becomes a real battle. Through the possible invention of so many bodily positions in close proximity, the installation provided an experience of the sensuality of the relationship with others that forges identities in the South. Meanwhile, the materiality of the forms of the refuge, flexible but firm, was more conducive to the awakening of consciousness than to scattered reverie. The experience was very convincing, and the strength and comfort of the installation facilitated people's immersion into a long and complex film, which is always a challenge in the hectic context of an event such as documenta.

In 2022, the Musée de l'Orangerie in Paris installed a series of sculptural seats in the temporary exhibition rooms in the basement. This initiative was the result of a dialogue between Cécile Debray, then director of the museum, and the artist Agnès Thurnauer. For several years, Thurnauer had been developing her series of sculptures entitled *Matrices chromatiques*, in which letters and words are created by carefully designing the space within forms. Debray suggested that she extend this series by creating functional sculptures to be installed in the rooms housing Monet's *Water Lilies*. The project was ultimately placed in other rooms and, thanks to the trust between the artist and the curator, took on an intermediate and delicate status between artwork and exhibition design. Not only did Agnès Thurnauer agree to move her sculptures from their originally intended location, she also adapted their dimensions to scale them to the human body for greater

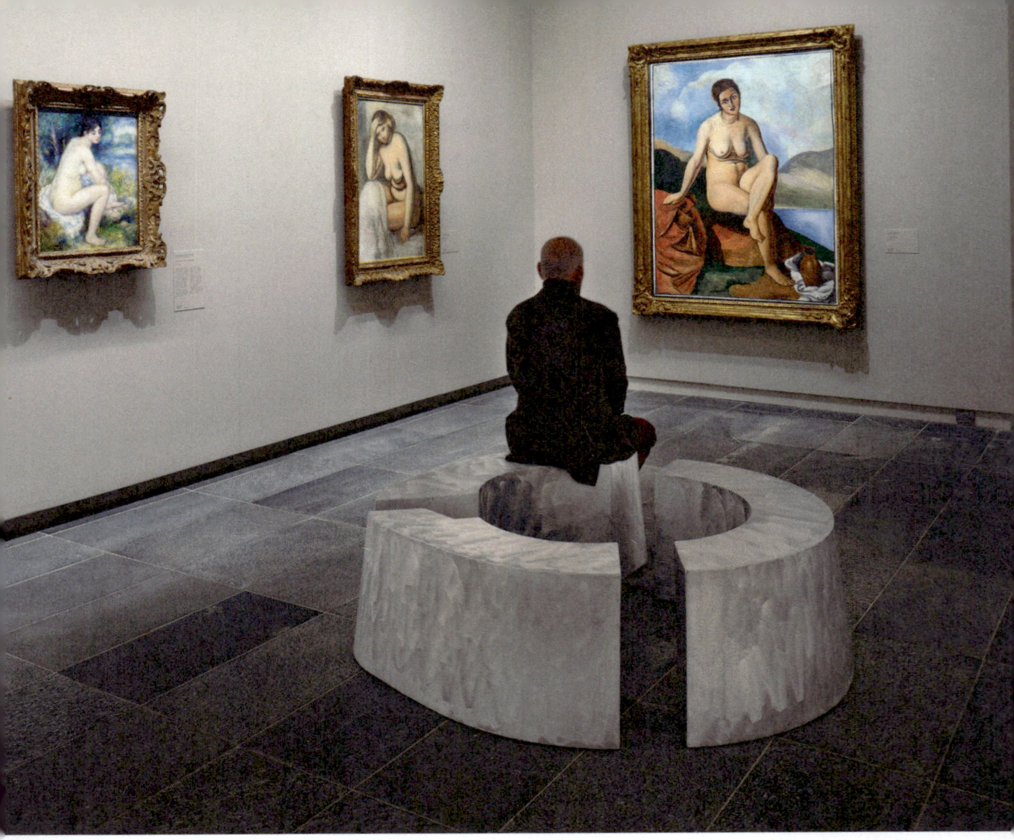

Fig. 27 *Matrices Chromatiques,* Agnès Thurnauer, Musée de l'Orangerie, Paris, 2022

comfort. Arranged in such a way as to offer seating areas facing the paintings, the matrices are not immediately recognizable as works of art, and it is only at the end of the tour that a museum label allows visitors to learn who created them. Handcrafted in a metalworking workshop, these brushed metal sculptures can be manipulated and moved around, and their arrangement changes throughout the day. The artist explains that the guards take care to put them back in place in the morning, even though handling them is not always easy, and that she accepts the risk of seeing the shape of the letters disappear as the day progresses. Nor are the *Matrices Chromatiques* necessarily viewed for their own aesthetic qualities, as they are primarily considered as seats. Nevertheless, they allow the viewer to shift their gaze away from the isolated paintings on the walls to observe a collection of works in relation to the passing bodies. Those who sit on these seats contribute to the overall atmosphere of the space, and watching people on them adds to the pleasure of rediscovering these nineteenth-century masterpieces in the collection. Seated on these sculptural letters that are so open to sensory reappropriation, we allow ourselves to be caught up in the generous spectacle of an ephemeral community bound by aesthetic desire and pleasure rooted in a broadened sensibility.

Through her focus on the dialogue between contemporary art and traditional artisanship, Anne Dressen, the curator at the Musée d'Art Moderne de la Ville de Paris (MAMVP), also paid special attention to seating for the trilogy of exhibitions *Decorum* (2013), *Medusa, Jewellery and Taboos* (2017), and *Les Flammes* (2022). At the entrance to *Decorum*, a sofa by Franz West invites visitors to lie down beneath the exhibition title, even if it means taking a nap instead of seeing the exhibition. People could also lie down at the end of the tour, as the exit takes you back to the entrance, exposing yourself to the gaze of others as you become part of the decor. Cat prints designed by Marc Camille Chaimowicz guided the exhibition route from this first wall and continued on a narrow carpet that crossed the spaces. Of course, visitors were not obliged to follow this path, but the visual and tactile contrast between this thick, soft material of the carpet and the hard museum floor enhanced the experience of the works. Benches painted by the artist dotted the route, half-sculpture, half-furniture, showcasing the bodies and emotions of visitors. Throughout his career, Marc Camille Chaimowicz has created numerous screens, chairs, and sofas, covering everyday objects with paint and inviting viewers to take possession of them. He has created styles of scenography that are somewhere between theater sets and domestic interiors, which can also discreetly infiltrate the narratives of the exhibition spaces.[85] For *Les Flammes*, an exhibition dedicated to ceramics, Anne Dressen invited Johan Creten to create rest areas, and he produced seats inspired by mooring bollards in ports entitled *Points d'observation,* all of which are the same size but feature different glazes. Positioned to favor certain viewpoints, they could nevertheless be moved by visitors. Johan Creten has played a major role in France in the reappropriation of ceramics by contemporary artists, and his choice to present his work through a seating area, on the margins of the museum at a time when this long-devalued medium was only beginning to be recognized, was a powerful gesture. These *Points d'observation* nevertheless stand out as sculptures as soon as you see them, even when bodies are resting on them, as we can still experience in the Dufy room of the MAMVP, where they were installed after their acquisition. Visitors to Raoul Dufy's famous *La Fée électricité* can now sit on these seats as they have been placed along the length of this large, curving wall panel. Children in particular easily make them their own, leaning against them or sitting down to draw.

Anne Dressen also chose to include two sculptures, tiled benches from Laëtitia Badaut Haussmann's *Daybed* series, in the *Les Flammes* exhibition. This series, which she began in 2015, is the result of the artist's research on Charlotte Perriand and, in particular, on a commission for benches for exhibition spaces that the architect received in the 1960s from Maurice Besset, curator at the Musée National d'Art Moderne, then located at the Palais de Tokyo. By studying period photographs, Laëtitia Badaut Haussmann observed that the rooms were more welcoming at the time and that the viewing positions afforded by the benches encouraged visitors to connect with the works on display. Perriand's Tokyo bench is quite low and broadens the field of vision, encouraging visitors to consider the artwork from a new perspective. When the museum moved to the Centre Pompidou in 1977, these benches were not reinstalled. A dozen of them were made available to the Louvre, others, poorly stored, suffered from the flooding of the Seine and disappeared; still others were discreetly dispersed, and one last example was kept at the Mobilier National, France's national furniture depository, but dissociated from its intended use. Thanks to her research, Laëtitia Badaut Haussmann found one of them and reinstalled it in the Palais de Tokyo exhibition space, accompanied by a letter recounting this story, which is all the more interesting given that Maurice Besset's decision to entrust the

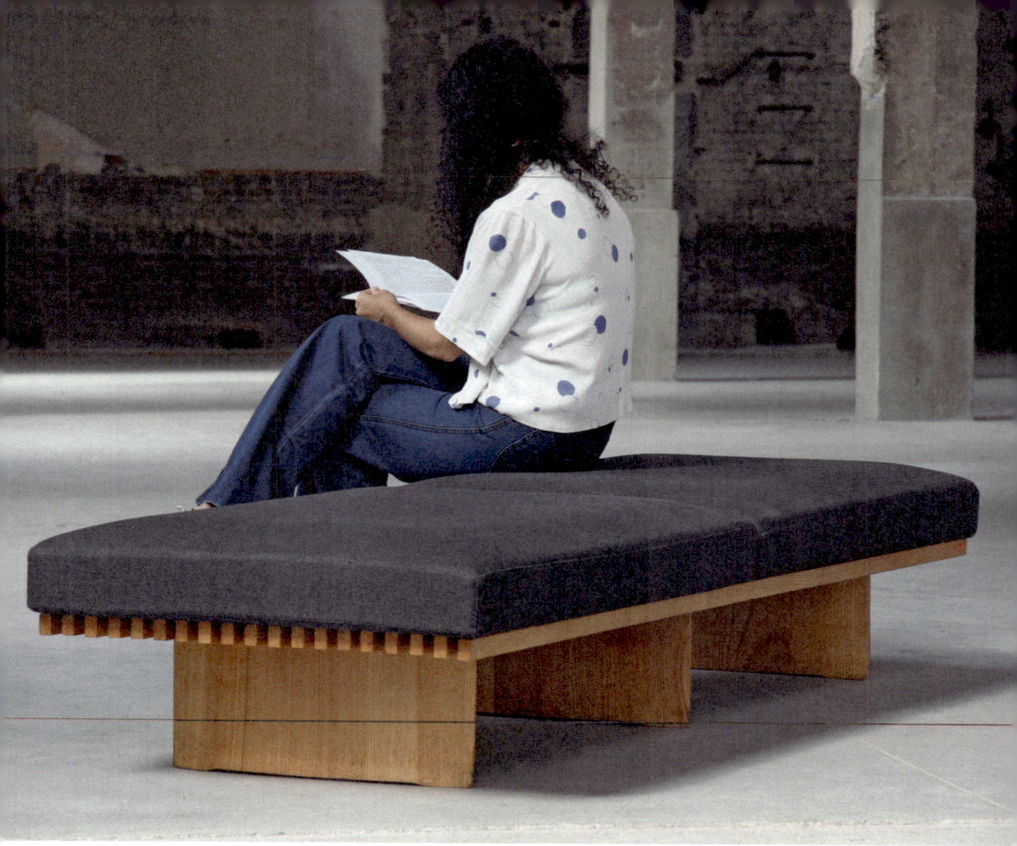

Fig. 28 *Dear Charlotte and Maurice*, Laëtitia Badaut Haussmann, Palais de Tokyo, Paris, 2012. Tokyo bench, Charlotte Perriand, 1955, reader: Julia Trotta

creation of the seats to Charlotte Perriand was part of his project to conceive the "museum of the future." Laëtitia Badaut Haussmann then went on to work on other seating projects, such as the series *L'amour est plus froid que la mort*, which she started in 2015 and initially consisted of soft sculptures suspended on metal framework. These works were reminiscent of Lilly Reich's scenography for presenting fabrics, and they gradually slid to the floor, encouraging visitors to settle comfortably into a dual interpretation of sculpture and design. The *Daybed* series plays on this same principle, changing less in form but just as much in status when they incorporate the function of seating in group exhibitions such as *Les Flammes*. The artist allows for broad appropriation of her work because when her pieces are acquired they can be exhibited as sculptures, used as pedestals, or serve as platforms for performances; the only caveat is that visitors are never prevented from sitting down. *Cœur* and *Squelette* (2019) are two chair sculptures, this time focusing on the expertise of the feuillardiers, whose craft has now almost disappeared. By twisting and shaping young chestnut trees, feuillardiers produced furniture and invented forms that inspired modern design. Working with them, Laëtitia Badaut Haussmann created these two chairs, which were inspired by her research on Charlotte Perriand during her stay at Villa Kujoyama in Japan. They are strongly reminiscent of the rattan furniture of Franco Albini and Franca Helg, particularly the Margherita chair designed for Caterina Marcenaro's apartment on the top floor of the Palazzo Rosso. First installed in the rooms of the Château de Rochechouart for her solo exhibition,[86] the works *Cœur* and *Squelette* appear as sculptures but also invite visitors to sit down and witness the dialogue between the artist's works and the museum's collection. Her 2023 project *Le Pavillon des amours (Pav.Lov.)* was a modular sculpture hosting assemblies of bodies gathered to talk, celebrate, and question love in contemporary societies, and it served as a continuation of this research by assuming a hybrid status between installation and exhibition design that welcomed spectators and participants.

This form of hybridization is also at work in Philippe Parreno's permanent in situ exhibition *Danny / No More Reality* at LUMA Arles. It was installed in 2021 when the LUMA tower opened with an evolving exhibition format that regularly incorporates new works. *Danny / No More Reality* is the result of close dialogue with the architect in charge of the art center's interior spaces, Jörg Schwarzburg, who selected fittings and materials for the diverse technical and design elements—carpeting, LED screens, electrical outlets, seating, labels, control modules—that are works of art themselves. While this list is made clear to curators, allowing them to distinguish between what is and what is not a work of art and to implement appropriate preservation strategies to care for a complex and fragile environment, the situation is much more confusing for visitors. It is therefore difficult to know whether the Brain, the control module whose glass constantly fogged during daily operations and which is now fogged to a lesser extent thanks to a mechanism inserted into the double glazing, is actually active despite this humidity. It is also difficult to define where the artist's scenography ends in the arrangement of exposed wiring, missing panels revealing technical parts, and open skirting boards for air circulation between the room and its architectural framework. In this staged space, the first part of the project is a mechanical ballet with an IKO robot fixed to an attached arm that sweeps the space with an associated sound shower in a wildly sensual choreography that also includes mechanical shutters, LED projectors, and a piano associated with a marquise, all of which play scores composed to create a highly immersive atmosphere bathed in sounds created in collaboration with the musician Arca. The flows move constantly from inside to outside thanks to heliostats installed on the exterior roofs that reflect the sun's rays toward another heliostat inside the gallery, creating a hypnotic *mise en abyme* effect. Live recordings bring in ambient sound, wind, birdsong, and construction site noises, which are integrated into a spatialized score where each machine expresses itself with its own voice. The seats take center stage, designed as a series of bleachers covered in blue fabric forming a circle. They invite visitors to settle into a comfortable position that immediately draws them into the spectacle, and there is a sense of involvement as people can add their own voice at any moment thanks to an artificial echo. Immersed in this "symbiotic organism"[87] that is highly scripted in space but also structured on a two-hour cycle that begins before LUMA opens to the public, visitors are immediately caught up in carnival-like mechanisms of seduction, but are also sometimes distanced by the effects of repetition, by long periods of non-event, by crackling sounds or, conversely, by dizzying accelerations. The seats also fulfill this dual role: initially welcoming, they become uncomfortable as they create a passive position and people must turn to see rotating images in opposite directions. Many visitors therefore prefer to stand up and position themselves outside this central module, near the piano or on the textured carpet, in order to be in a more active position, watching the other visitors seated in this motorized cinema. *Danny* ends after forty minutes of a show punctuated by breaks with a final theatrical moment in which all the acting machines are thanked during a final bow guided by the light of a spotlight played here through the reflection of the heliostat. The film projection of *No More Reality* then begins, after an indefinite period during which the machines remain present but, in the background, and the audience hesitates between getting up or falling asleep in the comfort of their seats.

## Moving exhibitions around

*Danny / No More Reality* is an in situ work designed to be permanent. LUMA's conservation team takes care of its technical management on a daily basis and regularly consults with the Parreno studio. Like the land art works managed by the DIA Foundation, *Danny / No More Reality* does not travel to other venues so visitors are required to come to it, providing an ideal setting for its physical and immaterial preservation, even though each work that makes up the project retains its autonomy and could one day be removed and relocated. By favoring movable, flexible, and modular materials in *Pav.Lov.*, Laëtitia Badaut Haussmann also addresses an important issue: how to transport and circulate works and exhibitions. Now more than ever, temporary exhibition design must address issues of environmental responsibility in its management of materials and their recycling, but also ensure the rational management of human and financial resources in an era of reduced budgets for culture and concerns about significant employee stress and fatigue. Furthermore, air conditioning cannot be the only solution to rising temperatures linked to the climate crisis. However, few museums, foundations, and biennials demonstrate a genuine commitment to change and innovation when it comes these issues. Recycling the scenography for a series of exhibitions has become common, with slight modifications to structures, colors, and visitor pathways so the visitor has a new experience and the specific needs of each project are met. This is generally a discreet part of the exhibition management and institutions do not devote much time to it. Artists sometimes expose this process and turn it into a conceptual act, as Pierre Huyghe did when he was invited to exhibit at the Centre Pompidou in 2013, following the Mike Kelley retrospective held a few months after Kelley's death. This Californian artist had a profound influence on Pierre Huyghe and his generation with his radical and exuberant exploration of art and exhibition formats. Huyghe decided to pay tribute to Kelley by leaving the exhibition display untouched: his works were installed along the same visitor route and the museum labels for Kelley's work had been left in place, creating emotional encounters and memories of the works in their absence. The visitor experience was profoundly disrupted by this departure from the strict formats of the temporary exhibition. Here, experiences overlapped, reminding us how museum spaces and the bodies of viewers are also places of memory and stratification, a question that is also at play in his piece *Time Keeper* (1999) that was featured in the exhibition, which used a spiral-shaped sanding tool to reveal the different layers of paint covering one of the museum's picture rails.

In 1953, UNESCO published *The Manual of Travelling Exhibitions*, edited by Elodie Courter Osborn, director of UNESCO's traveling exhibitions department. This small manual was taken up as a research subject by the exhibition design department of the Staatliche Hochschule für Gestaltung (HfG) design school and republished with numerous notes and appendices in 2018.[88] In the introduction, the principle of traveling exhibitions of collections is dated to 1850 and attributed to the Victoria and Albert Museum in London. In 1953, Elodie Courter Osborn noted a significant growth in this practice over the previous two decades, particularly following the end of the war. UNESCO considers the cultural exchanges enabled by sharing exhibitions to be an essential tool, since "a deeper understanding between peoples should assist in lessening tensions which ultimately flare into international conflicts."[89] The manual was produced with this in mind and sought to facilitate cultural exchanges. Elodie Courter Osborn's experience was important, as she had spent twelve years promoting, organizing, and devising traveling exhibitions in the United States and abroad to share the modern vision embodied by MoMA through the circulation of works and objects, as well as a large number of reproductions. Of course, the situation described in the manual in 1953 has changed considerably, particularly in financial terms; at the time, transport costs were a significant issue, but there is almost no mention of insurance costs, which are now a predominant concern. However, the guidelines and examples given for drawing up contracts, protecting works through various packaging techniques, the attention to be paid to communication and mediation tools, and finally the various possibilities for exhibition design make it a highly relevant subject for research today. The manual was intended as a practical tool and reproduces numerous diagrams with precise captions and photographs. Educational exhibitions based on photographic reproductions of works are also highlighted.

In terms of scenography, the proposed systems are simple, described in detail, and favor easily handled and transportable solutions in the examples given in the appendix, such as the interlocking frames used by the Palais de la Découverte, which are sturdy and reusable freestanding devices, and a shelf created for the MoMA *Good Design* exhibition (1950), about which the author observes: "The shelf is held in place by hinges and cord which allows it to drop to necessary level to support three-dimensional objects. Such panels can be used again for other exhibitions."[90] While the fairly wide selection of examples is interesting for the overview it provides of the period, unfortunately the exhibition designers are never named, the dates are not given, and the projects are represented by a single photograph, which does not allow us to go beyond a merely descriptive level. The research carried out by the HfG is therefore valuable and allows us, for example, to understand that the exhibition on design was a project put together by Elodie Courter Osborn with the help of Victor D'Amico, the director of the MoMA's education department. Furthermore, its wide circulation contributed to the dissemination of a vision of modern design as it was integrated into everyday life and was presented as the continuation of a long history of inventions in the form of functional objects. As Jennifer Tobias explains, Elodie Courter Osborn's close connection to the design world also explains the importance she attached to the practical issues and the place she gives to scenography, technical details, and graphic elements. During the same period, the American art historian Jermayne MacAgy curated numerous exhibitions of non-artistic objects, such as feathers (*Flight of the Image* at the Legion of Honor in San Francisco, 1952) and industrial objects (*The Trojan Horse*, *The Art of the Machine* at the Contemporary Arts Museum in Houston, 1958), which she staged within ambitious and highly inventive exhibition displays. Aware of their powerful aura, she aimed to produce "sympathetic"[91] effects. While she was fascinated by the aesthetic impact of non-artistic objects, she was also convinced of the importance of creating an immersive atmosphere in the exhibition that would immediately captivate the viewer. For her, scenography must therefore be specific to each project, because "using the same installation for one exhibition and the one immediately after would be like seeing someone wearing someone else's shoes."[92] The differing perspectives of Elodie Courter Osborn and Jermayne MacAgy reveal the complex nature of recycling elements of an exhibition display. By affirming their close link with the objects being presented, with the architectural context of the installation, and with the curatorial project, it becomes a challenge to integrate environmental and economic imperatives that are now much more pressing than they were in the past.

How can modularity and reappropriation be considered in temporary exhibition design projects? In his video *About the Relative Size of Things in the Universe* (2007), the artist Martin Beck proposes renting his reconstruction of the Struc-Tube system, an invention developed by the industrial designer George Nelson in 1948 for a traveling exhibition on companies that produce business cards.[93] The system is self-supporting, consisting of horizontal and vertical metal tubes that fit together to allow display panels to be suspended. George Nelson's inventiveness lay in his desire to produce a device that could be easily assembled and disassembled by hand, without the need for specific skills or tools. In Martin Beck's video, a man and a woman begin to set up the device and hang the first panel, entitled "the artist in social communication," when they are interrupted by an activist who asks them to join him in a meeting about working conditions. When they refuse, because they are overwhelmed by their own workload for the exhibition, he leaves, casting flyers on the ground. The installation resumes, this time with monochrome panels without any writing on them being hung on the structures. The second part of the video is devoted to dismantling the structure, with the same gestures, the same concentration, and the same interruption by the activist, accentuating the impression of emotional distance. Martin Beck associates the reconstruction of this display with a theoretical critique of the logic underlying simple modules that can be assembled by anyone and thus lose the specificity that links the work and its display, and its ability to convey an aura that makes an exhibition display device a valuable tool for collaboration between the artist and the venues. But, as Martin Beck explains in an interview with *Displayer* magazine: "Liberating the exhibition from the spatial constraints of the physical space comes at a price: the system is a typical product of Taylorist work organization and its drive for increased efficiency. This dynamic cannot be disregarded or hidden. If there is something like a democratization, it is a paradoxical one, constituted simultaneously by utopian and dystopian moments. Exhibition systems liberate by regulating, and they regulate by liberating. The emancipated spectator is the guided consumer and the guided consumer is the emancipated spectator."[94]

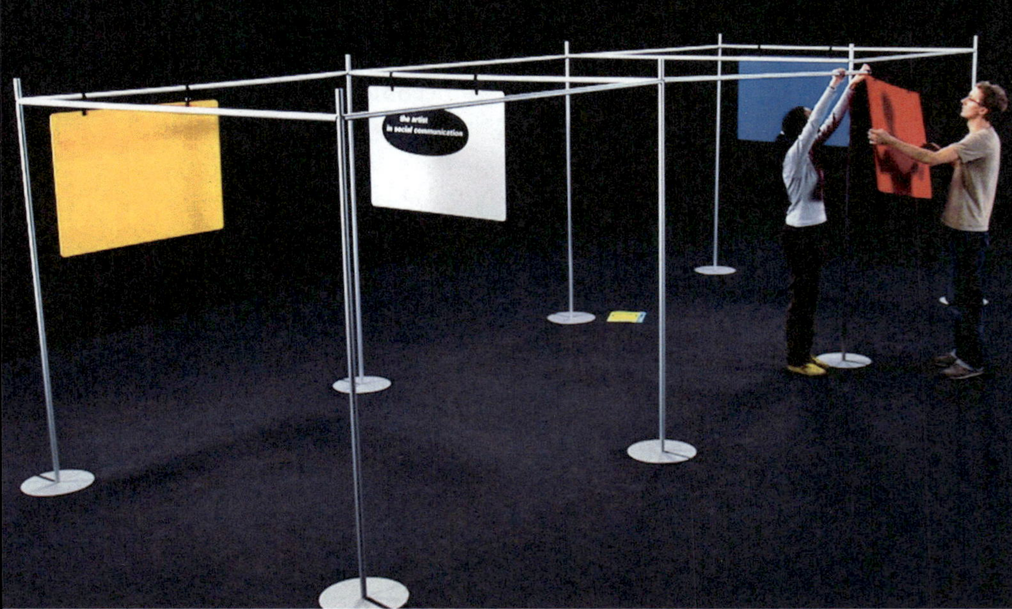


Fig. 29 Screenshot from the video *About the Relative Size of Things in the Universe*, Martin Beck, 2007

## The dialogue between art and scenography as a practice of hospitality

In her 2010 essay "How to Install Art as a Feminist?," Helen Molesworth examines the capacity of a museum's exhibition display to reintegrate women artists into their historical eras and the movements and contexts that have forgotten them, but also wonders whether such displays can imagine dialogues with contemporary artists based on the principle of a female bond or sense of sisterhood. The horizontal and rhizomatic feminist methodology envisages art history as a place of affinities between artists[95] and encourages us to rethink the museum as a tool for creating alliances rather than perpetuating conflicts. If art history is no longer a vertical line that we inherit and from which we must extricate ourselves in the Oedipal logic of the murder of the father, but rather multiple lines that unfold in several directions, through encounters and friendships, the ambition of museography must shift away from the model of linear writing punctuated by leaders, and instead invent a coexistence without demarcation, a connection capable of embodying the sense of community and proximity that reinforces artistic energies for visitors. The figure of the artist is no longer conceived on the model of the genius who draws inspiration from their predecessors and then distances themselves from them in acts of rupture, but rather as a movement of rapprochement with a family chosen from among different generations, in a complicity sometimes experienced in direct dialogue but more often imagined through the relationship between the works. However, as Helen Molesworth clearly expresses in her essay, the difficulty lies in achieving this shift in museum displays: "Art history needs its objects of study to be displayed, and thus the history of the museum can be seen in part as a struggle for how to display works of art."[96] In a transformed vision of the exhibition as a relationship between works, the viewer is invited to perceive them in a broader, multidirectional way, in a state of contamination that requires a very precise exhibition design so as not to create the sensation of circulating within a faceless crowd. By pointing out the importance of the articulation between works, of the meaningful relationships produced by the hanging, Helen Molesworth makes a profound connection between museography and scenography issues. Constructing an exhibition is in fact a work of producing perspectives, laying paths of discovery, and creating atmospheres and sensory experiences of the works in an environment that both contains them and that they help to produce.

In 2023, I traveled to Hélène Bertin's studio in Cucuron, a small village in the south of France, to prepare a group exhibition that I was curating[97] and to borrow some of her pieces. Her sculptures live in her domestic space, readily integrating into the functional realm by supporting clothes or crockery. Cultivating a lifestyle that celebrates artisanship and the pleasures of the senses, Hélène Bertin combines her mask sculptures, bouquet sculptures, and costume sculptures, often created with her friends and neighbors, with everyday fruits, vegetables, objects, and books. More broadly, her work takes the time to welcome and make visible those in the shadows, those who remain invisible for many reasons, including the rejection that artisanal creation has long suffered at the hands of contemporary art. When she discovered the work of Valentine Schlegel (1925–2021), a talented sculptor and ceramicist whose contributions had largely been overlooked, she eschewed the invitations and budgets that had been allocated to her own work and focused on this forgotten artist, embarking on a long-term research project that led to a publication and an exhibition with the CAC Brétigny.[98] The catalogue *Valentine Schlegel: je dors, je travaille*,[99] which has won several awards and has already been reprinted four times, has played a major role in lifting Valentine Schlegel out of obscurity.

That day in Cucuron, Hélène Bertin showed me some racks she had designed to display her costumes, as well as a set of sculpted frames. These devices are pieces that function for her own work, but which she wishes to make available to other artists, and she offered me the chance to use them as display tools for the exhibition I was curating. It was a wonderful opportunity to explore their capacity for hospitality. The exhibition I was working on at the time highlighted the work of Marcelle Cahn, a deceased artist who is gradually being rediscovered, in a dialogue with contemporary artists guided by the connections between them. Our discussion led to an idea that was immediately adopted: Hélène Bertin's frames would house a series of works on postcards that Marcelle Cahn produced in the latter part of her life, in great poverty, using simple collage techniques on urban views transformed in a poetic and critical manner. These sculpted frames turned the display tool into a space for encountering the work of a woman artist who was rendered invisible by her era. In the exhibition, the museum label names this relationship between the frame and the work as a gesture of hospitality from one to the other.

Producing display tools for a group exhibition involves establishing connections that anchor a project in space through forms that serve as

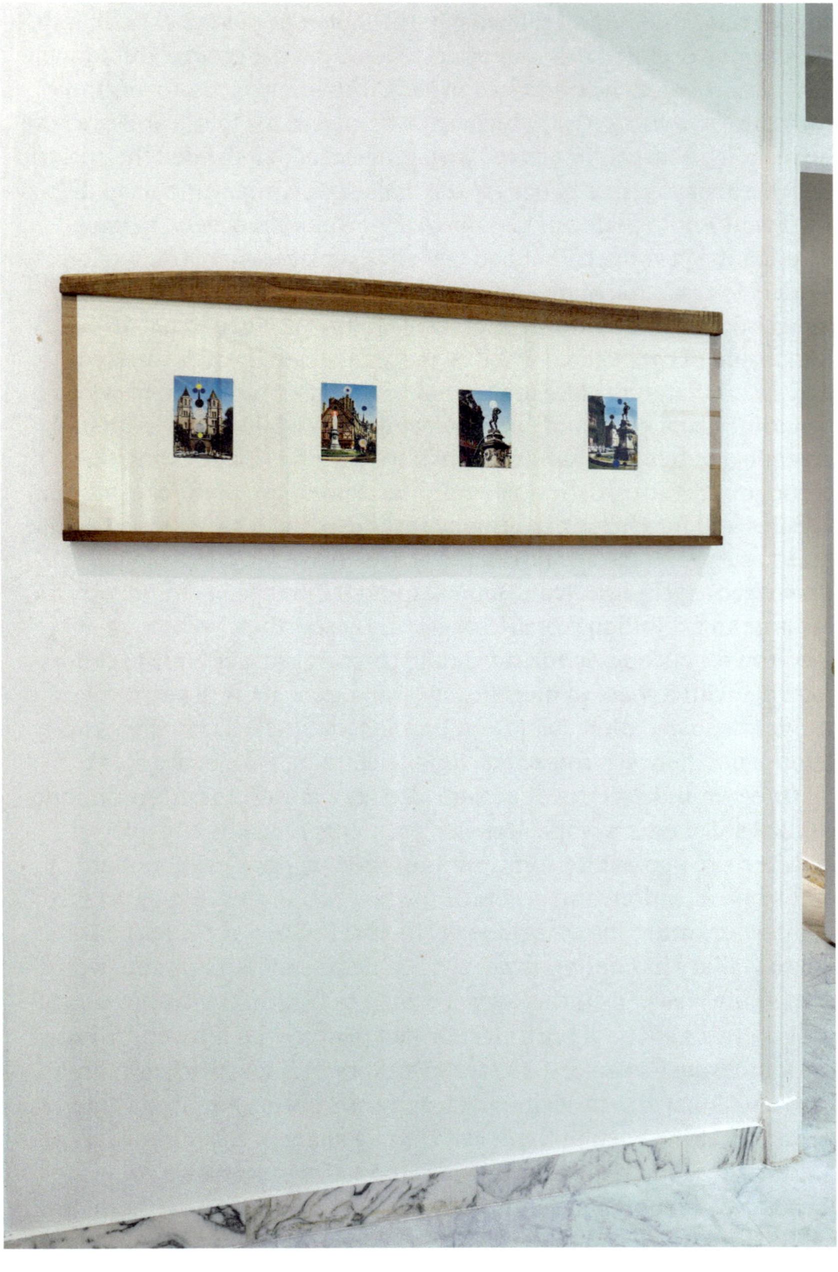

Fig. 30 Frames by Hélène Bertin displaying postcards (1972–81) by Marcelle Cahn. Exhibition view *Faire*, *nager*, *s'envoler*, La Gaya Scienza, Nice, 2023

supports for the works. Following in the footsteps of Marcel Duchamp, Jean Dupuy explored this concept extensively in the group exhibitions and performances he organized in New York in the 1970s, for example with the *Grommets* series, which he presented in his loft in SoHo, where he installed a tarpaulin pierced with grommets that divided the space in two. He invited artists to occupy the makeshift compartments to display their works or to perform. Visitors to the exhibition needed to look through the grommets that had become eyepieces, sometimes climbing ladders to reach the higher ones and gain different perspectives. The images documenting the project testify to the playful and participatory dimension of *Grommets*, as well as the great diversity of the artistic endeavors that took place in the compartments. The design provided a beautiful visual unity and overall effectiveness while offering artists a great deal of freedom for their individual projects. By investing the scenography with artistic and curatorial expression, both for exhibition formats and for Fluxus performance evenings, such as with the one-meter square rotating stage he offered artists to use for *3 Evenings on Revolving Stage* in 1976, Jean Dupuy explored the capacity for display to become an exhibition scenario or event. Display thus becomes a medium for encounter and hospitality, bringing artists and spectators together with a sense of humility. By giving each artist the same place within the installation, Jean Dupuy avoids hierarchies and effects of domination between the works, thus celebrating a collective spirit.

Direct or indirect dialogues are also very important in Dominique Gonzalez-Foerster's work. Her environments revisit the history of architecture and exhibitions, draw on the imaginaries of modernity and tropicalization, and embrace science fiction to bring figures from the past or future into the present. In *Alienarium 5* at the Serpentine South Gallery in London in 2022, a 360-degree metapanorama welcomed the viewer as if they were coming to a park. On the circular walls, a vast gallery of portraits showed people who have contributed to Dominique Gonzalez-Foerster's work, even if only through inner conversations: artists, visionaries, activists, philosophers, writers, poets, curators. Each of them can claim a share of the authorship of *Alienarium 5*, and the hospitality offered to them was a way to bring to life the nourishing and reinforcing dialogues in the present moment of the exhibition while establishing their creative complicity. This brightly colored metapanorama, blending portraits with alien bodies and extraterrestrial landscapes, facilitated encounters. It invited visitors to settle in and draw narrative threads between the assembled group of friendly looking identities. Through a series of science fiction

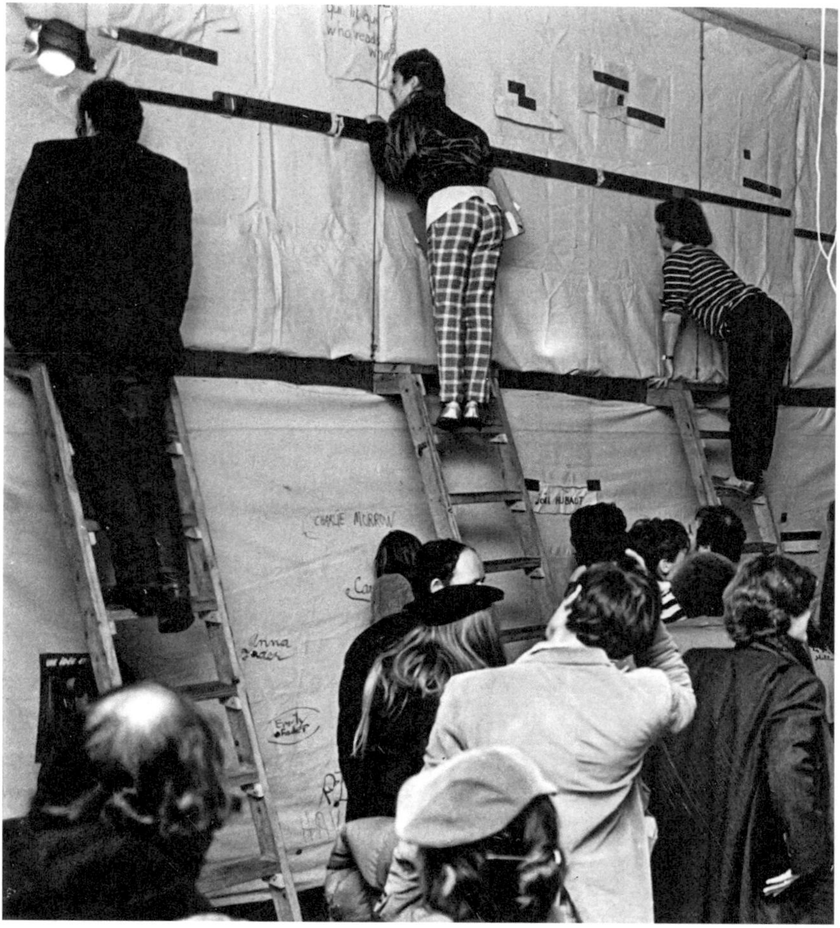

Fig. 31 Exhibition view *Grommets #5*, Jean Dupuy, Grommet Studio, New York, 1980

imaginings, the cut-out faces were mixed with sculptures, flowers, plants, and lush shells. As is often the case in Dominique Gonzalez-Foerster's work, everything was laid out flat and horizontally in this panoramic composition: scales were blurred and perspective effects forgotten, ushering viewers on a joyful, dreamlike expedition. A soundtrack composed by Julien Perez contributed to the experience by deploying different modes of perception that go beyond the visual to create moods that elevated people from their everyday life. Inspired by Hilma af Klint's spiritualism, Dominique Gonzalez-Foerster took visitors on an immersive and mediumistic journey, inviting them to sit on a carpeted floor or on cushions reproducing book covers. By evoking her bedside books, as she had already done more directly with her *Tapis de lecture* installation in 2000, Dominique Gonzalez-Foerster once again highlights the importance of the circulation of ideas and transforms the space of the solo exhibition into a cohabitation. All the figures portrayed on the wall provide valuable insights for overcoming the challenges of our contemporary world, whether it be the weakening of individual and social bodies or the rise in climatic and geopolitical disasters. As in a park, people could lie down on the carpet and become one with the landscape to recharge their batteries, to feel alive in an environment that contains them, and to get to know these thinkers and artists whose ideas and imaginations are instruments for the struggle. The exhibition became a place for sharing intelligent and militant thinking, and the axonometric plans the artist used when working on this project testify to her way of appropriating the tools of scenography: designing an exhibition this way means thinking of spaces as places, designating different colors to identify different affects, drawing intertwined threads to evoke densities of trajectories. For example, the choice of the picture rails is the product of a vision that is applied to a space. The plans were drawn up with architect Martial Galfione, a long-time collaborator, and served to describe and share their vision for the exhibition during the long period of preparation, but they were also a tool for the conceptual verification of a project, allowing the artist to be confident in the ability of a vision to function as an exhibition. The book *Alienarium 5*,[100] with graphics inspired by a vinyl record sleeve, is generous in its reproduction of these plans and working diagrams, and it shows how Dominique Gonzalez-Foerster uses them as a mental space, a tool for shaping ideas even before they become a technical tool. In 2021, at the beginning of the process of preparing for the exhibition, the architectural layout of the Serpentine South Gallery was used to create a digital

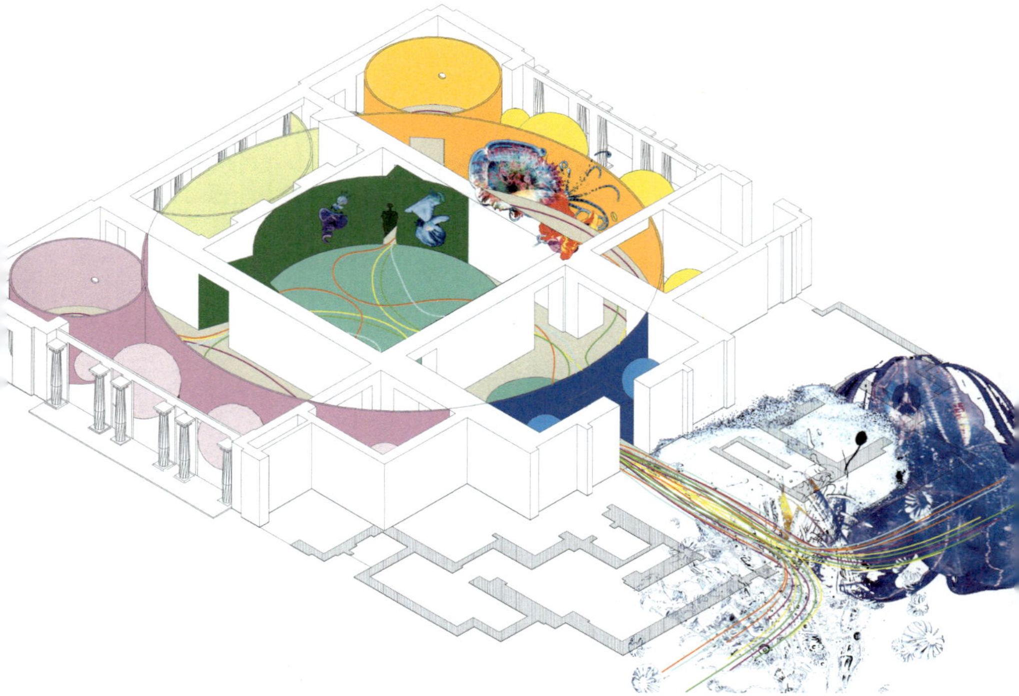

Fig. 32 *Alienarium* 5, plan, Dominique Gonzalez-Foerster, May 2021

drawing that conjured up an imaginary Alienarium, which became a very effective tool for communicating the intention of the project while being far removed from the usual modes of representation in exhibition plans. Dominique Gonzalez-Foerster likes to refer to these plans as scores, and they could also be described as "creatures," as Philippe Parreno, an artist with whom she has a close relationship, does in the interview that was conducted for this book.[101]

Another recent example of the ability of exhibition display to generate situations that facilitate hospitality is the scenography of the 2022 Venice Biennale entitled *The Milk of Dreams*. Despite the fact that the biennale is dedicated to contemporary art, the curator Cecilia Alemani made the bold choice to include several historical works by female artists in the international exhibition, conceiving the event as a space for dialogue. To complement this approach, she invited the Italian studio Formafantasma, and its founders Andrea Trimarchi and Simone Farresin, to design the scenography for the entire collective exhibition and she explicitly named them in the communication campaign about the project, which is unusual. The primary challenge of the collaboration was to simplify the visitor's experience, as people often feel overwhelmed when confronted with the breadth of artistic proposals offered during the Biennale,[102] a risk that was even greater as the curatorial project emphasized the effects of layers, porosity, and strangeness inspired as much by science fiction as by Surrealism. Because the brick walls are protected in the Arsenale's exhibition spaces, the challenge is to design a display layout that is consistent with the artists' individual projects, but also with the structure of the long building. In the spirit of the curatorial vision organized around historical focuses and dialogues with contemporary creation, the Formafantasma studio designed five time capsules that functioned as smaller exhibitions within the main exhibition, with a specific color for each one that helped observers to grasp the works as a whole. The designers conducted rigorous research into materials, which resulted in the choice to use textiles in all the capsules, but each time in a different form. They also took charge of the issue of recycling/upcycling the materials at the end of the event, in collaboration with the Biennale organization. These capsules drew on the classic vocabulary of scenography through the extensive use of display cases, more in line with the museography of a permanent exhibition or period room, which are displays that combine decorative style with the style of the works on display in order to allow visitors to immerse themselves in an artistic context. By creating environments that envelop the works in

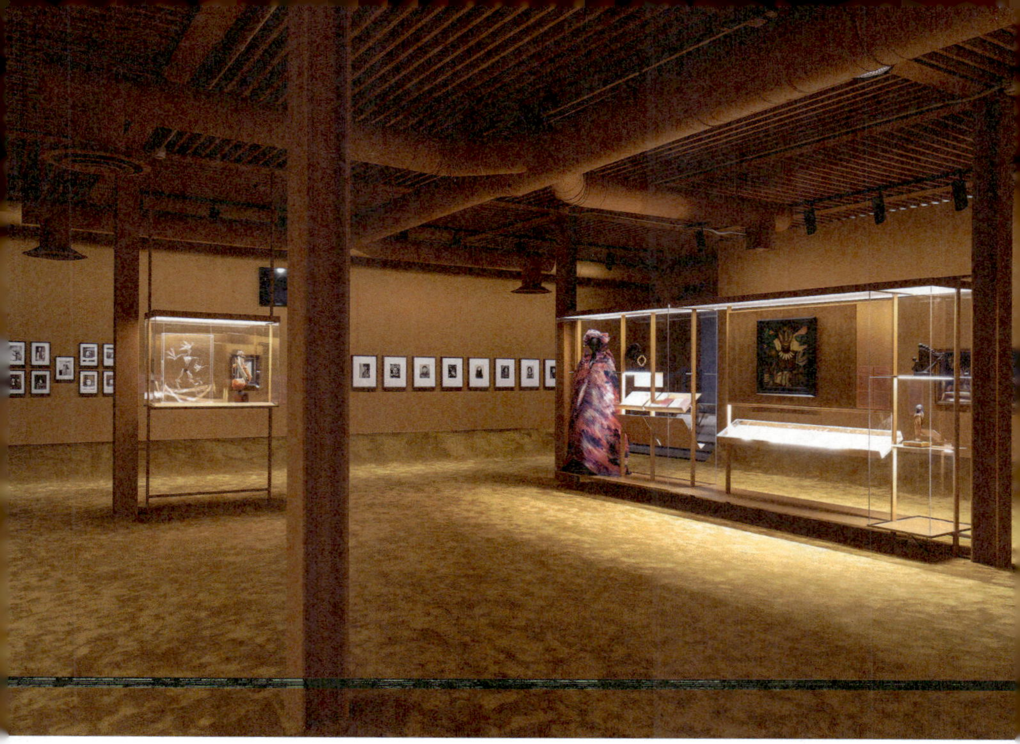

Fig. 33 Exhibition view *The Witch's Cradle*, time capsule, exhibition design by Formafantasma, Arsenale, Venice, 2022

a complete ambience, Formafantasma's intention was also to facilitate historical contextualization. The first capsule, entitled *The Witch's Cradle*, brought together female artists associated with Surrealism, Futurism and the Bauhaus movement, and it was particularly indicative of this approach, as the walls and floor were covered with ochre-colored fabrics and carpets. The corners were smoothed into curved surfaces, transforming the room into a cavity or vessel inspired by imaginary realms from science fiction, which, together with the figure of the witch, are central elements of Cecilia Alemani's feminist curatorial approach. The capsule was not a journey through time disconnected from the present, but an experience that encompassed the bodies of the viewers and anchored the female artists of the early twentieth century in our contemporary world.

In her essay "The Carrier Bag Theory of Fiction" (1986), Ursula K. Le Guin humorously deconstructs the heroic tales of prehistoric man as hunter that form the basis of the narratives that underpin patriarchal societies, and advocates replacing them with stories of gathering, an activity delegated to women. By inventing containers such as baskets and bags to transport wild oats or fruits so that they could be shared and preserved, humanity wrote its most beautiful story with neither bloodshed nor destruction; Ursula K. Le Guin also notes a similar role for writing that assembles, harvests, shares, and reveals another possible humanity, nourished by counter-narratives. This text was the starting point for the exhibition *Vieilles coques et jeunes récifs* at the FRAC Île-de-France in Paris and Romainville in 2024. Curated by Céline Poulin and Alicia Reymond, the exhibition questioned the biological, technical, and technological supports invented to sustain tired bodies and enable their possible transformations and regenerations. The curators constructed a two-part exhibition at two sites, inviting the architectural team of Régis Bagdassarian and Rita Elhajj to assist them in creating a scenography. As with Richard Hamilton's *Man, Machine and Motion* in 1955, the research into elements adapted for the human body led to an exhibition that was itself made into an apparatus. From the moment visitors entered the exhibition space, there was an ideological shift; the work wasn't presented alone on a pedestal or as the culmination of an isolated creative act, but rather as a collective space for gathering emotions and stories. The walls and floor were placed in tension by supports for the paintings that were reminiscent of those designed by Franco Albini and Franca Helg or Carlo Scarpa. A painting by Jimmy Beauquesne, *Purpose, Episode 1, Closer to Them* (2020), opened the section of the exhibition at Le Plateau in Paris. It depicts an embrace between Justin Bieber and a young man, both of whom prevent their gaze from being drawn to a sky that is ablaze. The painting evokes the dramatic context of a threatening climate and social conflagration that is difficult to confront, and is reminiscent of the European ruins that were the context for work by the Italian rationalists in the 1950s. Today, as then, transforming the museum and the exhibition remains essential for imagining tools that connect alternative, non-dominant narratives and strengthen collaboration by broadening the fields of action and support. The challenge is to ensure that the art is not imposed upon the space, while also preventing the display from assuming such an artistic presence that it overshadows the works themselves. Instead, the exhibition structure should expand the narrative logic of the works by mobilizing meanings embedded in what supports, frames, and positions them; the display should nourish and enhance the subtext. Régis Bagdassarian and Rita Elhajj designed a variety of arrangements, pieces of linoleum on the floor, picture rails, displays for hanging paintings and sculptures, which combined to create a common atmosphere of tension and support dissociated from the walls. Sometimes the works already had their own arrangements, such as Hatice Pinarbaşi's paintings that were presented on the wall and supported on the sides by crutches, so the display choices extended the vocabulary of the work into that of design by creating lateral support structures. Conversely, the work was also modified according to the scenography, as Hatice Pinarbaşi replaced the metal crutches on one of her paintings with wooden ones in order to emphasize the association of materials between the work and the exhibition display. Dialogue is a central issue in this relationship between art and exhibition design to ensure the supporting structures do not become tools of domination and oppression.

Lady Chatterley's violent rejection of the act of display is the perfect expression of what motivates this line of research: to separate the term from a social history where the staging of reality was exclusionary, vain, and contemptuous. Certain museums and exhibitions played a role in this phenomenon because they served as places of segregated bodies and appropriated objects and works that were looted during colonial expeditions, places of rejection and separation. It is sometimes difficult for the curators of museums whose history is intrinsically linked to the colonial past to pursue decolonial policies while also considering the future existence of these same institutions. The curator and researcher Karen Archey concluded a lecture at the 55th AICA[103] congress on the challenges of decolonizing the Rijksmuseum in Amsterdam by projecting an image of a museum on fire, questioning whether the destruction of the museum might be a possible way to confront its history. This destruction was envisaged as a thought experiment in the context of the restitution of collections to new museums built in formerly plundered territories that would merely echo the designs of museums in the West and thus reproduce those models. By making the film *Dahomey* (2024) to document France's restitution of twenty-six royal treasures from the Kingdom of Dahomey back to Benin, the filmmaker Mati Diop sparked collective reflections that had not been previously possible, as the event was barely discussed in France and this first step was not followed by further restitutions. The camera follows the silent departure of the works from the Musée du Quai Branly – Jacques Chirac. Enclosed in dark crates, the statues are given subjectivity through a synthetic voice speaking in the Fongbè language, using storytelling to convey their questions about the journey ahead. The vibrant and joyful welcome given to the returned treasures in the streets of Cotonou, announced on billboards and truck tarpaulins, is one of the most memorable moments in the film. People dance and sing, dressed in colorful traditional costumes, and representatives of the dispossessed tribes cross the threshold of the museum with majestic dignity, despite the masks imposed by the Covid pandemic. However, it is difficult to fully rejoice when seeing these statues take their place in the cold conservation facilities that the Beninese museum had to adopt in order to allow this tiny fraction of a material heritage stolen by colonization to return to its territory of origin. Both joy and anger run through the gatherings filmed by Mati Diop at the university in Benin, where people questioned why only a tiny portion of objects had been returned and why they had to be locked away in air-conditioned display cases. This resonated with our own questioning: How can we emancipate exhibition display from patterns of domination and transform it into a support structure in the face of the climatic, decolonial and political challenges confronting us today, which require us to transform traditional models? The testimony of Clémentine Deliss, who attempted to transform the ethnographic Weltkulturen Museum in Frankfurt, which she directed between 2010 and 2018 before her contract was not renewed, is invaluable. Her book *The Metabolic Museum* (2020) conceives the museum as a body and recounts the curator's attempts to remedy its metabolic blockages by reinventing it as a laboratory, a postcolonial museum-university, and a research territory offering hospitality to artists, philosophers, and students while welcoming the public with its body (the question of seating is addressed as a central aspect from the outset). The book ends with the "Manifesto for the Rights of Access to Colonial Collections Sequestered in Western Europe" (Dakar 2018), a powerful rallying cry to overturn existing museum models, their display schemes, showcases, and scenography that contribute to the distancing and abusive regulations inherited from colonial models: "No more museological pyramids! That 'absent air conditioning,' those 'incompetent curators,' et cetera, et cetera."

These positions of dominance and political issues surrounding exhibition display were very much present in the conversations we had, including those with Grace Ndiritu and Monster Chetwynd. This book was constructed as much from historical research and analyses of recent exhibitions as from long-term conversations with artists and exhibition designers between 2023 and 2024, in their studios and at their exhibitions, at the crossroads of art and life. The discussions were invigorated by ongoing projects and personal encounters and provided an opportunity to begin sharing the questions and historical journeys evoked here.

# Philippe Parreno

## Exhibition design as creature

*Philippe Parreno (French, born in 1964) is a pioneering artist in the use of the exhibition as a form and has continually explored its choreographic and temporal dimensions, its links with architecture, and the potential of new technologies. Exhibition design is present in many aspects of his work, particularly in the way he incorporates its tools—lighting, signage, seating—to blur the boundaries between artworks and their surroundings. Our conversation began with a discussion of the history of exhibition design—from Herbert Bayer to Edoardo Persico, via Carlo Scarpa and Franco Albini—which prompted Philippe to share drawings and simulations, stages of his work that had previously been unseen. An examination of these materials nourished our conversation, which took place in his studio in Paris in November 2023.*

MR Your artwork is inextricably linked to exhibitions, as this is the format in which it unfolds. The temporal and architectural dimensions, as well as the psychological and organic ones, are key elements, and the ensemble is clearly permeated by a plurality of considerations linked to exhibition design.

PP An exhibition always responds to a space, but also to a given moment in time. For the project to have its own structure, I need to design it independently of the architecture into which it fits, as an organic and autonomous entity. For example, if we look at this plan for my exhibition at the Gropius Bau in Berlin in 2018, what we see are two eyes—two film rooms—equipped, on the right and left, with ears—blinds and movable shutters, two pianos, and external microphones. The east and west wings can be seen as the creature's membranes. The central, higher part houses the circulation of the waves of sensitivity of the "beast" as well as a pond measuring approximately 20 meters, as water is an essential element for any

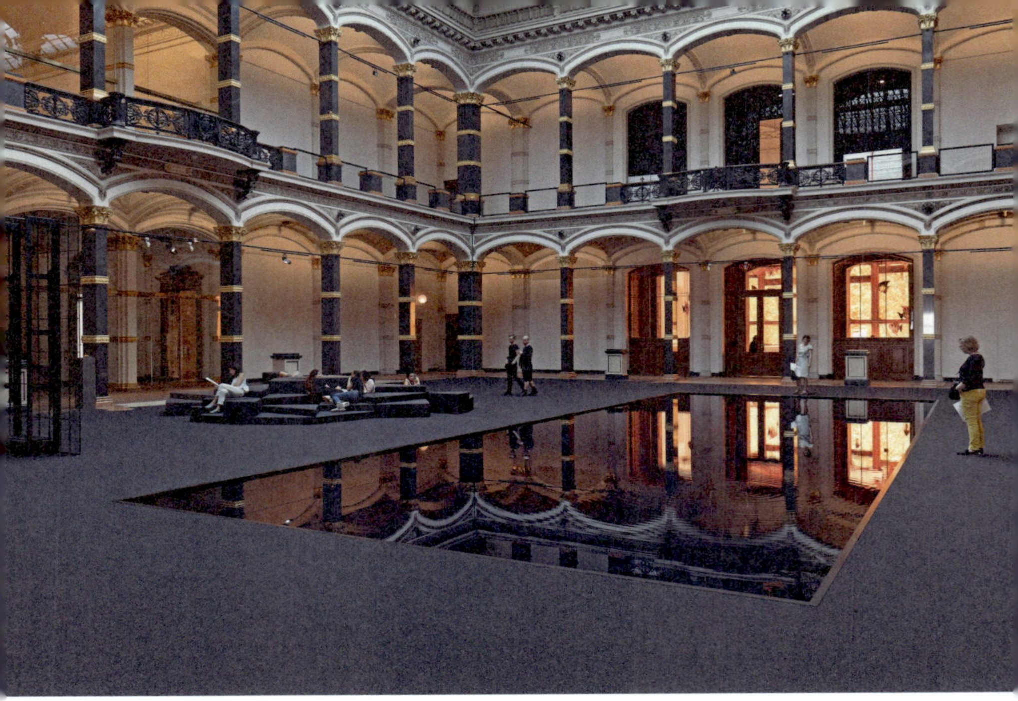

Fig. 1 *Philippe Parreno*, Martin-Gropius-Bau, Berlin, 2018

organism. Finally, the digestive system, the bioreactor, came to digest the exhibition. There were also other parasitic elements that ran through the exhibition, like when an elephant takes a bath.

MR The plans for this exhibition layout are fascinating. They create an animal structure, interpreting the exhibition's technical tools in an organic manner. This is a vision that you work with, but it is never revealed as such to the visitor.

PP No, because I make these plans when I feel that a project is taking shape and that it needs to be able to stand on its own.

MR The viewer actually has a more fragmented conceptual experience when visiting the exhibition than what we see here on the plans, thanks to your use of space-simulation software. Your career as a young artist began in Grenoble, where you worked in the production department of the Le Magasin contemporary art center. Is this where you acquired the technical tools of exhibition design and began integrating them into the creative process?

PP Le Magasin nourished my way of thinking about art because it was a place of experimentation and knowledge production that was very much removed from art as an object. In fact, I rarely went to the Musée de Grenoble. In a way, I discovered a manner of seeing through the technologies that were emerging at the time, as well as through music. At Le Magasin, art was like a promise of transformation of spaces, of mixing sensations, of transversality, like with science fiction and cyberpunk literature.

MR You take a highly technical approach to exhibiting, as demonstrated by the design simulations you just showed me.

PP This technical aspect of the exhibition came about very gradually: when I started out, video projectors were expensive and not very good quality. It was difficult to get decent images and sound in an exhibition space. We used home devices to create these relationships with temporal spaces, without any budget. At that time, Daniel Buren was one of the few artists who insisted that he should be paid to do an exhibition.

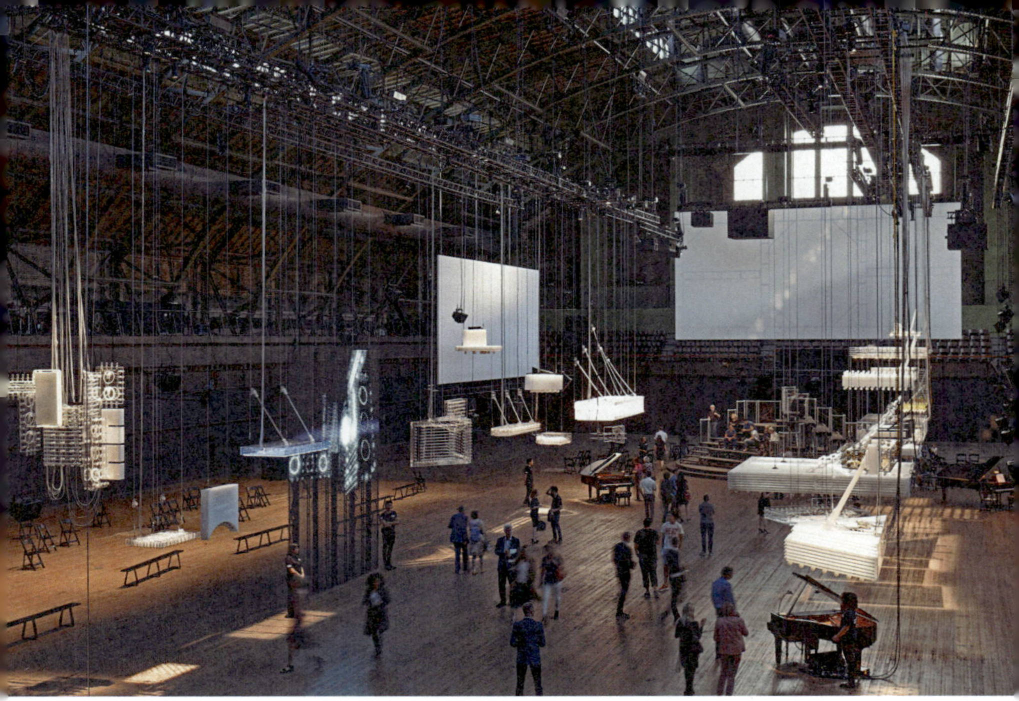

Fig. 2 Philippe Parreno, *H {N)Y P N(Y} OSIS,* Park Avenue Armory, *New* York, 2015

MR Despite these difficulties, you approached the exhibition as a place to experiment with space and perception, initially using inexpensive technical solutions, then increasingly sophisticated technologies.

PP Indeed. For example, with the project at the Armory in New York in 2015, I conceived the space as a basilica-like structure. If you remove the architecture of the venue, you find a cruciform structure that stands on its own, in a mineral way, different from the organic way that the exhibition structure existed at the Gropius Bau. In the same vein, the exhibition at HangarBicocca in Milan that same year was conceived as a constellation, an orbital structure where each event was a planet revolving around a central system, with satellites. The exhibition plans offer a way of visualizing this dynamic, including sounds, with constantly changing systems of attraction/repulsion.

MR Here, the plans are not just a preparatory tool, but a true conceptual matrix. Do you use them in your dialogues with curators and staff?

PP I showed them to the curator, Andrea Lissoni, but I don't do anything else with them. However, I am increasingly interested in the exhibition structure becoming something in itself, in the spirit of the Nouveau Roman, where the description becomes the thing itself.

MR The plans also become a memory, a dynamic archive of the exhibition. You often undertake important, long-term collaborations with cinematographers and musicians. Do you also maintain this type of ongoing dialogue with exhibition designers?

PP No, I have never met any exhibition designers. The only person I have worked with on this aspect of exhibition staging is Tino Sehgal, notably for my exhibitions at the Palais de Tokyo and the Bourse de Commerce in Paris. I wanted the bodies in these spaces to be connected to the overall system. I will also be involving him in the exhibition I am currently preparing in Seoul.[104] It will be divided into six *épokhè*, which is the time it takes to become aware of what we are experiencing in a new social moment—as described very well by the philosopher Bernard Stiegler. Each room will be an *épokhè* that is blind to the others, separated from the others. I like the idea that a person can take care of it, can connect to it through their body, and be penetrated by it. I am also going to have a 13-meter-high cybernetic tower

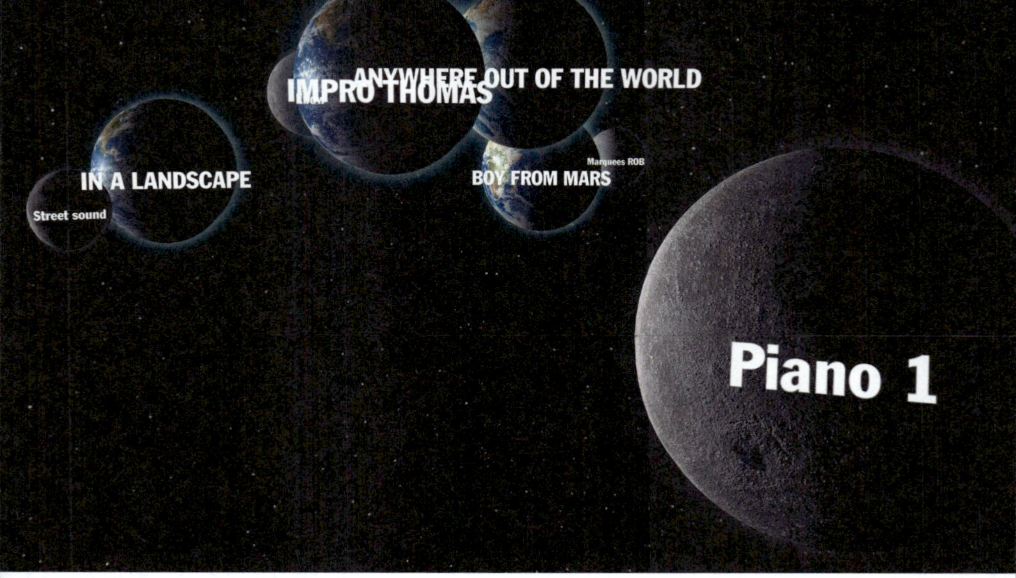


Fig. 3 3D simulation, HangarBicocca, Milan, 2015

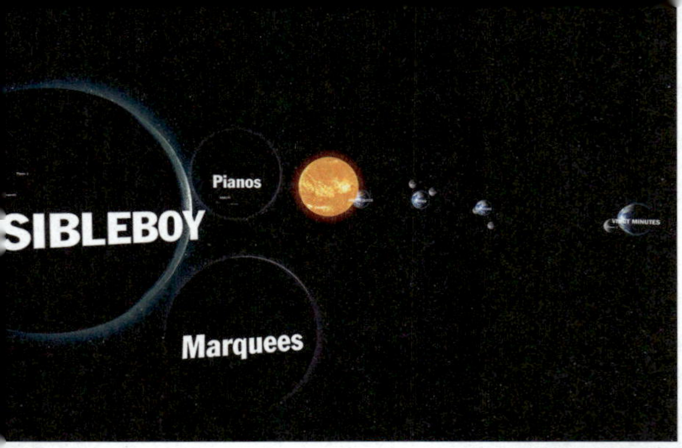


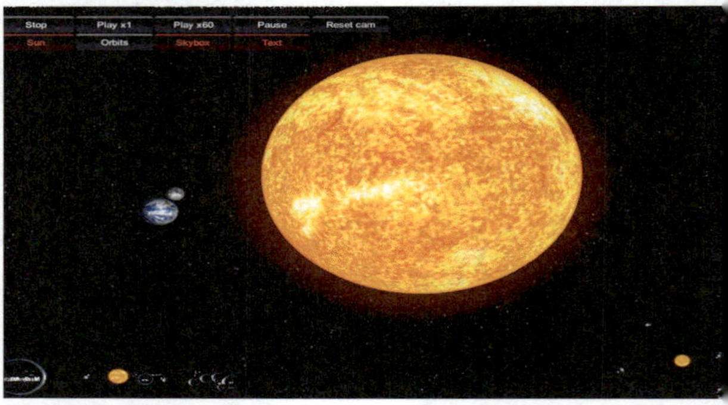


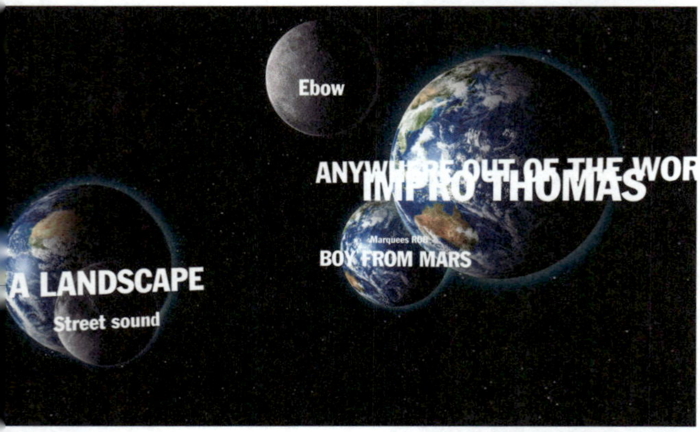


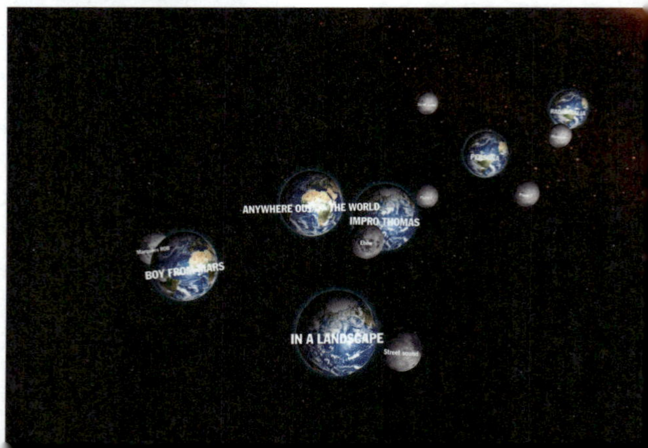


Fig. 4 3D simulation,
HangarBicocca, Milan, 2015

built called *Membrane*. It will be equipped with around fifty sensors providing information on the magnetic field, the level of the earth's crust, the wind, the temperature, atmospheric pressure, etc. All this spatio-temporal data will produce random movements and non-visual perceptions. Each *épokhè* will be connected to this membrane and sensitive to one signal spectrum. So we will hear different tones in these rooms, which will communicate different events and produce an analogical language in space, with undertones of lamentations. The sound must be linked to a feeling in order for us to be moved by these forces. Earlier, when you mentioned Herbert Bayer, you talked about how his exhibition designs conveyed a directed path, certainties linked to political commitment.[105] I believe that today, on the contrary, exhibit-ions are created as places of uncertainty, which has become particularly evident after the Covid-19 pandemic period, when we faced an unprecedented collective loss of bearings, of suspension of knowledge. In this context, I am interested in working with occult forces. In the 1960s, research conducted with crystals led to the invention of liquid crystal displays, but it was also linked to an esoteric dimension in language and communication. At the Leeum Museum of Art in Seoul, the cybernetic tower will function as a modular synthesizer that will redistribute waves in acoustic rooms controlled by a person, and the ensemble will create a pattern that may, at some point, go beyond the format of the exhibition and the experience of the work itself.

MR With *Anywhen*, at Turbine Hall in London in 2016 and 2017, I remember that we lost our sense of relationship to the work, which burst into a multitude of light beams, creating a great deal of uncertainty about what we were witnessing. The hanging wall panels and suspended video projector made us expect the climax of a cinematic moment, but it didn't happen where we expected it to. We were immersed in a temporal event where architecture, atmospheric data, and invisible machines came together, connecting us to multiple forces that were impossible to control. Your exhibitions are places that disorientate us and immerse us in relationships that extend beyond the usual patterns of knowledge.

PP Sometimes you can be connected to something, caught up in a space, but you can also be immersed in a substructure, and I try to create a coexistence between these different movements and levels. The experience is similar to a moiré effect, where something is trying to make itself understood but is seen in a particular way because the viewer's sensibility and sense of time—without beginning or end—come into play. This is yet another interpretative framework, and it is the combination of all these frameworks that produces this vibrating effect, this charge, as in Edoardo Persico's descriptions of the *Salon de la Victoire* that you showed me earlier.

MR What is fascinating about his descriptions is the attention devoted to atmosphere and perceptual experience, which was very rare at the time. But, coming back to your way of thinking about the place of a body in charge of a space, I would like to ask you about meditation: Is this practice also a way of working on these presences of bodies in space, these openings toward invisible forces?

PP I have been practicing meditation for years, in a fairly simple form, and I have talked a lot with David Lynch, who is a great practitioner, about what it teaches us in terms of rhythm and attention. Do you meditate too?

MR No, but swimming in the sea creates a fairly strong perceptual reversal in me, a kind of temporal dilation. When swimming with a mask and snorkel, you also learn a lot about breathing and rhythm, you lose your bearings between the sky and the sea, the light passes through the mediums and disrupts your senses. As I live in Nice, it's an experience that's a big part of my life. I'd also like to discuss your position as responsible for the exhibition's *mise-en-scène* in the group exhibition *Dancing around the Bride*[106] that was based on the influence of Marcel Duchamp's work. Was it a good way to understand the role of "generator-referee" that Duchamp himself played in the *First Papers of Surrealism* exhibition in New York in 1942?

PP I would very much like to return to the position of director and scenographer, as in those examples of early exhibition scenography that we looked at together. That would allow me to do my job without including my own work. The only opportunity I've had to do this was with the *Dancing around the Bride* exhibition about Marcel Duchamp and those who gravitated around him—the Black Mountain College, Robert Rauschenberg, Jasper Johns, and the couple Merce Cunningham and John Cage. The post-war context in the United States was a special moment when bodies, motifs, and ideas were exchanged. I was interested in the complexity of creating an exhibition with dance and sound, and in the need to find ways to collaborate with these memories. That's how I created the floor structure where you can hear the sound of Merce Cunningham's dancers (*How Can We Know the Dancer from the Dance?*, 2012). Cunningham worked on the idea that there was no relationship between music and choreographic movement, that the two things had to exist separately. The dancers had to produce their own rhythms through accentuated movements, which led me to the idea of recording the sounds they produced while dancing and then playing them back on their bodies using small speakers. They thus danced to their own movements, creating a certain cacophony that was recorded and broadcast in the exhibition space.

MR: You can feel the ghostly presence of these bodies moving in an expanded temporal and acoustic space. So you were acting as a conductor, both in staging the works of these historical artists and in creating works that engage in dialogue with these tutelary figures. This project of yours is especially interesting for the research I have been conducting over the past few years. It's not often an artist puts themselves in that position.

PP You also have to be allowed to do it. I really want to return to this format, this realm of exhibition design.

MR Are you also interested in the concept of display? How do you understand this term?

PP For me, display describes what is used to make something understandable, like a museum label does. What interests me is when there is no longer any difference between what describes the thing and the thing itself, as with the graphic designers M/M, where the text and form become part of the object or image in a kind of cross-contamination. We are not seeking to stage an object, but to reinvent the object to such a point that it perhaps even becomes superfluous. It is this tension that is interesting. Earlier, when I mentioned the Nouveau Roman, I was thinking back to Robbe-Grillet's story *The Erasers*.[107]

MR I had never thought of this idea of display as description, and it is inspiring in the tradition of the Nouveau Roman. How do you approach the question of describing your exhibitions, memories, and archives?

PP It's complicated. At the Palais de Tokyo, we published a book with photographs by Darius Khondji, who followed the exhibition script to recreate the visitor's path. Right now, I'm working on a publication that follows up on the *Danny / No More Reality* project at LUMA in Arles. The exhibition becomes a practice that generates something in itself that happens and repeats itself. Sometimes we keep the intermediate stages, but ultimately it's a process that doesn't always need to be documented. I keep the photographs, but I never look at them; I'm not interested in revisiting the exhibition matrixes like the ones I showed you.

MR Yet it is fascinating to delve into this orbital system of the exhibition with you. The software allows for a mental experience, a dynamic description. Do you develop a different scenographic matrix for each project?

PP Yes, they are intermediate stages of work that have their own function, like the orbital system at HangarBicocca. Or like the tower I am currently developing for Seoul. I am interested in the idea that the exhibition design becomes a creature in its own right.

# Rosa Barba

## The use of display as annotation of space

*Rosa Barba (Italian living in Germany, born in 1972) experiments with cinematographic devices in open spaces where spectators, sounds, and lights circulate freely. Her projects draw inspiration from astronomy and the scientific exploration of the world, as well as questions about the ideologies that underpin them. These questions are often expressed through patterns that reveal the importance of circulation and conversation. Her exhibitions are complex environments where the conception of space and its temporalities is a central issue. The interview took place in Paris in May 2023.*

MR We are in your installation *Hear, There, Where the Echoes Are* at the Centre Pompidou, surrounded by mechanical movements of screens, projectors, and glass plates that produce visual and aural effects and a captivating atmosphere. How did you work in this specific space in the south gallery?

RB I always try to respond to the architecture of the place where I exhibit, to project the exhibition outwards, and I love spaces like this one, with its huge glass façade, which I like to think of as a membrane of the building. I started to move outside the museum space with the White Museum project in Vassivière in 2010. In the piece *Hear, There, Where the Echoes Are*, which I will be performing with drummer Chad Taylor tonight, the different elements of his percussion activate the shutter systems in front of the projectors. There is an immediate response, a direct link between sound and cinema, both of which are created at the same moment. One of the projectors will be moved to project images onto a screen outside the building, through the bay window. Even though I work with films, I don't want to exhibit in a completely dark space. I invite daylight and the movements of the sun so that the space slowly darkens. The projections are integrated into

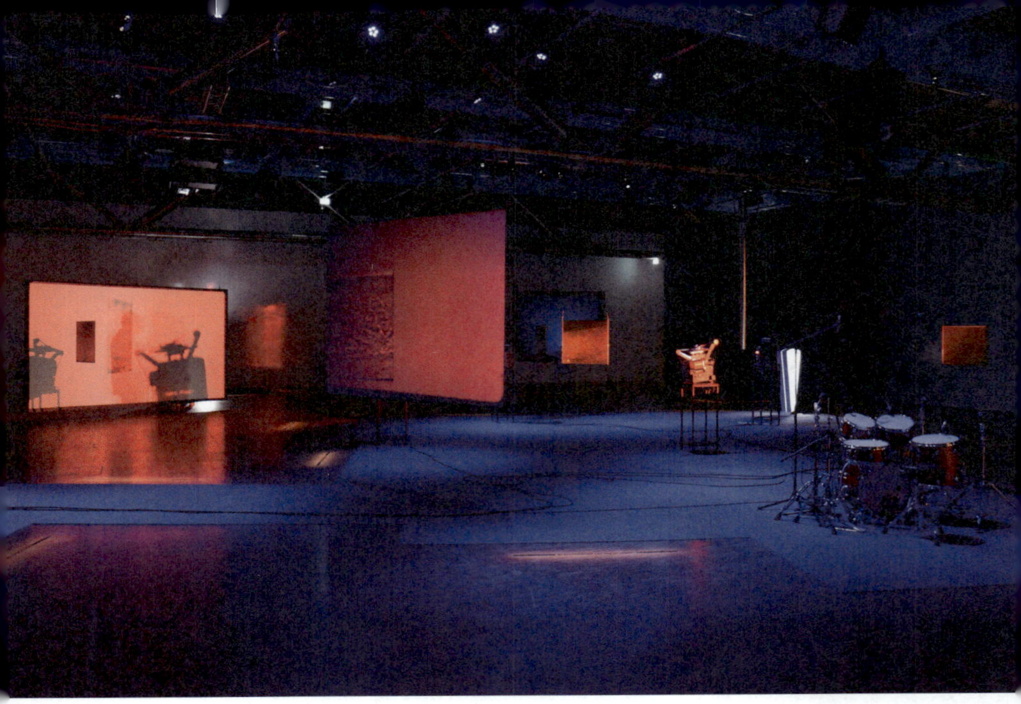

Fig. 1 *Hear, There, Where the Echoes Are*, Rosa Barba, Moviment, Centre Pompidou, Paris, 2016–23

the interior and exterior of the architecture, in a gradual progression, as they are initially very faint in the daylight before becoming increasingly present, as when film photographs are developed. And this is repeated in a loop, as the light returns day after day in a perpetual movement.

MR Yet this sensation of a perpetual loop is produced by moving, fragmented, or intermittent light.

RB This step involves abstracting the observed object, removing information in order to try to represent it in a different "light." The abstraction also comes from the perspective, vibration, and idiosyncrasies of the person handling the camera or projector, while simultaneously incorporating the space of non-information created by the intermittent light. The flickering has several layers, the sound produces a vacillating materiality, and it is this state that is also found in your mind. The voices of the choir singing during the performance further increase the vacillation, as it is impossible to program human voices precisely, to harmonize on an exact tone.

MR This state of uncertainty creates a sense of disorientation that is reinforced by the environment: upon entering the space, the viewer does not know where to go or what to look at among this array of machines, lights, and bodies. We feel as though we are inside a complex cinematic machine that integrates movement and action. In a way, it is only a covering laid on the floor that defines different areas between the instruments, the projectors, the performers, and the audience.

RB With the floor covering, I wanted to define a scene, a setting that would contain all the works. The museum also uses it to establish a kind of safety zone. It's like a drawing, allowing visitors to get up close to the work while providing guidance on how to walk around it.

MR The project is very precisely staged, as can be seen on the plan, but it breaks with certain conventions in that the carpet does not mark out a path for the viewer to follow, but is instead reserved for the artworks and performers. In addition, *Hear, There, Where the Echoes Are* has two parts, an exhibition and a performance, and during the day, since the space remains open to the public, visitors can watch a rehearsal of the performance, and see you working with the musicians and technicians.

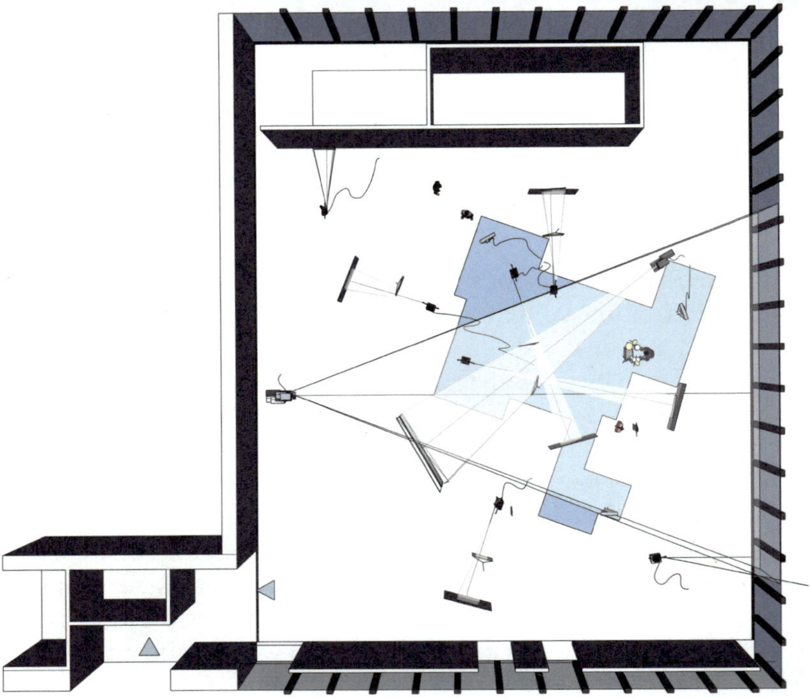

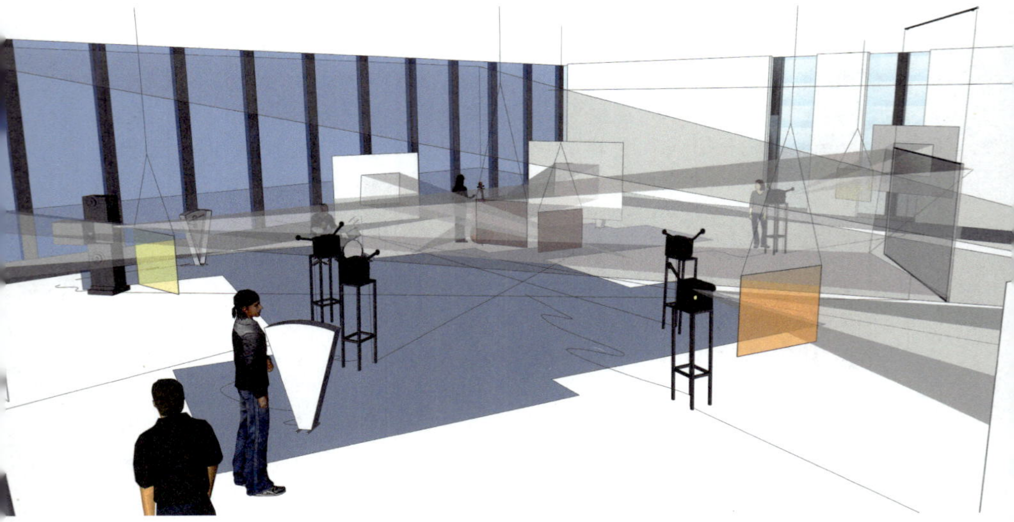

Figs. 2–3 3D plans, *Hear, There, Where the Echoes Are*, Rosa Barba, Moviment, Centre Pompidou, Paris, 2016–23

RB In a way, it becomes an active space that dissolves between performance and exhibition. I am always interested in the moment when a piece can become performative in itself and create a time frame. Here it is done with two sequences since we have some sculptures that light up and others that turn off. I've done this for different formats, the largest being at the Neue Nationalgalerie in Berlin, where fifteen different works were choreographed and sequenced to form a 45-minute loop. Even in such a case, I try to include a moment of live performance, but here in Paris, as it was a two-day exhibition, the project was more focused on the performance itself.

MR I have a very clear memory of the choreographed aspect of your exhibition at HangarBicocca in Milan. Could you talk about that?

RB It started very early on, with a piece I created in 2009 for the Venice Biennale, which was a choir itself: *Coro Spezzato: The Future Lasts One Day*, with five 16 mm projectors showing texts. I had been thinking about the idea of a Renaissance choir where there was no hierarchy between the singers, wondering what people might talk about in that kind of environment, in a choir or a church. The projectors were manipulated to project the films in slow motion and at different speeds, as well as the sound of the motors, and then the texts appeared. Sometimes they were synchronized, so that they sang a chorus, then they separated again. When I was invited to curate an exhibition as an artist at the Museo Nacional Centro de Arte Reina Sofía in Madrid, I created an exhibition-conference, which was a continuation of this creative research, using the same type of techniques with different pieces from the museum's collection. The projector beam changed, sometimes accelerating in the same synchronized mode, and at one point all the text appeared at once, creating a kind of chorus, before separating again.

MR In your role as artist-curator, how do you approach a display space?

RB I was fortunate enough to be able to visit several times during the year to study the collection. I had the idea of a conference between works of art within an exhibition. I drew a diagram that was displayed at the entrance to the space, detailing who was talking to whom. The works of art were more important than the authors, who were in the background and were not all contemporary. I looked for themes that spanned the ages, so that one or the other could take up an idea and bring it back into another conversation from different angles, given that times had changed, like Valie Export in relation to feminism, which opens up new discussions about the body. I wanted to see how ideas evolve and how voices can be added to these conversations. Then I implemented my own exhibition techniques: I choreographed the exhibition as I do with my own work, which I did not include directly. But I was present through my strategy of thought, through the orchestration of the whole.

MR How did it work? Was it a conceptual exercise in orchestration?

RB Yes, but also a real orchestration of time, with video works that turned on and off. For example, Martha Rosler's work appeared just as David Lamelas's work turned off. So you were led to look directly at something, and then something happened behind you, like in a call-and-response game.

MR As an artist, what did this experience of curating bring to your work?

RB I have always been very interested in how works of art fit into contemporary conversations and how that can be expressed. While working on this project with the Reina Sofía, I realized that I enjoyed studying the layers of conversation that aren't really addressed when focusing on specific works of art. This was a source of great inspiration, and I began making the three films of *The Hidden Conference*, which are currently on display at Tate Tanks in London.

MR For *The Hidden Conference*, you filmed the architecture of different museums, questioning their ideology of transparency and interrogating their storage spaces, where works of art have their own invisible lives. In the film, you move the racks to reveal hidden paintings. How did you choose them? Did you plan their appearance or was it accidental?

RB The three films are very different. At the Neue Nationalgalerie, I had to work quickly and I was alone, so it was a reaction to what I was seeing in the space. I didn't have much time to think and do research, so it was more about my relationship with my camera as it encountered works of art. I was invited into a setting that was already in place.

I was just an observer of that specific moment, entering the space and starting to see connections and film them. If I had come later, the works and settings would have been different. Of course, the exhibition was then designed more as a dialogue between the films, where I worked like a conductor.

MR Extending this idea of working with the buildings where you exhibit, and making the machinery active, I'd like to talk about the power of display, which you make extensive use of. You create sculptures by exhibiting motors, materials that seem random. Yet they become something else through an artistic process that uses exhibition as a tool, by suspending colored glass panels, for example.

RB The lenses themselves are in motion and project light into space.

MR The elements are sculptural pieces, but they also contribute to the creation of an environment; they are active accessories for a choreographed exhibition.

RB What I'm also looking for is to breathe with the architecture.

MR Could you explain your way of working through this duality of elements that are both perceived as sculptures and used as tools to create an atmosphere of light and sound?

RB First, I work individually on the sculptures, fragmenting them and assembling them in different ways, then using them as tools or elements to create another larger, fragmented space along with the architecture. It can become a single piece. I have always been interested in theater, but also in contemporary dance, and there are all these elements that come together when the pieces occupy the space. Here, for example, with curator Jonathan Pouthier, I chose to use a piece from 2009, *One Way Out*, composed of a system of pipes that seems to be part of the architecture of the Centre Pompidou.

MR It creates a confusion, an infiltration, which is made possible by a very precise arrangement of time and space.

RB I'm also interested in how sound can have its own level. In *One Way Out*, it was an optical sound on film that is aspirated by a fan and hits the metal tube, so that the sound is modulated by real objects and movements. The projector is essentially used to bring the image into existence, but the rest is entirely taken care of by the air and the tube that modulate the sound.

MR These physical movements and the sound create a hypnotic, disorienting experience.

RB Disorienting and orienting are ways of modifying the parameters of space and reflecting it, while also playing with the materials that exist there, such as the glass façade, and introducing multiple layers, with a continuous loop for each room. The colors are those used in astronomy and cinema. These aspects of my research converge in my work.

MR I would like to mention Lina Bo Bardi's exhibition design for the Museu de Arte de São Paulo (MASP), where she framed the paintings to install them on glass easels, revealing the backs of the canvases and creating conversations between them in an open space. I thought back to this arrangement when I entered your installation, where I observed the backs of the screens, the conversations between the elements, the projections on glass, and the bodies moving around in the midst of it all. For Lina Bo Bardi, it was a way of de-hierarchizing the elements, since everything becomes sculpture, and of composing a space in which the viewer has an active, but also more complex, position, because there are an infinite number of possible paths, and therefore just as many decisions to make. This echoes what you write in your book *On the Anarchic Organization of Cinematic Spaces:* "The audience is always made unsure of how to read the work and how to position themselves in relation to it. This discomfort forces the viewer to make decisions—to take a stand—thus becoming an active actor."

RB Thank you for that reference. It's true that, very early on, I wasn't interested in the frontal approach to watching a film in a cinema. I wanted to see everything in a non-hierarchical way, without hiding the objects, the projectors, the source of the light. So I started arranging all the elements involved in the film in the space and giving them a place. For example, at HangarBicocca, I used the distinctive ceiling structures and transformed them into islands where the works were located. It felt like a single work, but all the pieces had their own island, open enough to allow them to communicate with each other.

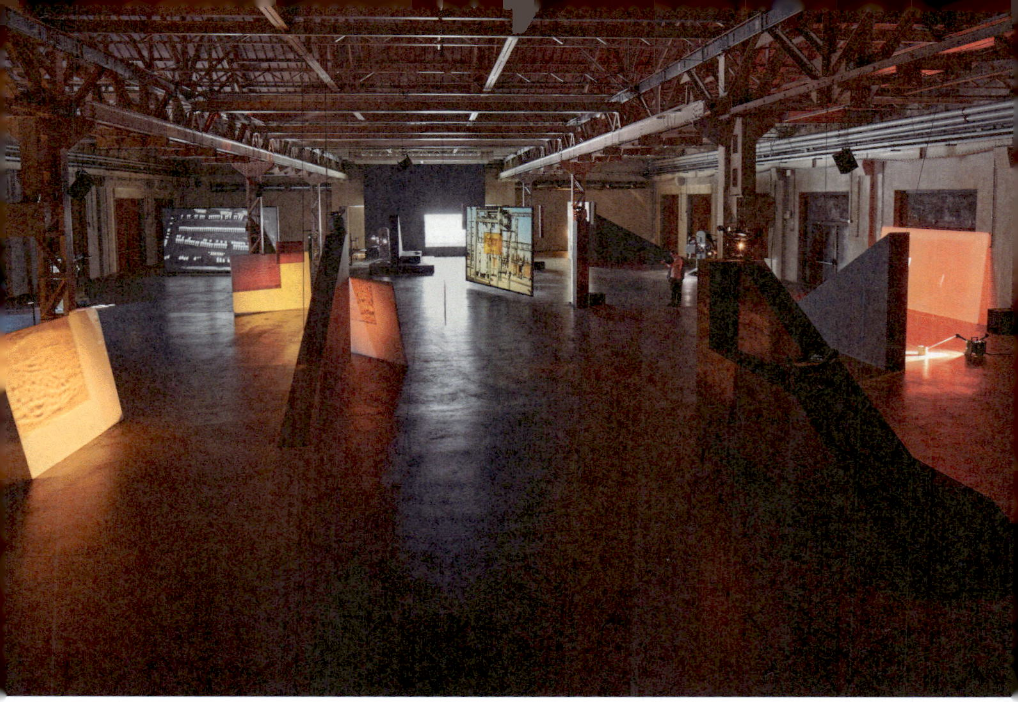

Fig. 4 *From Source to Poem to Rhythm to Reader*, Rosa Barba, Pirelli HangarBicocca, Milan, 2017

I try to create a layered experience through fragmentation, which is different from immersion. Of course, when it comes to performance, the balance between fragmentation and immersion is unstable, but that's my starting point.

MR Franco Albini and Franca Helg, Carlo Scarpa, and Lina Bo Bardi designed specific displays to show the backs of paintings, sometimes requiring the active participation of the viewer. In their museums, there is always a back-and-forth between contemplating a work and observing what is in the background, what is behind and around it, all in a collaboration with natural light and the play of reflections. The creative research carried out during this period of exhibition design seems to me to be very close to what drives your work.

RB Scarpa was a great inspiration to me. The Palazzo Abatellis in Palermo is an incredible example of how display can be used to annotate space. The same thing happened when I went to São Paulo and saw Lina Bo Bardi's glass easels. In both cases, it wasn't just about creating a space, a setting for the artworks, but also about studying how they interact with the architecture, how they mark certain positions, which I understand as annotation.

MR At the Palazzo Abatellis, Scarpa played with colored backgrounds, which we also find here in your project for the Centre Pompidou.

RB Yes, and these colored glass panels are set in motion by motors in the ceiling that cause them to move slightly. The light moves through the space, leaving the gallery through the glass façade and returning to it, gathering other light information along the way.

MR These movements create a blurring between architecture and art, between the exhibition and the works of art, which echoes your personal work when you exhibit projectors as sculptures. This is an experience we often have with Carlo Scarpa, who places as much emphasis on façades, lights, or walls as on works of art. At the Centre Pompidou, this experience was reinforced by your decision not to show any films.

RB This decision was linked to the attention I wanted to focus on sound frequencies without any visual distractions. Light projections from research in astronomy and cinema seemed to me to be the appropriate "film" for this occasion.

# Katinka Bock

## The plan as a promise

*Katinka Bock (German, born in 1976, lives and works in Paris) develops work that combines sculpture, installation, and photography in a dialogue with architecture, usages, and environments. She creates narratives between materials, their origins, and the contexts she encounters, taking charge of the balances and imbalances of spaces and atmospheres while fully integrating the dimension of scenography into her work. The interview took place in her studio in Paris in May 2023.*

MR  Your exhibitions create intricate relationships between sculptures, photographs, and architecture. It is an orchestration that plays on punctuation and fragile balances. How do you view your approach to inhabiting the exhibition space?

KB  I often hear people say that I produce softness and fragility, but I think what I'm really trying to do is make precariousness visible. When something is in balance, it holds, but it's a precarious state, as we see in many social systems. The duration of the exhibition is not experienced by the artist, but by those who work there and experience the changes in light and atmosphere, as well as events like possible water leaks and their consequences.

MR  This possibility of flooding in your exhibitions occurs through the inclusion of taps connected to the buildings' water systems, which drip, creating an instability that echoes social precariousness. For me, it also brings to mind Carlo Scarpa, who I think about a lot when I visit your exhibitions. When he designed the Olivetti store in Venice in 1958, he anticipated the flooding associated with the phenomenon of *acqua alta*,[108] and instead of fighting against the rising waters, he invited them to circulate through the space by creating different floor levels and playing with reflections. Like you, he attached great importance to the movement of natural light and water, anticipating and orchestrating their manifestations as much as possible. Does this comparison make sense to you?

KB Yes, I really like looking at what Carlo Scarpa did, the layout of the Olivetti store, but also the Palazzo Abatellis in Palermo.

MR For the Palazzo Abatellis, Scarpa experimented with display, playing with effects of depth, incorporating colored backgrounds, and creating fields and counterfields. He designed visual layers with great pictorial and sculptural power, which are a source of inspiration for many artists today. Could you elaborate on what attracts you to his work?

KB Looking at these installations helped me, particularly the way he stages the front and back of objects and paintings, or the fact that there is never a general system, such as a uniform height. You have to start over each time, to adopt the role of a novice to find the right way for two things to come together, which Scarpa does magnificently.

MR In the museums designed by Scarpa, each room has a specific hanging system, which is also possible because they are permanent collections where the works have had time to find their place and are still available for us to see today.

KB In Scarpa's day, there wasn't yet the standardization of hanging systems that resulted from industrialization. Artisanship was important; you had to come up with solutions, and Scarpa did so with remarkable freedom and finesse because he was very familiar with artisanal practices.

MR In this context, I'd like to talk about your approach to pedestals, which are also designed specifically for each piece, with a certain lightness, like when you see a lemon balanced and held in place by a string.

KB I don't like pedestals in general, so they always have to be part of the artwork, like legs or hands, something that holds it up and cannot be amputated. I work in fragments; I often have shapes that I want to make without knowing where they will go or what their identity will be, and it is the pedestal that will give them that sense. I also look a lot at sculptures in churches, particularly the drapery or structures that serve to hold the figure in place, in addition to the base. This is

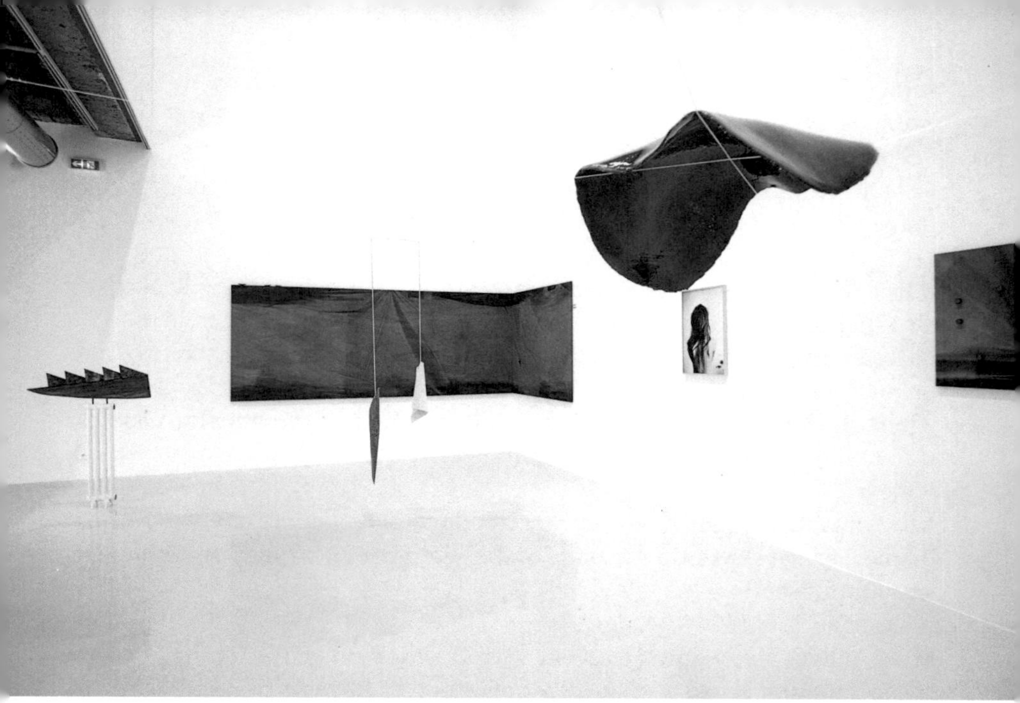

Fig. 1 *Tomorrow's Sculpture*, Katinka Bock, IAC Villeurbanne, 2024

something that can be seen in some of my sculptures, such as my 2022 work *Insomnie*, where I extended the wings to form the base. I am deeply inspired by artists from earlier periods, such as Donatello, who were already grappling with the same issues that concern me: how to make a figure stand upright in a space?

MR The Germaine Richier exhibition at the Centre Pompidou in 2023 also highlighted the way in which the sculptures generated their own bases as extensions of the bodies, integrating the sculpture's system of balance, for example in *Torse II* [Torse de femme, Muhlethaler] (1941), where the hand clings to the picture rail and the legs are transformed into metal supports set on the floor.

KB Absolutely, Germaine Richier developed a system where the display device slips into the body of the sculpture. It's a metamorphosis without secrets.

MR What I also wanted to evoke with the example of the lemon is the humor and sense of absurdity that emerges from its presence among the sculptures.

KB What is absurd is that the lemon needs to be changed as soon as it becomes lighter, so as not to disturb the balance of the mobile and to avoid a catastrophe. In exhibitions, someone has to climb a ladder every week to take care of this sculpture, and it's obviously comical to give so much attention to a lemon, which is the culmination of this grand sculptural gesture. It's like a mechanical watch that needs to be constantly adjusted.

MR There are opposing movements: the sculpture leans toward the lemon, which is a supporting structure that allows it to balance in space, but conversely, the presence of a lemon that has not withered and lost weight is necessary to prevent it from collapsing. This reciprocity is important.

KB And it is cords that hold the lemon in place.

MR Which brings us back to the systems of wires used to secure objects in museums to prevent theft, systems that must usually remain hidden.

KB But in my case, I'm not trying to hide the wire. It's made of linen and is visible, like in old systems for closing packages. I'm also thinking of the strings that hold the fruit in still lifes, the *bodegones* by painter Juan Sánchez Cotán (1560–1627), which are suspended in a cinematic black space.

MR You also observe movements that take place outside the field of art, which you then incorporate into your work as a sculptor.

KB I particularly like to observe people who work manually in a specific field, such as tailors or cleaning staff who have perfected repetitive movements. I look at how they hold objects. For example, in Sèvres, I observed a woman who had perfected her turning stick by adapting it to her shoulder in order to create plaster form, a technique used for making slip cast. Everything made perfect sense in relation to her morphology, I could have watched her for hours.

MR These are fascinating connections to the body, and it reminds me of the way you take care to welcome emotions when you start a project by talking to the people who work there.

KB I try to learn something about the place from them, asking them what's missing. Sometimes it's water, heat, or a lack of connection between two spaces, and I invent installations that offer temporary solutions to remedy the problem. I'm interested in collaborating with the institution. For example, *Kalendar* is a series of 50 or 100 paving stones arranged at the edge of the exhibition space, which changes over the course of the days because every morning a guard takes a paving stone from the end and places it at the beginning. I like to share responsibilities, as with the lemon. The institution accepts the possible risk that something will be forgotten.

MR I'd also like to return to the way you shift balances by considering your exhibition at the Fondation Ricard[109] dedicated to your photographs—which you don't usually exhibit on their own—and where ceramics ended up occupying the margins. Small green ceramic elements hung on the edges of the picture rails or on the walls, with a rather vague status. Can we say that these elements from your sculptural practice have the status of display elements?

KB The invitation I received was clear: to show my photographs and not my sculptures. So I had to come up with a system of display, which initially took shape through a set of double-sided panels with fabric and aluminum, suspended in space and creating a kind of musical score. I thought a lot about books, but also about Scarpa, who often showed the backs of paintings and created units using colored backgrounds. When I work, my sculptures are often scattered throughout the space, and here, the ceramics serve a similar function. I also thought about the way we mark texts when reading: these baseboards—pieces of green ceramic—are used to annotate and highlight. They are notes for reading aloud: to catch your breath, pause, lower your voice; they are like exclamation marks or parentheses. For example, I created a line between a series of photographs and a rather massive door to mark the beginning of the reading, to guide or contain the energy of the photographs. A kind of barrier.

MR How did you work on this spatial arrangement?

KB I started with what was there: ceiling suspension systems marked on the architects' plans, and I drew lines to see how to distribute the panels in the space, creating a partition. I try to imagine spaces without resorting to simulations. I prefer to test things directly on site and then adjust.

MR So it's a visual composition that is nourished by what you observe, your intuition, and your verification in the space, without collaborating with an exhibition designer?

KB No, I have never worked with an exhibition designer, but that's not because I don't want to. And, of course, I collaborate with the teams at the venues, I show them my drawings on the plans, which are promises to me.

MR That image of plans as promises is very poetic. At the Fondation Ricard, the suspended installation also reminded me of the inaugural exhibition at the Neue Nationalgalerie in Berlin in 1968, where Mondrian's paintings were hung on suspended picture rails in Mies van der Rohe's glass building. This exhibition design produced some amusing images, with the feet of the spectators sticking out from under the paintings. I thought about this a lot as I walked around your exhibition on the evening of the opening.

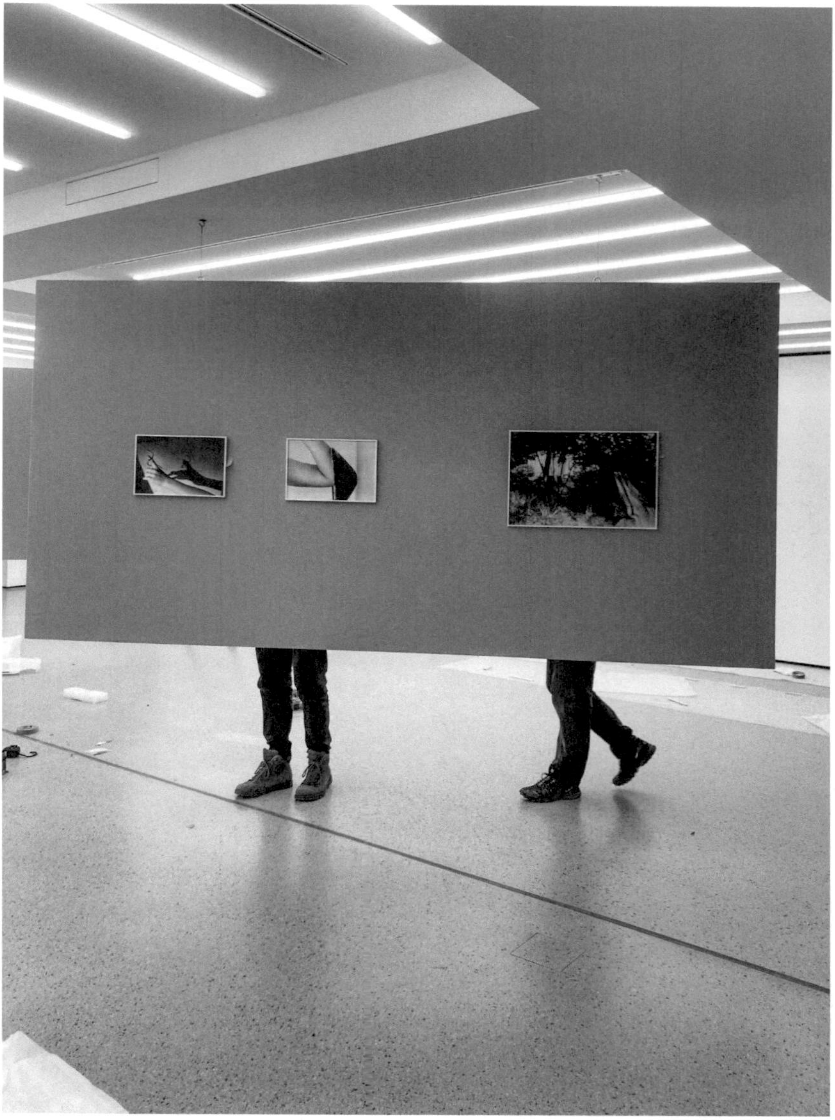

Fig. 2 Exhibition set up, *Der Sonnenstich*, Katinka Bock, Fondation Pernod Ricard, Paris, 2023

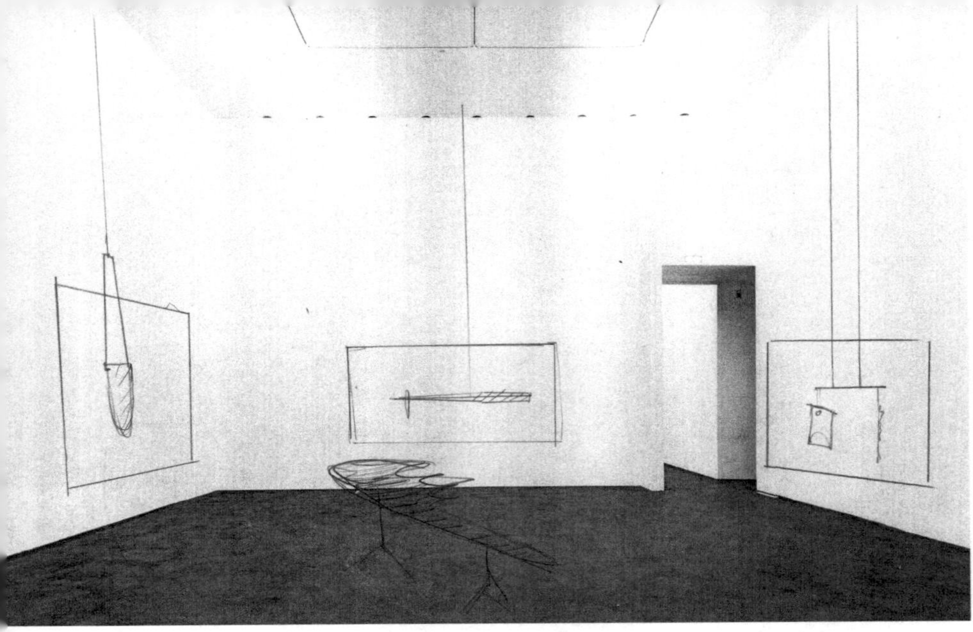

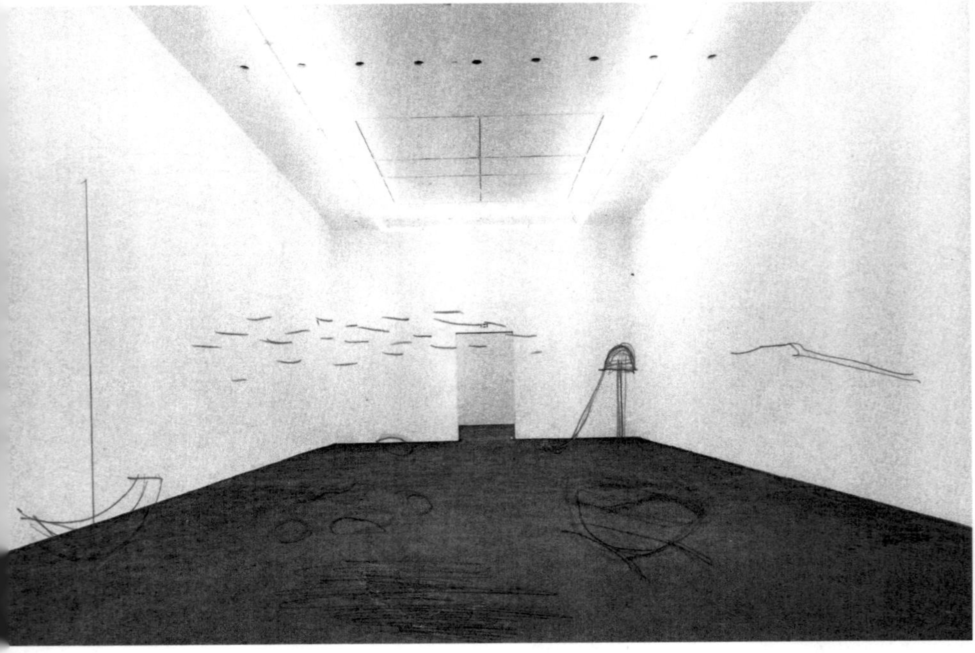

Figs. 3–4 Preliminary sketches, *Silver*, CRAC Occitanie, 2024

KB Of course, I had that in mind when I thought of this installation, but also voting booths or changing rooms, where you can also see feet sticking out.

MR The positioning of the suspended picture rails allowed for a multiplicity of viewpoints and orchestrated the images as different compositions.

KB That was important, and I had also thought about the views you get at intersections in the city. I like to create these constructions in dialogue with others, and for this exhibition, I asked the curator Christophe Gallois, whom I know well, to work with me, because I knew we would have interesting things to discuss. The installation is a tremendously creative moment.

MR How did you come to the decision to introduce color?

KB Color is something difficult, it's an area I approach with restraint.

MR There is a lot of chromophobia, a fear of colorful spaces in contemporary art.[110] Your decision to bring color into the space has changed the perception of the images on display, which are in black and white.

KB The decision to introduce color came quite late, when I was in residency at the Villa Medici in Rome. This is where I truly realized that every material has a color. Before that, I always thought about shapes and how materials reacted, not colors. As a result, in the plan I drew for the Fondation Ricard space, I added color to the picture rails and integrated them into the promises.

MR Looking at them, we can also appreciate the importance of the floor, an element that often features in your work, whether in the form of rolls of earth crushed by cars or water dripping onto the floor.

KB The primary surface is the floor; it's where things naturally find their place.

MR But it's also a place in itself. When you place a roll marked by the passage of a car, you feel the gravity of bodies falling, shapes being crushed, lives coming to an end.

KB Bodies and territories. Very often, institutions oppose work being done at the level of the floor: you can't pierce or damage it.

MR Of course, we are aware of the problems Hans Haacke faced after destroying the floor of the German pavilion in Venice in 1993. Nevertheless, when you really consider the question, the floor takes on a very important role. How do you choose whether to place a piece on the floor or on a pedestal?

KB Both are possible, but they produce different works. For example, with the sink, it was important that it be seen from above, but also that it be at a certain height in relation to the body.

MR So it's the position of the bodies looking at a work that guides you?

KB Yes, and that's why the studio is important, to take the time to observe. A few months ago, I asked a friend and artist, Mathieu Cherkit, who cleared an incredible garden near my studio in the countryside, how far he was going to go with his clearing. He told me that you had to wait and take the time to see what was happening before continuing. You can't do everything right away, otherwise you destroy things, and I think that's very true. You often have to live with the works for a while before making certain decisions.

MR Coming back to your pedestals, I'd like to draw on the research carried out by the artist Céline Condorelli in her 2009 book *Support Structures*, where she gives meaning to the structures that are used as support: here, when I look at this spoon, I really feel the presence of the pedestal that supports it, in the strongest sense of the word. Céline Condorelli points to the place of bodies that support, and bodies that support other bodies, in states of accumulation and precariousness that echo your vision, where the act of sculpting is also a way of making visible those who are invisible.

KB Yes, exactly, I seek to express the precariousness of social conditions, to make visible those who support and that which supports. Of course, it is also a political position to show everything that is there, without pretending that miracles can happen. The threads and crutches that allow us to maintain balance must remain visible.

MR There is an epiphany of the visible when entering your exhibitions, but when one approaches, one understands what is happening, one discovers what is behind, which is contrary to the logics of traditional exhibition design that seeks to conceal the act of mounting and securing a work. I recently visited your exhibition at the CRAC in Sète,[111] and I was struck by the way you orchestrated very different points of view that encourage visitors to retrace their steps, to move in several directions, to alternate their body positions and perspectives. You first put us in a state of shock when we discover imposing sculptures suspended from an architecture that is accentuated through them, then in a state of strolling and seeking when we turn around before leaving a room, discovering the back of the images. We then seek to better understand the compositions and identify the interplay between the photographs, the sculptures, and their arrangement in space. There is a certain pleasure in slipping into the corridors behind the suspended picture rails, spotting the visual openings and the precisely composed layers, or discovering the presence of a spoon behind a wall that achieves the impossible balance of its handle piercing the wall of the previous room. This creates a sense of suspense, a dramatization of the experience, which is difficult to perceive when one encounters your exhibitions only through photographs. It is somewhat similar to the installations of Carlo Scarpa or Lina Bo Bardi, where the images that circulate are always frontal, while wandering through the spaces they created invited the visitor to move their body and gaze freely. In your exhibitions, the design combining architecture, panels, sculptures, and photographs can give the impression of a solely frontal view, but the margins, the reversals, and the shifts in perspective are very important. For example, you talk about the two sides of your panels as two different "climates." Can you elaborate on these inversions?

KB These suspensions have two distinct sides: one covered with green fabric, the other with aluminum plate. The contrasting surfaces give the photographs different "temperatures" and "moods." It is not just a question of color, but also of material, texture, and resistance. This atmosphere is quite powerful and influences the interpretation of a work. There is no neutrality, and above all, the front and back tell us that we can be two people at once. How fortunate! In other pieces, I further emphasize the atmospheric nature of the works. I exhibit fabric, panels, or metal objects outdoors for several months. For example, on the roof of the Copan,[112] on the terrace of the Centre

Pompidou, or in a garden in Shanghai. These materials evolve in very specific ways over time due to the weather, thus recording time and space and revealing a climate map. Windows open up the exhibition space. The climate is interesting because it is diffuse; we cannot possess it, control it, or hold it, but it affects us everywhere, physically, mentally, and politically. One more word about the double-sided supports for the photos: not only is the double surface important, but so are the edges. I have inscribed a kind of broken line on these suspended works, one composed of glazed ceramic baseboard tiles. These baseboard tiles serve to punctuate, emphasize, and structure the space, offering a way of reading it. It is like reading a book, where the text mingles with our own thoughts in a dialogue, or like reading a text aloud, giving it intonation and accent.

MR In another exhibition, in Romainville,[113] you used the same hanging panels that you had used to hang the photographs at the Fondation Ricard, but you incorporated the memory of that first moment by filling in the holes, like a sculptor. Can you tell us about that?

KB I often keep the edges, cutouts, and scraps from my ceramic and wood pieces. These scraps lie dormant in the studio for a while, obsolete, before I rediscover them and give them new life. I used white ceramic buttons, originally circular scraps, to accentuate the holes in these aluminum sheets. I didn't fill in or camouflage these attachment points, but I enhanced their presence, making them the central subjects of a story. I was keen to include these climate panels in this exhibition, *Palomar*, knowing that the technical holes were irreversible and that I wasn't going to hang photos on these suspensions.
I didn't have a solution yet, but I was confident that I would find one. I often work in a sufficiently open and risky environment where problems are not completely resolved. I took my box of ceramic buttons to the exhibition installation and, in the end, the score wrote itself on these surfaces. The meaning of its writing comes from an experience, an event, and, slowly, these panels shifted from being a display object to a work in their own right.

MR I would like to conclude this discussion with the position of bodies in your exhibitions, which are solicited horizontally but also vertically through the suspended sculptures which, as you say, are loudspeakers that whisper in our ears. The positions of the images, sculptures, and bodies are changing; you often shift them from one exhibition to another, and you also play with the reversal of frames and images in space and in your films. How are these movements constructed?

KB We perceive a space or an object as large or small, high or low, depending on our size and the height from which we are looking, usually standing and moving around in an exhibition. Ultimately, this plays out in a fairly limited register around the human scale. I always come back to this body: my own, specifically, when I work, and the universal body that shows, holds, passes through, brushes the ground, or seeks flight. In the exhibition space, I am free to reverse the decisions I made earlier. I allow myself the option of changing my mind (so important in life!) if it makes sense to do so. So the sculpture *Personne* is sometimes lying down, sometimes standing up, sometimes in relief horizontally on a wall. The space lets me know what I should do. A hat becomes a bowl. A body suspended by a thread or the same body lying on the ground, which is our primary surface, says two completely different things. It is social gestures and places that are at play. Think of people sleeping on the street. Or the bust of Voltaire watching authoritatively over readers from its lofty position in a library. A film or photograph is easier to turn upside down: the hair will not flop down as it would in real life. It is a notion of abstraction and distancing that I introduce by turning things upside down. In an exhibition, I trust the visitor; I am certain they will find their way. I do not dictate how they should read or visit the exhibition. The pieces or details that are perched high up may be spotted by only a few people, but they are just as important. And perhaps, in another exhibition, they will find themselves at the center...

# Tatiana Trouvé

## Setting the gaze in motion, bringing worlds into dialogue

*Tatiana Trouvé (French-Italian, born 1968, lives and works in France) brings together drawing, sculpture, and architecture, engaging materials and chance forms in an ongoing dialogue. Her exhibitions inhabit spaces, connect energies, and incorporate what lies beyond the frame, offering poetic experiences of the environments they traverse. This conversation took place in her studio in Montreuil in November 2023.*

MR Your solo exhibition at Galerie 3 of the Centre Pompidou in summer 2022, *Le grand atlas de la désorientation*[114] [The Great Atlas of Disorientation], has been an important reference for this research. Your gestures in space seemed to enter into dialogue with historical figures of exhibition design such as Lina Bo Bardi, Lilly Reich, and Carlo Scarpa. Could you speak about what connects you to them?

TT Carlo Scarpa never overwrites what already exists; he weaves it together with his own interventions in a very subtle way. In his staircases, for instance, the old always remains beneath, everything reappearing almost transparently. In that sense, he's very close to Lina Bo Bardi—there's a similar sense of interpenetration. They also share an openness to flows and to vegetation within architecture. I've always been struck by Lina Bo Bardi's life: a deeply committed woman who left Italy for Brazil and absorbed its lush vitality—something carried first and foremost by nature, by vegetation growing with an energy she had never encountered in Italy, and which she then integrated into her architecture. She isn't always easy to read—there's something elliptical about her writing, with grand statements that merge into a kind of poetic language—but everything resolves with remarkable coherence in the work itself. And she never builds monuments to herself, but spaces where everything can coexist—viewers, works, objects. It's a profoundly poetic architecture. Scarpa, for his part, doesn't try to resist the rising waters in Venice—he welcomes them into the Palazzo Querini Stampalia. It's both intelligent and poetic.

At first, my exhibition at the Centre Pompidou was meant to focus solely on sculpture. But another show of my drawings, scheduled at the same time, was postponed, so I decided to include them. Galerie 3 is actually ill-suited to light-sensitive works, as three quarters of its walls are glass. Paper is like skin: if drawings are exposed to daylight, they deteriorate, they wrinkle, they fade. To prevent that, the exhibition would have had to be almost entirely dark, which I really didn't want. I wanted reflections between the street and the interior, to let sunlight in. On the floor, I used a principle similar to my *Les Dessouvenus* [The Unremembered] series: I start with bleach stains that guide me and prompt me to discover what they might become. I also worked with diagrams that correspond to different ways of moving through the world—not just human ones: from Aboriginal dream paths to the trajectories of ants or wolves. These lines lead us to wander between different perceptions of the world.

MR That floor drawing was indeed very important: it subverted the idea of a scenographic path, traditionally conceived as a single route, turning it into something layered and complex. You also introduced suspended walls, playing with colored backgrounds and multiple viewpoints, again expanding perception and bringing bodies into the experience.

TT When I work, I always have several drawings going at once, and my gaze moves between them. It's a very spatial way of seeing, which I then extend to the visitor. During the Renaissance, it wasn't unusual to make very large paintings and then cut into them—one painting could become several. There are countless possible framings within a single image, each capable of becoming a new composition. That idea was very much present in this exhibition.

MR Did you develop the project through models?

TT Yes, I love making architectural models, I do one for every exhibition. But it's also a trap, because it imposes an elevated, distanced viewpoint. Once you enter the space, your body gives you a completely different measure—it almost feels smaller.

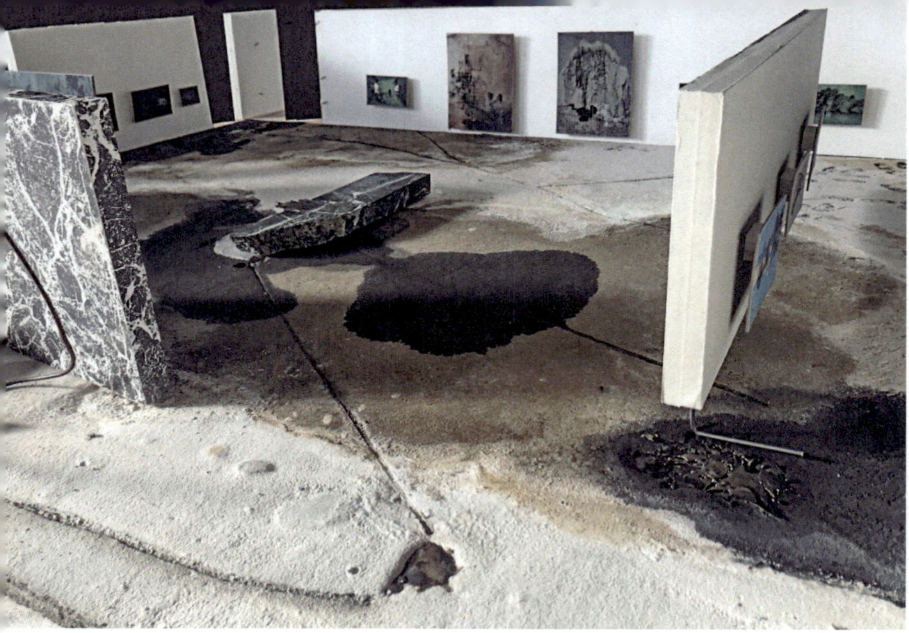

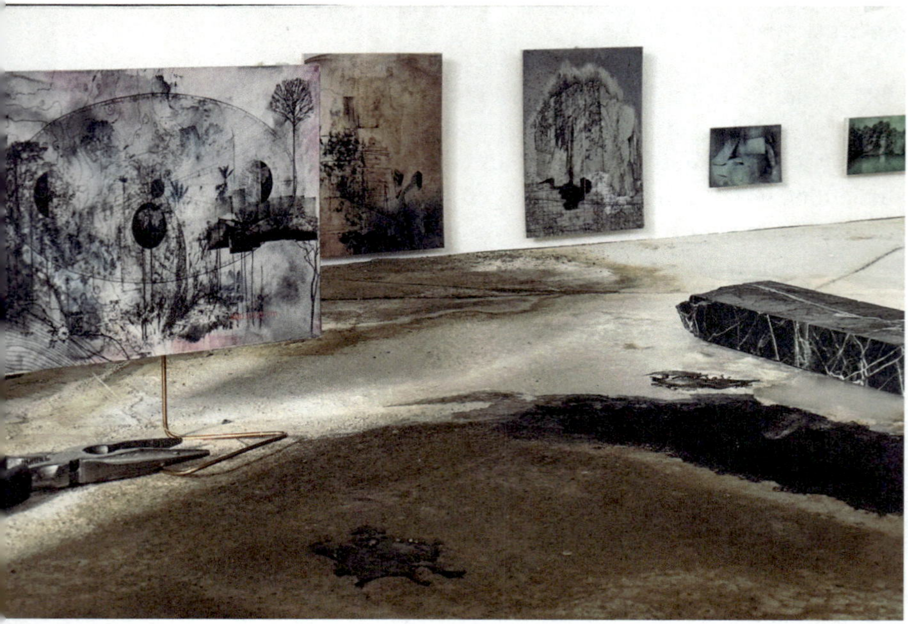

Figs. 1–2 Model, *Le grand atlas de la désorientation*, Tatiana Trouvé, Centre Pompidou, Paris, 2022

MR And you're entering a space already inhabited by other bodies, which changes everything.

TT Exactly. I hung the drawings at many different heights. What mattered most to me was this sense of suspension—a gaze in motion, circulating, alive, rather than fixed in static contemplation.

MR Like in the gallery of the Museu de Arte de São Paulo designed by Lina Bo Bardi where, unlike the often-reproduced photographs taken from a dominant, empty viewpoint—as detached from experience as a model might be—you're immersed in a mobile field of vision, shaped by the presence of other bodies, which is made highly visible by the transparency of the glass easels. Your exhibition also had a strong scenographic dimension through the use of curtains, which had a powerful presence in the space and reminded me of how Lilly Reich transformed decorative and industrial elements by revealing their sculptural qualities.

TT I like to bring in decorative elements that don't have any inherent value, and shift them so they can be used as a medium—almost like paper. These aren't major interventions: I don't paint them or turn them into artworks. But they become part of a whole.

MR You're incorporating what usually remains outside the frame of the exhibition—in this case, technical tools, or, in your series on museum guards' chairs, *The Guardians*, those bodies that institutions tend to render invisible.

TT Yes, there are many off-frame elements here—the curtain that separates us from the outside world is itself a kind of interaction. I'm interested in the position of museum guards as they're never placed randomly, but in spots from which they can oversee everything, with a panoramic view. I like reversing things, inviting us to look from their position, because in a way they carry our gaze.

MR The curtains were also set at a distance from the glass façade, allowing vision to circulate in that in-between space.

TT There was this sort of buffer zone, with these sculptures installed between the curtains and the windows that could be seen both from the inside, as silhouettes, and the outside. My only regret is that the museum had to apply film to the windows, which limited visibility from outside, except at dusk. You could also see the sculptures from both sides of the curtained area, but visitors couldn't enter because they were too fragile.

MR  As a visitor, you really wanted to step into that space.

TT  I would have liked to allow even freer movement.

MR  What is the status of these curtains? Are they scenographic elements?

TT  For me, they're extensions. In the same way, I used unfinished drawings, bleaching and smoothing out the paper to hang smaller drawings onto it, alongside other finished drawings of the same format. The blank drawings were just as important to me as the others. It's a bit like *Mapping the Studio* (2001) by Bruce Nauman, where you realize that there's an entire life unfolding in the studio at night when no one is there—mice passing through, a cat, the distant sound of a coyote. The studio absorbs all these dimensions, day and night, and everything in it carries equal weight—a dirty rag on the floor as much as a good pencil. That's the intensity of a studio that I try to bring into an exhibition, so that it becomes a full aesthetic experience. That's why I hung a small drawing at a height where it's almost impossible to see properly, but it's a spot of color that draws you in. You make the effort to look, and in doing so your attention shifts elsewhere, gliding across the curtains, and so on. It's this circulation that matters to me. These "undrawn" drawings are like dust thrown into the air and held there. The curtains themselves functioned in a similar way—like surfaces or backdrops marked with stains that let light through and tint the space, altering how the drawings are perceived. You don't see them as you would in a catalogue or on a white wall.

MR  I'd like to come back to the floor drawings: how did you compose with these different kinds of paths that you bring together?

TT  At first, I imagined using the cast shadows of the suspended drawings, but the tests weren't convincing. So I proceeded as I do in my drawings—by throwing blue and black India ink onto the floor, which then served as a kind of map. I first made a full-scale mock-up of the gallery floor in a large studio in Lyon, and then reworked those stains back in my studio, turning them into drawings.

MR So everything begins with the floor. That really came through when moving through the exhibition. The sun—the shifts of natural light hitting certain areas—also seemed to reinforce those impressions. How did you work with that?

TT Completely by trial and error. We couldn't accurately calculate where the light would fall because the architect didn't have sectional drawings of the buildings around the Centre Pompidou. So we didn't know at what time the sun would be blocked by neighboring structures. I worked from rough estimates based on the architects' memories of previous exhibitions. I tried to anticipate how the light would move, but it wasn't an exact science.

MR There was clearly an element of chance in those moments of alignment. It reminds me of my visit to the Museo Canova by Carlo Scarpa, where I was struck by the precision of a ray of sunlight falling onto a sculpture.

TT I once made a sundial in a park, this time based on very precise scientific data, so it still works today—when there's sun, of course. I love the idea that, at any period in time, sunlight will always fall in that exact spot.

MR It also brings to mind your 2009 installation *350 points à l'infini* [350 Points to Infinity], where weights suspended from plumb lines point in different directions, each with its own force.

TT Normally, a plumb line always falls straight down. There, it became a set of inclinations, forming something like the base of an inverted world. We tend to think of infinity as being above our heads, but here it is below us. If there are so many different gravities, it means there are just as many worlds beneath our feet.

MR That shifts the structure of the exhibition itself, which is usually based on a perspectival model—designed for an upright body of a certain height looking at what's directly in front of it.

TT  I'm very interested in the scale of bodies. For a long time, I made very small sculptures. That came about after I saw a documentary about a little person who explained that the world around him had never been designed to his scale. He experienced life as a foreigner, and began dressing like a tourist—because if his body didn't correspond to those environments, it was as if he were living on another planet. By adopting that role, he could move through life without adversity, exploring a world that wasn't his own. I found that reversal incredibly beautiful.

MR  The suspended elements in your exhibition at the Centre Pompidou also overturned hanging conventions, where paintings are typically installed at eye level—around 1.5 meters.

TT  I wanted to show how the gaze moves while drawing. I'm constantly influenced by everything around me in the studio. It felt more interesting to show how a world comes into being than to present the world of a single drawing—which, however complex, is only a rendering of something much larger. I'm currently working on a Grand Paris project for the Bagneux station with the architect Marc Barani. I'm creating a floor that functions like an inverted architecture, incorporating different types of road surfaces through a range of materials—asphalt, concrete, tile, stone. I'm also integrating manhole covers in bronze or in cast iron that evoke planets like Mars or satellites like the Moon—like hatches opening onto other worlds. It's also about bringing together materials that would never normally meet, like asphalt and bronze. People will walk across it, but they'll also be able to see it from above, where the drawing of this kind of cosmology becomes more legible.

# Daniel Steegmann Mangrané

## Exhibition as overflow and dissolution

*Daniel Steegmann Mangrané (b. 1977, lives between Spain and Brazil) is an artist who explores the exhibition as a living environment—a space for transforming perception and our ways of relating to the world. His work engages a sensitive and inventive use of the different dimensions of exhibition design. This interview took place online in May 2023 and continued by email.*

MR When visiting your shows, I am always struck by the way you approach each exhibition as an environment in itself.

DSM At its core, it's what we artists all do: whatever medium we choose, in the end we make exhibitions. What surprises me most is that the exhibition—despite having its own specificities, its own language, and being such a powerful medium—is not more widely used across disciplines. The sciences do engage with it, but rather timidly; philosophy or poetry, for instance, could also venture into it.

MR The exhibition is also a way of thinking. While it's a ritual shared by all artists, you explore a more specific dimension by inventing formats and displays.

DSM I think many artists do this, but not very consciously. I'm very much attracted to the way Dominique Gonzalez-Foerster, Philippe Parreno, or Pierre Huyghe, to name a few from the French scene who approach the exhibition-as-medium very deliberately.

MR For you, this awareness also seems to involve an interest in the history of exhibition design.

DSM I'm not a scholar, but I am very interested in it. I remember a beautiful display I saw in Frankfurt, at the Weltkulturen Museum,[115] where the director, Clémentine Deliss, had commissioned Austrian designer Mathis Esterhazy to create a very elegant set of display furniture. The units were modular and mounted on wheels, literally demonstrating how the exhibition, and the readings and meanings of the collection—even in a historical museum, since it's an ethnographic collection—are dynamic, reconfigurable, mobile, and constantly subject to change. In addition, she would regularly invite contemporary artists to intervene within the collection. I also recall Benjamin Meyer-Krahmer's proposal to present an exhibition of empty historical displays, dissociated from the works. What's striking is that when these displays were originally created, they were considered neutral, almost invisible—whereas in the exhibition they would have taken up a great deal of space and likely appeared quite spectacular. Today, many artists and curators are stepping back from the supposed neutrality of the white cube and trying to engage differently in relation with spaces and audiences, with the presence of bodies and how they occupy space. These are attempts to break away from the earlier modern notion of a disembodied eye floating in space, observing autonomous art. Everything around us affects our perception, our understanding, our vision.

MR The exhibition is a porous space that affects us.

DSM Exactly, that's what has led me, for instance, to develop a series of works using curtains. They are sculptures but they can still be used as curtains, to divide space. I like that they retain their original function.

MR Visitors can pass through them like beaded curtains, and they also have openings cut out in geometric and organic shapes. Passing through a curtain, crossing a threshold, separating spaces while allowing them to permeate one another, producing a work while fulfilling a function—these are all ideologically charged gestures.

DSM These curtains come from southern Catalonia, where I spent my summers as a child. There, they are widely used in butcher shops and at the entrances of homes preventing flies from coming in but allowing the breeze to pass. Kriska aluminum curtains can be passed through and quickly close again behind the viewer, producing a characteristic metallic sound. The cut-out openings come from a catalogue of shapes that invite recognition but resist clear interpretation. The curtains thus create an interplay between full and empty, continuity and interruption, invoking states of transition and engaging with notions of corporeality and immateriality. Most of these curtains are site-specific or at least site-responsive to a given place, deriving their form and color from their relationship to the space—both in reflective and contrasting manners. They divide space, creating a here and a there, while structuring both the gallery and the viewer's body position within it. The viewer is compelled to stand and move in relation to them and to the new spatial configuration they produce. They become more aware of their own movements and of their own body in space.

What's important to note is that these curtains never impose a rigid separation: just as the eye can pass through them—their porous materiality making them transparent—they can also be freely touched and crossed at any point. The curtain is therefore more a soft filter than a barrier, showing that even a very light, subtle architecture can nonetheless organize space, time, and movement. Even a work in its own right, the curtain can function as an exhibition display device, separating spaces and organizing their flows. It operates both as an independent sculpture and as part of a larger installation, creating a work that dematerializes in the relationships between the viewer's body, their movement through space, and the curtains—making transit and transience its material essence.

MR By reclaiming the function as a work of art, you're also opening the way to design, which you explore as an artist. I would like to come back to the design you created for the group show *Infinite Garden* in 2017.[116] I was surprised to learn that the catalogue for this show started with a text from the curator Emma Lavigne about your scenographic contribution—symbolically a strong gesture, as it gave it center stage.

DSM I was myself surprised when Emma Lavigne invited me to design the exhibition, as I had never worked on that scale before. I understood that I had to approach it like an architect, whose client has specific needs that must serve the project. Rather than limiting my artistic freedom, taking on that role allowed me to approach the exhibition with a different perspective, and to open up different kinds of conversations.

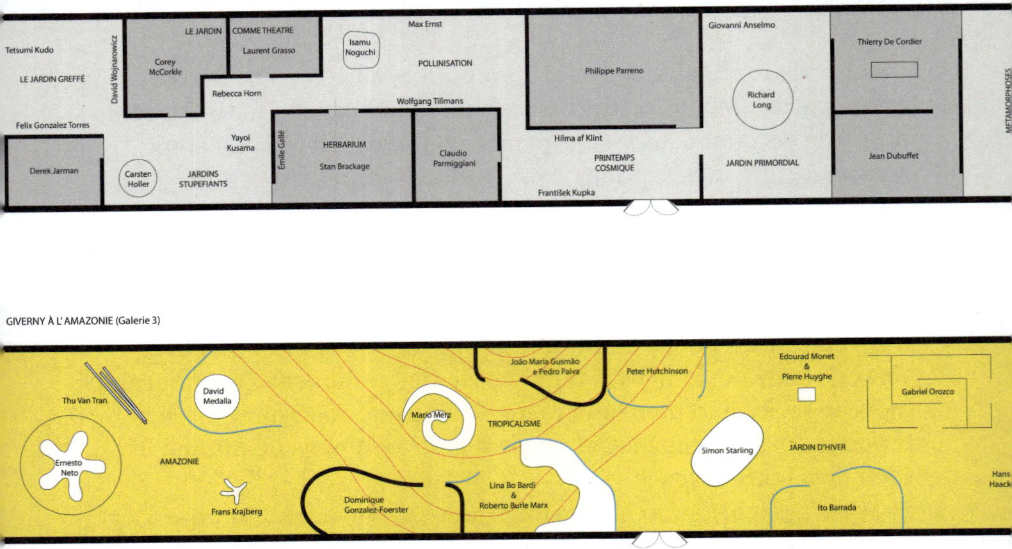


Fig. 1 General map of *Jardin infini. De Giverny à l'Amazonie*, Centre Pompidou-Metz, 2017

MR In what way was it different?

DSM Some differences were obvious, others more subtle. It was essential to be careful and dedicated to the works so they could be properly presented, but I also knew this didn't necessarily entail a white wall or a neutral display. Still, I would never have imposed my aesthetic ideas over the needs of the works. There were several pieces—by Hans Haacke or Frans Krajcberg—that I wanted to place directly on the carpet. The technical and curatorial teams were not entirely convinced; they felt that a plinth was necessary, both to protect the works and to separate them from the architecture, which was quite bold and colorful. I suggested placing them on the floor and sending photographs to each artist, asking for their opinion and letting them decide. There was also a very beautiful work by Jim Hodges, *Through This* (1996), a bouquet of artificial flowers, exploded and delicately scattered across the wall. The gallery walls were painted in different shades of brown, and I was convinced it would be beautiful—that it would create something like a galaxy. But the curators had doubts, understandably, since the artist had always shown the work on a white wall. So I made a simulation using the seven shades of brown and explained why we wanted to present his work alongside those of Felix Gonzalez-Torres and Tetsumi Kudo: to form a trilogy bound by a shared relationship to death, within a space immersed in a darker atmosphere. I also simulated the installation on a white wall to show how much it would stand apart and recede within the overall composition. Of course, there was still the option of placing it in the upper gallery, in a different atmosphere, but that would have slightly betrayed the work's meaning. Hodges understood this very well and swiftly approved the proposal, leaving us free to choose the exact tone of brown. As for Haacke and Krajcberg, they also understood and appreciated the idea, and in the end, we didn't use any plinths.

MR This reminds me of a conversation I had with Dominique Gonzalez-Foerster in the initial stages of my research, about her scenography for the exhibition *1984–1999. La Décennie*, which also took place at the Centre Pompidou-Metz in 2015. She explained that her position as an artist designing the exhibition gave her greater freedom to develop her vision. You managed to convince both the artists and the institution—do you think your position as an artist helped?

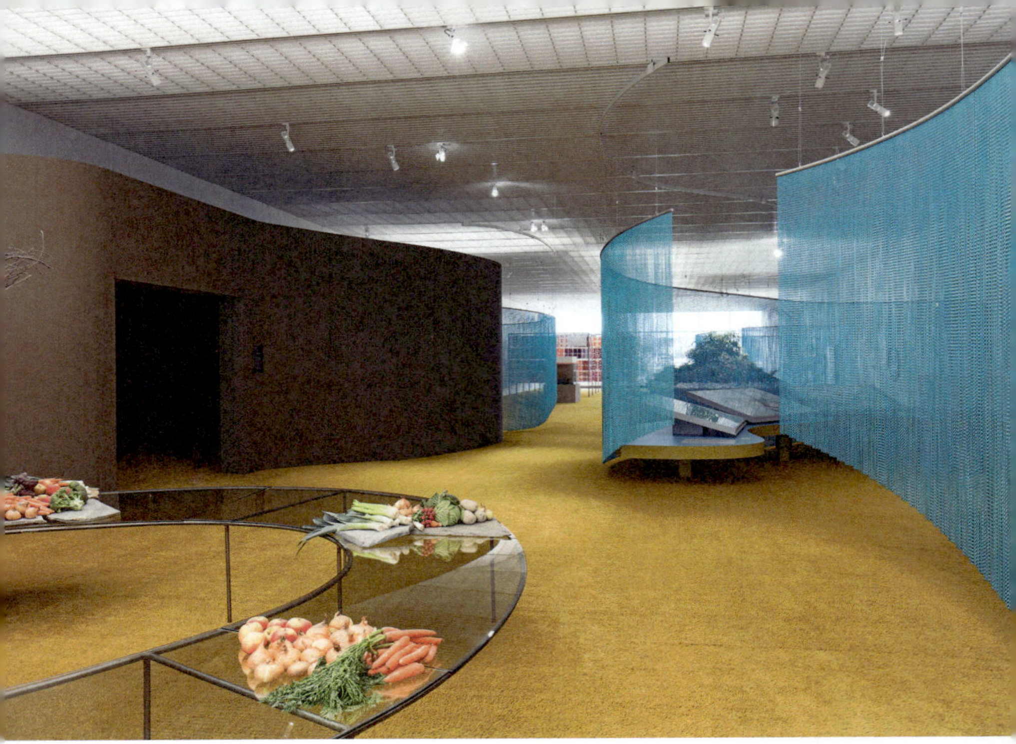

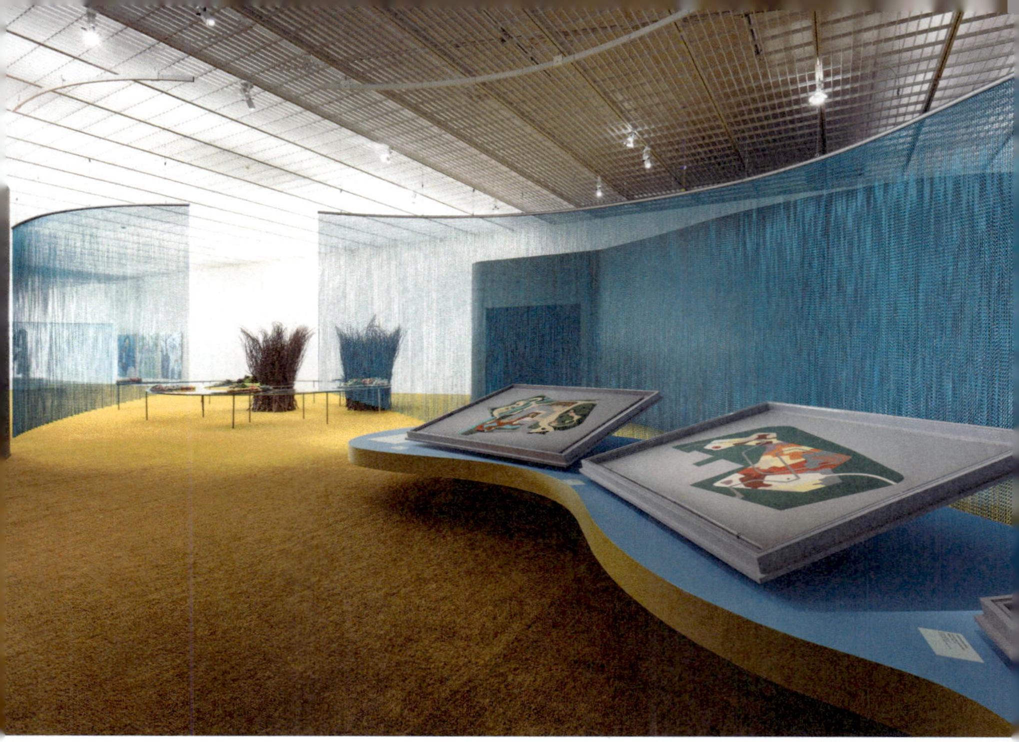

Figs. 2–3 Daniel Steegmann Mangrané, *Jardin infini. De Giverny à l'Amazonie*, Centre Pompidou-Metz, 2017

DSM Certainly. But it's also true that I was somewhat naïve about the institution, as it was my first time working with such fragile and valuable works, like paintings by Claude Monet or Georgia O'Keeffe. I imagined we would hang them and then move them if necessary as the project evolved—but of course that wasn't possible. They arrived accompanied by conservators from the loaning institutions who remained on site until the works were installed, and after that they couldn't be touched. But that naïveté also allowed me to propose ideas freely. Emma Lavigne was incredibly courageous—not only did she believe in my ideas, she made them possible within the institution.

MR Close relationships and forms of complicity between institutional directors and exhibition designers have always been important. They're what made the most experimental projects possible, already in the time of Franco Albini and Franca Helg, or Carlo Scarpa.

DSM Institutions are shaped by the people who work in them—and those relationships are indeed essential.

MR Atmosphere was clearly central to this project, as you've pointed out—in the use of color and lighting, but also in the way you worked with the museum's floor.

DSM The floor was treated topographically, with a difference in level of almost one meter between the highest and lowest points. It was quite subtle, but you could feel it as you walked. In the lower gallery, the space was painted in darker tones, and the works resonated with destruction, death, decay, and World War II. As you moved up to the upper level, you encountered sunlight, pollination, fertility, spring...

MR The catalogue of *Jardin infini* doesn't reflect this, since it was published for the opening. However, the floorplan of the exhibition is reproduced at the end, which is quite unusual and points to Emma Lavigne's desire to cast a light on the scenographic project.

DSM I really appreciate the way Emma Lavigne places the viewer's sensory and poetic experience at the forefront of her exhibitions. Perhaps because she comes from a musical background rather than the visual arts, she brings a sense of drama and staging that I value greatly. She isn't afraid to speak about beauty, death, or love. It's unfortunate that institutional constraints and publication timelines didn't allow installation views to be included in the book. Adding the floorplan was therefore a way of acknowledging the importance of the scenography in the overall project.

On the plan, you can see that the lower gallery space was divided into several enclosed boxes, with large open spaces in between, and the ceilings had varying heights. This created the sensation of having both interior and exterior spaces. So even though you were in a museum, moving through the gallery felt like wandering through a desolate, ruined village—made up of many small houses with intimate, almost solo exhibitions, alongside larger areas resembling open squares with collective sections. The architecture constantly forced the viewer to choose between turning right or left, producing a disorientation on the horizontal plane. By contrast, in the upper gallery, you were immersed in a bright, solar, colorful, vibrant atmosphere, with no right angles, allowing for very fluid movement. While downstairs your movement was shaped physically along a horizontal plane, upstairs the topographical elevation of the floor created a disorientation on the vertical plane. On the floorplan, this elevation appears in the contour lines. The slope was very gentle, but it made visitors acutely aware of their bodies and movements in space.

MR This project reminds me of the scenography Herbert Bayer designed in 1942 for Edward Steichen's exhibition *Road to Victory* at MoMA, where he also introduced a raised floor to generate movement and guide the viewer's awareness—first toward a sense of isolation and difficulty during the ascent, corresponding to the early years of the war, and then toward a sense of momentum during the descent, echoing the United States' entry into the conflict, where the viewer felt carried by a collective force.

DSM That's a beautiful project I didn't know about, thanks for sharing it.

MR In that project, the power of scenography to shape not only the visitor's physical path but also their sensory and intellectual experience is very evident, raising the question of its potential to function as a tool of manipulation.

DSM I'm very fond of these lines by Fernando Pessoa: "What in me feels, thinks." We think through our senses, our emotions, through our bodies and movements—the mind is a muscle. By altering the conditions of the viewer's body, by proposing new ways of sensing, you can affect their mental state, their emotions, their thinking, their way of acting or interacting, their perception of space... The capacity to produce such transformations is what makes the exhibition such a rich medium. What matters, to me, is that an exhibition goes beyond simply illustrating ideas—that the experience overflows. An exhibition is an experiment in articulating reality through art. What matters is not what happens inside the exhibition, but how you confront reality when you leave it. As Godard said, the problem is not to make *political* films but to make films *politically*—and if you make ecological art, make it ecologically.

MR In the *Jardin infini* catalogue, Emma Lavigne writes that you conceive the exhibition "as a metonymic field in which this renewed conception of the living can unfold, informed by the multinaturalist perspectivism of the Brazilian anthropologist and philosopher Eduardo Viveiros de Castro, which abolishes distinctions between all forms of life, between the human and its surroundings." Some of your works are also direct collaborations with the living—they are inhabited by it.

DSM Western ontologies tend to define things through divisions: between the non-living and the living; the living between plants and animals; the animals between rational and irrational; body and mind, nature and culture, subjects and objects... But as science, philosophy, and ethics evolve, these divisions are quickly dissolving. Amerindian cosmologies begin from a completely different premise: for them, everything is human. This doesn't mean that everything is a human being in the biological sense, but that humanity is the shared ontological condition of all things, and that everything can therefore be a subject. "Point of view" is not something subjects have over objects; rather, it is the point of view that creates the subject and grants it agency. Perhaps even more fundamentally, it is the point of view through which a thing is apprehended that defines its ontological actuality. Depending on the perspective from which it is viewed, a vessel may be the embodiment of a deity, a ritual object, or a simple pot. Likewise, a person changes depending on whether they are seen by their child, their enemy, or a panther. And perhaps, for a spirit, a person might appear as a vessel. Eduardo Viveiros de Castro calls this process Amerindian perspectivism. What makes it relevant here are its far-reaching implications for art: if there are no longer fixed subjects and objects, then there are no longer artworks and spectators, but rather dynamic relations of mutual transformation. Similarly, if everything is human, the traditional nature/culture divide is reconfigured entirely, with new agents and actors involved. This strikes me as a far more compelling, engaging, and intriguing way of thinking about art.

MR You lived in Brazil for around twenty years and, like Lina Bo Bardi, your time there has shaped your work. She is a figure only now being rediscovered in Europe, where she remains relatively little known. What does she represent for you?

DSM I admire her deeply—for who she was, for her political commitments, her generosity toward the public, her courage in refusing to conform, but also for her understanding that viewers participate in an exhibition with their whole body, in a mobile, non-frontal way. When you see the display at MASP in São Paulo, with paintings mounted on transparent glass easels, it's incredibly beautiful. It feels like something from the future. You move through art history with works that seem to float toward you, in a very intimate and personal relationship that also reveals the backs of the paintings—which are sometimes just as beautiful as the front and very rarely seen. And yet, despite its radical and imposing nature, this display allows for a direct interaction with the works. In the end, it is more neutral and discreet than most exhibition designs, which are often far more rigid and overbearing.

MR The way you describe it resonates with what she tried to achieve—it's remarkable that this display still works so well nearly seventy years after it was created.

DSM As I said, it's not a work of the past, but from the future.

MR In the photographs taken at the time of the museum's opening, reproduced in a small catalogue,[117] there are multiple views of the display featuring visitors. We are more familiar with that striking image of the installation when empty, but this inhabited series is very important, as it reveals how bodies position themselves in an intimate relationship with the works. Your description is also valuable for the personal dimension it brings in, and that is often what is missing from exhibition catalogues, which rarely convey these kinds of experiences.

DSM That's true. For *Jardin infini* it was also important for me to imagine people detaching from the works and wandering through the space, almost as if in a park. And that did happen: some people spent time on the turf, lying down while still within the exhibition, and continued to experience it by talking, pausing, lingering. Most of the time, I'm looking for that moment of detachment—when the viewer stops engaging with individual works and begins to engage with their own presence in space, to dissolve into it... I think that's when things start to become truly interesting. It's a pity we don't have images of those moments.

MR This was also the case in your exhibition *A Leaf-Shaped Animal Draws the Hand* at HangarBicocca in Milan in 2019–20. I clearly remember spending a long time observing visitors moving through the exhibition, wandering in a state of attention that was sometimes diffuse, sometimes focused on a particular display, fully immersed in a living environment.

DSM In that exhibition, this was also closely linked to the transparent partitions dividing the spaces: they housed the works, but you could see through them into the rest of the exhibition. This created relationships not only between the works sharing a space, but also between works and neighboring visitors that could be seen through the screens. It made the proximity of other bodies and gazes very tangible.

MR You've just opened the exhibition *A Leaf Shapes the Eye* at MACBA in Barcelona, continuing a project initiated at Kiasma in Finland. How did you approach these two iterations in such different contexts? And more specifically, could you talk about how you conceived the space, the visitor's path, and the display?

DSM *A Leaf Shapes the Eye* is a good example of everything we've been discussing. It shares many of the spatial solutions and strategies of *Jardin infini*, but applied to my own work. The space was covered with blue artificial grass, and we created a gentle topography throughout, bathed in a bright blue light that matched the color of the grass. This installation is a work in its own right, titled *Landscape of*

*Possibilities*, which serves both to host the other artworks and welcome the viewers. Through this use of color and space, I try to prompt an immediate recalibration in the viewer—to make them pause and sense that they are entering a completely different environment. It's striking to see how this transforms the way people engage with the works, the space, and their own presence. As Kandinsky said, color is a powerful language that speaks directly to the soul. Brazilian Neo-Concrete artists considered the sensorial a democratic point of access to the work—but one with emancipatory potential—and I naturally align myself with that tradition.

Personally, I want the viewer's full attention, full engagement—I want their whole body and mind. I want them to be entirely absorbed by the work or the exhibition. I spend a lot of time thinking about how to intensify their experience and capture as much of their time and attention as possible. To do this, I work with scale, lighting, color, and space, choreographing all these elements. For instance, I create systems of internal references or echoes—like a ritornello in a musical composition—that guide the viewer's attention across the room, to another previous moment. Suddenly, their body is in one place and their mind in another. There is a split. Something breaks, and may or may not need to be pieced back together... There is a profound difference between physical and psychological presence in space, and the exhibition can highlight and exploit it. These are just a few of the possibilities the exhibition offers as a medium.

# Ulla von Brandenburg

## Eating the exhibition

*Ulla von Brandenburg (German, born in 1974, lives and works in France) works at the intersection of art and scenography, creating spaces, films, and performances that inhabit exhibitions. Attentive to architecture and to bodies, she produces work that engages with the histories of art and cinema, draws on psychology and alternative pedagogies, and attempts to transform galleries and museums into heterotopias. This conversation started in her studio at the Karlsruhe Academy in January 2024 and continued on the occasion of a public talk at the Le Parvis art center in Tarbes, in May 2024.*

MR For several years now, we have been engaged in conversations about the porous and productive relationships between art and scenography—about the ways exhibition spaces can be inhabited, contaminated, departing from formats inherited from museums, which were originally conceived as spaces guaranteeing the autonomy of the artwork. In your exhibition *Le milieu est bleu*,[118] you installed at the entrance a red curtain marked by the imprints of paintings once hung in a dense, tightly aligned arrangement typical of traditional museographic displays.

UvB I studied in Hamburg, and I was struck when the director of the Kunsthalle said, after the museum's renovation, that the best moment for him had been when all the paintings had been taken down and only their traces remained. He knew which painting had produced which trace, and I really liked that idea of an invisible presence. In 2018, I was invited to Switzerland, to the Musée Jenisch in Vevey—a museum dedicated to drawing—and I conceived six rooms in six different colors, each linked to specific museographic periods. For example, at the Louvre there is a dark red that's very present in the collections, to which this curtain refers. At the Musée Jenisch, the drawings were placed on the floor, whereas at the Palais de Tokyo the curtain was presented without the works, raising questions about what was at stake in that absence.

MR That absence becomes a way of installing other kinds of presence, which detach themselves from the frame and the wall.

UvB I like the idea that one cannot tell whether the paintings were there before, which gives the impression of arriving at a somewhat indeterminate moment.

MR You studied at the Karlsruhe University of Arts and Design (HfG), which specializes in scenography—how did that shape your trajectory as an artist?

UvB My studies were very important, particularly my teacher Johannes Schütz, who worked with Jürgen Gosch, an important figure of the 1980s. He had a very pared-down approach to scenography, stripping things back as much as possible in order to reveal something with great precision. He had us work extensively with 1:20 scale models, a format used in theater in Germany, and I assisted him on several productions. I was able to see how a project shifts from model to stage. I'm very glad to have had this grounding in thinking about space for my practice. Even today, it is space that determines my projects, and I have just begun a series of fictive models that are ends in themselves, with arches, walls, stairs. One can see influences from Adolphe Appia, Constructivism, El Lissitzky, the Bauhaus. I make them in ceramic and then glaze them.

MR These models remind me of the installation you created in 2016 for the exhibition at the Centre Pompidou, in connection with your nomination for the Prix Marcel Duchamp, in which visitors could sit on a stair-like structure to watch a film shot on the stage of the Théâtre des Amandiers in Nanterre, where a set similar to the installation had been built for the actors. Your work often features this kind of *mise en abyme* between spaces, films, the exhibition, and the stage.

UvB At the Théâtre des Amandiers, the team built the stage from my plans in order to shoot the film, but there was never any performance. The staircase makes it possible to question what it means to move from one level to another, and there were three levels of steps, so one

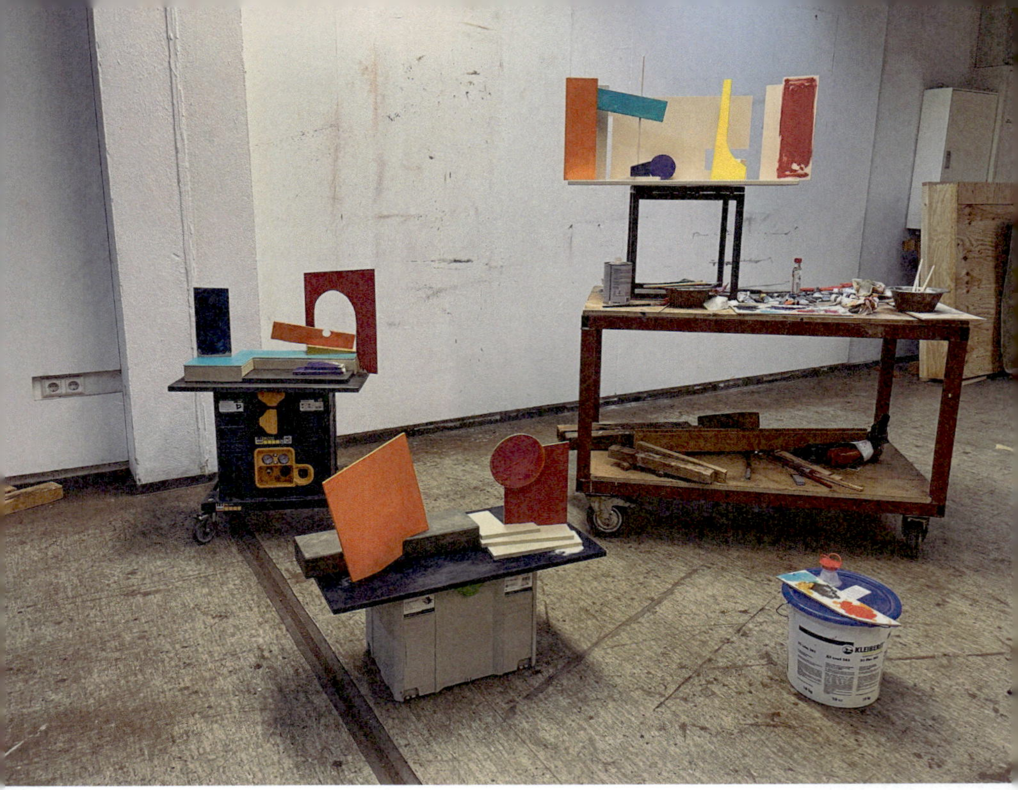

Fig. 1 Models in Ulla von Brandenburg’s studio, 2024

could choose how to climb the pyramid. After that, the film was shown in different spaces, and the design of the stairs was modified each time according to the site. These models are a new variation on that idea of wall/steps, and one of the forms, which resembles breasts, was inspired by a stay I had in Iceland last summer, where I was struck by a landscape in which the hills looked like breasts. I felt as though I were inside a vast installation by Niki de Saint Phalle!

MR Why do these models remain at this scale?

UvB Because they are mental projections, imaginary representations that do not need to become anything other than ideas. The scale itself is not clearly defined, which keeps the fiction more open. It is a new line of inquiry, in which the model is no longer just a cardboard stage destined to be discarded.

MR You also cultivate this sense of uncertainty in your exhibitions: one often enters from behind or from the side of curtains, without knowing what serves as a projection surface, what is set, what is artwork, creating a disorientation of the gaze and an ambiguity between what constitutes the work and what constitutes the scenography. I'd like to come back to how you produce these atmospheres in places with a strong architectural presence, such as the Palais de Tokyo—your way of placing spaces within spaces, of installing your own "hut," your own space within them.

UvB At the Palais de Tokyo, I often referred to the notion of hetero topia as described so well by Michel Foucault—spaces within spaces, bubbles that shift us elsewhere, into a kind of declaration of independence. The architecture of the Palais de Tokyo where I exhibited takes the form of a large, quite imposing arc. So I decided to create my own space within it, something that could have been anywhere, by constructing five different geometric environments using curtains that came from other contexts, other exhibitions—like the blue circle from Antwerp, where I presented a baroque theater outdoors for five months. As a result, the curtains retain traces of rain and sun. Each space also had a specific designation, and six performers would activate them every weekend according to a precise set of actions.

MR The presence of these performers contributes to your ambition to create inhabited spaces, to propose different states and moments of exhibition, in which the viewer feels invited to merge with the space—to be absorbed into it, to digest colors and sensations, and then to leave carrying something of them.

UvB I like the idea that the viewer comes to eat the exhibition, but also that they are eaten by it. The audience is, in a way, "staged," but I always leave movement open—there are multiple paths to take, different possible perspectives. And when the performers are present, they are on the same level as us; there is no separation. At the Palais de Tokyo, I wanted to bring in the countryside through haystacks, which have so often been represented throughout art history. At one point, the performers adopted the pose of a tableau vivant to look at the haystack and recreate those representations of rural life found on museum walls. The public was invited to do the same by photographing themselves with the haystack. And since the performers were only present once a week, I made dolls to replace them the rest of the time. They were always left in the last position in which they had performed, in order to preserve a trace of their bodies.

MR You recently opened a two-person exhibition with Farah Atassi at the Fondation Pernod Ricard,[119] located on the ground floor of a glass-fronted office building—also not the easiest space. How did you approach making it habitable?

UvB It's a complex space because it has very different ceiling heights. With Julia Mossé, who has been working with me on scenography in my studio for the past five years, we decided to emphasize the great height of the first space by installing very tall fabrics, and to accentuate the narrowness of the second space by using color to create a labyrinthine sensation.

MR In doing so, you completely transformed this space—which was designed as a neutral, transparent white cube—by painting the walls and partitions in vivid colors.

UvB The white cube is obviously an artificial idea, since a neutral, history-less space does not exist. So I try to detach myself from these spaces, particularly through color. At first, I drew on color theory—for example, the psychological test developed by Max Lüscher. Color functions in a way similar to music: it cannot really be grasped cognitively; it has to be approached through other means. Everyone responds differently, but it can still produce effects. The curtains I installed at the Fondation Ricard draw on designs by Sonia Delaunay from her *Atelier simultané* [Simultaneous Studio], which I enlarged to the scale of the space—zooming into them to let the vibrations of large colored surfaces take effect.

MR Could you say more about your dialogue with modernist figures such as Sonia Delaunay or Anni Albers?

UvB There are several important figures for me within modernism, including Sophie Taeuber-Arp and Lilly Reich, who did not confine their approach to a single medium. With Sonia Delaunay, for instance, her drawings migrated onto costumes, textiles, curtains, furniture, even cars. I really like this idea that art is not separate from us—that it isn't just hung on a wall, but can go everywhere, that we live within it, and that it can, at best, transform the way we live. All of these women also actively worked toward the de-hierarchization of the arts: Sophie Taeuber-Arp, for example, made furniture and her own clothing.

MR This de-hierarchization is also at work in your practice, particularly in your films, which—although shot on analogue film, in dialogue with cinematic tradition—can be projected onto fabrics, curved supports, or at floor level, without the protection of a black box. Films are an important element of your exhibitions, but they don't dominate; they are fundamentally interwoven.

UvB Yes, and I also often create mirror effects, where what we see in a film is replayed in the space. At XNL Piacenza,[120] for example, I projected the film onto the very curtains with which it had been shot, so that visitors would find themselves in the same space as the actors—so that there would no longer be any boundary.

MR We are inside the fictional space—and in that sense, we are "eaten" by the exhibition.

UvB At a certain point, the actors are also quite literally eaten by the curtains, since the fabrics come alive and swallow them. I work with 16mm film following the principle of in-camera editing: the camera is stopped to make bodies disappear into the curtains—a trick that functions like a magic act, recalling the early days of cinema, and Georges Méliès.

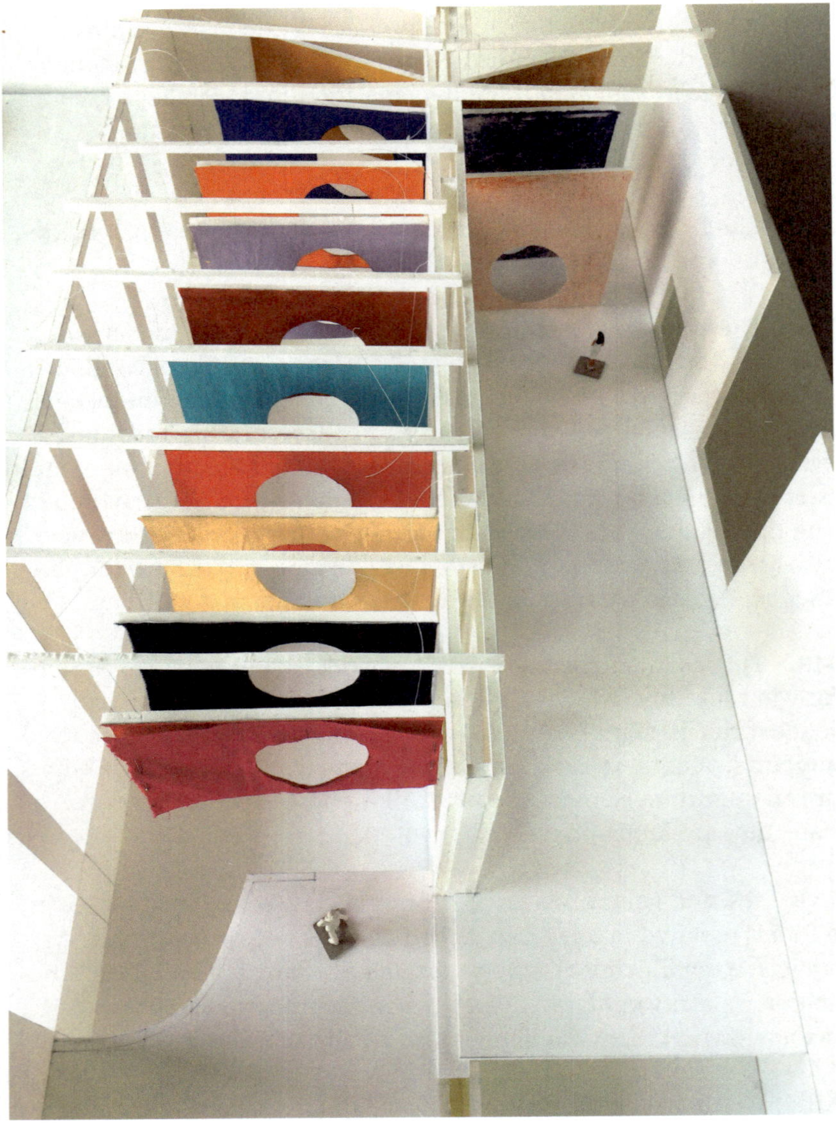

Fig. 2 *Das Was ist*, model for *Le milieu est bleu*, exhibition, Palais de Tokyo, model by Julia Mossé, 2020

MR Could you come back to your use of curtains—how you work with them?

UvB The curtains always come from different contexts and are treated according to specific processes. Some are made and painted using theatrical techniques, with layers of acrylic. The orange curtain, for example, is a sail from a boat in Sydney. I have also painted fabrics in my studio with my assistants, and dyed them in large vats. I then reuse them multiple times, adapting the scenography to each site.

MR You also work a great deal with folds in the curtains, and with knots and ropes.

UvB I'm very interested in folds, which are inherent to fabric—a material that is constantly in motion. The fold is the sign that another fold is always possible, that there is always a hidden part and a visible part, as Gilles Deleuze expresses so well in *Le Pli / The Fold*.[121] Ropes allude to theater, but also to the maritime world. In the beginning, it was often sailors who worked in theaters, because they were the ones most familiar with ropes and knots. I like to look at all these fabrics in theaters as sails, with the idea that they carry us somewhere—into our minds and into our bodies.

MR Earlier you mentioned Lilly Reich among the modernists you're "re-digesting." In collaboration with Ludwig Mies van der Rohe, she produced spatial compositions using curtains—most notably the *Café Samt & Seide* in 1927—offering great flexibility of arrangement and a certain autonomy of architectural space, while creating very strong formal atmospheres. She often sought to free herself from walls and partitions, allowing the materials on display to stand on their own within the space, affirming their aesthetic dimension. There are affinities between what Lilly Reich began to develop—at a time when women were dominated, particularly in architecture—and your exhibitions, where you draw forms independent of walls using curtains that take on geometric shapes, visible from certain elevated viewpoints or in your models.

UvB The "huts" I construct with curtains are indeed circles, arcs, triangles—and, as with Lilly Reich, they are spaces set within another space, offering different heights and viewpoints. The staging effects also vary greatly depending on the quality and color of the fabric;

there are significant shifts depending on the point of view, and perspectival effects evolve as one moves through the space.

MR To design your exhibitions, you produce models that are not shown but are an important stage in thinking through and imagining your projects.

UvB Yes, and I really enjoy looking at models—like those by Alberto Giacometti, which I discovered not long ago, or those by Salvador Dalí.

MR Artists like Giacometti or Constantin Brancusi gave as much importance to the plinth as to the sculpture itself, and producing models belongs to this way of thinking about space as the site of the work. At what scale do you work?

UvB At 1:50. It's important for me to move beyond drawing or the screen and to have this three-dimensional aspect. In the part of my studio where I store my curtains, there are drawers containing fragments of those same curtains at 1:50 scale, which I then use differently each time. When I work in theater, however, I use a 1:20 scale.

MR In this history that we continually "digest," I'd also like to mention the exhibition *E.R.O.S. Exposition inteRnatiOnale des Surréalistes*, at the Cordier Gallery in Paris in 1960. The Surrealists transformed the space into a cave, a cavity that incorporated the viewer by immersing them in an atmosphere inspired by ghost trains. The walls were covered with tarpaulins, the floor with sand and mirrors, and a soundtrack composed by Radovan Ivšić diffused erotic breaths and moans, while paintings and sculptures were hung all the way up to the ceiling. The aim was not simply to show Surrealist works, but to produce a Surrealist, subversive exhibition—one that immersed the viewer in a liberation of desire. These questions of bodily emancipation and sexual liberation are also important in your work, and I'd like in particular to mention your 2023 film *Le Bal sous l'eau* [Under Water Ball], which stages a community living in an underwater cave.

UvB Within this historical perspective, I would also mention *Hon* by Niki de Saint Phalle—a large sculpture presented in 1966 at the Moderna Museet in Stockholm, which invited viewers to enter through the vagina of a reclining, pregnant "Nana." Inside, one could see a small museum with reproductions of paintings by Paul Klee or Jean

Dubuffet, but also an aquarium filled with goldfish. My film *Le Bal sous l'eau* shares affinities with *Hon*, in that the idea is for a theater troupe—embodied by puppets—to transform into living beings in water, freeing themselves from the vices of the terrestrial world and becoming sexually emancipated, with oversized sexual organs, including a vulva from which the characters are born. Underwater, gravity is completely different—we make love better, everything is softer. These are long-standing themes, important in the 1960s, but already present in thinkers like Charles Fourier, which have greatly inspired me. The idea was that without sexual liberation, no revolution is possible, as Emma Goldman[122] says: "If I can't dance, I don't want to be part of your revolution." Today, the sexual liberation of 1968 is no longer really noticeable, and I wanted to imagine a much more advanced society made possible by living underwater. The characters sing about all this on stage, in a spirit of love, while behind the stage other things are also taking place. The film is shown on a symmetrical platform, with a curtain on one side and the projection on the other.

MR Underwater, one also experiences a transformed, stretched sense of time; one quickly feels close to other living species, and can imagine hybridizations between human and animal bodies. Water also makes us more aware that we are always immersed in a milieu—which is of course also true of the atmosphere, but becomes more perceptible in water.

UvB Water is also a heterotopia that transforms our relationship to movement: it allows for floating, but also introduces resistance. It's something I had already begun to explore in the film I made in 2019 for the Palais de Tokyo, *Personne ne peint le milieu* [Nobody Paints the Milieu], where objects are submerged in the sea. I would very much like to film underwater with actors.

MR At the Palais de Tokyo, on a wall label in one of the rooms, you also mentioned the idea of "inhabiting an exhibition," which resonates with my own research. What do you mean by that expression?

UvB I mean the place of the human—but also a contradiction, since no one truly inhabits an exhibition the way one inhabits a house. For the Palais de Tokyo, it was something of a dream: that the performers would live their lives within the exhibition, and that the public would at some point encounter spaces different from those they are used to—like entering an orange circle. I am always trying to create emotional spaces, using color and the music of the films that are projected. Sometimes it is silence that produces the atmosphere—you hear footsteps more clearly. During one of the performances that took place in *Le milieu est bleu*, we filled a box with words, evoking a sonic presence contained within the object. The milieu is where we are.

MR To produce this quality of inhabited space, you also often work with the floor and with seating.

UvB Yes, for example in *Sweet Feast* (2018) at the Whitechapel Gallery, I made a film based on an exhibition that had taken place in the 1970s in that same venue, which presented confectionery specialties from different European countries. At the end of the exhibition, they invited children to come and eat them, and they were completely overwhelmed. What also interested me was that the Whitechapel was one of the first art centers to work with children, with the idea of trying to transform society through art. I created, on the floor, a colored mountainous landscape that people could climb, walk on, slide across barefoot, and settle into in order to watch the film. The fabrics were sponsored by Kvadrat, a historic company that collaborated with major designers to upholster many of the pieces of furniture we know so well, and encouraged them to introduce color. It was with them, for example, that Charles and Ray Eames began using colored textiles. In the 1970s, around the same time as that exhibition at the Whitechapel, Nanna Ditzel also designed colored landscapes with different floor levels, seating, and curtains to accommodate different generations, who could each choose their ideal spot. I conceived the floor of my exhibition in that spirit. In the *E.R.O.S.* exhibition you mentioned earlier, I really like the fact that they used sand—a material that destabilizes the body—which is also something I was trying to do with these reliefs. I'm very interested in working with the floor, but it's rarely possible, for reasons of budget and, of course, environmental constraints. At the Palais de Tokyo, I was able to cover the floor with recycled wood, but that's quite a rare possibility.

MR Have you had the opportunity to work with this scenographic dimension for other artists, or with curators?

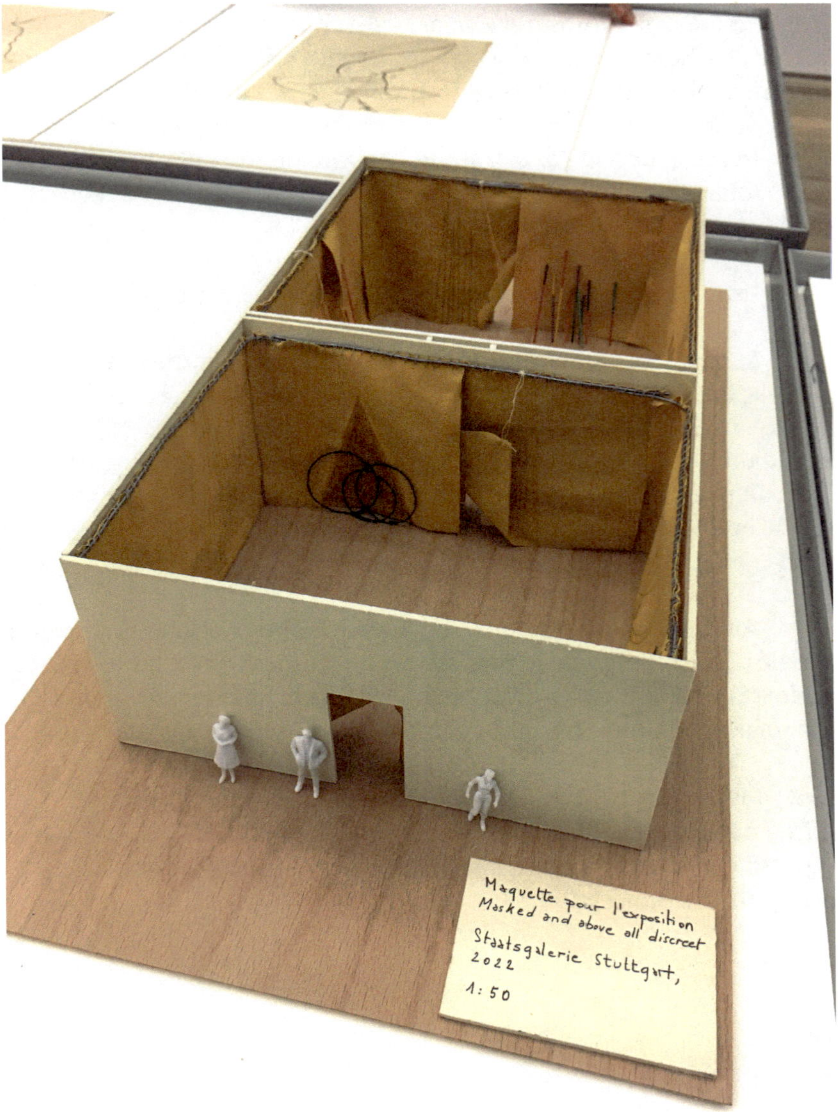


Fig. 3 *Bad Timing*, model by Julia Mossé, 2022

UvB Yes, for the exhibition *Hall of Half-Life* at the Steirischer Herbst in Graz,[123] where I created a scenography with walls painted in triangular forms. I was also exhibiting my own work, but the idea was to host other works. I like the idea that my works can be modified and remain open. In 2023, for *Bad Timing*, at the Den Frie Centre of Contemporary Art,[124] Julia Mossé and I also designed the scenography at the request of the curator Anna Weile Kjær.

MR How do you work from that position as a scenographer?

UvB At first, I was a bit reluctant to intervene only on the space, without including my own works—even though, of course, my intervention itself becomes a work. The curator determined how my spaces would interact with the works in the exhibition, sometimes creating difficult proximities—for example, when she installed a textile work inside one of my spaces, and the two tended to weaken each other. But in the end, they came together well.

MR You fully qualify the space through your intervention, but within a logic of hospitality, since your spaces host other works. Producing an atmosphere and creating relationships—that is precisely the definition of scenography, though of course the risk is to create confusion.

UvB My idea for the scenography was that each space should be different—a rectangle, a U-shape, a semicircle—and that each would be used in a specific way. I think some spaces worked better than others in this project.

# Céline Condorelli

## Behind artworks and in front of architecture

*Céline Condorelli is a visual French-Italian-British artist working across installations, sculptures, exhibitions and architectures that foreground display and the relationship between art and publics. She develops group and solo exhibition and research projects that explore questions that link art and display, the work and its supporting structures, and the space and the bodies that inhabit it. She is a professor of Scenography and Exhibition Design at the Hochschule für Gestaltung in Karlsruhe (HfG), where this conversation took place in January 2024.*

MR  Display occupies a vital place in your work process. You've said, for example, that your 2021 installation *Thinking Through Skin* at Nottingham Contemporary was both "a display, an artwork, and a way of thinking." You live in London but speak French fluently, so I'm interested in the way you use the term "display," which has migrated from English into French.

CC  Using "display" rather than "exhibition design" or "scenography" is a way of not distinguishing the way an exhibition is made from the exhibition itself. Display is inherent to what is shown; it forms the exhibition. It is not an external expertise that comes in to determine how the works should be arranged; but it exists within the work. Display occurs the moment when the work starts being installed, it is what brings it into being. Choosing the word "display" allows it to remain inseparable from the artistic process. In his text *The Exhibition and the Display*,[125] Martin Beck explains how display—which can consist of a highly technical mechanism (such as a specific screen, a bracket, type of hook), a device—is a moment of contact between form and the social. The encounter with art and the way we approach it (including: Do we buy a ticket? Are we greeted by a text?) takes place through display.

MR Display connects the outside and the inside, suggesting the personal, social, and emotional trajectories that draw us into an exhibition.

CC It is a question of thinking through the encounter: who is exposed to the work and how. Display is therefore a working method that includes a technical aspect, such as hanging height, and allows a work to be approached through specific aspects rather than from an overall perspective.

MR How did you develop this method? What led you, as an artist, to adopt this approach, not merely to practice it but also to reflect on its theoretical nature?

CC As usual, it's a combination of chance and micro-decisions that, twenty years later, end up shaping one's practice. I studied architecture and theory and began working as an artist from those perspectives, which is different from going to art school. My studies gave me a technical way of seeing, and a process grounded in material thinking. I approach artworks not out of a need for self-expression, but out of a desire to understand how to change spatial relations and alter what I call "existing conditions." The *Support Structures* project was an attempt to grasp what support means, and what it means to want, as an artist, to take up such a position: behind artworks and in front of architecture, while embracing the specificity that connects them.

MR Could you discuss this research project and the resulting publication that appeared in 2009?[126]

CC It was a collaborative project conceived with the artist-curator Gavin Wade that began in 2002 as a long-term project developed in phases. The first one, in support of Art, questioned hierarchies of labor within the workforce inside the art world. It came up through important encounters, such as with Kathrin Böhm, an artist who at the time was also working with an art and architecture collective whom I am very much still in dialogue with. We were supported by a fantastic grant that no longer exists, "RSA Art for Architecture Scheme," which funded long-term collaborative projects between art and architecture (we received a modest grant from 2003 to 2006). We decided to understand support structures through the creation of an art project as a methodology, that would allow us to develop a

cumulative practice-based knowledge as artworks and exhibitions across different sectors of society: support for art, support for education, economic support, democratic support. We got and invented artist residencies within some of these support institutions.
For example, in support of Education we were artists-in-residence at the University of Essex, and in support of Economy we were self-declared artists-in-residence at The Economist Building, where *The Economist* magazine is published. Through these residencies, we tried to understand what support structures could be within their context and how they shaped what they sustained. What interested me, for instance, was the fact that there had been no genuine reflection on how the history of the frame—which is a formal history, a history of the artifact—has conditioned artworks. I had Jean-Claude Lebensztejn's essay "À partir du cadre"[127] [Starting Out from the Frame] translated into English, and we subsequently published it in the book *Support Structures*. We were also thinking about how financial support structures influence artistic production, and this angle was developed by Andrea Phillips, who wrote an essay for the book. Each of these sequential, cumulative projects became an exhibition, leading eventually to the founding of Eastside Projects[128] in Birmingham—an artist-run space founded by six artists and curators—where we attempted to put into practice what we had developed, turning it into a long-term support structure. It still exists today (I was one of its directors for ten years).

MR What is particularly beautiful about this creative adventure that explores the idea of support is that it brings together technical, economic, and logistical support with friendly support and hospitality—something that occupies an important place in both your thinking and your work.

CC Absolutely. I felt a chapter on friendship was missing in the book, which is why it later became a project in its own right, titled *The Company She Keeps*, accompanied by a separate publication with the same title. The very notion of "support structures" has become much more present today, at least in the art world, but in 2003 it was not understood as relevant or important. When I proposed this topic for my PhD (which I pursued in Visual Culture at Goldsmiths), it was considered problematic because it was not recognized as belonging to any specific discipline, and I'll never forget this "not a subject in its own right." I spent literally years trying to demonstrate that what is

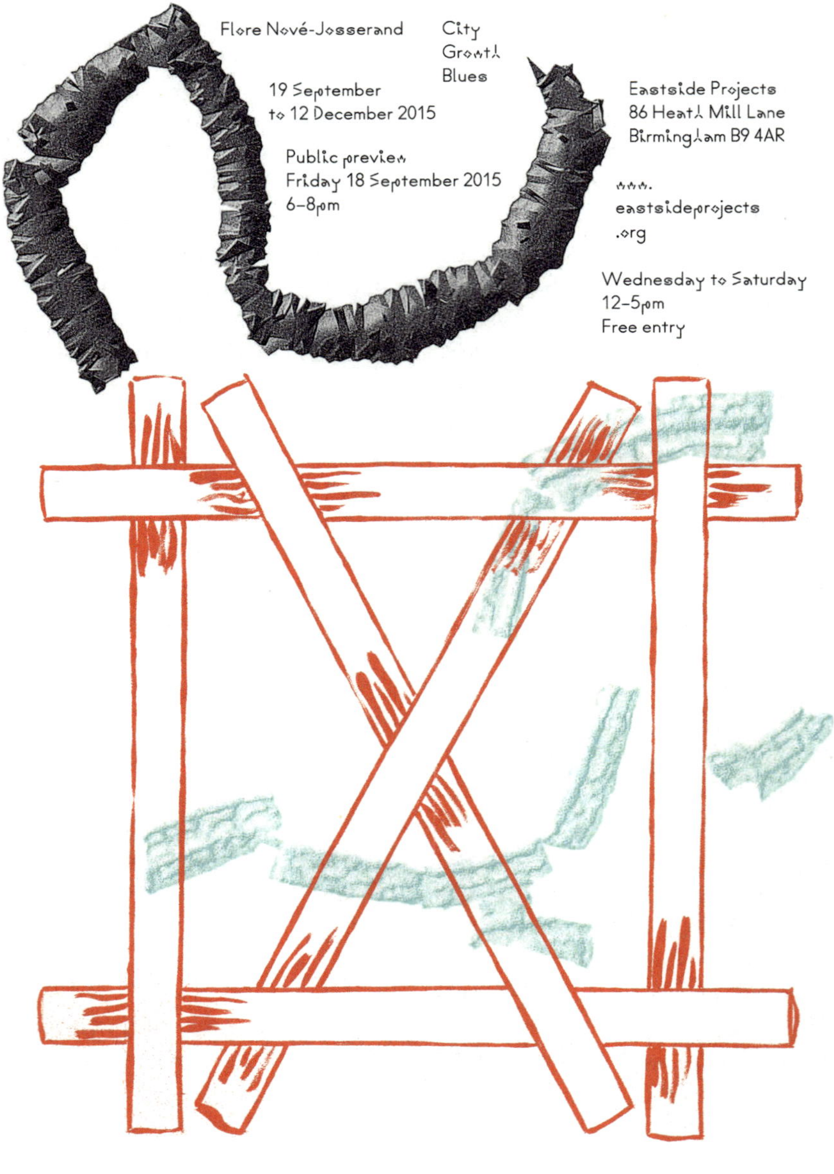


Fig. 1 *Display Show*, poster, Céline Condorelli, 2015

# Display Show
# 19 September to 12 December 2015

## List of works

(∞)
HAIM STEINBACH
'∞' (1994)
Black vinyl
Dimensions variable

(1)
CHARLOTTE CULLINAN
AND JEANINE RICHARDS
'Abstract Mirror Paintings' (2015)
Mirrored vinyl, plastic, steel scaffolding, industrial paint

(2)
AMALIA PICA
'Stage (as seen on Afghan Star)' (2011)
Cardboard, wood, tape, spotlight
54 × 279.4 × 279.4 cm
Exhibition copy, courtesy Coleccion Patricia Phelps de Cisneros

(3)
NATHALIE DU PASQUIER
'Painting with no title' (2013)
Oil on canvas
100 × 100 cm

(4)
CÉLINE CONDORELLI
'After Image (Gray and Bayer)' (2015)
190 × 275 × 0.3 cm
Aluminum screen parts, cut vinyl on existing window, wall painting

(6)
CHRISTOPHER WILLIAMS
TecTake Luxus Strandkorb grau/weiß
Model no.: 400636
Wood/plastic
154 cm × 116 cm × 77 cm
Weight: 49 kg
Manufactured by Ningbo Jin Mao Import & Export Co., Ltd, Nigbo, Zhejiang, China for TecTake GmbH, Igersheim, Germany
Model: Zimra Geurts, Playboy Netherlands Playmate of the Year 2012
Studio Rhein Verlag, Düsseldorf, January 31, 2013
(Zimra resting) (2013)
Selenium toned gelatin silver print
86 × 94.6 × 3.8 cm
Edition 7 of 10, 4 AP
Certificate of Authenticity
WILCH0387

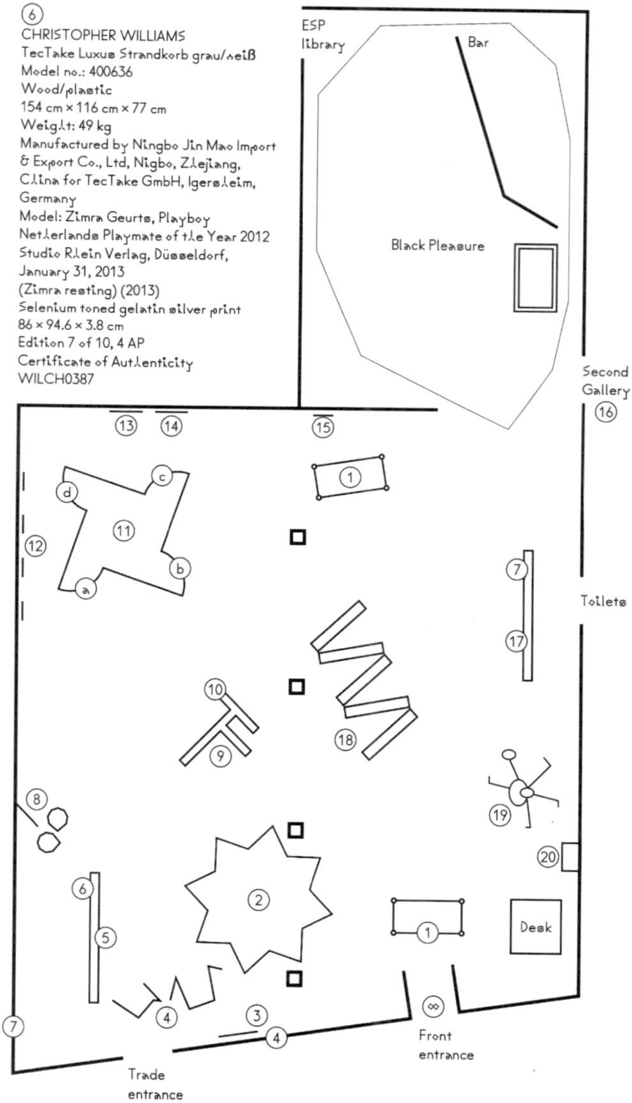


Fig. 2 *Display Show*, map, Céline Condorelli, 2015

specific about support structures is the type of relations it establishes. And yet at the time, terms like collaboration were becoming indispensable, but support was not yet recognized. It has now entered mainstream discourse in both good and bad ways. This is what often happens to feminist projects: one arrives with a term that doesn't resemble specialized knowledge because it is too "soft." Making this term available to others also means making it useable, habitable, which in turn makes it easier to use it for oneself. What I mean by that is that producing the book *Support Structures* and founding Eastside Projects allowed us to realize the kinds of exhibitions we wanted to make—for instance, by layering artists' works cumulatively, with some works staying for long periods of time and others being disappearing quickly.

MR Did the artists you invited to exhibit understand your approach?

CC Some artists did, others less so. It was not always obvious to them why we didn't invite them into a blank, white space, or why we refused to do the work of erasing, removing, and repainting to provide a "neutral" space for them. Of course, we worked with artists we had affinities with, but we also decided to make a manual to facilitate the relationship with guests and artists. This manual explained that the space functions cumulatively, that things such as the front door handle and the toilets are also artworks, and consequently, that any artist enters a space where things began before them and will continue after them, and that they are working within a collective flow.

MR Which implies expanding the notion of authority.

CC And this doesn't suit everyone, of course. Sometimes we cleared white walls for works that absolutely required it and were important to exhibitions. These works then left, while others stayed for ten years, becoming walls or backgrounds for subsequent works, being recycled in very specific ways. In 2009, we published *Support Structures* through a considerable collective effort, and from that point on we could work without constantly having to justify or explain how we worked, which allowed us to pursue greater ambitions with our projects. We carried out a series of typological exhibitions titled *Display Show*, *Curtain Show*, *Abstract Cabinet Show*, and *Puppet Show*, the latter going on to tour in different institutions. This allowed me to develop new exhibition formats and vocabularies, which has been very important for the continuation of my practice.

MR Was this when you began historical research on the founding figures of display, people who you placed into dialogue in *Display Show*?

CC Gavin and I were already discussing Lilly Reich and El Lissitzky with the *Abstract Cabinet* from the start of *Support Structures*. In the second phase, we created a giant curtain for The Economist Building, which allowed us to sculpt spaces for meetings and work, and to reshape them as needed. At Eastside Projects, we commissioned Barbara Holub to make a curtain, which led to *Curtain Show*. We started from Lilly Reich and looked at those who referred to her, like Ines Schaber or Simon Starling, constructing a narrative that allowed us to introduce other artists.

MR Through this project, you also help disseminate Lilly Reich's work, which remains relatively unknown today.

CC Yes, and we create connections like curators, while also inventing what is missing by intervening as artists. For example, we worked with Grace Ndiritu, who presented one of her films in which she wraps herself in African textiles, nominally from a place of origin related to her, but actually produced in Birmingham African market.[129] Since the Eastside Projects building was originally a garment factory, her film links multiple histories. In parallel, after teaching at architecture schools in London, I became professor of display at NABA, the art school in Milan, where I conduct extensive research on the Italian museum architects like Albini, Scarpa, and BBPR, going with students into the archives of Franco Albini, Gianni Colombo, and Achille Castiglioni. Through this research, I develop a specific vocabulary around display and supporting artworks, which informs my practice to this day. I continue to create displays, such as *Disobedience Archive (The Republic)* at Castello di Rivoli in 2013, or furniture for café baubau for GfZk in Leipzig, which allows me to develop a typology of exhibition formats: the archive exhibition—*Castello di Rivoli*—the exhibition as art school—*Cell Projects*, 2010—or the exhibition as garden—*Talbot Rice*, 2022—and so on.

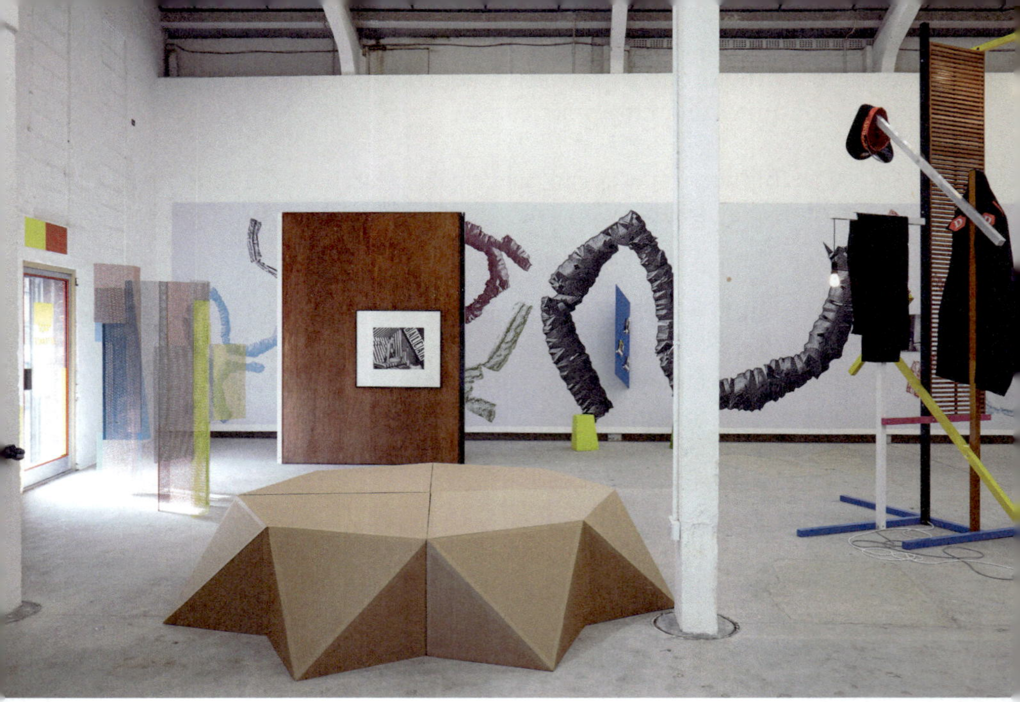

Fig. 3 *Display Show*, Eastside Projects, 2015, Stroom Den Haag, The Hague

MR Would you say your artistic project is to work with display, to provide support, to create tools for encounter and relationship?

CC I try to develop a specific knowledge of this mediation role that I have chosen for myself, in which the exhibition itself is an artwork, and the artist mediates between the museum, the public and form.

MR You also develop a critical mediation approach. It is not just support for what already exists, what is visible—the work, the public, the institution—but also for what is rendered invisible or made fragile.

CC Yes, and each exhibition is also a prototype, an attempt to introduce an element that is missing. The exhibition as art school is a return to one of the now forgotten but historically primary roles of the exhibition and the museum, which was for artists to get an education. Looking at it from today, it is difficult to even imagine that this was such an important function that museums would have artists days every week. The exhibition as garden, or as playground, are also attempts at creating more inclusive exhibitions for different audiences, and not just the privileged spectators of Herbert Bayer diagrams, who know to observe respectfully from a distance.[130] Are there other valid ways to enter exhibitions, with the visually impaired or with children for instance, who might physically engage with form? The exhibition as garden interrogates the relationship between the botanical garden and the museum, which are both contemporary exhibition formats, but since plants have been removed from museums for so long, their relationships need to be rediscovered. So each project is a study, some more in-depth than others.

MR Your engagement with Lina Bo Bardi recurs frequently, particularly her approach to thinking about the museum in close relation to nature, as well as a site for teaching and education.

CC Some projects derive from Lina Bo Bardi's work, especially as you say the attention she gives to plants, to the public garden, and to folk arts. I have been obsessed with her building in Salvador de Bahia, which was entirely constructed around an existing mango tree. I have tried to work on these three aspects, though the relation to so called folk arts is still ongoing. I recently returned from Morocco, where I am working on carpets and the rich history of abstraction made by women since time immemorial, which inspired many (male) twentieth-century artists. This year, I plan to work with an Inuit collection at the Remai Modern in Saskatoon and hope to collaborate with Inuit artist-run centers in Canada. I work in chapters, each project being a phase in a longer trajectory beyond the temporal constraints of exhibition invitations. I owe this approach to Antoni Muntadas, whose project *On Translation* made me see a way to work on long-term issues if you structure your thinking in that way, so that each exhibition or commission adds a new layer to a line of thinking. The figure of Lina Bo Bardi is recurrent across my projects and signals continuity within the same research. Some of her forms also reappear in designs and mechanisms, like her stage-like shape in Bahia, which articulate a relationship to putting on show but also brings the outside in, even if in my case it is for more of a Japanese garden than lush nature.

MR You also explore the colonial histories of plants that you integrate into your garden installations, giving cues through titles like *Props*, *Corps-à-corps*, *Brise-soleil*, etc.

CC There are indeed micro-histories, and the *Props* expose how plants were present in MoMA exhibitions for eighty years, in painting and sculpture exhibitions, which is something that would be unthink able today. Exhibitions were decorated with these subtropical, colonial plants from temperate zones, and that were used to make the exhibitions a little more livable. They tell another exhibition history, one in which exhibitions were livelier, designed to be comfortable, since plants served to domesticate and decorate the institution. They convey an idea of comfort for the human body.

MR This also relates to the democratization of art and visitor flow management, which often prevents visitors from lingering too long in front of a work. An important aspect of my research is restoring the notion of bodies within an exhibition, especially through seating, which I'd like you to discuss, as you address this frequently.

CC I have indeed created many seating elements, and loved finding Joel Sanders and Diana Fuss's text "Notes from the Museum Bench,"[131] which I found in a catalogue published by Bard College titled *Interiors*, and I have referred to many times.[132] I found in it a history of museum visitors and how they are expected to behave through that of museum benches. This history started with maximal comfort: movable seating

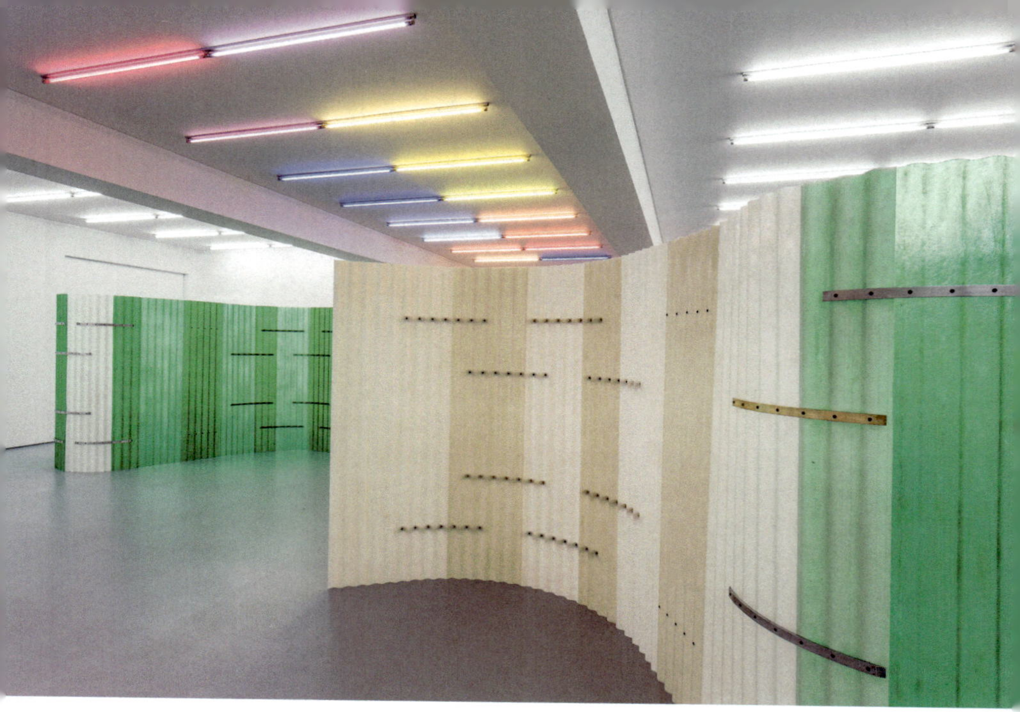

Fig. 4 Céline Condorelli, *Epilogue and Grazie e arrivederci*, Galeria Vera Cortês, 2017

that allowed you to choose where to sit, or large heated sofas for spending the day. Over the twentieth century, these sofas gradually disappeared and were replaced by ever-narrower benches to preserve sightlines and not interfere with wall works, until eventually nothing was provided, or uniform benches were installed in the center of rooms from which one cannot look at art. This is a process of gradual alienation of the human body. If you are not used to it, it creates intimidating experiences. Exhibition photographs are taken without bodies, so as not to "interfere" again; the truth is the human body has needs: for warmth, cooling, seating. It seems crucial to reintroduce the body and intimacy into culture, to allow closeness and touch. I call the seating sculptures I make *Spatial Compositions*; it's a tribute to Władysław Strzemiński, co-founder of one of the first artist-founded museums in Europe, the Museum of Art in Łódź, who insisted that the museum of the future should not resemble those of the past and that one must build rooms to house future works. He created the Neoplastic Room, and in the rare photographs of it that survive, I noticed a form on the side (besides the plinths for Katarzyna Kobro) that to me suggested seating. I imagined that in this museum of the future, there were not only spaces created by artists for artists, but also seats to welcome the human body. From this idea, I began a series of seating sculptures that attempted to reconstruct the form in the archival images, which was only partially visible. In the Neoplastic Room, these were called *Spatial Compositions*; there were two, so I started from *Spatial Composition 3* for the museum café/exhibition in GfZk in Leipzig, all variations of the same form. I had initially only seen drawings and photographs of them in the archives, and then when I finally saw the structure resembling a bench, it was clearly a display and not for sitting, however I continued the series as a small correction or interpretation to history. I still call the seating sculptures I make *Spatial Compositions*, even when drawing inspiration from other sources, such as Eileen Gray's deckchairs. With these deckchair-shaped *Spatial Compositions*, I start from the idea of the exhibition as a garden of leisure, from free time, or non-work. The deckchair comes from transatlantic ships or the terraces of a recovery clinic—it is a piece of furniture at the opposite end of a work desk, and for me a way of entering the idea of free time within culture.

MR That reminds me of the Tripolina, the very comfortable leather chairs Franco Albini and Franca Helg placed in the Palazzo Bianco in Genoa. Once seated, it's hard to get up—like a deckchair.

CC When I was invited to the Albertinum Museum in Dresden, I started by looking for all the benches that had been in the galleries at some point in its history. They were difficult to find because they are not conserved as such; it was necessary to search through exhibition photographs if and when they were any, look at older exhibition views, and also jog people's memory. One was found that had remained in a studio, recycled as a footrest, another had been salvaged by a curator who took it home, one more ended up in the storage. They were restored and reupholstered in the same fabric so they would be recognizable as part of a single intervention, then installed in relation to the collection with new *Spatial Compositions*. One bench which was lower than the rest was placed in a room with all the paintings hung at children's eye height.

MR And what became of these benches afterwards?

CC They entered the collection, thus changing category.

# Monster Chetwynd

## Transforming space with simple means and a great deal of energy

*Monster Chetwynd is a British artist, born in 1973 and now based in Zurich, who has at different moments in her life and artistic trajectory gone by the names Spartacus Chetwynd and Marvin Gaye Chetwynd. Her performative work draws on expanded forms of theatricality within the exhibition and appropriates the tools of scenography—circulation, sets, lighting—with remarkable vitality. This conversation took place in early 2024 at Cabaret Voltaire, which Chetwynd had transformed for a year into a large-scale installation incorporating chairs, tables, workshops, and parades.*

MR Your exhibitions and performances transform spaces with great generosity, blur the boundaries between art and popular culture, and give bodies a central, joyful, and subversive role. Your sources of inspiration are many—from carnival and the Middle Ages to alternative communities and pedagogies—and your work intertwines art and life. How do you work with the exhibition space, which can sometimes seem far removed from the energy that surrounds you?

MC I think I'm quite opportunistic—I don't want to fight against the space. As a student, I first organized performances in the apartment I was renting, then, when I was invited to perform in nightclubs and theaters, I quickly realized I didn't like the stage: I rehearse very little, and the frontal viewpoint doesn't suit me. Nightclubs also have their downsides: I remember, for instance, drunk people knocking us over while we were wearing masks, which was very stressful. That's why I actually appreciate the white cube, it's a contained space that can be oriented, something you can play with. Each time, I start by the paths visitors naturally take in a gallery, as well as the emergency exits and more broadly any constraints the building presents—like parts of the ceiling that may be visually interesting but from which nothing can be hung. I also keep in mind a list of projects I haven't been able to realize because of spatial constraints, and I see whether any of them might fit the site. I feel close to Kabuki theater, to Bertolt Brecht, but also to parades and various forms of dance. I'm looking for ways to create a playful, surprising situation for the audience—one I fully inhabit myself, because I really enjoy being part of the audience. I often observe how audiences are treated in different contexts. I'm fascinated, for example, by the stage machinery in the Colosseum in ancient Rome, where they had such ingenious entrance and exit systems. All of this is also closely tied to the hospitality of a place. I'm very sensitive to the opportunities each site can offer. Galleries provide controlled lighting and many advantages, but it's harder to create an intimate experience in them.

MR To create a welcoming intimacy you work with scenographic elements such as lighting, sets, and seating, in a kind of visual abundance similar to the one surrounding us here at Cabaret Voltaire.

MC I love suspending elements to create shadow play, in the simple, economical way of Josef Svoboda, who used models and sheets of paper to cast striking shadows on walls (as well as groundbreaking innovations with dry ice). What I try to do is transform space with simple means but with a great deal of energy—like in carnivals, where people work for three months for a celebration that lasts three days.

MR In 2019, I invited you to lead a workshop with students at Pavillon Bosio in Monaco, where I teach. You combined the energy of making—each student created a cardboard creature—with the liberation of the body through very intense warm-up and improvisation sessions. Do you often begin your projects with these bodily warm-ups, and what role does the collective workshop play in your process?

MC When I was studying anthropology, I was interested in analyzing when and how social bonding happens in a community. The way I transform spaces aims to create experiences that generate such connections. What we experienced together during that workshop was very intimate and fun, but it happened at a very particular moment—you invited me into something that isn't usually part of my practice. Workshop programs in galleries or museums are often artificial, disconnected, and impersonal. They stem from a statistical approach to audiences, designed to attract specific groups. Of course, they are necessary to broaden the sociological reality of audiences, but they come afterwards—and it's very rare that I'm invited to begin a project with a workshop.

MR How, then, do you approach spatial constraints in order to create this collaborative energy?

MC I don't mind being in situations others might find uncomfortable or strange. These difficulties don't bother me, because I immediately see what can be used—what can become a resource for doing something else. I take a lot of time to observe, to understand how spaces function, and when I move to a new country it usually takes me about two years before I can really do anything there. I am impressed by Glenn Murcutt. He grew up in Papua New Guinea, in a close relationship with his environment. When he starts to design a building he spends a long time camping and living on the piece of terrain to research it. He studies the way wind currents travel across the land and how it is to live there without a building to retreat to. When he builds, he draws on long observations of nature and works almost exclusively with wood and metal. I admire that way of working—and that there are clients willing to wait for his projects, creating conditions of stability without the need to produce more. At the moment, I'm working on an exhibition at the Mudam in Luxembourg, a museum where you can't touch the walls and where the floors can't handle heavy loads. These kinds of architectures are very challenging—but the point is to make something out of them, to try to transform them.

MR Your work is also deeply connected to the living world, inviting viewers to take part in experiences that free the energies of the body, of language, by connecting with the non-human. We've just been looking together at photographs of the galleries of the São Paulo Museum of Art (MASP) at the time of its opening, where bodies occupy the space among the paintings and glass easels, and reading texts by Lina Bo Bardi in which she stresses the importance of opening the museum to the outside world, integrating pedagogy, workshops, popular arts, and not separating it from nature. She had also planned a playground for children on the museum's esplanade and invited a circus to set up there. All of these commitments seem very close to your own vision.

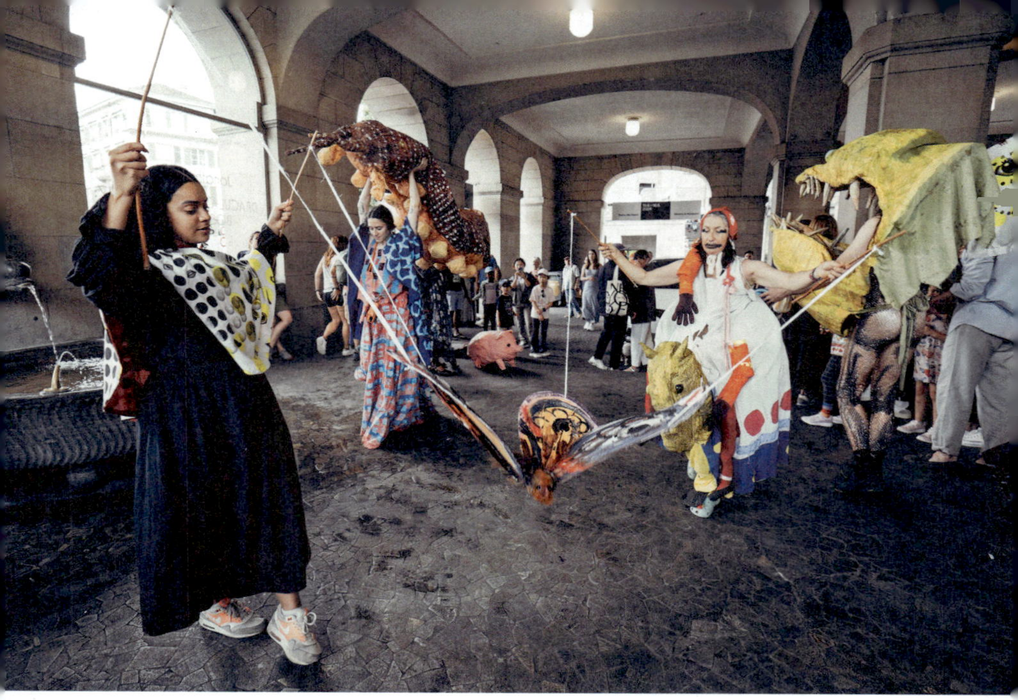

Fig. 1 *Performance Journey to a Sacred Place*, Art Weekend, Monster Chetwynd, Zurich, 2024

MC I love those photographs, where viewers seem to be dancing within the museum's modernist architecture. Usually, we see these spaces empty, with works on the walls dominating the space and commanding our attention, whereas with the glass easels you sense a decolonization of vision—they become objects you can move around. Today, the challenge is to produce real change in how art and museums are conceived, in a climate that resists it—where people would rather install an explanatory plaque than remove a statue. It's striking that, from the very beginning of Lina Bo Bardi's project for MASP, the aim was to create an open, plural, inclusive, and decolonized space.

MR How do you go about activating such transformations?

MC By always working through a kind of bricolage—avoiding expensive materials, using papier-mâché, working through simple, instinctive, rapid processes. It's a way of never intimidating audiences. The downside is that I don't have any particular technical skill or "value" in the conventional sense, but the upside is that it connects me to punk, inclusive, and subversive energies. When I was younger, I could feel hurt by judgments about my lack of skill, but I've come to understand how deeply political it is to make everyone feel capable of doing things, within a playful energy. I've often noticed how difficult it is to create genuinely joyful situations: I've visited exhibitions that aimed to do so but ended up feeling sad or dull, or overly controlled despite their claims to subversion and excess.

MR That's a criticism that was made of Allan Kaprow, whose participatory, playful happenings were often quite controlling.

MC In a happening, the artist makes decisions, imposes rules, and when you see empty play spaces, it's hard to understand their meaning. It's the same with the pavilions of Dan Graham, whose work was very important to me when I was younger—especially his 1984 film *Rock My Religion*. I've visited several of his pavilions, and each time I experienced them as cold sculptures, not playful at all, despite his intentions. At one of his talks, I shared this view, and through the discussion I realized the issue often lies in the maintenance of the works—for example at Dia, where one of his pavilions was supposed to be presented alongside children's cartoons and bean bags, but wasn't. When I create semi-permanent works, like playgrounds, I pay

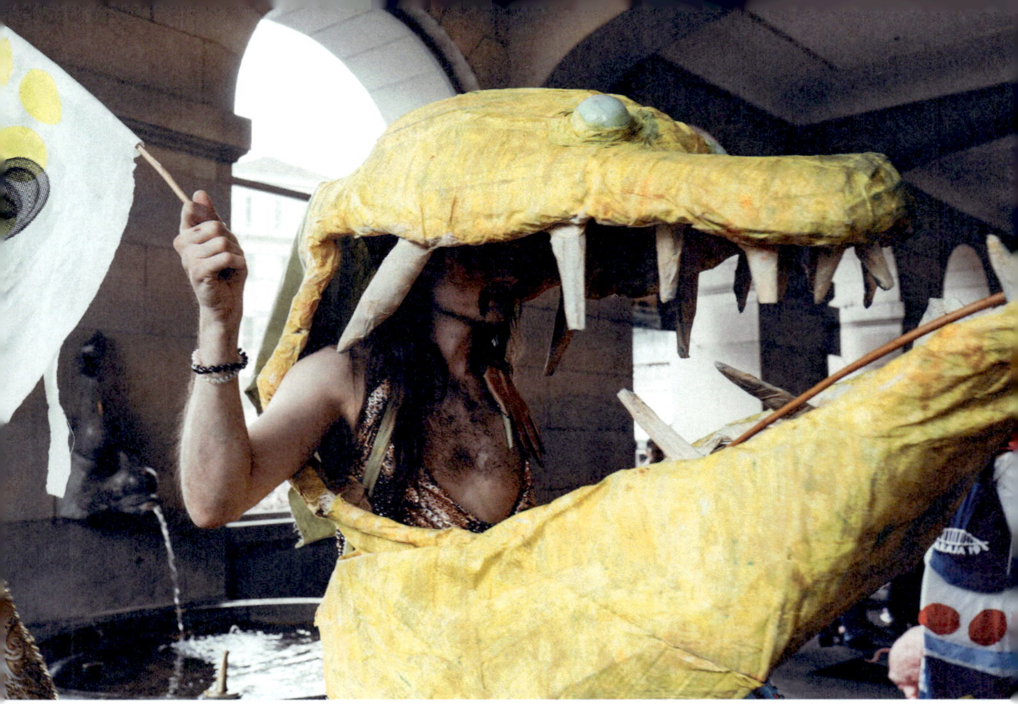

Fig. 2 *Performance Journey to a Sacred Place*, Art Weekend, Monster Chetwynd, Zurich, 2024

close attention to ensuring people can continue to experience them over time while preserving the project's intention.

MR How do you ensure that?

MC I always think about people who arrive with negative energies, often linked to some stress in their personal lives. I try to introduce a second, more hidden layer that might allow them not to remain stuck in that initial judgment—to open up, to become receptive. Transforming the space is really key. I should also mention my love of the circus, I adore it in all its forms, even the most traditional ones.

MR What inspires you in the circus?

MC I'm fascinated by how transitions and set changes are handled between acts: a spotlight focuses attention on a clown while, elsewhere, the rest of the team is dismantling one set and building another. Something is always happening—even during the break, when sweets and programs are being sold. I love that machinery, the way this tightly knit community, where everyone knows exactly what they have to do at any given moment, captures the audience's attention. And it's very clever that it all takes place in a traveling tent that can reproduce the same tricks anywhere.

MR The magic of the circus is closely tied to its performative nature. How do you create that same intensity in an exhibition, which can't rely on that performative tension?

MC It's more difficult in a static space, of course—there's a certain solitude in the museum. At the moment, I'm working on animated sculptures that might introduce a more interactive, playful dimension.

MR The circus is also a place of deep complicity between humans and animals, which is important in your work.

MC Of course. For me, it's very simple: humans are animals—we belong to the same group.

MR How do you convey this decolonial and decentered perspective in your exhibitions?

MC Because I studied anthropology, I have a different relationship to museum displays—we studied them as such. We would go to the British Museum to attend lectures in front of these objects, fully aware of the sadness of their decontextualization, knowing they should never have been taken from the communities they belonged to. These questions of decolonizing the museum, which are only now emerging in the art world, were already very present in anthropology at the time. A few years ago, with my students, I also enjoyed reading *Inside the White Cube* by Brian O'Doherty (1976), which articulates these issues so clearly. In Zurich, where I teach at ZHdK, I take my students to the NONAM – North American Native Museum, which presents indigenous artists' works as it would those of any contemporary artists, including videos where they explain their processes and use of materials—creating a meaningful dialogue. Coming from anthropology gives you a different awareness of display culture than approaching it solely from within art.

MR That resonates for me with Lady Chatterley's anger at her husband's use of language, in the novel by D. H. Lawrence that I'm commenting on in the essay part of this book, which becomes for her nothing more than a "display of nothingness." In her rejection of display, one hears an awareness of the separation of emotion produced by the staging of language—something that echoes the deep sadness we feel when faced with displays of objects detached from their uses, contexts, and beliefs.

MC I love that book—*Lady Chatterley's Lover*—especially its analysis of the coal mining industry in Britain, but also its critique of literary circles, the relationship between the husband and his nurse, and of course Lady Chatterley's sexual emancipation.

MR What interests me is how display is tied to a colonial, dominant, and capitalist history—one that needs to be overturned, as Lady Chatterley does when she dances naked in the rain in the forest.

MC Last year I made a film about the Crystal Palace (*Who Named the Lily?*, 2023). At first, I only wanted to focus on its kit form engineering—the use of metal and glass—but I realized I couldn't separate an object from its context. The architecture of the Crystal Palace is inseparable from colonialism, everything was designed to display might and intimidate people. I had to rethink my project as I learned more about the context and the ideology of functionality. It was unsettling at first,

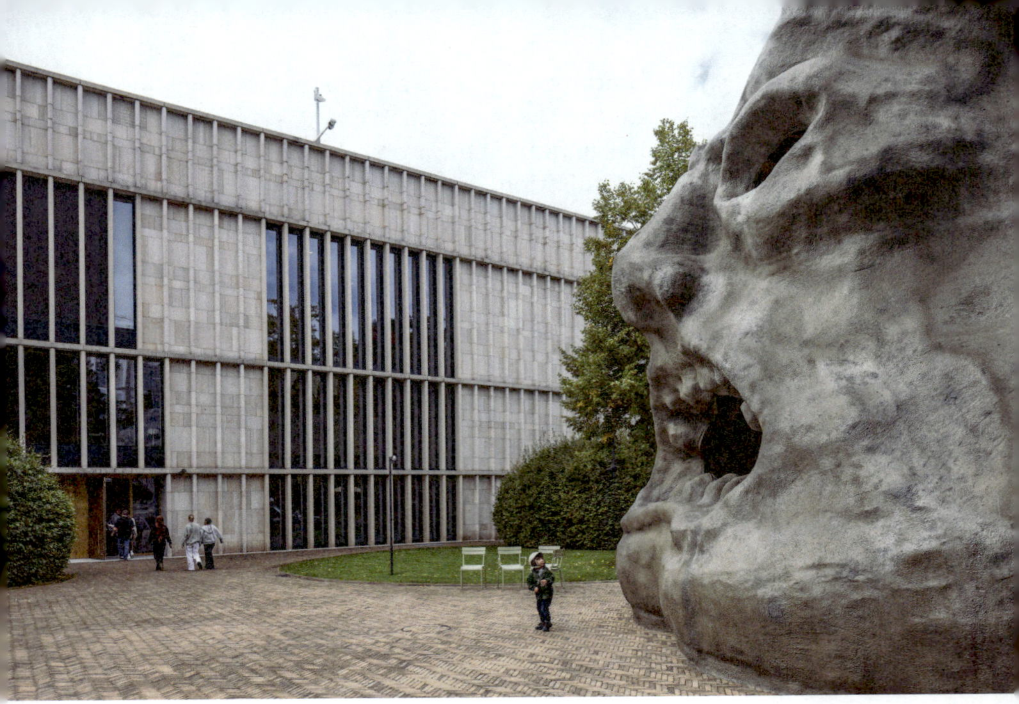

Fig. 3 *Zardoz*, Monster Chetwynd, Zurich, 2025

but I'm very glad I went through that process. It's the difference between the comfort of ignorance and the sometimes painful difficulty of a learning trajectory—which is by far the better option. Working on this project taught me a great deal. The Crystal Palace was designed by Joseph Paxton who was originally a gardener, and he drew on his experience of building greenhouses. I also met Antoine Picon, who spoke to me about the relationship between architecture and craft, and about the technical innovations developed for the Crystal Palace such as hollow cast-iron columns that allowed rainwater to be directly channeled to the ground—and which they still bothered to paint in an elaborate color system. This research has led to another project I'm currently working on: a 20-meter-high head that will be installed in the gardens of the Kunsthaus Zürich in summer 2025. This head will function as a pavilion that visitors can enter and have tea in. I'm working on it with architects Andrei Jipa, Angela Yoo, and Lian Staehelin, at the invitation of curator Raphael Gygax. I drew inspiration from the science-fiction film *Zardoz* (1974) by John Boorman, with all its humor and absurdity. It's incredible for me to be invited not only to exhibit in museums and perform, but also to create children's playgrounds or build pavilions in gardens.

MR These types of spaces create opportunities for different uses and aesthetic experiences, addressing audiences who don't necessarily have to pass through the symbolic and economic threshold of a museum entrance.

MC That's very important to me—I pay close attention to audiences. This project is also informed by my experience of the Serpentine Pavilions in London, commissioned each summer from a different architect. I remember in particular the one by Oscar Niemeyer: a triangular form that framed the park in a very calm way. It may sound strange, but I truly felt that pavilion belonged to me—and I'd like the one I'm building to produce that same feeling in others. I thought the reference to the head in *Zardoz* might raise concerns at the institution, but actually they love the idea of placing this head next to the Kunsthaus. So it won't just be a physical construction, but a psychological one as well.

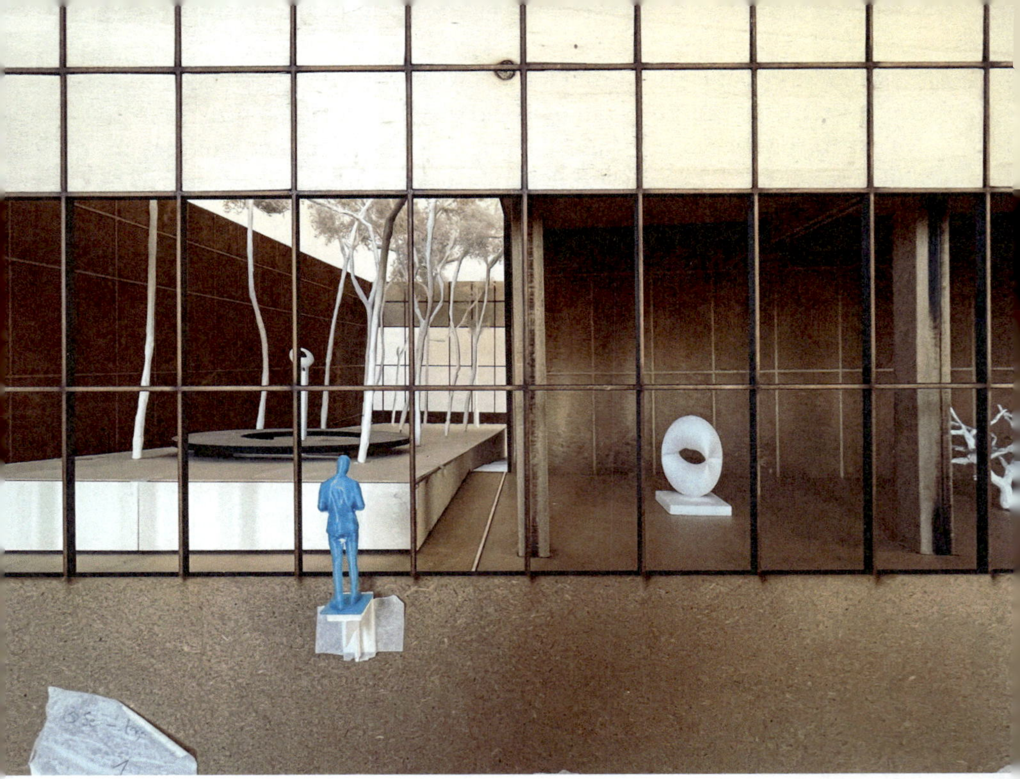

Fig. 1 *Les jardins de la sensibilité aux conditions initiales (Les jardins de Cyrus)*, model, Berger&Berger, 2024

# Berger&Berger

## The sculptural dimension of scenography

*Blending the practices of art, architecture, and scenography across the fields of performance and exhibition-making, Berger&Berger (French; Laurent P. Berger, born 1972, a graduate of the École nationale supérieure des Arts Décoratifs, and Cyrille Berger, born 1975, an architect trained at the École nationale supérieure d'architecture de Paris-La Villette) develop a reflection on the intersections between these fields and on the shifts made possible by their shared gestures. The interview took place in Paris in May 2024.*

MR Before us is a model that evokes a stage backdrop, but is in fact that of a sculpture garden, *The Gardens of Sensitivity to Initial Conditions (The Gardens of Cyrus)*,[133] a project associated with a railway station that you have been working on for several years as part of the Grand Paris commissions, and which is due for completion in 2027.

LB (Laurent P. Berger) It is indeed the model of a work conceived as an exhibition of objects and plants—requiring us to think through questions of scenography, display, viewing, and circulation—and which is integrated into a public-use building, the new Aulnay–Val Francilia station.

MR This project echoes the research we conducted together at the Pavillon Bosio—where we both teach—on the exhibition as garden and the garden as exhibition, in which we notably discussed Roberto Burle Marx.[134] Lina Bo Bardi also explored these issues extensively by incorporating vegetated spaces into her museums.

LB These are tutelary figures of modernity for us, in their handling of materials and their writing of space at the interface of different artistic fields. For Lina Bo Bardi, it was a matter of thinking together the treatment of the building, the scenography of objects, and the vegetation outside. The same applies to Roberto Burle Marx, who approached landscape design as a painter.

CB (Cyrille Berger) In these Grand Paris commissions, artists were selected to produce a work for an architectural setting, and we chose to work from the idea of the garden—which is part of the station's architectural logic—by conceiving it as an exhibition. We combine sculptures in traditional materials—stone, cast iron—with vegetal compositions, themselves considered as sculptures.

LB The analogy also lies in the way the plant is treated. It's like an exhibition with different typologies of works, arranged for example here, in this part of the garden, on a sloping ground that functions like a large plinth on which a vegetal carpet is laid out, then another plinth—this time mineral—at its center, and finally a small ceramic sculpture, in a play of *mise en abyme* where each element supports another and becomes its base. The garden itself, within its architectural enclosure, is the first plinth; the sloping vegetal carpet is the second; the mineral plinth the third; and the ceramic sculpture crowns this stacked arrangement. It becomes difficult to determine where the architecture ends and the garden begins, or where the plinth gives way to the work.

CB These accumulations are also enriched by the technical constraints inherent to the architectural structure. Elements linked, for example, to ventilation and smoke extraction in the station's public spaces become plinths for the sculptures. They may appear as ordinary elements, either detached from or, on the contrary, integrated into the scenography—or even be read as sculptures in their own right, incorporated into the whole. We have five gardens: two fully open, contained by high-rise buildings on either side; two semi-covered gardens; and one entirely covered mineral garden at the center, beneath the station's glass canopy.

MR We find again the interplay between inside and outside that you explored in the installation you created for the exhibition at the Nouveau Musée National de Monaco in 2018,[135] where you connected the museum to the exterior—by leaving a window open in one of the rooms—in order to place sculptures within a different atmosphere.

LB Exactly—we have equivalent principles here, with open sections and others with glazed façades facing the street.

MR This principle of transparency in façades can be found in many museums, creating a dialogue between artworks and the outside space—something Tatiana Trouvé explored very effectively in her exhibition at the Centre Pompidou in 2022, by organizing a gallery of sculptures visible only to passers-by. It reverses the usual relationship to the exhibition.

CB Yes, though it also evokes the shop window.

MR Do you conceive this project as a permanent exhibition?

LB It is indeed very different from a temporary exhibition. As it happens, it is the only station in the Grand Paris network—out of sixty-five projects—to incorporate a garden, conceived by the architect Aldric Beckmann as an enclosed garden, without visitors.

CB We are working alongside a landscape designer, a structural engineer, and a civil engineering specialist. One of the interests for us is also to test different techniques in ceramics and cast iron, which require specific reflections on fabrication and implementation, and are fully integrated into the process.

MR This kind of technical collaboration is one of the major challenges in projects combining architecture and vegetation, as can be seen, for example, at the Sant'Agostino Museum by Franco Albini and Franca Helg, which had to close due to the fragility of its glass walls—damaged in part by water infiltration from the terrace garden, with its plants and trees that Albini had integrated into the museum.

CB Maintenance issues also often arise, as Daniel Buren experienced with *Les Deux Plateaux.* But here the advantage is that the garden was already part of the initial program, and maintenance and upkeep had been anticipated. We are not imposing any exceptional constraints.

MR How did you select the plants?

CB It was primarily for formal reasons, since the whole project stems from the idea of revealing the presence of mathematics in all things, with specific species corresponding to the different climates of each garden.

LB This project grew out of research we conducted when we took part in the competition for the extension of the Institut Henri Poincaré, which allowed us to discover this heritage. We like to step back from drawing, composing instead from pre-existing forms—in this case, forms drawn from mathematics such as minimal surfaces or Euclidean geometries, which maintain a relationship to infinity. These formulas describe surfaces that are, in theory, without thickness or material substance, and it is precisely this paradox that interests us: as soon as we give them thickness in order to represent or fabricate them, they begin to shift, to alter, and it is through that process of alteration that forms emerge which we could never have invented ourselves. The drawing almost happens in spite of us, following a logic of its own.

What interests us is that they appear ethereal, but are in fact systematically altered as soon as thickness is introduced in order to render them. These are inaccessible gardens, which one traverses visually, in a contemplative manner. The project is experienced in a cinematic way, by moving along a 50-meter walkway that allows the five gardens to be observed in succession. For the interior mineral garden at the center of the station, we treat the ground with polished asphalt and a composite material combining aggregates of white faience, black marble, and transparent glass, in a play of mixed materials that recurs across many of our architectural projects. We also integrate a sculpture into the ground—one that disappears beneath our feet into a void, of which only a flat surface remains visible, embedded within the mineral carpet.

MR This produces an inversion effect: on this very beautiful floor, reminiscent of that of a museum, you make sculpture disappear, while multiple sculptures are displayed in the gardens.

LB This removal of sculpture from inside the station also stems from the impossibility of integrating it into the program, because—somewhat surprisingly—the fire brigade, whose approval is required for the realization of the work, feared that sculptures in this space might "captivate" users and slow down a potential evacuation. In the outdoor gardens, we therefore imagined vegetal carpets functioning as plinths, and a succession of supports that unsettles the relationships between elements—where the sculpture begins and where it ends—in a very Constantin Brancusi-like gesture. We selected plant species whose tones will evolve with the seasons and which will gradually form small mounds over time—as in the case of Zoysia, for example—thus altering the initial design. Naturally, we are working with species that require little maintenance and minimal water.

MR Light is an important component in your work. How are you approaching it here?

LB We chose to rely solely on natural light and on the station's own artificial lighting, calculating the reflections of sunlight on the surrounding façades to ensure the balance required for the plants and to anticipate the kinds of atmospheres that would emerge.

MR Did you try to calculate light trajectories in order to integrate them into the scenography, as Carlo Scarpa did at the Museo Canova in Possagno?

LB We mainly tried to incorporate it into the composition of cast shadows from the buildings surrounding the garden, in order to anticipate the play of appearance and disappearance of the sculptures. We decided that the project would remain largely invisible at night, except for the two covered outdoor gardens, which will be lit from above with standard fixtures, extending those used by the architect in the station's public spaces. In the evening, a homogeneous, gallery-type lighting will take over in these areas, offering a different reading of the vegetation, but without producing the kind of spectacular effect typical of heterogeneous garden lighting.

MR These garden-exhibition spaces will therefore be traversed by the gaze but devoid of human bodies, since they can only be seen from an interior walkway crossing the station and from the street through the glass façades. They will nevertheless be inhabited by animal presences. How will you integrate them?

LB Of course, we would have liked to develop this biotope in a more elaborate way, but that wasn't possible within the constraints of maintenance. There will be flowering plants, and therefore pollinating insects, and so on. I was very struck by an enclosed tropical garden on Line 14 of the Paris metro, at Gare de Lyon, with this phenomenon of an inaccessible jungle—a kind of mysterious diorama never trodden by humans—where plants have their own undisturbed environment.

The species will then develop autonomously within this garden. These are highly scenographic mechanisms, since one looks at them as one would at the theater, through a frame.

MR It is also interesting to think of it as a permanent exhibition because, as with Carlo Scarpa, it allows one to conceive relationships between sculpture, painting, and architecture over an open temporality, while being freed—thanks to this enclosed garden principle—from issues of wear and vandalism that usually affect sculpture in public space.

LB Exactly. The different gardens also allow for the creation of distinct atmospheres, as in Scarpa's rooms. Here, for example, we will have a shaded garden composed of twelve honey locust trees and a carpet of ferns of varying heights, following a geometric pattern inspired by drawings by Roberto Burle Marx for Rio de Janeiro. Two sculptures will be included, one of which will be camouflaged among the trees.

CB To return to the idea of a permanent exhibition, we worked from mathematical forms that are not tied to any immediate present and that, like gardens, belong to a long history.

MR This recalls the project of Donald Judd, who advocated for the permanent installation of his works, allowing his sculptures to find their place rather than being subjected to the usual flux of temporary exhibitions.

LB Yes, he is indeed an important figure for us, as is Isamu Noguchi, whose work we have studied closely. We conceived a set of enduring forms—sculptures in stone, cast iron, and ceramic—made with carefully chosen materials that can withstand time and the elements, and around which the plant life will evolve. This coexistence sets up a contrast between what shifts with the seasons and what endures: plants that swell and spread, grow, change color, sometimes disappear, set against the sculpture that remains. At the same time, we fully embrace the idea that unforeseen alterations will occur—a species taking up more space than anticipated, a shoot eventually spreading to partially cover a form. This isn't something to be resisted; it is integral to the project. Rather than fixing an initial image, we aim to establish the conditions for a process of change that we can only partially control. We do not place vegetation within a false naturalism; the garden is shaped by human hands. We take, for example, the motif of the *futaie*—a forest landscape cultivated for exploitation—and apply it in an ornamental context.

MR This is a project that evokes the idea of the total work of art, as it brings together art, scenography, landscape, and architecture. Do you see it as a model for an ideal museum?

LB A museum is a place dedicated to conservation and to publics, so it is somewhat difficult to conceive it in those terms.

MR At the same time, you are creating a protected space—a permanent exhibition-work that will be encountered by a large flow of station users.

LB Yes, in that sense it is interesting, even if we cannot predict how what we are projecting—within a delicate balance—will be perceived in a place that combines everyday transit with large-scale commerce.

MR I would now like to return to the scenographic project you developed for the group exhibition *Arcimboldo Face to Face*[136] at the Centre Pompidou-Metz in 2021, and, prior to that, to your installation *No tears for the creatures of the night* at the Biennale de Lyon in 2017.

CB Initially, for the Lyon Biennale curated by Emma Lavigne, we wanted to stage a theater piece. The project then evolved into an architectural replica of Aldo van Eyck's Sonsbeek Pavilion (1966), placed in the space like a sculpture. This structure is small enough to be almost an environmental sculpture, like those of Jean Dubuffet. It contained three sculptures—one by Marta Pan, one by Étienne Martin, and one by André Bloc, which had been slightly damaged and removed from its garden setting—all inhabited by a short story by Alain Robbe-Grillet, *La Chambre secrète,* about an imaginary painting, read by the actor Frédéric Fisbach and broadcast throughout the installation via loudspeakers. Three sculptures were very few for such a space, which produced an experience of wandering through an empty labyrinth, with the idea that an invisible painting was also being "hung" through its sonic evocation. We worked in particular with light, choosing to open all the glazed bays and to add a layer of artificial light that shifted through the space, creating very luminous

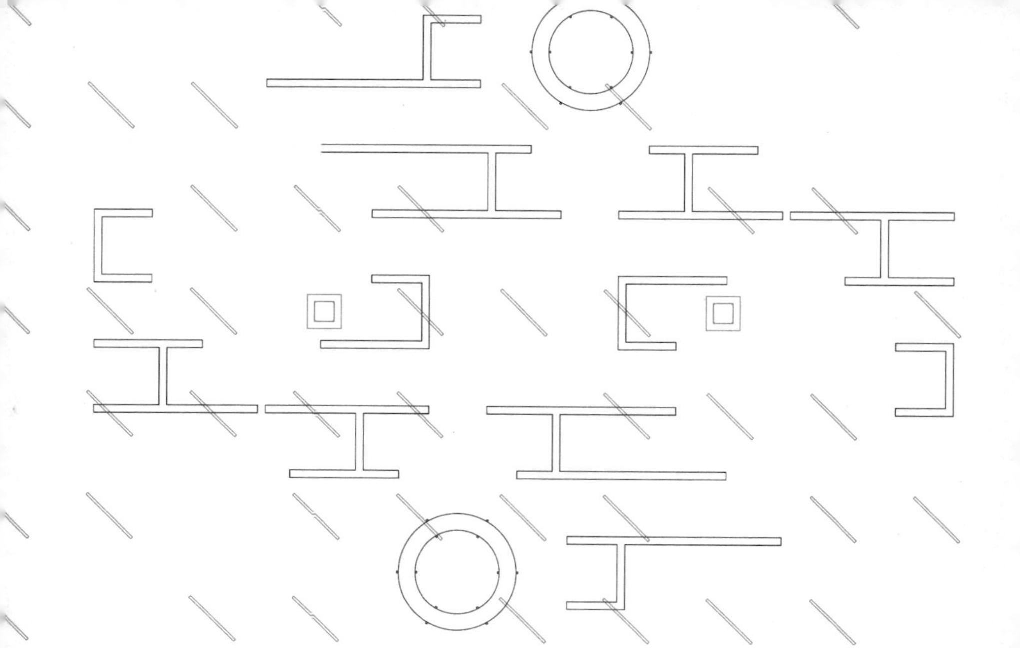

Fig. 2 General plan, revised

atmospheres on one side and darker ones on the other. At times, the text produced a sense of disorientation as it resonated with the experience of the space or the sculptures.

LB Each of these three sculptors was important in their dialogue with architecture. They were contemporaries of the construction of the Sonsbeek Pavilion, which itself went through multiple versions. I think the aim of that museum was to create a situation of immediacy between the outside and the inside, to place the exhibition in a direct relationship with its surroundings. In his drawings, Aldo van Eyck produced a variety of versions of the pavilion, and therefore of possible scenographies, with different hangings, proportions, and relationships between works. Our project was to create a new version—one that van Eyck did not draw, but that we imagined as possible. We're very interested in using concrete blocks because they are, at first glance, the most antithetical material to what one would expect for displaying artworks. Typically, one thinks of light, neutral walls that recede into the background. Concrete, on the contrary, asserts itself—it has a presence, a weight that stands in contrast. And it is precisely this contrast that interests us: it establishes a relationship to reality, to raw materiality, that we consistently aim for in our projects, including in theater, where we try to avoid purely decorative effects in order to produce something more concrete and grounded. Concrete also brings an architectural dimension to the scenography. These walls no longer resemble a temporary display device, but something constructed, enduring—as if the exhibition had always been there, intrinsically bound to the building that houses it.

MR Van Eyck was doing this at the same time as Albini and Helg, who created self-supporting cinderblock niches that allowed them to move away from the wall.

CB That was indeed very influential for us, and something we pursued further in the scenography for *Arcimboldo Face to Face* at the Centre Pompidou-Metz, introducing greater variation and complexity. There too, we built a scenography out of concrete blocks, creating a striking contrast between this raw construction material and paintings in classical formats such as those by Giuseppe Arcimboldo.

LB We worked in the Grande Nef, a gallery overlooked by three others, forming a layered organization within a hexagonal building.

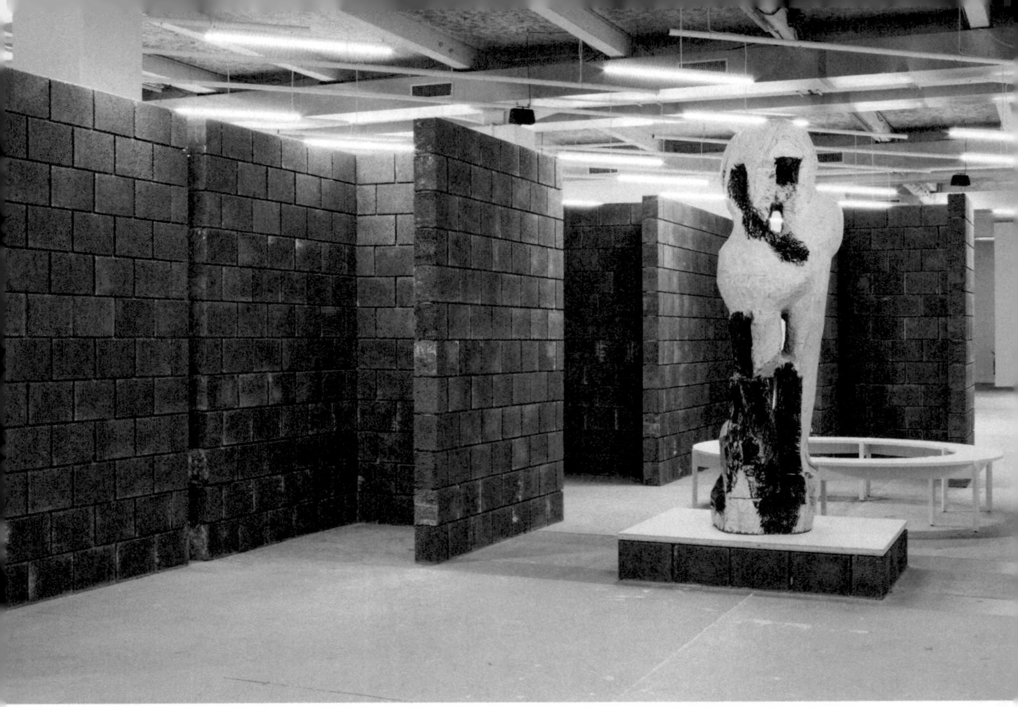

Fig. 3 Installation view, *No tears for the creatures of the night*, Berger&Berger, Biennale de Lyon, 2017

We took this framework as our starting point and reduced it to see what it would produce in space. From there, we developed a composition that resembles the gesture of a permanent museography, since it is intimately tied to the building. It is then up to the curatorial project to take place within it.

MR Was it flexible enough to adapt?

LB The curator Chiara Parisi wanted to work very freely with her corpus, creating unexpected encounters between works, and we developed the hanging together.

MR You have a strong rapport with Chiara Parisi, which probably also enabled this close collaboration, much like that between Franco Albini and Caterina Marcenaro.

LB Yes, we have known each other for a long time, and we were able to work hand in hand, even if we did not influence the selection of works—apart from the choice to include a representation by Man Ray of the Marquis de Sade, in which his face is depicted in bricks.

CB Nor was the exhibition conceived as an art-historical survey; it was driven by a great freedom of interpretation. Arcimboldo is highly rhizomatic and allows for encounters across very different fields, within a transhistorical perspective. Chiara Parisi also had in mind an exhibition by Pontus Hultén at the Palazzo Grassi in Venice in 1987, *L'effet Arcimboldo,* which already proposed dialogues between Arcimboldo and the Surrealists, for example.

LB We therefore began by removing all the partition walls that had gradually obstructed the glass walls during previous temporary exhibitions, in order to recover the gallery as it had been conceived by Shigeru Ban when the building was inaugurated in 2010—as a large, unadorned void—while taking into account the constraint of natural light coming through in order to conceive the exhibition. We placed the exhibition walls in counterpoint to the natural light, creating a gradation that made it possible to adjust the hanging based on the fragility of the works. Of course, there are also adjustments and a degree of porosity within this conceptual framework. We introduced openings arranged according to a scheme radiating from the center of the building, though this underlying structure wasn't perceptible to

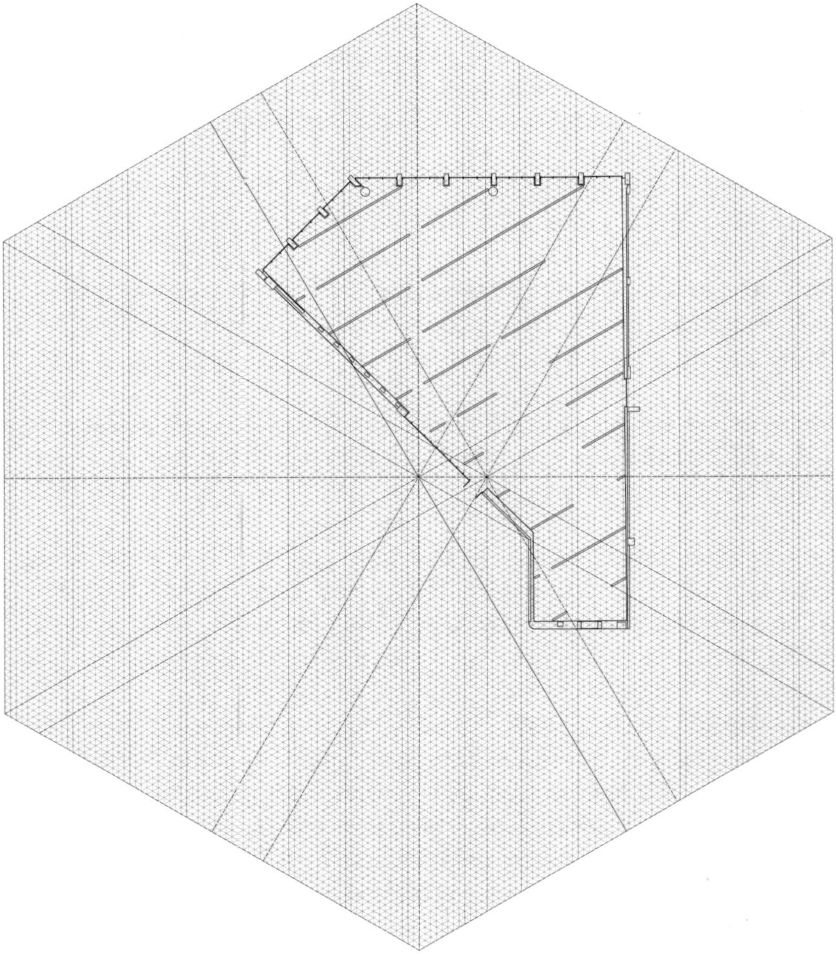

Fig. 4 Grid and axis plan *Arcimboldo Face to Face*, Berger&Berger, 2021, Centre Pompidou-Metz

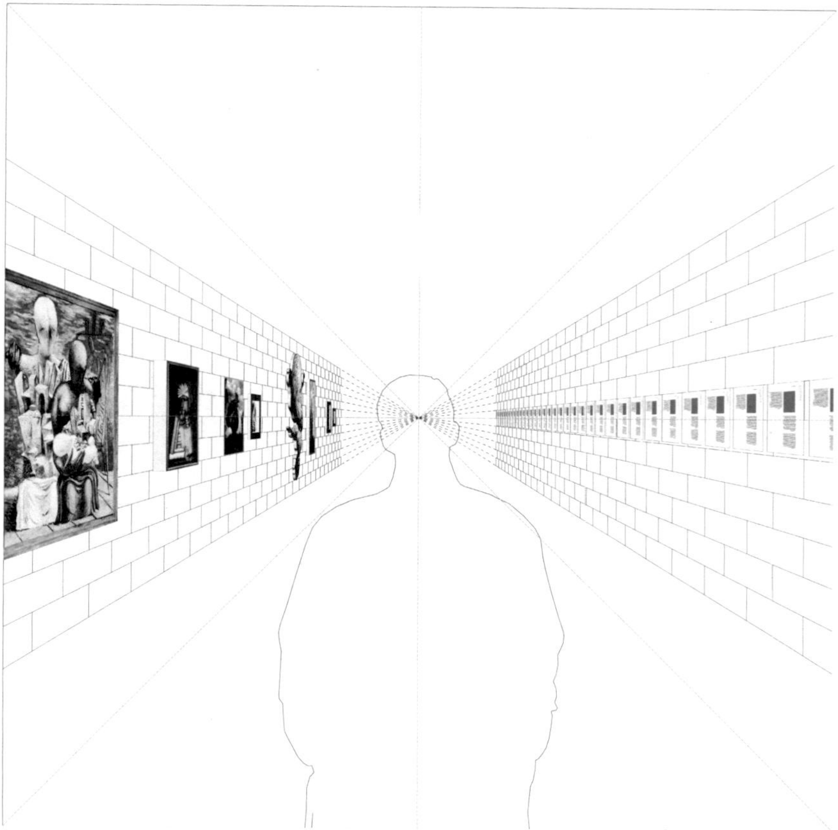

Fig. 5 Vis à Vis illustration *Arcimboldo Face to Face*, Berger&Berger, 2021, Centre Pompidou-Metz

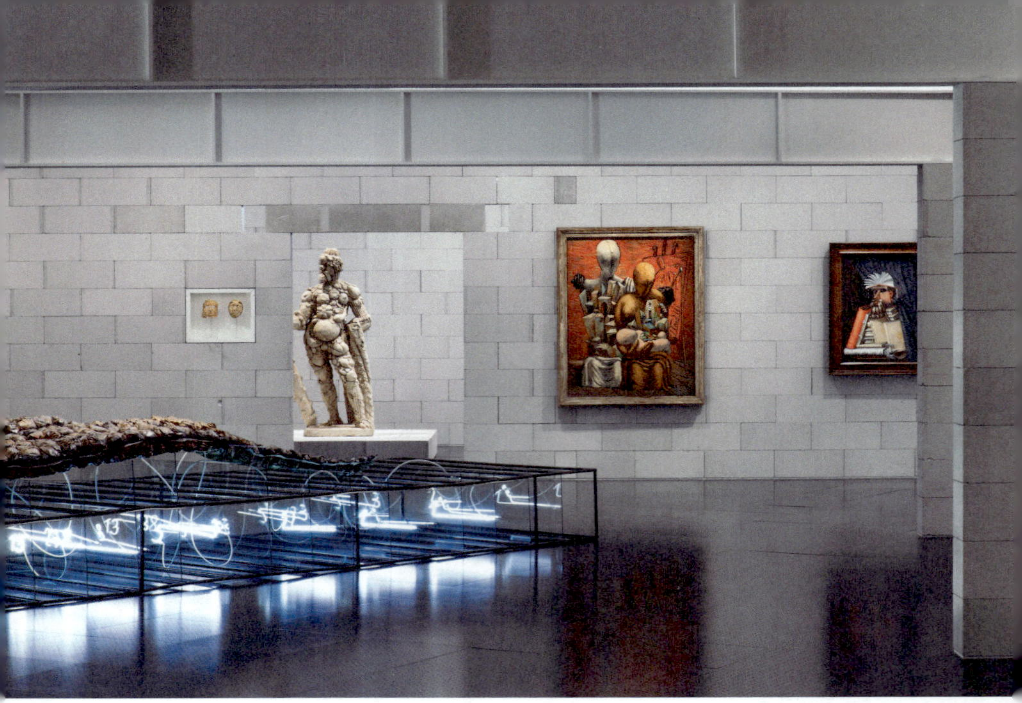

Fig. 6 *Arcimboldo Face to Face*, Berger&Berger, 2021, Centre Pompidou-Metz, Metz

the viewer. As can be seen in the drawing that follows, the axes of the hexagon split and marked the vanishing points of the composition. We then chose to dissociate the works from their labels, placing the labels behind the viewers, so that the works were presented on one side of the wall, and the captions on the other. The principle is of course inspired by the glass easels designed for the MASP by Lina Bo Bardi. This produced very striking juxtapositions, which we first tested in 3D in dialogue with Chiara Parisi through numerous exchanges. We created passages using concrete beams as lintels, and since these were slightly shorter when produced, we worked with these discrepancies, fully integrating them into the spatial composition. The design is total, block by block, in order to fully control the sculptural dimension of the scenography. We occasionally also hung works on the white lateral walls of the gallery, though this remained exceptional, and we played with different heights, sometimes even extending beyond the cinderblock walls. Entry into the exhibition is located two-thirds of the way through the space, via a lateral access point that requires the visitor to position themselves within an already constituted whole unfolding on both sides. It is precisely at this point that the principle of display is inverted: in the bright section on the left, the works are facing the visitor while the labels are behind them; on the right, one moves into the darker section, where this relationship is reversed. We felt it was important that the visitor's first view upon entering be entirely occupied by the works, without labels, without texts, without mediation—a purely visual experience that immediately places them in a direct, frontal relationship with the works themselves.

MR Today, scenographic projects are increasingly expected to incorporate the possibility of recycling materials—how did you approach this in your case?

LB It is not yet possible to recycle concrete blocks within the economy of scenography, but it exists at the scale of architecture through specific channels. For this exhibition, everything had to be dismantled afterwards, but since the exhibition period was long, this seemed acceptable. That said, we had initially developed a first version of the project using individual, lightweight easels, which could have been reused for other projects. This raises other issues facing institutions today, notably the crucial question of storage.

# David Douard

## Inducing a feeling that something unstable is happening

*The sculptor David Douard (French, born in 1983) plays with the visitor pathways when he designs his solo exhibitions by disrupting spaces and appropriating elements such as picture rails, lights, and seating. The boundary between artwork and display is often blurred. Recently, he has also taken on the role of designer and curator for group exhibitions. This discussion took place in Paris, where he lives and works, in March 2024.*

MR You appropriate design elements for your exhibitions. I'd like to talk about how you do this because, from my perspective, it seems to be driven by a subversive energy: the picture rails, tracks, and grids are never there to support the works, they are gutted or overturned. Meanwhile, the pedestals and bases direct the gaze to blank walls and the lighting creates atmospheres that do not actually illuminate the works.

DD An important influence for me, and one that helped me embrace this subversive dimension, was George Maciunas and the *Flux Year Boxes*. These were containers used to store items and then it became an exhibition of the boxes themselves. It is a project where there is no separation between the object and the staging, between the extension, the environment, and the object. I am very interested in the Fluxus movement due to this idea of capturing a flux in an object that is obsolete as a consumer item but which is reactivated amid the life that surrounds it, for example, in the interaction with the observers themselves, like Joseph Cornell or Robert Filliou. Their use of space was very powerful and it was a source of great inspiration, especially George Maciunas, who spoke of his desire to create labyrinths, to begin an exhibition at the end, or who said that the middle, which is the nerve center, must always be a disappointment. In my exhibition at Frac Île-de-France, the end of the visitor's pathway was obscured, you couldn't access it, but there were still things to see and the street entered the exhibition space. Is this subversive in terms of exhibition design? I don't really know, it's too early to say, because I'm just beginning to understand what I was doing with graffiti, which was very important in getting me out of a difficult situation in my life. I come from Perpignan, where graffiti is very common, a response to a desire to express oneself and exist in society. I'm dyslexic, I had a lot of trouble reading and writing, so graffiti also allowed me to appropriate language as a form of authority and repeat it until it lost its meaning. When I started sculpting at art school, I sought to bring the fluidity of language to sculpture, and I found the same energy in art that I had found in graffiti.

MR The way you constructed the exhibition layout at the Frac Île-de-France, and in particular the end where the glass wall of the Frac was open on the street side but closed on the interior side, preventing passage, blurred the boundaries and made them more porous with the flow of passersby and the public space. It also reminds me of Dan Graham and his reflection on the need to invert the positions of gaze by playing with transparency and opacity in an attempt to subvert the relationship between bodies and images in public space.

DD Like many of my generation, I devoured the works of Michael Asher, Dan Graham, Gordon Matta-Clark, and others who fully integrated the contexts into their exhibitions. Today, it no longer makes sense to do the same thing, so instead I play with placing stigmata in our present. Exposing the picture rails and playing with the pathway of the viewer is I think still important as a convention of art history, but it is not an end in itself, unlike in the 1960s when these strategies emerged. Today, practices are drifting toward something else, toward the present, incorporating more emotions and personal feelings into these conventions that were supposed to be mirrors of institutions. I also really like the work of Dominique Gonzalez-Foerster because of the way she has made spaces poetic and domestic. In her rooms, which are reappropriations of space, I rediscover my experiences of the street and walls: graffiti, like a bed or a cushion, is a way of appropriating a place.

MR Can you tell us more about how you conceived the layout of your exhibition at the Frac Île-de-France contemporary art archive?

DD I asked the director of the Frac, Xavier Franceschi, if there were any unused storage areas, anything that was "off-limits." He showed me a space that I turned into an entrance by simply removing some partitions. I wanted visitors to immediately feel a sense of physicality upon entering a room where they weren't supposed to be, but was nonetheless part of the exhibition. It was an act inspired by Michael Asher, who expanded the practice of sculpture by tearing open a ceiling in the 1970s.

MR In your exhibitions, your sculptures adopt a work-like function, serving as places of hybridization and overflow, while the exhibition design is an extension of this. Can you explain how relationships of contamination between them are established?

DD Objects have a physicality; they are sometimes already assemblages, chimeras, but they are also surrounded by emptiness, which allows these pieces to be activated. Placing a sculpture near a colored wall, a partition, or a light box creates confrontations between their organic nature, filled with fluids and information, and which can become something very objective at a distance of one meter. Playing with these constraints is a way of putting them at peril, of not giving them too much aura, and of making them more resistant. I love creating very narrow spaces for the viewer, where they don't really know if they should go in or not, or how to view the object. More generally, I like to try to create a fluid experience of architecture, like in a dream where you can go boating in your bedroom. I use a lot of "hard" forms such as mounting grids and plexiglass, as these constraints are necessary for the fluidity of my imagination, in a spirit of constant contamination. I like it when a sculpture takes the pulse of its constraints and spits them back out, becoming one with them. It could even eat a wall of the space.

MR Beautiful image! That's why I mentioned a subversive approach to exhibition design earlier. Design is initially a tool to facilitate a visitor's pathway, to clarify the place of the work and the gaze of the observer, but you turn it into a tool to disturb spaces and bodies. What interests me is that you are an artist who integrates exhibition design in your artistic process, which is quite rare, you do it in a way that is antithetical to what we experience in terms of the exhibition design we see when we walk through a museum such as the Musée d'Orsay, for example.

DD When we worked as a group of friends on the exhibition at the Palais de Tokyo, we liked to say that we loved the aesthetics of Gifi

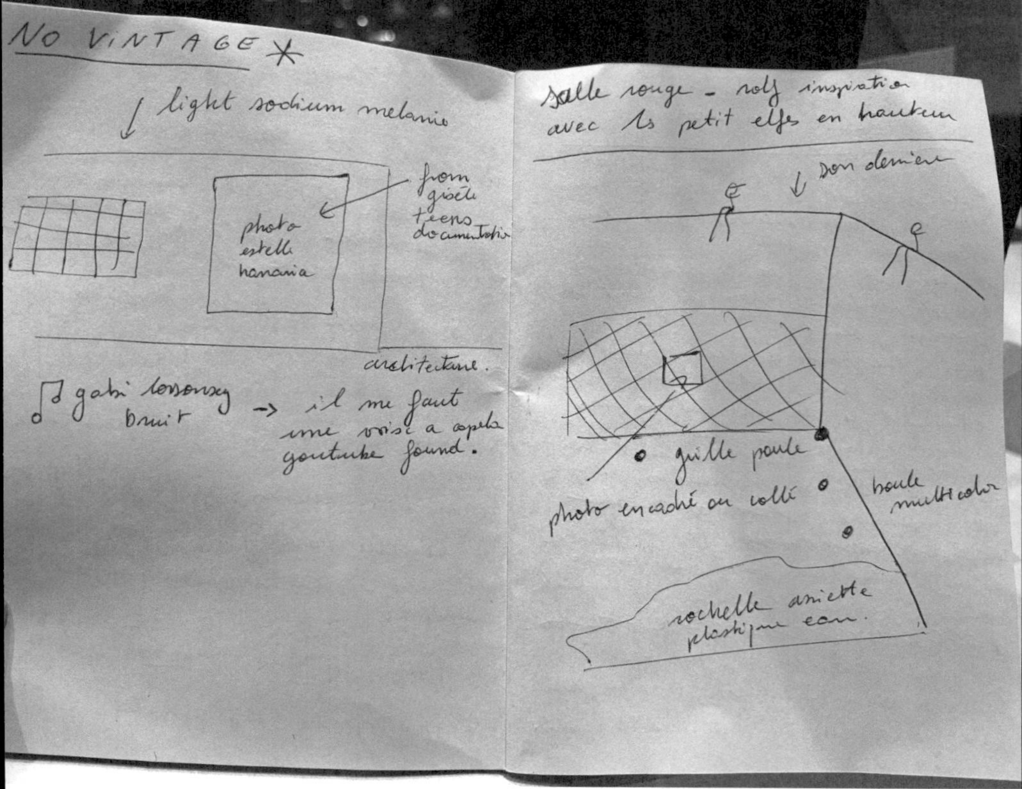


Fig. 1 Preliminary sketch, David Douard

home goods stores, which are the epitome of consumer seduction. At the Palais de Tokyo, I created lines to follow so that I wouldn't have to deal with too many questions, so that I wouldn't have to think about the visitor's journey in terms of seduction.

MR The entrance was through a red arched wall inspired by the slaughterhouse system filmed by Georges Franju in 1949 in *Blood of the Beasts*.

DD What interested me was that you didn't know where to enter. When I use curtains, I always leave a 36-inch gap so that you never know whether you can go in or not. The entrances that are officially available always require opening a door, so there is a strong mental experience that can also be irritating. When you arrive at the object, you have already experienced a sensation that has to do with where it is located, its context. I often arrange my pieces like grids, and we go from moments of excitement and surprise to moments of disappointment, which, for me, is the perfect balance, because then we can position ourselves on the object from this objective state of disappointment. The object is stripped down to the bare minimum so that we can look at it as it is.

MR You also used an image in the Frac Île-de-France exhibition of a hand held close to an ear in a moment of whispering, which points to the idea of the experience being contaminated by rumor.

DD You never know what can happen between the mouth and the ear. Whispering and the laughing joker mask are also two things that, as a friend once told me, make it impossible to know whether someone is being mocked or being asked to play. I probably lose some visitors who are annoyed by the disruptions and the exhibition design, but I'm still interested in people having a choice of where to sit.

MR With rumors or whispers, the idea is to distort language and space through gestures that destabilize the architecture: openings in the picture rails are left unfinished, grills hang crookedly, and the lights are often too bright.

DD Yes, I think that cutting a hole in a wall with a jigsaw and leaving the dust on the floor, or leaving the rail exposed, tells a story. I even try to haunt spaces. I also use the sound of clapping or applause as a way

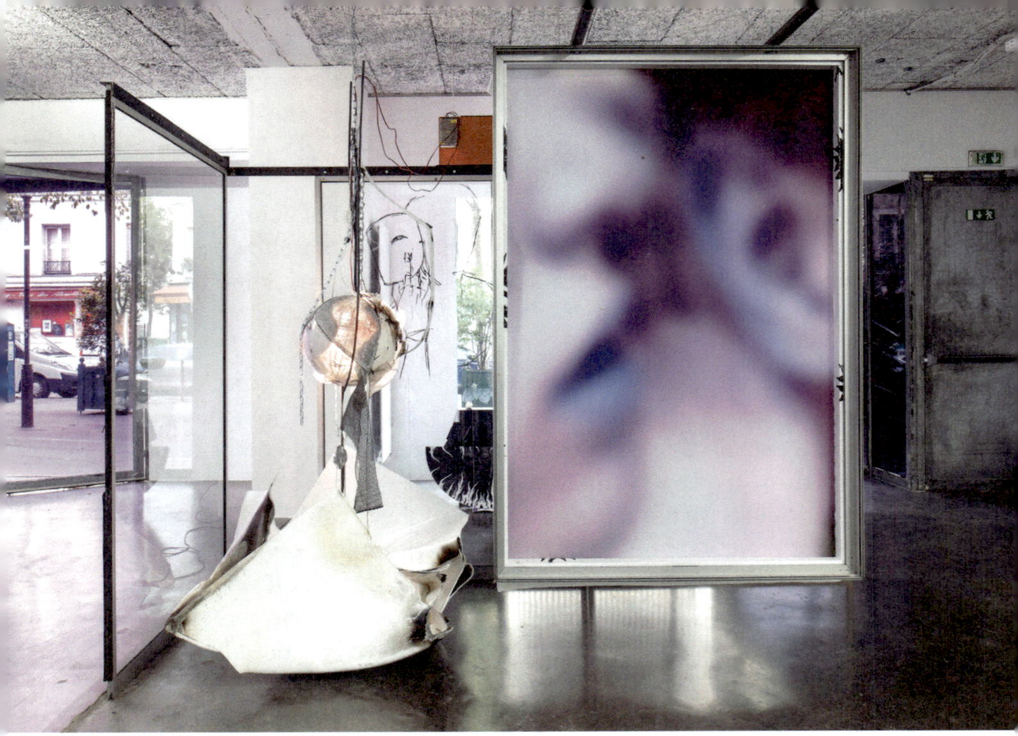

Fig. 2 *O' Ti' Lulaby*, David Douard, Le Plateau, Frac Île-de-France, Paris, 2020

to initiate a game that attracts the visitor. This is interwoven into the exhibition design. If you pay attention, you hear these claps and follow them, only to realize that nothing is happening.

MR Nothing occurs directly in the foreground, but of course, a lot of emotions emerge behind us, through ricochet, transparency, and reflection, like when we sit on seats facing a slightly varnished white wall where a video is reflected.

DD I am very interested in airport waiting areas, which condition us to do nothing, which is so important. One day, I spotted some armchairs with a very distinctive tongue-shaped design that had been set aside to be thrown away. I wanted to salvage them, but I arrived too late. The Aéroports de Paris remade them so that I could include them in my exhibition at Frac Île-de-France. Visitors could sit on them facing a bare wall, but it wasn't completely bare because it was varnished and you could see the reflection of videos being projected behind it. These were videos of scenes of self-exposure that I had found on the internet and chosen because you could hardly see anything in them. Installing airport seats in front of a white wall is a way of creating a moment for oneself in an exhibition, of perhaps allowing the viewer to rest a little from their busy life. When he went to see Marguerite Duras' films, Guillaume Dustan said, "I feel good because I'm sleeping." I think it's not bad if a work leaves us room to sleep, to escape. It's very kind, ultimately, and it makes us wonder what we take away from an exhibition when we leave. The spaces I like best are the ones that give me room to let go and make life a little more beautiful, as Filliou said.

MR When it comes to your visitor pathways, you combine these moments of emptiness, rest, and wandering with moments of intensity and visual shock.

DD I am also interested in extremely bright areas because they question the resistance of the object itself in an interstitial context. At the center of the Frac Île-de-France, in the heart of the exhibition, there were sculptures with a box on a wall covered with stripes, and I tested the resistance of the objects. When they are put under a spotlight, how do they hold up? I also like the fact that the intention we put into an object is the same regardless of its size… I think a lot about stuttering in the way I put together an exhibition. When we stutter, we are unable to say something in its entirety, so we spit out little bits that we repeat several times in different ways to get it said. Stuttering ricochets through space. It's like a rhythm that kicks in and makes us dance with objects, which are genuine in their shortcomings. The exhibition design allows me to emphasize this. I love it when a small object manages to corrupt square meters of space. I also work with light, which hurts the eyes and puts us in a delicate position when looking at the object, as it forces us to squint or shut our eyes. Light allows me to create voids. I often use sodium lighting, streetlamps, but also grow lamps, so that ideas can germinate in objects. This allows me to create a focal point, as with sound and the color of walls. My father was a horticulturist, and I saw this way of nurturing something that grows, where the challenge is not just to make the tree grow tall, but to maintain a structure around something that is germinating. As a teenager, I was inspired by movements such as the Invisible Committee and Anonymous, which carry out underground actions without being visible, germinating silently while wielding great power. In an exhibition, I seek to create devices that have an ongoing presence, something alive, but whose purpose is not immediately apparent. If I capture my initial subject in sculpture, it dies. I use exhibition design to convey the feeling that something is happening, but in an incomplete, elusive way, like the poetry I often include in my pieces, which is a flux, a stream of writing, a blog exchange that takes place beyond the space and can never be read in its entirety. By capturing fragments, we also complete the rest. I also really like Marcel Broodthaers's book, which contains the idea of a text and allows it to be read, but in an incomplete way. The object becomes a somewhat fantastical ornament of writing.

MR You once told me that you were also inspired by Constantin Brancusi, who already incorporated the pedestal into his creative research into sculptures, particularly in the way he arranged his pieces in his studio.

DD I often visited Brancusi's studio, which opened my eyes to what a work of art is when it is finished, and to the importance of the process. The pedestal and the frame are questions to be posed and mastered, in order to tame these constraints and embrace them. Today, we think not only about the pedestal, but also the location, the financing, etc. Contemporary art defies many circumstances because it has become aware of the conditions in which it exists. Christopher

Williams approaches this in a good way. He is an artist who produces hyper-realistic, perfectly framed photography, but who always confronts his work with the design layers of the exhibitions that preceded him in the institution that hosts him, accepting the fact that, as a result, the aesthetics no longer belong to him. I also really liked Neïl Beloufa's exhibition *L'ennemi de mon ennemi* at the Palais de Tokyo in 2018, which formalized the idea that an institution's exhibition space contains an ideology and that the artist's role is to scratch beneath the surface to see what the institution is hiding.

MR What happens to the display elements after the exhibitions? Are they sometimes permanently associated with the sculptures, for example, when they are sold?

DD No, for me it's important that objects stand on their own, and that installations remain contextual, linked to a space.

MR So that's the distinction you make between the interventions you make on the exhibition design and your artworks? The former are contextual and ephemeral, while the latter are permanent and autonomous? It's interesting to think about what distinguishes them, even though you conceive of them as being porous.

DD That's what distinguishes my approach from Michael Asher's, whose protocols can be updated, but which don't really have anything autonomous left afterward. These ideas inspire me, but I'm somewhere else, closer to Dominique Gonzalez-Foerster. I am currently working on a group exhibition for the Fondation Ricard, *Crumbling the Antiseptic Beauty*, which will bring together some of my artist friends. I am designing the space based on the daily dialogue I have with these friends, which is an incredibly powerful experience. The exhibition design will reflect this dialogue, everything will coexist together, with overlapping elements. I'm really interested in this, and I've also just been invited to do a solo exhibition in Rome, which I'm trying to transform into a collective project in a very different way. I question what it means to invite an artist to exhibit: I could buy a catalogue by Martin Wong, who is now deceased but used to do graffiti, then tear it up, draw on it, staple it, put it in a display case, and that artist would be present.

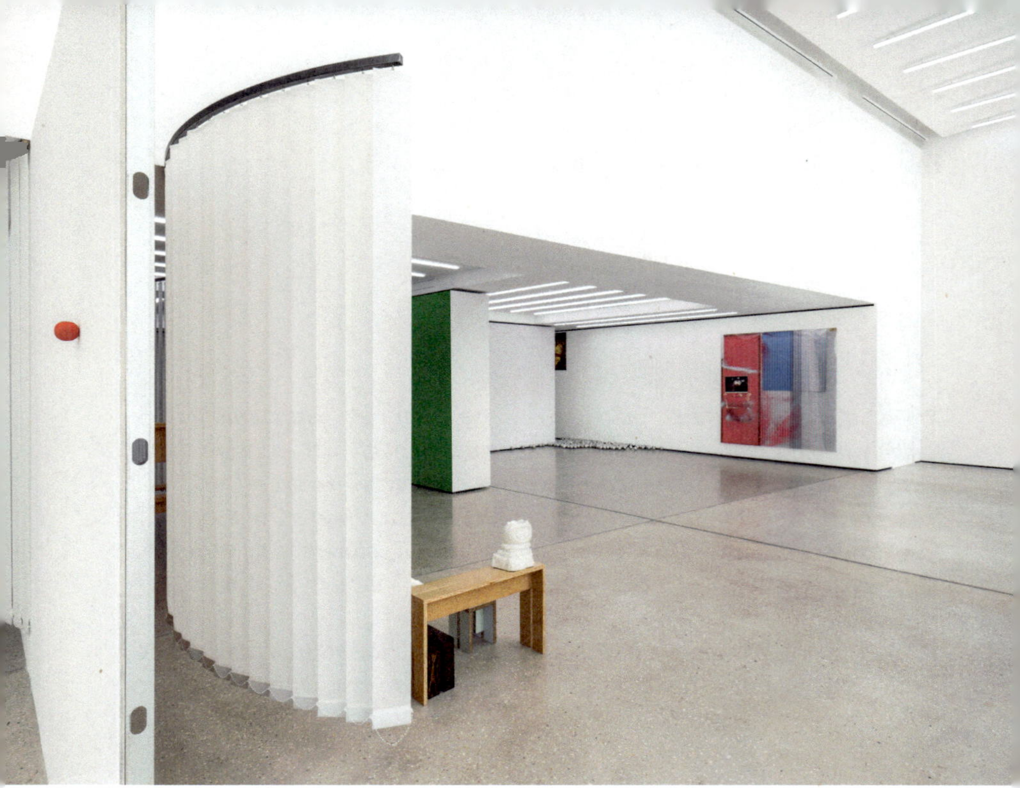

Fig. 3 *Crumbling the Antiseptic Beauty*, curated by David Douard, 2024, Fondation Ricard, Paris

# Diogo Passarinho

## Building an emotional space

*The architect Diogo Passarinho (Portuguese, born 1983) has a studio in Berlin where he works with Gonçalo Reynolds with a creative vision that focuses entirely on exhibition design in the contemporary art sector. We first met at Laure Prouvost's exhibition* Above Front Tears Oui Float *at the Nasjonalmuseet in Oslo, an artist he has been collaborating with for some ten years. We then had the following conversation in Nice in 2024.*

MR You studied architecture in Portugal but your studio is entirely dedicated to exhibition design for contemporary art, which is uncommon. Can you tell us about your beginnings?

DP I started working with the artist Laure Prouvost when I set up my own studio in Berlin after conducting several exhibition design projects with other studios. She contacted me because she had been invited to do an exhibition at the Consortium in Dijon, which is a very complex building. We decided to create a labyrinth with double walls and double doors, where the idea was to disorient the visitor. My perspective was to not worry too much about whether the works were presented correctly, focusing instead on creating an experience. We wanted the public to feel they might see something or miss it, or that they could find themselves stuck in a space without knowing how to exit.

MR Laure Prouvost always plays with the public in her work and enjoys false leads and misunderstandings. Could we say that in her case the display devices are a continuation of her work?

DP Yes, and you could even say that sometimes the exhibition design becomes a work of art. You can climb it, touch it, sit on a sculpture to watch a video—it's very dynamic and completely the opposite of the cold and hygienic atmosphere of the white cube, a

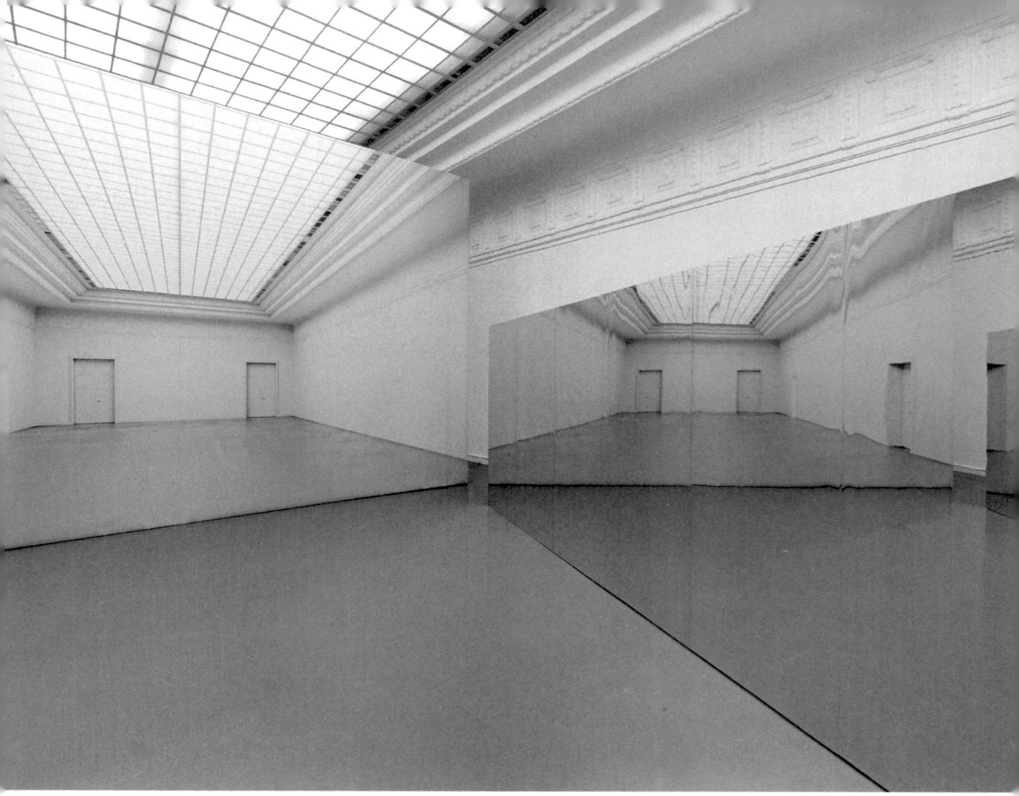

Fig. 1 *All dressed up and nowhere to go*, Jimmy Robert, exhibition design by Diogo Passarinho, Staatliche Kunsthalle, Baden-Baden, 2022

space that doesn't encourage artistic experience, because, without an emotional connection with the works, we lose the possibility of remembering what we saw. Since then, we've collaborated on numerous exhibitions. We speak the same language and I'm proud of our bond and the trust we have in each other.

MR You also played with the building's white-cube atmosphere in your post-pandemic collaboration with Jimmy Robert for the *All dressed up and nowhere to go* exhibition at the Kunsthalle in Baden-Baden in 2022.

DP The project consisted of using mirrors to create an overdose of white-cube energy in a nightmarish way so there was an atmosphere of great solitude that placed the visitor at the center, inviting them to become a performer. The labyrinthine architecture was composed of a stage, a backstage area, a dressing room, a new space and a trompe l'oeil image. It brought on a sensation of intimate emptiness within the institution's exhibition space, where the visitors were first confronted with reflections of themselves. The title, *All dressed up and nowhere to go*, questioned themes like belonging, the place we each occupy, and our perspective on others as well as their own perspectives. Performance, as one of the artist's practices, was dissected in time and space and could be experienced as an installation or event that moved through time.

MR As in this example, exhibition design can be used to control the atmosphere and the public's sensations. What I like about Laure Prouvost is that we always know she's using ruses. She trusts the public to take part in the game without completely forgetting they are dealing with tricks and trompe l'oeils. This way, she can make us believe she made a hole in the brand-new floor of the Nasjonalmuseet in Oslo, but she also always finds a way to show us the hidden reality at some point, so as to not leave us in a state of illusion.

DP For me, Laure's vision is like a child's dream, such as when she invites us to float on a cloud or seeks to communicate memories of the feelings we had at that age. Our most significant collaboration was of course the French pavilion in Venice in 2019, where the primary work was a road-trip film that traveled across France, revealing its identities, genders, and migrations, and ended in Venice. Travel was part of the process, and, for Laure, it was important that the experience begin before entering the pavilion. So, we plunged the whole building into a kind of fog and then asked visitors to look for the way in, as the main entrance was closed. You had to find a door at the back of the building that first led to the basement, which was important to the idea of immersion, and then go up to the main spaces by crossing a room with an incredible floor that looked like liquid water and led to the film. Laure wanted the visitor to enter the belly of an octopus, so we transformed the main space by installing a tent that looked like a parachute hanging from ropes, which completely erased the usual aesthetic of the space. We also raised the thickness of the carpeting on the floor by 2 centimeters every meter as you got closer to the screen, so that when you were in the dark space, your legs would start to feel uncertain, you didn't know where to put your feet, you could lie down and feel you were inside the octopus. Then, when exiting the belly, you were met with several tentacles and you had to decide whether to go right or left. In fact, you could only see half the pavilion, one half with blue energy, the other with red, each with its own videos. You had to either go backwards or start all over from outside if you wanted to see the other tentacle. Laure was interested in the fact that people could then talk to each other and realize they hadn't seen the same thing.

MR I also would like to talk about a project carried out through a dialogue with the curators of the Van Abbemuseum in Eindhoven, *Delinking and Relinking*, which was a "multisensory presentation of the collection." This highly impressive exhibition was organized in different sections with the exhibition design playing an important role as it provided support for powerful curatorial ideas around the decentering of perspectives and accessibility. For example, paintings were placed very low on the walls in a room that had metallic benches at the center, which were also low. Color was also very important in the design, which was in sharp contrast with the hegemonic white wall of the contemporary art museum. Does the dialogue you have with curators differ from the one you have with artists, and, if so, why? Could you tell us more about the context of this project?

DP The financing for this exhibition came from the national lottery and their conditions were that the show had to be highly inclusive. When the Van Abbemuseum asked me to collaborate, I responded that I always try to make the work accessible but that I am not an expert and that we would have to collaborate with people who are personally affected by art's inaccessibility. We thus worked with a multisensory

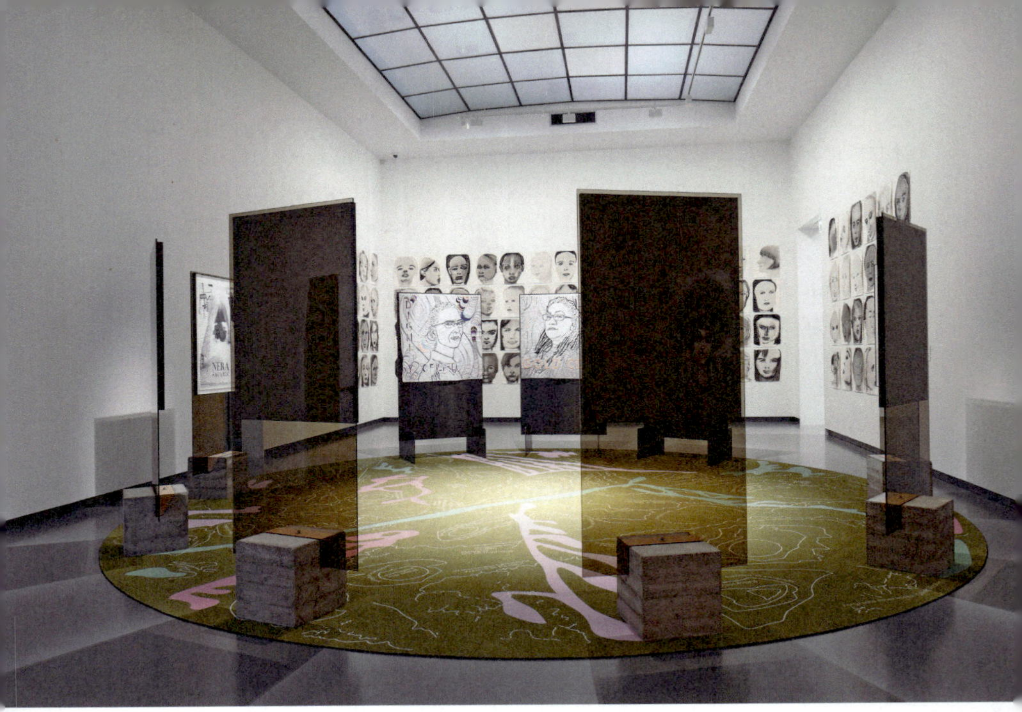

Fig. 2 *Delinking and Relinking* in the Van Abbemuseum collection, exhibition design by Diogo Passarinho, Eindhoven, 2021

team, that for example included a blind designer, who helped us in combining visual, auditory, and sensory experiences. Some of the tours are guided by these experts, injecting new life into the exhibition. Some curators also embraced these questions relative to the thousands of artists and artworks in their collection, and it became clear that there were few women represented. We immediately realized that the presentation had to show these women and that we needed to take advantage of this opportunity to make the problem more visible. The exhibition starts by highlighting individual figures who are the ghosts of the collection, with questions regarding gender, colonialism, and the environment deepening as you go from room to room. At first, the people in question emerge from the wall, you find yourself face-to-face with them, and we chose specific subversive individuals. The curators also decided to place the Cuban artist Wilfredo Lam in the center of the room and to place Picasso in the corner, since he had already seen Lam's work when he painted the piece, and they thought it was time to flip their positions in history. It's a tiny gesture to try to bring a modest change to the way we tell art history.

MR The contextual narrative was also intimately associated with the pieces, since you created specific design elements, such as adding documentation, photography, and letters to the works' presentation. You also made the radical decision to remove the frames, and created a very specific exhibition design for each room, including one which revisited Lina Bo Bardi's glass easels, which she developed for the MASP, the Museu de Arte de São Paulo.

DP In that specific room, we staged an explosion of feminist figures, with Marlene Dumas and two activists at the center. We decided to create a circle and to use Lina Bo Bardi's MASP easels, which were already in the museum following another exhibition. The graphic designers also created a rug, a place to sit down during group visits. The project took two years to produce but is still ongoing as it is a semi-permanent exhibition (2021–26).

MR You played a central role in this exhibition, even though it was a joint endeavor. Is your position as an exhibition designer recognized in the art world today?

DP A good exhibition is not made by one person alone, even though the art world likes to think of it that way. I no longer work with artists who don't recognize that, but I also like when the public doesn't notice the exhibition design, when it is completely integrated with the work. A few times, artworks were purchased with the exhibition design, like when a video is bought as an installation with its display, or a poem is bought with the wall mounting that presented it. For example, I created ten spatial installations with The Otolith Group and the videos were purchased with the technical drawings so they could be shown. The group offered that we share the proceeds, but I refused because I thought they deserved the money. I also gave them the drawings so that they could use them anywhere. Receiving positive energy and giving it back is very important to me. With my studio, every year we produce one or two projects for free for an artist who can't afford it, and sometimes this marks the first step in a successful working relationship.

MR We know that the dialogue between curators and museum directors was essential to historical exhibition designs. Could you explain the type of relationship you have with curators?

DP When dealing with a personal exhibition, the design is usually considered apart, but when the exhibition is collective, as in a biennale, the curators truly understand that the design can be the connection between certain pieces. I've had different experiences, with curators who trusted me and there were no contentious issues, or the opposite. Most often, I work with the people who are implicated in the process, and sometimes they even call me for personal exhibitions because they understand what such a collaboration can bring to the artist. Many curators focus on the exhibition's concept and struggle with the space; they are always a little intimidated by it and I invite them to send me anything that can be helpful for understanding their vision. Some curators have played a decisive role in our studio practice, like Natasha Ginwala, Annie Fletcher, Defne Ayas, or the late Vincent Honoré, who saw Laure Prouvost's show at the Consortium and asked me to work with him at the Hayward Gallery, at the Baltic Triennale, and at the MO.CO. He knew that space could help tell stories, and it starts with trust. It's the same for artists; if they are confident in their work, they can invite others to play. When I first started my practice, I worked on many projects where I wasn't credited, and this angered me because such projects are temporary: they are on display for a few months and then they disappear.

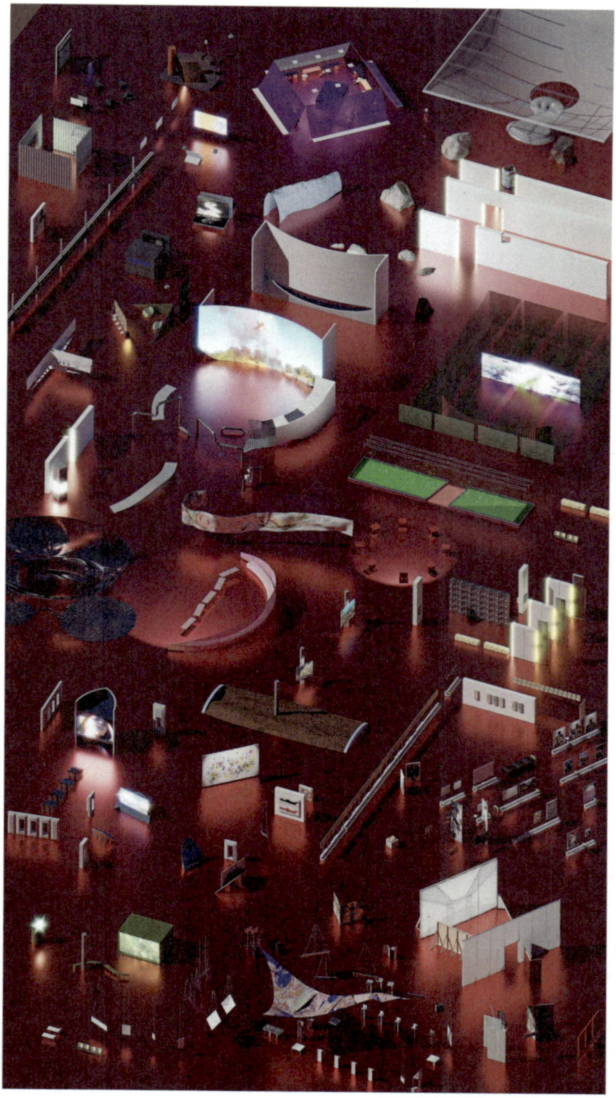

Fig. 3 *Emotional Landscape*, Diogo Passarinho Studio, 2015

MR Today, figures like Carlo Scarpa, Franco Albini, and Franca Helg are gaining recognition in the art world because they've produced many permanent projects that are still visible.

DP Yes, and because their work was playful. Their exhibition design is an experience, and, even if the details have become a central focus, I think the overall attention is helpful because we have remained in the Kunsthalle's white cube model for too long. If you think historically, for a long time museums were colorful, with the paintings presented in different contexts, and this idea of the white cube is both somehow "recent" and ineffective. There was also a period where Scarpa, Albini, and Helg were not only invited to create the exhibition design, but also entire museums: they drew doors, windows, floors, lamps. People are also obsessed with this period because Scarpa, Albini, and Helg were able to collaborate with artisans in a way that is no longer possible today, since everything relating to architecture must go through years of validation, be certified, etc. For example, when I worked with Vincent Honoré for the Baltic Triennale, the main space was a magnificent museum in Vilnius dating back to 1967 that now houses the Contemporary Art Center. They had decided to cover the ceiling of the main hall and paint the floor gray. By way of spatial intervention, I offered to find existing skylights, some of the original floor, and to use materials found in storage as walls, responding to the exhibition's title, *Give Up the Ghost*. Of course, these museums prefer artificial lighting as it is easier to control, but a biennale is mainly composed of independent productions, and so we didn't have to go by the same curatorial rules.

MR How do you define your method of developing an exhibition design?

DP I always try to address everyone, from a six-year-old child to my grandmother, and to create emotional landscapes. The visitors go on a voyage that is sometimes confusing and complex, but the key is for it to be an experience they will remember. Even if you don't see all the artworks, the energy is there.

# Benoît Maire and Marie Corbin

## Display as a possible form of sculpture

*Benoît Maire is a French artist (born 1978) whose conceptual and sculptural practice has, in recent years, extended into the fields of design and scenography through his collaborations with Ker-Xavier. This conversation took place in Bordeaux in July 2024, during a visit to the exhibition* Cronos, *a collaboration between the CAPC Musée d'art contemporain de Bordeaux and the Musée des Arts décoratifs et du Design (MADD). Benoît Maire curated the exhibition, which was constructed from objects in the MADD collection for presentation at the CAPC, and also contributed to its scenography within Ker-Xavier, a structure in which he collaborates with scenographer Marie Corbin, who also took part in the conversation.*

MR How would you define your relationship to scenography?

BM I think every artist is already the scenographer of their own solo exhibitions: deciding whether to place a sculpture on a plinth or against a wall, whether to include a handout or wall labels—these are already scenographic gestures. But perhaps scenography only really exists when one places oneself in the service of another artist?

MR When there is a kind of external position?

BM I'm a drifter, a poet, a designer, a coffee drinker, a husband—all at once, within a kind of social game—and the position of "artist" doesn't interest me particularly. When I work with categories, as in the exhibition *Foncteur d'oubli* [Forgetting Functor] at the Frac Île-de-France in 2019, where I brought together art, architecture, and design, it is precisely to show how one can move from one to the other. So yes, I am a scenographer, if you like, when I take on that role and adopt a certain analytical distance in relation to the objects I handle. But within that distance, I am also—once more—something else: a philosopher, a cinephile, a coffee drinker.

MR What interests me is how the projects you develop integrate an artistic vision into scenography by drawing on its technical tools and its specific vocabulary—the display case, the plinth, the route through the exhibition...

BM When I think about scenography, I imagine a structure, a strategy for making certain objects visible, which is already the work an artist does when deciding how to present their works in a given space. In the exhibition *Cronos,* the scenographic gesture is quite clear: it stems from an emphasis on the idea of a "route" through the exhibition, and therefore on making corridors for circulation visible. Like a canoeist navigating an artificial river, with eddies, accelerations, and slowdowns, each visitor to the exhibition becomes a kind of Tony Estanguet, a well-known French canoeing athlete and sports official. In fact, the image of the river works well because it is also used by Heraclitus as an allegory for the flow of time, and chronology—with its timeline—is precisely what the scenographic structure brings into view. The aim of the scenography is to foreground something that doesn't exactly belong to the MADD collection, but is one of its conditions of possibility: time. So you have a scenography that "shows" time by allowing it to be experienced within a spatial arrangement, while the objects in the collection are reduced to the status of "witnesses." In a way, I am mistreating the collection because I only present it as a set of objects bearing witness to a phenomenon, which is the true subject of the exhibition (and what the scenography works on). And that subject is—as you can probably guess by now: EL TIEMPO! As for the overall look, the form and the materials, the decision to create a white environment with organic plinths is connected to an exhibition I did with Falke Pisano in 2008 at Croy Nielsen in Berlin, titled *Organon and the Audience Perception.* I created tables with orthogonal forms mounted on wheels, which could be moved through the exhibition and generate a specific affect.

MR What kind of affect?

BM I wanted to produce the affect generated by a white space in which objects are placed on white surfaces. It would have been very different if those surfaces had been red. For me, it's like the idea of the plane according to Gilles Deleuze. In 2018, I made a video titled *Letre* in which I filmed two philosophers, Anne-Françoise Schmid and

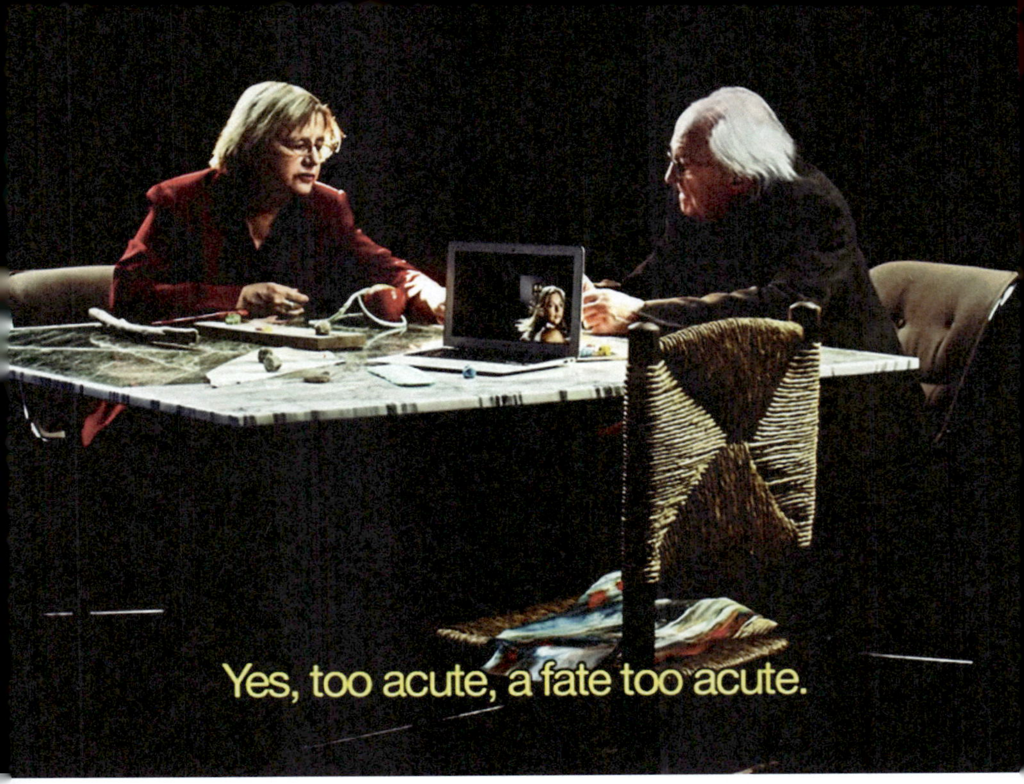


Fig. 1 Video still *Letre*, Benoît Maire, 2015, 16'55, starring François Laruelle and Anne Françoise Schmid

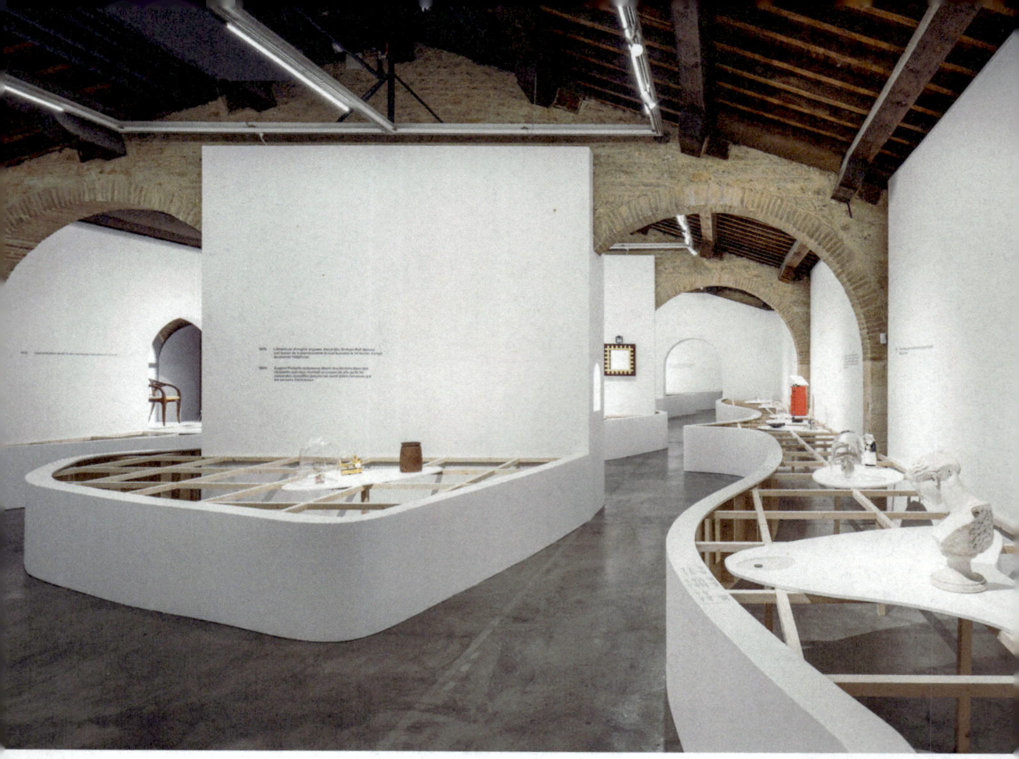

Fig. 2 *Cronos*, with the collection of Musée des arts décoratifs et du design Bordeaux, CAPC, 2024–25, curator: Benoît Maire, exhibition design Ker-Xavier: Marie Corbin and Benoît Maire, blown glass bells design: Jochen Holz

François Laruelle, seated around a marble table that I had made. They sit on either side of the corner of a plane on which various objects are arranged. At one point, Laruelle says: "Objects fall—they are always liable to fall—and from that point of view, the plane is both the source that generates the multiplicity of objects, and also, in a sense, a point of death, perhaps a zero point, the death-point of objects, their tomb. This plane is also a tomb for objects!" Laruelle also points out that, on a plane, there are always sides of objects that one does not see. In *Cronos* at the CAPC, I included clocks and, contrary to the way such objects are usually displayed in museums, I decided to show their backs. The object is conceived as a witness to a form of life at a given moment, and I choose to deactivate its function and its ordinary use. What expresses this intention in the scenographic structure is that I place them in a position where one sees a side that is not normally visible in everyday use—the back, which is quite ugly, in raw wood rather than gilded like the rest. Ha ha, little eighteenth-century bourgeois object: you are only gilded where it shows... This points to certain perspectives on the form of life that produced it. The scenographic structure of *Cronos* is therefore first of all a plane, a grid, on which there are islands, archipelagos (I really like this concept as Jacques Derrida discusses it in relation to *Robinson Crusoe*), onto which objects fall somewhat arbitrarily, revealing certain faces that usually remain hidden, in order to reveal something about the period in which they were produced. The other important idea in the scenographic structure was to create corridors of time, corridors within time, inspired by a very popular French film, *Les Visiteurs.* Once these ideas were established, my collaboration with Marie Corbin within Ker-Xavier allowed the project to take shape while taking into account all the museum requirements, all the necessary rules that, ordinarily, as an artist, I try to bypass. In the end, with a project like *Cronos,* I have the impression that I am producing an artwork constrained by scenography rather than a scenography as such.

MR So you conceive your scenographic gesture as an artwork?

BM It is an artistic structure constrained by museum requirements related to the circulation of visitors and the conservation of objects.

MR Constrained in a positive way?

BM No, in a negative way—but negation is neither good nor bad. Negation is simply one aspect, one moment within a dialectical process. And in this work, my artistic requirement enters into a dialectic with the requirements embodied by Marie, who represents the voice of the museum. Marie always says that, as a scenographer, her aim is to take care of the objects, to present them properly. In our work, she is the guarantor of the various constraints of the space; she communicates them to me, and we work things out together to produce a constrained form. For me, that is not the goal—to respect the objects. I want to assert an artistic proposition, for which I choose objects, albeit in a somewhat approximate way. What seems interesting to me are the relations between the objects and the sentences I have written.

MR Do you feel closer to the idea of display?

BM Yes, I have always worked with display, from the very beginning—for example with *Éléments pour une discussion après la fin des néons dans une exposition* [Elements for a Discussion After the End of Neon Lights in an Exhibition] in 2006, in which I placed wooden panels with objects on the floor that served as the basis for a discussion with Alain Badiou. At that time, I spoke of "display,"[137] as Éric Troncy did, and what interested me was the idea of the displaced object. Display is a possible form of sculpture.

MR A derived form, but not a constrained one?

BM It is a possibility of sculpture, but without the classical idea of modeling. At a certain point, this possibility of sculpture borrows from the shop window a way of formulating the space of visibility, which it reintegrates into contemporary art. In my view, when we speak of scenography, we are speaking of another profession, whose role is to accompany an autonomous art form. In *Cronos,* I thought of the project as a display, and with Marie we turned it into a scenography.

MR In "display," there is also this idea of laying things out flat, which is very close to the processes you have described.

BM I have always liked the table, the plane, and the chair. In *Cronos,* we conceived a basic grid.

MR In your gesture, you also disrupt certain codes of scenography, for instance when you hijack the format of the wall text, which is usually reserved for biographical information or quotations.

BM I do this especially with conceptual artists in mind, such as Lawrence Weiner in the 1960s. Making a sentence appear in black Helvetica on a white wall, lit quite strongly and evenly, is a recognizable "manner" of conceptual art—let's say classical or even traditional (almost conservative)! Even the didactic text at the entrance is completely twisted. In the exhibition, there is the technical time of the objects on display, which unfolds over 800 years; then the dates written on the wall, such as "1957, birth of Nathalie du Pasquier," which introduce human time; and then geological time, embodied by natural artefacts from my personal collection that I added.

MR Why did you add these "natural expressions"?

BM The conservation constraints of the MADD required the objects to be placed 1.2 meters away from the visitor, and I was bothered by the fact that nothing could be placed closer. So I decided to take eight elements from my personal collection—fossils and minerals—and place them in these empty spaces. In this way, I introduced geological time—the most distant from us—and placed it, paradoxically, closest to the visitor.

MR While walking through *Cronos*, and observing the auratic effect of the white cube on some of these utilitarian design objects, I thought of the *Machine Art* exhibition at MoMA in 1934, where Philip Johnson used similar auratic effects of the white cube to make viewers feel the sculptural dimension of an airplane propeller or a spring, much as you do by placing industrial objects such as a glass from the Orangina brand.

BM I did play with the white cube effect, and I think this proposal owes a great deal to the aesthetic of the artist Falke Pisano, to whom I was very close between 2006 and 2010. She worked on modernism, and with her I made several pieces, including *Organon* in 2008. I wanted to recover that modernist affect, but with softer forms. However, the CAPC is not a white cube, and we also worked with the forms of the vaults, for example, which are widely used in decoration—and I love that. We opened up certain walls as well to create windows within the

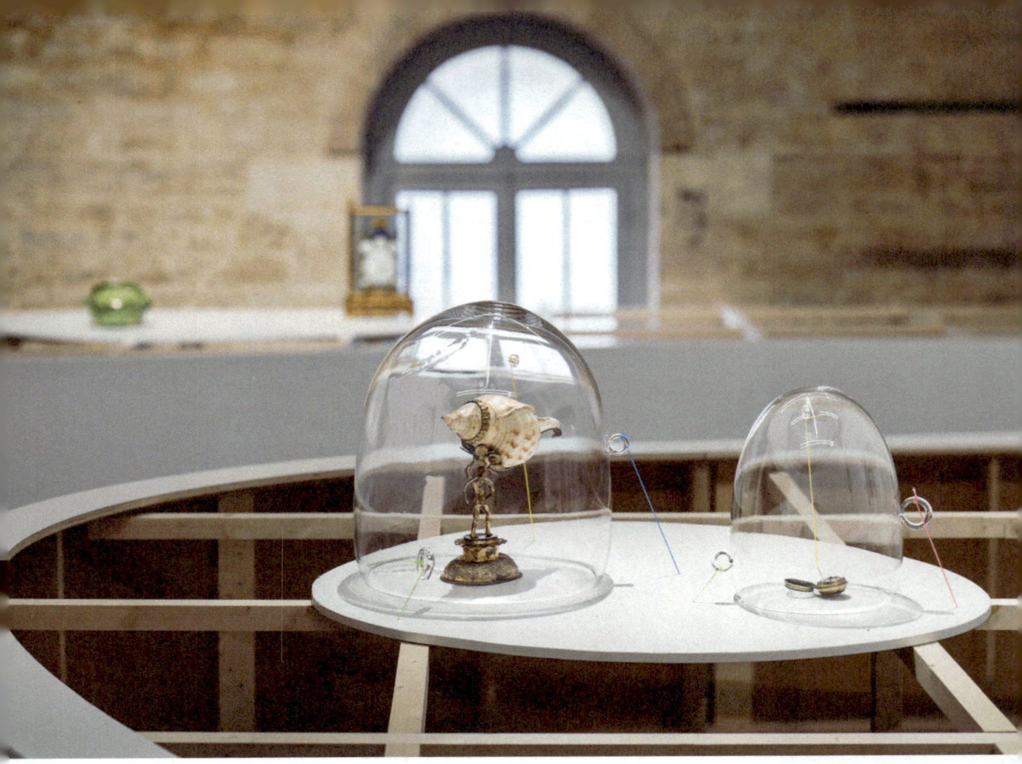

Fig. 3 *Cronos*, with the collection of Musée des arts décoratifs et du design Bordeaux, CAPC, 2024–25, curator: Benoît Maire, exhibition design Ker-Xavier: Marie Corbin and Benoît Maire, blown glass bells design: Jochen Holz

exhibition, allowing the architecture of the building to enter into the overall proposition.

MR Marie Corbin, you're a scenographer and you've worked with Benoît Maire on all the scenographic projects as well as the 1% commissions within Ker-Xavier. What exactly is this structure through which you collaborate?

MC It's a collective I founded with architects, with the idea of producing projects without individual attribution. Benoît joined us for the design side, and now it's just the two of us: Benoît is the artistic director, and I oversee production and construction. For *Cronos,* he knew straightaway he wanted to create a chronology by showing objects that have passed through time. We developed the scenography together around these ideas of time corridors and islands, which I then adapted to the practical requirements of the checklist. The exhibition is on view for a year, and certain objects needed to be protected under glass domes. We decided to have these domes blown, using an age-old technique that has itself endured over time, while dealing with the constraint that they had to be fixed to the plinths. We then invited Jochen Holz, a London-based glassblower, to collaborate and turn this constraint into a meaningful gesture. I produced 3D elevations for each object, also taking into account the maximum dimensions of the kiln used by the glassblower Simon Muller (Arham Glass) with whom I'm collaborating regularly in France. From there, Jochen Holz proposed these glass rings, glued to the domes and fixed to the plinth with colored cables. The fact that some domes were large enough also allowed us to imagine dialogues within them between smaller objects when their materials were compatible (for instance, we couldn't place a metal object together with a textile one). The list of works selected by Benoît also evolved in relation to the budget, once we had a clearer idea of the cost of these domes. This is also where the overlap between the roles of curator and scenographer becomes particularly valuable, as it allows the project to evolve in response to constraints and decisions to be made in both directions. We also worked closely with the technical teams who produced the scenography, because it's important to me that this collaborative logic extends to the technical side as well. They made suggestions based on what they had in stock and quickly produced a prototype, which helped guide our decisions.

MR Usually the wires used to secure objects are concealed within the scenographic setup, whereas here you've reversed that with this use of color.

MC The idea was to assert these display constraints inherent to museum objects—and even to aestheticize them.

MR The route through the exhibition also includes a niche.

MC The niche was already there, but we re-proportioned it based on the building's stone arcades. We also opened up certain walls to create a strong dialogue with the building by emphasising proportions.

MR The first project I visited where Ker-Xavier was credited for the scenography was *Foncteur d'oubli,* the group exhibition at the Frac Île-de-France in 2019, which you also curated, Benoît. Could you come back to that project?

BM It was actually an exhibition that contained three exhibitions: a solo show by Christopher Orr, where I placed one painting on each wall at 1.5 meters from the center, following a precise scenographic logic; a group exhibition of historical and contemporary design displayed on plinth-like platforms—the traditional museum format for showing design—on which I placed chairs and various pieces of furniture; and finally, a contemporary art exhibition that spilled out into the remaining spaces, with both existing works and others produced for the show.

MR What did bringing these three exhibition formats together produce?

BM It produced misunderstandings, discrepancies, visual aberrations—and that's what underpins my work. In *Thèbes,* my solo exhibition at the CAPC in 2018, the works were installed according to precise hanging rules: all the paintings were hung at 1.5 meters, and the photographs at 2 meters, placed adjacent to the door. These two systems intersected and produced an aesthetic discrepancy—a kind of clash that was nonetheless justified by rules. It didn't "work" in the usual sense, but it was interesting because it asserted itself through heterogeneous rules and pushed the exhibition into question.

MR In *Thèbes,* you also said that you used mythology as a constraint on the exhibition. Does this idea—that scenography imposes a logic of constraint on your work as an artist—relate to this same production of discrepancy that runs through your work?

BM Yes. But perhaps the only true scenography I've done is the one I created for Julien Carreyn, who, over the course of our conversations, asked me to take charge of one of his exhibitions at Galerie Crèvecœur. I decided to print his images in large formats, which he doesn't usually do, to build tables to display other images he produces on plexiglass (that's where I started making tables), and to reuse carpet from the previous exhibition, which I placed on the walls to create a black room for his video. I was both curator and scenographer, but you could also say it was a conversation between two artists.

MR Your position recalls that of Marcel Duchamp in the Surrealist exhibitions, which he described as that of a "generator-arbiter." Even if the point is less to define your role than to think about how scenography can function as a tool for thought—as when you speak about creating discrepancy and tension. Scenography involves technical constraints, safety requirements, and mediation, but it can also become a conceptual lever within an artist's practice. Did you place yourself in the service of Julien Carreyn's artistic logic?

BM In fact, I intensified certain elements already present in his work, but which he usually leaves implicit. It's my reading: I enlarged images, placed his photographs in relation to ceramics, introduced vintage design pieces as seating for viewing his videos... I'm very interested in interpretation as a way of speaking about art. The paintings I'm making now are also readings of other painters—interpretations, appropriations, reformulations.

MR They are like collages in space, visual readings. More broadly, your work in space is highly composed.

BM Yes—and my studio is also highly composed.

MR Do you revisit your own work within these compositions, as Brancusi did in the space of his studio?

BM Yes, it's like a living environment, with new objects entering the family and others leaving.

MR In *Cronos,* you placed *Chaise du soir* [Evening Chair], one of your sculptural-design pieces from 2019, for the invigilators, along with a label. It's quite rare to consider seating for guards within an artistic logic. In *Foncteur d'oubli,* you also included two chairs by Diego Giacometti, produced for museum visitors and guards—one beneath a work by Oscar Tuazon, the other at a table with other works, including one by Mélanie Matranga. You've often exhibited chairs while exploring the porous boundary between design and sculpture.

BM In the performance *Drawing Attention* in 2008, I placed two wooden chairs facing each other and sat on one of them with a stack of books. Each book had the word "Medusa" in its title. I would wait for someone to sit opposite me, then draw their face while staring at them without looking at my drawing, and then pin the sheet to the wall. I've collected many chairs, included them in exhibitions, and eventually started making them.

MR You draw them, but you also assign them a function—like a chair for a performance or for guards. Earlier, you were talking with a guard who was asking about a piece, and you told him you'd done that job yourself at the CAPC when you were a student.

BM A chair is a sculpture constrained by use—it's the sculptor at rest, with less freedom, and therefore able to play more lightly, like moving from philosophy to crossword puzzles.

MR And yet it's very difficult to design a chair.

BM Making a good chair that actually fulfills its function is indeed complicated—but making something that looks like a chair is easy. The most comfortable office chairs are often the ugliest.

MR By choosing a chair for the guards, you also give a place to the body and include it within the exhibition's script.

BM The chair is a metonymy for the body. When I include a chair I've made, I'm also incorporating my own presence into the exhibition. In *Thèbes,* I placed side by side a museum chair—by

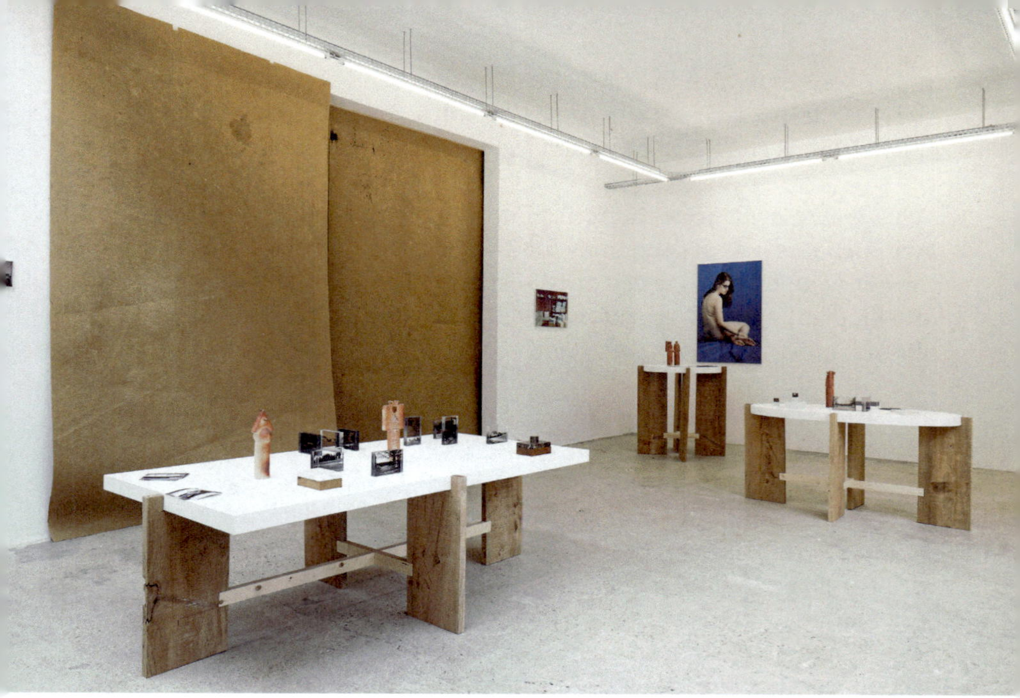

Fig. 4 *Photographies du soir*, solo by Julien Carreyn, exhibition design by Benoît Maire, Crèvecœur gallery, Paris, 2016

Mallet-Stevens, which the CAPC usually uses—and an armchair by Pierre Dariel, who was Mallet-Stevens's editor. I was creating an image of two friends conversing through their shared, immortal death.

MR You also use your chairs as plinths, which makes me think of Frederick Kiesler's scenography for *Art of This Century* by Peggy Guggenheim in 1942. He designed seating that could also be flipped into display supports, and even staged himself with them in photographs.

BM Or we could mention Donald Judd... Another artist who influenced me greatly is Guy de Cointet, who used very simple objects to create humorous performative dialogues. The way an object can become something else has shaped my relationship to sculpture and performance. Joseph Kosuth is also a major influence, with the chair, the photograph of the chair, and the definition. That very Platonic work is extremely powerful—an icon of conceptual art. Malevich too, of course, with his *Red Square on White Ground* (1915), and his display methods that revolutionized exhibition space. Another image that inspires me is Malraux in his office, with images laid out in front of him.

MR The images are laid out flat in front of him, like on a table—which is also, in a way, how Georges Didi-Huberman has defined scenography. I'd like to suggest another reference image: Edward Steichen working on the exhibition model for *The Family of Man* in 1954, which Quentin Bajac discusses in his text for the book *D'après maquettes* that I edited in 2023. You've also often worked with arrangements laid directly on the floor.

BM Yes. For instance in the exhibition *Letre* at La Verrière in Brussels in 2014, where I placed everything on the floor. The idea is that the floor is a kind of fallback plane. My dialogue with the curator Guillaume Désanges was very stimulating—he pushed me toward a certain radicality.

MR Earlier, when we were talking about influences, you didn't mention any scenographers. Are you familiar with Carlo Scarpa or Franco Albini?

BM Franco Albini, no—but Carlo Scarpa has been very important. His scenographic designs have an incredible delicacy. I saw the exhibition pairing Carole Bové and Carlo Scarpa at the Museion in Bolzano in 2014–15, where Scarpa's display structures asserted themselves in their autonomy, in their sculptural force. The Castelvecchio Museum, which Scarpa designed, is also an extraordinary experience as a visitor. And, like what Lina Bo Bardi achieved, they're definitely the GOATs of scenography!

# Grace Ndiritu

## Display as a powerful tool to engage the viewer

*Grace Ndiritu (born 1982) is a British-Kenyan artist who uses shamanic methodologies in exhibition-making as a way to broaden our modes of perception, question the legacies of colonialism, and reinvent the museum. Exhibition design also constitutes a privileged tool for redefining spaces, guiding visitors, and creating atmospheres that expand our perception of the world. This conversation took place online in 2024, following an initial encounter and a visit to her exhibition at FOMU in Antwerp.*

MR I would like to start with your view of museums as dead spaces in need of reactivation. You point to their inability to respect the agency of objects—their ability to act—as well as to their difficulty in fostering a living relationship with the public. You place strong emphasis on exhibition design and scenography as a tool for healing both the museum and its audience.

GN I'm very interested in ideas of "holistic living," grounded in alternative modes of thought, and in the notion of the "Total Art-work." Everything I create as an artist is also part of my life. I spent a great deal of time in different places and within alternative, spiritual, and indigenous communities. My family is from Kenya—I am half Maasai, half Kikuyu, two distinct tribes. I've been exposed to a lot of different spaces and architectures. I grew up in Birmingham, then went to art school in Amsterdam, where I initially studied textiles. More broadly, I'm interested in ways of living and being: how we work, sleep, eat, think—everything conceived as a whole. I began creating exhibition designs to encourage people to slow down and reconnect with their senses—not just the five bodily senses, but also the sixth, intuition—using different tools: interior design, architecture, scent, color, fabric. In many of my exhibitions, I ask visitors to take off their shoes so they enter the space in a very different way from how they usually experience exhibitions. I'm also interested in using all these

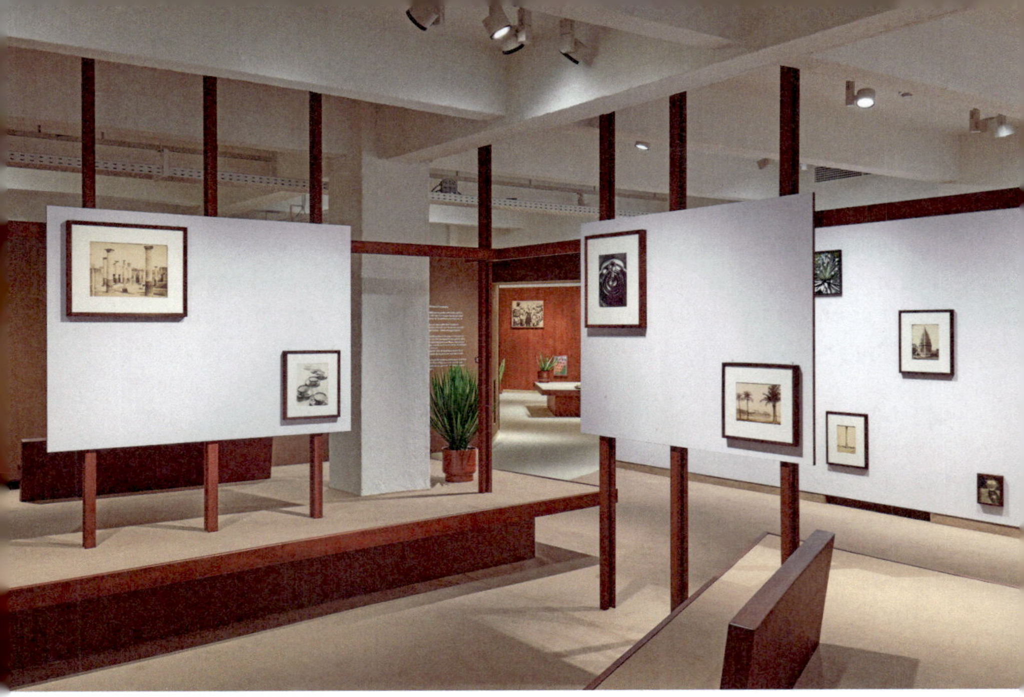

Fig. 1 *Grace Ndiritu Reimagines The FOMU Collection,* Grace Ndiritu, 2023–24, FOMU, Antwerp

elements to build a connection with the audience and to invite them to engage with the world differently.

MR When I entered your exhibition at FOMU in Antwerp, I was struck by the absence of distinction between your works and the overall exhibition, which included a massive wooden installation made up of panels, display structures, benches, and plants. There seemed to be no hierarchy between the photographs and the spaces.

GN I'm very interested in placing plants, photographs, seating, and carpeting on the same conceptual level. I always conceive an exhibition as a trajectory. I think about how people enter the space, whether or not they take off their shoes, how they will breathe, do they need to listen to something—an audio recording, a meditation. I work through it step by step. Textiles are also important to me. I use them in the space to make people feel at home—I grew up in a house where we collected textiles for the pleasure of it. I want visitors to feel that the museum belongs to them, and I use color and textiles to enhance that feeling. We live in a century where museums are more democratic, but they still need to move closer to people. Whenever I visit a museum, I like to wander around and sit on the floor. For the exhibition at FOMU, which is an institution dedicated to photography, I was invited to share my perspective as an artist rather than as a photographer. I had three spirit guides in mind: Anni Albers, Tina Modotti, and Georgia O'Keeffe. Only Modotti is strictly a photographer, though I think of her as an activist. O'Keeffe is a painter and I was mainly inspired by her house, which I visited, and how every object is placed. The Albers room I created is really about the production of textiles, and how these connect to her travels in Mexico.

MR At the entrance of the show, visitors were greeted by a photograph of the inside of Georgia O'Keeffe's house, showing a very beautiful association of objects, textiles, and plants.

GN Even though I'm not a photographer, I started an encyclopedic series of photographs titled *A Quest for Meaning,* which uses shamanism to connect with different ways of seeing through images. In 2010 I went on a shamanic journey to the upper world, and I saw our planetary system from very far and very close, as if I was zooming in and out. When I came back to this reality, I realized that's the way a camera sees the world. I then started to think of images as a constellation. Such non-linear temporalities are central to my way of designing exhibitions, in which images are hung at different heights, without labels, and mix together different geographies and histories to create a total work of art—much like shamanism, which generates new realities by drawing on different worlds. At FOMU, I installed *A Quest for Meaning* in a room lined with wooden panels that reinforced its sense of totality.

MR Could you specify how you apply these non-rational methodologies to exhibition design?

GN Take for instance my show at S.M.A.K. in Ghent, which was designed around several trajectories for visitors to follow. This relates to my understanding of architecture as a form of spiritual technology—meaning that it can reveal certain qualities that we might not perceive solely with our eyes. It's also connected to the idea of the "medicine wheel," a sacred Native American circle, as I guide visitors through different stages of transformation—north, east, south, west. At S.M.A.K., the north was daytime: a time for contemplation; the east, community: a time for protest; the south, ecology: a time for play. Then there was a transitional zone, and in the west, feeling: a time for change. I conceived the west as a temple—an environment that functions like a modernist structure, where paintings or sculptures can be displayed, but which also enables dialogue, conversation, and community.

What I mean by architecture as a spiritual technology is that, while it has a function—creating a specific space to host objects—it also produces collective spaces. My exhibitions explore how we value ourselves and objects, and how we can slow down by returning to contemplation and reimagining the museum as a sacred space. Not in a religious sense, but as a place to step away from the madness of the world and to be, quite literally, with oneself. In 2017, I wrote an essay titled "Ways of Seeing: A New Museum Story for Planet Earth,"[138] on the importance of reclaiming spaces of freedom and contemplation—such as the library, the museum, the park, and the church. Everything else is driven by consumption or productivity. This is where my ideas about architecture as a spiritual technology began. I ask the audience to work a little bit harder, as there are no wall labels. I want them to construct their own narratives from what they see, without focusing on the rational part of their brain.

MR This reminds me a lot of El Lissitzky's *Abstract Cabinet* (1927–28), in which he arranged paintings on the walls as a spatial composition—much as you do—but also gave the viewer an active role, allowing them to move panels and reveal or conceal certain works. Is this a reference that influenced you? Have you ever seen it?

GN No, I work in a completely different way. I usually visit museums to get a sense of the spaces, then I embark on shamanic journeys during which I have visions. I'm very interested in traditional indigenous architecture. My way of negotiating architectural space is different because I am guided by my spiritual visions and how these interact with my experiences of traditional indigenous spaces. I try to extract their energies and bring them into the museum. My interest in art history and exhibition design is more focused on world's fairs, such as the Paris one, or the Eames Pavilion in the 1950s in New York. The Bauhaus is also important in thinking about the total work of art and holistic living.

MR I also sense a lot of affinities with Lina Bo Bardi's vision.

GN I never went to São Paulo but I have seen her work in books and videos, and I'm interested in the fact that she worked in a country with an indigenous population and I wonder how she was influenced by them. It's also interesting to note that Anni and Josef Albers traveled extensively to Mexico, and visited temples there. I think museums and exhibition designs are the contemporary version of prehistorical caves. As artists we're always connected to the creation story and, in Western culture, it goes all the way back to the cave painters. But most of the artists that interest me—such as Georgia O'Keeffe or Andrea Zittel—have been, lived, or worked in environments where time slows down, like the desert. I believe in the notion of deep time, which is why I use shamanism as a tool in my work and in my life—from getting into a trance in front of a camera to teaching, to doing shamanic performances with people. At S.M.A.K. in the temple space, I held one such performance, *Labour: Birth of a New Museum,* with a group of pregnant women. It was about making their unborn child the art audience of tomorrow, and to connect them to the museum. Architecture can offer that safe and serene space, allowing you to go deeper than you normally would in a museum.

MR Have you ever collaborated with architects or scenographers?

GN Yes, on occasions, like at FOMU in Antwerp where the space is massive, but I'm always very specific: I know what type of wood I want to use, which colors on which wall, what type of seating and carpeting to install, so in the end it's not really a collaboration. At the Wellcome Collection in London it was the same, I knew I wanted to use the wooden panels from the Medicine Man Gallery, founded by Henry Solomon Wellcome during colonial times, where he kept a lot of human remains. The gallery had been closed, and I decided to reuse those panels. I started using wood in 2014, when MACBA in Barcelona commissioned me to do my first photography project, *A Quest for Meaning,* for which I designed a set of frames. Some were regular frames, others were simply bars from which the photos hung like fabrics. I used a particular kind of wood, bubinga wood, and since then I have become very interested in its uses. This also connects to my own memories: my grandmother lived in an adobe hut in Kenya, which had a fire burning in its center and stones around it. We would go in there—she would sing, tell stories—and the hut was a sanctuary. That's what I tried to create with *The Temple,* a balance between my left and right brain. Much of my work is about balancing the rational, analytical side with the creative one, so as to resist easy categorization or critique. To do that, one must draw on something else, which I would call "intuitive sciences." For instance, at FOMU, I placed all the photographs following my own intuition, at different heights. Children experience a completely different display from adults. Hanging is a powerful tool for engaging with the viewer.

MR You also use audio guides to slow down the pace and create a sense of safety by establishing a direct dialogue with the audience. It's a didactic tool that artists rarely use, often fearing its reductive effect. How do you approach it?

GN I first used it for my exhibition at the Wellcome Collection. The tapestries on the walls reproduced photographs from the collection, taken between 1915 and 1973 by curators posing with African objects in intimate scenes—images that were not intended to be made public at the time. I turned them into tapestries, and the audio guide became a way to make people pause, reflect, and meditate on colonial violence in front of the images. I invited visitors to close their eyes and breathe in a specific way while I provided historical information about objects that were largely looted from Africa, then to open their eyes again and look at the tapestry anew. It's about thinking through empathy—embodied

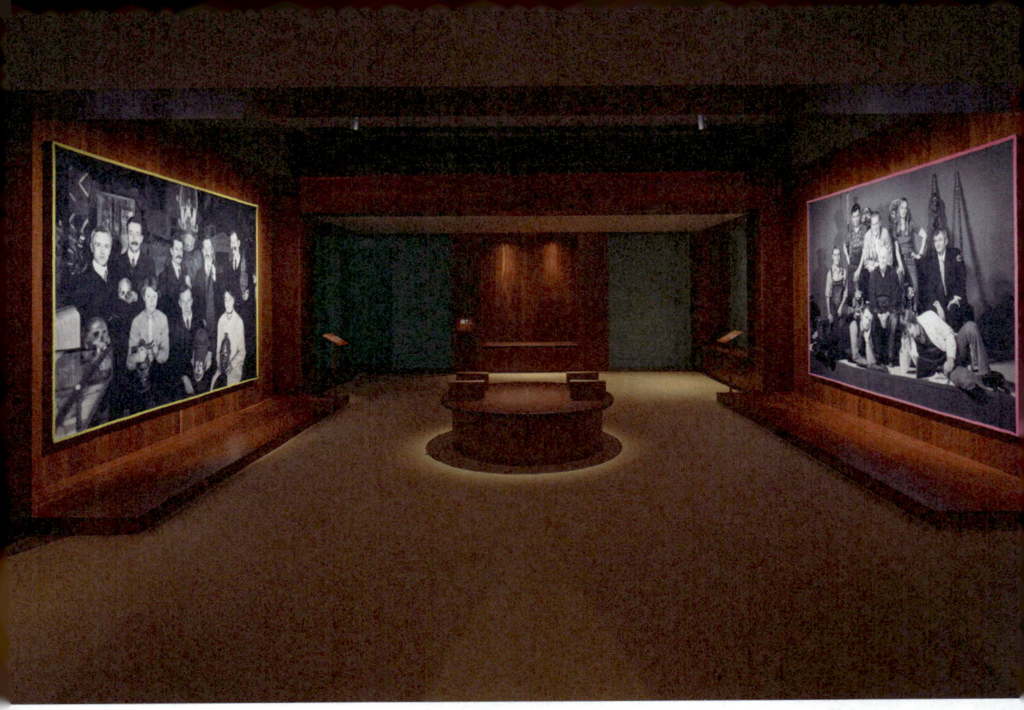

Fig. 2 *The Healing Pavilion*, Grace Ndiritu, Wellcome Collection, London, 2022

learning—which I've practiced for many years, whether teaching meditation in art schools or creating holistic rooms where one can read academic texts while meditating. Creating an audio guide was a natural next step.

MR When visitors take an audio guide, they usually expect to be guided, to follow instructions and receive explanations, often in a passive way. How do you deal with those expectations?

GN The first difference is that I guide myself as a viewer. At FOMU, we also produced French and Dutch versions with actors who tried to emulate my delivery. There's a specific pacing, where I ask people to look at certain images, to follow particular trajectories, so they move through each stage of transformation. When I write the script, I have all the historical information and wall texts, and I combine them with meditation. Wellcome is an institution deeply committed to accessibility for all types of disabilities, so there were many discussions around active looking. If I ask people to close their eyes, they need to have access to sight; if I ask them to lie down, they cannot be in wheelchairs—so I had to negotiate these aspects.

MR When I visited your exhibition at FOMU on a Sunday afternoon, there was a very large and diverse audience. I was struck by how much time visitors spent in the exhibition, and how easily they followed your instructions—taking off their shoes, sitting where you asked them to, closing their eyes, and sometimes even falling asleep during the meditation…

GN Amazing! The wooden structure in the first room is inspired by Zen temples: the benches and tables, where visitors can browse books, are quite low to create that atmosphere. I was happy to see how calm and relaxed people were there. Many friends told me they had dreamed about the exhibition, which means they shared that shamanic journey with me.

MR It's also important to mention that the exhibition was divided into different chapters, each using display in a specific way—with different colors and hanging methods, but also different ways of guiding the visitor.

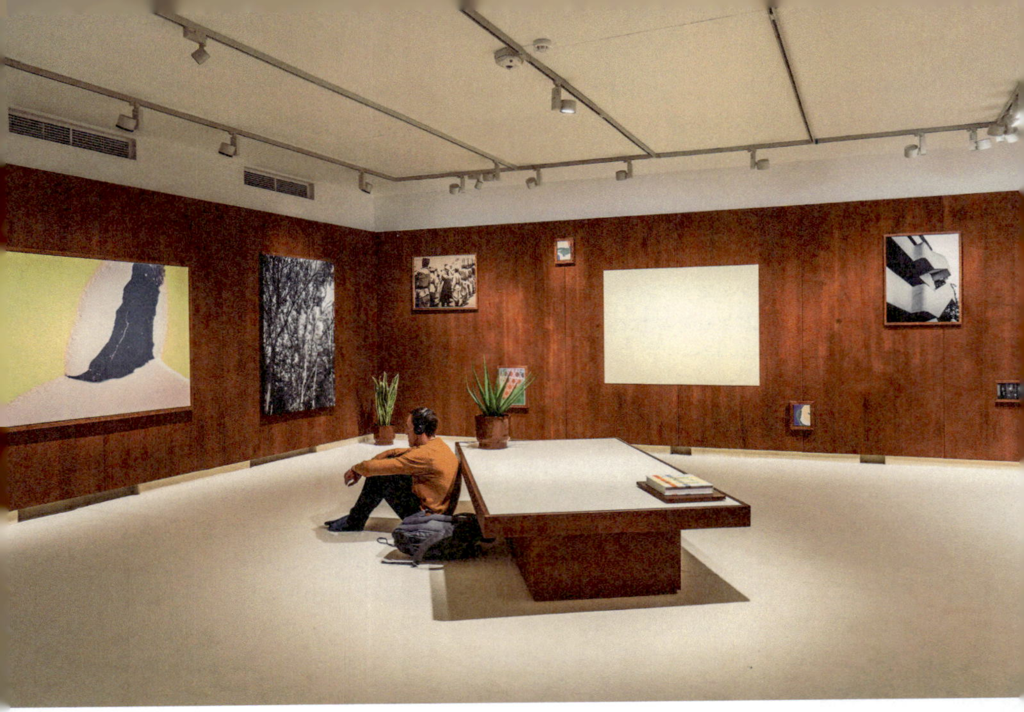

Fig. 3 *Grace Ndiritu Reimagines The FOMU Collection*, Grace Ndiritu, 2023–24, FOMU, Antwerp

GN The overall idea was to create a constellation using images from the FOMU collection alongside my own work, but without portraits. There were only objects, animals, interiors—without any categorization, as that is a Western mode of thinking. I wanted to create harmony and equality, and to encourage a different way of seeing the world. Then there were three colored zones, each focusing on different themes: the lilac zone is for instance about travel, suns, animals and textiles; the blue zone is about architecture, exterior and interior—each approached in a very intuitive way. The museum holds many photographs, but also objects such as cameras, and a large number of stereographic slides. I wanted to connect these with nineteenth-century textile and photographs taken by Anni Albers of temples in Mexico. At the time, the museum had just completed the restoration of the Kaiserpanorama,[139] which had to be included in the exhibition. But I was able to change its velvet panels, choose the wall colors, and introduce plants so that it truly became part of the exhibition. I also selected each stereographic image inside it, linking them to the categories I had in mind. So the FOMU project functioned as a combination of different exhibitions where visitors were meant to spend time. I was told that many came back several times.

MR Plants also featured in the exhibition, but more as props since these were made from plastic.

GN FOMU has a lot of restrictions because the photographs are old and fragile, sensitive to light and heat, and that actual, living plants produce condensation and moisture. At S.M.A.K., where I made *The Temple,* we exhibited Lois Weinberger's *Garden,* which uses living plants that continued to grow throughout the show, but all the works in that exhibition were modern and contemporary art, which made it possible. At FOMU, however, I was happy with these artificial plants, which looked very realistic.

# Pauline Curnier Jardin and Rachel Garcia

## Producing a scenography to present a film

*Pauline Curnier Jardin (French, born in 1980) develops film and performance works imbued with a theatrical dimension. Her creative process is informed by the exhibition itself and she creates visually powerful worlds by manipulating spaces to broaden interpretations. By drawing on reality, her work facilitates upheavals, reveals marginalized bodies and exposes what is usually kept behind the scenes. Her regular collaboration with the scenographer Rachel Garcia led to a second conversation at the Freestanding Joys symposium in Porto in November 2024, an excerpt of which is included at the end of the interview.*

Rome, May 2024

MR I have a very intense memory of the first installation of your film *Bled out* at the Hamburger Bahnhof in Berlin in 2019 (Preis der Nationalgalerie), where you created a dark and highly theatrical forest environment that echoed the film's final scene. After walking through the forest to get to the place where the film was projected, we were invited to sit on two benches that you had engraved with inscriptions echoing those seen in the prison cells where you filmed scenes inspired by Jean Genet's *Un chant d'amour* (1950). The installation was a way of extending the film's decor while producing something different for the exhibition. Today, we can begin this conversation by discussing a model that you made in 2023 for the Centraal Museum in Utrecht for a brand-new version of the installation of the same film. This time, visitors entered the space in a completely different atmosphere, much more colorful, first facing a huge suspended garter belt whose decorations become a small garden.

PCJ I wanted to create a different setting for this film. I stretched out a net and then placed a garter belt and flowers, it was a composition inspired by women's lingerie, particularly the Victoria's Secret brand. Visitors must walk around the installation to reach the imitation wrought-iron benches I bought in Holland. The hydrangeas and their colors are reminiscent of those small German or Dutch gardens with their distinctive aesthetic, where roses and geraniums blend with the asphalt and green grass. I also like the inexpensive design of garden centers, which are the equivalent of the women's sections in DIY stores.

MR  You offer new interpretations each time: in the first version, the dark forest served as an extension to the ending of the film, whereas the version presented in this model stages the beginning with its trashy and slightly kitsch aspect.

PCJ  I think that with this film, I allowed myself to do this because it is so cinematic that it doesn't need a specific installation, and so it's a way of expanding its meaning. Here, I think I'm emphasizing the surrealism of this collective orgy in prison. In the time between the two different installations, I had the powerful experience of developing a permanent piece, a fresco and a film, for the Casa di Reclusione Femminile della Giudecca, a women's prison in Venice, a space where there was no longer any irony. I worked with the inmates on this fresco, and we used a slightly divine, soothing blue-violet color from the film *Black Narcissus*. I showed them works by artists such as Niki de Saint Phalle and Dorothy Iannone, and the drawings facilitated the expression of their emotions, even if anything related to sex or violence was self-censored.

MR  What role does scenography play in your work?

PCJ  In the exhibition, I use it to lure the viewer in, for example by having them enter through a hand or walk on a placenta (which may be a heart) in *Grotta Profunda Approfundita* (2017). I am inspired by cabarets and my experiences in music halls, where I performed as a child for several years. When I make my films, the scenography also serves to give amateur actors tools to produce a performative presence. This was the case, for example, when I filmed my grandmother (*Solo pour Geneviève*, 2018), where I used the fan in her bedroom, her motorized chair, and the black-and-white tiles as design elements. This established connections to Flemish painting, where we find the same tiles, and by integrating these decorative elements into the installation space where the film was screened it imbued the exhibition with a domestic dimension.

MR Do you often make models?

PCJ Yes, and that's thanks to my collaboration with the theater scenographer Rachel Garcia. I've been working with Rachel Garcia since the filming of *Grotta Profunda—they* designed the costumes for the movie. They taught me a lot, particularly how to develop a language of materials, and they contribute technical skills that I don't have. I also worked as a prop master in cinema, as a prop assistant, and I studied at the École des Arts Décoratifs in Paris, even though I only did two years. All of this has given me a methodology. It's important for me to think about the exhibition design that supports the text or film, and the model is a tool for collaboration with Rachel Garcia, but also with my assistants and collaborators when we think about the space, as well as with institutions.

MR Your models are DIY and the scales are approximate because they do not necessarily refer to a specific location. They are conceptual models with proportions.

PCJ Yes, and sometimes even if they are made to scale, they still have errors, but it's a great tool for bringing ideas to life, which allows me to position objects in a space.

MR In the interview with Kristina Schrei published in your monograph,[140] you say that the installation is a stage for your film. Can you elaborate on this idea?

PCJ It's a stage in the cinematic sense. The first "kino" idea, "kino palaz" in the architectural sense, that I worked with was for the *Dynasty* exhibition at the Musée d'Art moderne de la Ville de Paris in 2010, where I created an installation for the opera of objects *Le Salon d'Alone*. For this project, I went to the archives of the Film Museum Potsdam to research cinemas in Berlin before the city was bombed, to observe how the rays of the projectors, the light, and the eye were staged in the architecture. Using the logic of an installation, I then pursued this idea of building a cinema for a particular film, for a story, for a play, in the sense of space and theater.

MR So your installations are like film-inspired architectural structures, but they are also linked to the spaces where you build them since they evolve with each presentation.

PCJ Yes, the location will always dictate certain elements and the initial ideas come from visiting the spaces. At the Venice Biennale, where I presented *Grotta Profunda Approfundita*, there was a pillar in the middle of my space in the Arsenale, and I transformed it into a "Kissing Corner"—a mediator told me that he had once seen visitors making love there! When I was invited to Kiasma in Helsinki and saw the giant vaulted space that was the result of a striking architectural statement by Steven Holl, I realized there was already an aura of entertainment about it and I thought I would finally be able to create my *Luna Park*! I immediately placed my *Colosseum* (a huge sculpture that combines the shape of the Colosseum with a wedding cake and contains a projection space inside) and then I wanted to create a multi-stage journey for *Qu'un Sang Impur* and install *Luna Kino* in this amusement park. I have been living in Rome for five years and am influenced by these ruins that are so accessible to everybody, that can be traversed by night or by day, in a kind of total democracy of settings that are open to all bodies. People blend in with a grace that matches the setting, which makes this city beautiful not only for its architecture but also for the way those who live there move with an absolute awareness of the strength and power of the scenography, both in the center and on the outskirts, since the ancient ruins continue well beyond the center of Rome. This is the Roman Empire in its full splendor, but also its violence and barbarism, with its aqueducts and brothels.

MR The eroticization of bodies, pornography, cross-dressing, and emancipation are central themes in your work, particularly in the projects you are leading with the Feel Good Cooperative, a group you created with trans sex workers during the Covid-19 pandemic. Returning to this model you made, you used the motif of a garter belt, which refers to the commodification of eroticism and the female body.

PCJ The market does everything it can to speculate on sex, but some things always slip through the cracks. Other people's sexuality and degree of emancipation are indefinable. In classic men's pornography, the female body is subordinated and subjugated, but reality is much more complex, and so the associated market carries with it the

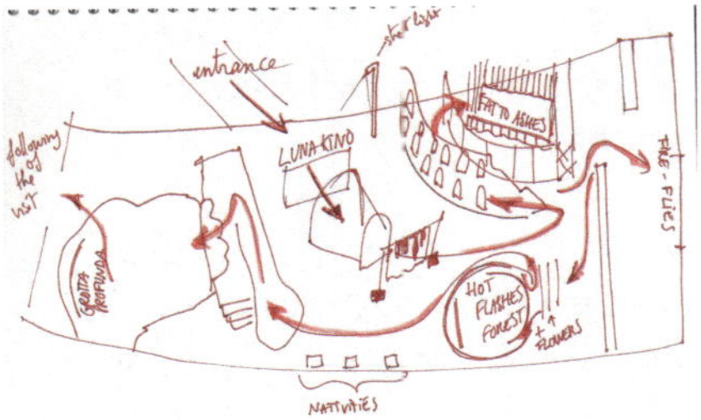


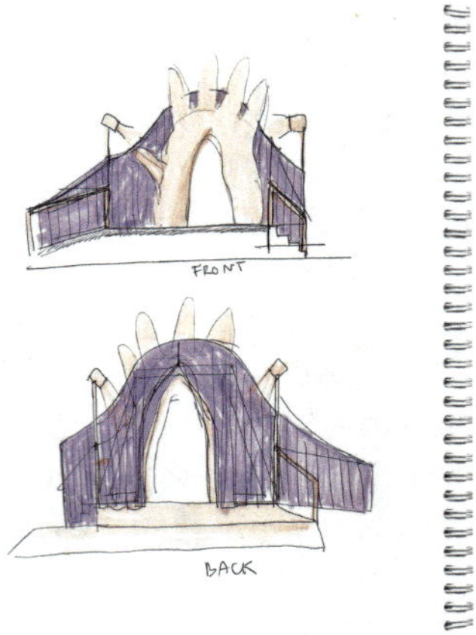


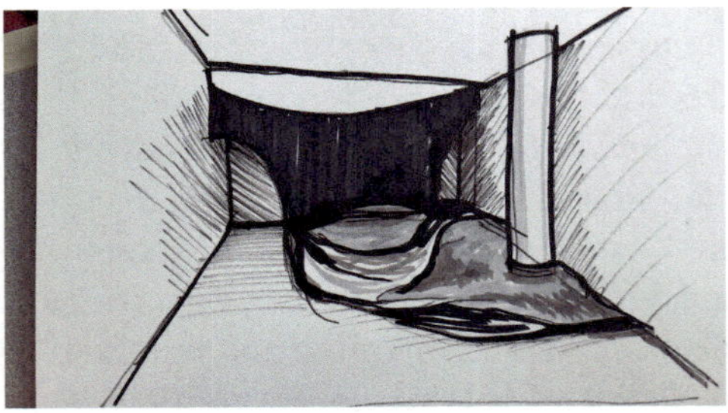

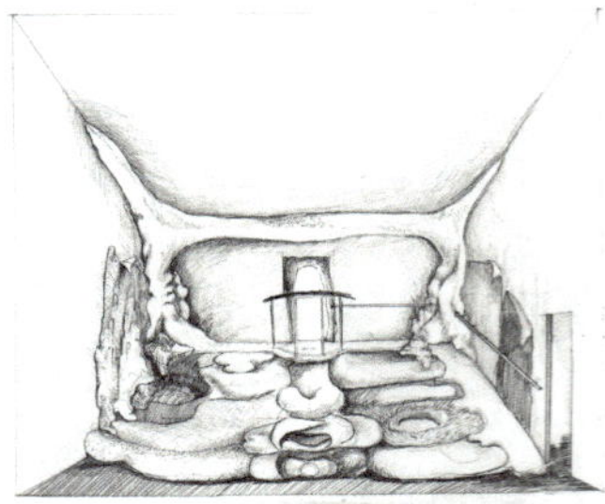

Figs. 1–4 Drawings by Rachel Garcia

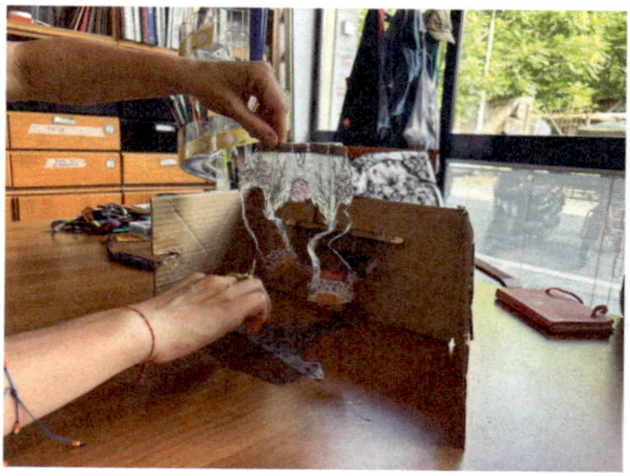

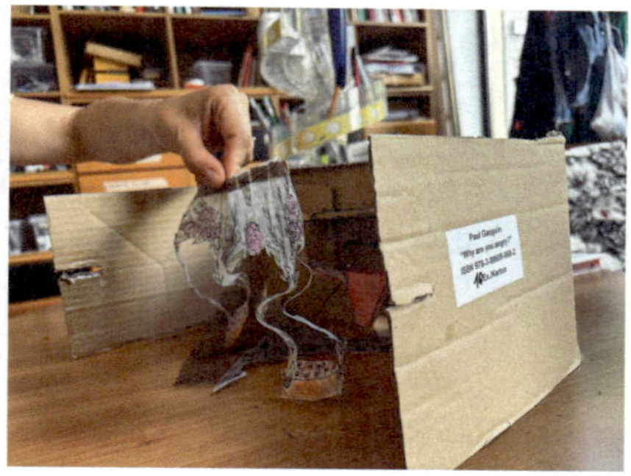

Figs. 5–6 Model by Pauline Curnier Jardin

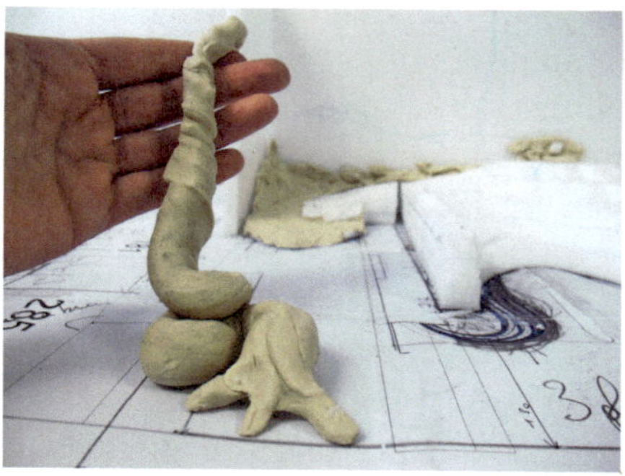

Fig. 7 Model by Rachel Garcia

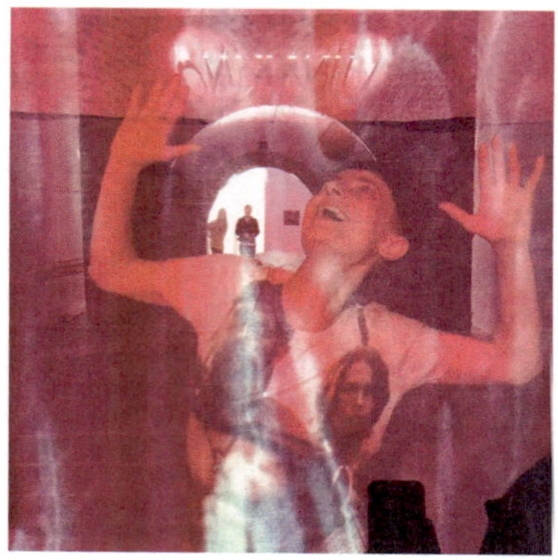

Fig. 8 Photograph from Rachel Garcia by Pauline Curnier Jardin during a set up

ambiguity of these issues. We are in a wonderful moment of feminism with the "whore revolution," which associates all the attributes of the whore with a feminist, radical, lesbian perspective. This is embodied, for example, by María Galindo or Itziar Ziga. It's something I experienced growing up in Marseille with the figure of the *cagole* and which we also see in Italy as a behavioral premise for many women.

MR The scales are often monumental in your installations; they play with the spectacular. How do you handle this dimension so as not to create an overwhelming effect?

PCJ The spectacular is also something expected in the art world, and creating *Colosseum* was a way of responding to the National Gallery Prize I won in 2019, which offered me an exhibition in such a large space within the Hamburger Bahnhof that I had to respond on that scale. The Roman Colosseum is THE spectacle, that of death, with a round architecture without a roof or angles that stages pure and bestial violence, the survival of the fittest. I am not competing with the object itself, the Roman Colosseum, but I do embrace an irony I have about myself, about my means, which are a form of mockery—and I believe that the link with the "mock-up," the action of making a model, is one of the elements that motivates my work. It's a way of poking fun at one's fears, not necessarily in a mean or aggressive way. Faced with these enormous symbols of power, one can only take up the same weapons and turn things upside down, like David and Goliath, or in the spirit of the carnival.

MR Your *Colosseum* is truly impressive in size, but it's also ridiculous and funny, since it's a big, soft cake. When you go inside, the feeling changes as you find yourself immersed in a film that plunges you into violence with scenes shot during ceremonies honoring the martyrdom of Saint Agatha, whose breasts were cut off, and others during the Cologne Carnival and the slaughter of a sow in central Italy.

PCJ The scenography was indeed intended to make people laugh, but after entering the satin setting, a sort of giant candy box, the film begins and it is a distressing experience because it addresses the structural violence of erotic relationships, human relationships, and more broadly, the relationship of European societies to their own bodies and the bodies of others. I grew up in Arles, so the arena is also a place for bullfighting, a place where animals are killed. Furthermore, gladiatorial combat in Ancient Rome was a homoerotic spectacle of great significance. It's the most vicious and violent film I've made. It was done just after I had my second child, after that moment when the body turns inside out, when you step outside yourself as when you're angry. It's like the story of the glove in *Grotta Profunda* that you put on and take off: turned inside out, it retains the trace of the act and the skin in their absence. It's also linked to my caving experiences, those anxious memories of entering the bowels of the mountain with my own body. I arrived in Rome via the Villa Medici, in the context of representing France at a time when I also won the German national prize, a country I needed to leave at the time, so I sought to slip into the bowels of Rome and escape these national patterns by meeting sex workers that I wanted to collaborate with, which led to the creation of the Feel Good Cooperative.

MR You also told me earlier that reading Paul B. Preciado had been important in that regard.

PCJ Yes, of course, and in particular his 2011 book based on his thesis *Pornotopie: Playboy et l'invention de la sexualité multimédia*. However, it wasn't a premeditated choice to work with trans sex workers: the Feel Good Cooperative project is more the result of my experiences in Rome. Stalker, an artistic and urban collective that has been organizing explorations of the city of Rome since the 1990s that cross both physical and social barriers, was important because it was through one of the group's founders, Lorenzo Romito, that I met Serena Olcuire. She is an architect, urban planner, and transfeminist researcher, and she wrote her thesis on the geography of sex work in Rome, analyzing it not only from the perspective of institutional policies but also from the bodies and narratives of the individuals involved. It was with her and Alexandra Lopez, a sex worker, photographer, and now artist, that we founded the Feel Good Cooperative.

MR Do you also work collectively on scenography within the Feel Good Cooperative?

PCJ Absolutely. During the engraving workshop we did for *The Death of the Pope*, a video installation and series of engravings inspired by our visit to St. Peter's Basilica when Pope Benedict XVI's body was lying in state, we had the idea of organizing our own art school for our projects. For the exhibition in early 2024 at MACRO in Rome, the five of us built a balcony during a workshop with a blacksmith. We designed the balcony as a minimalist space measuring one square meter, serving as a direct transition between the bedroom and the street, and thus as a symbolic place of sex work. We watched the Chanel commercial with Prokofiev's music, where we see lots of women, each more beautiful than the next, shouting "egoist" from balconies until a man's hand appears and puts a bottle of perfume in their place. We laughed a lot, and we also read Jean Genet's *The Balcony*, even though it wasn't an easy process, watched Jean Genet's film *Un Chant d'Amour*, and shared Serena Olcuire's research on the balcony from an architectural and urban planning perspective.

MR When you were invited to exhibit at the Centraal Museum in Utrecht in 2023, you created an environment in a room using the museum's collection, which you curated and staged. Can you tell us how that went?

PCJ My main contribution was the installation of my series *Peaux de Dame*. I began the piece in 2018 at the Villa Santo Sospir in Saint-Jean-Cap Ferrat, invited by Eric Mangion, and envisioned it as a reaction to the homoerotic cult of Jean Cocteau, who painted and drew on the walls. My approach was to spread *Peaux de Dame* on the beds, seats, and carpets to take possession of these spaces. Since then, I have installed *Peaux de Dame* in very different environments; sometimes they are on the walls, sometimes associated with installations, and sometimes spread out on the floor, as in the CRAC in Sète, where they were even crushed on the asphalt.

MR Do they always play a disruptive role in spaces?

PCJ Yes, and in Utrecht it was wonderful because I was able to connect them directly with the works in the collection, creating scenarios in the exhibition space inspired by the idea of a cabinet of curiosities (Wunderkammer). The curator checked in regularly, but she gave me a great deal of freedom, even when I decided to hang a painting by Max Ernst on a pole dance pole. I was also able to work on the floor, which is covered with a painted wooden surface, removing parts of it to incorporate the pole.

MR You opened other avenues of interpretation for the collections while working on elements such as the floor, which you temporarily modified, but with strong undertones of infiltration. Your scenography became an installation.

PCJ It was a wonderful collaboration. I was also able to use a chair by Rietveld and cover it with a Peau de Dame fabric.

MR And you covered it to the point that it was barely recognizable.

PCJ They let me bring their collection to life in a different way. I painted the walls blue to create a swimming pool atmosphere, and, as an echo of the painting of Saint Sebastian that was on display, I included a monitor showing an excerpt from my film *Qu'un sang impur*, in which the character Giorgetto has the impression that old women are bleeding again, that their menstruation has resumed, in a delirium directly inspired by this religious myth.

*Conversation continued at the Freestanding Joys Symposium in Porto, as part of the Pauline Curnier Jardin exhibition at Galeria Municipal do Porto, November 2024*

MR Rachel Garcia, you trained in dance and practiced this art form for many years. Is this important for your work in exhibition and theater design?

RG Yes, I have always tried to link dance with scenography and, more broadly, with architecture. I started out as a cabaret dancer, and I created costumes, objects, and spaces for my dancer friends. It was through one of these friends that I met Pauline and discovered her creative world, which immediately intrigued and captivated me. I first suggested that we do a performance together with a set made entirely of cakes. It never happened, but it was a way for our worlds to intersect.

PCJ I remember that conversation very well, which took place in my kitchen thirteen years ago, with you shaping the cakes and me imagining the sounds. We continued to work this way, starting by developing imaginary spaces with our hands that we could enter together. Six months later, I was invited to create a piece for the Le Printemps de Septembre Festival in Toulouse, where Rachel lives, and that was the beginning of this long collaboration (*Grotta Profunda*). From the very start, we realized we had many common influences, such as Forced Entertainment, Grand Magasin, and Royal Deluxe, which combine circus, street theater, and dance, and are also companies that toured the towns where we grew up.

RG For *Grotta Profunda*, I first worked on the costumes, and then on the installation *Grotta Profunda Approfundita* for the Venice Biennale, which is an extension of the film. That's what we do most often now: Pauline makes a film and together we create a space that allows the audience to be part of the film. We create objects and spaces that are related to our body sizes, while allowing ourselves to develop monumental spaces, the size of giants, an unspoken dream of transgressing my female gendered upbringing. *Grotta Profunda* is made from materials used for playground floors, which we were very familiar with at the time because we were mothers who brought our children to these places and waited while they played. We discovered these lumpy, conglomerated materials that stimulated the audience's senses, sparking curiosity and making them want to touch them, like Hansel and Gretel's cakes, a further shared point of reference.

PCJ Yes, because this act of touching is also dangerous, a little scary at times, and we embrace its pornographic aspect, departing from the issues of morality that go with candy and cakes. They give immediate pleasure, and the films always play with heavy issues while having beautiful colors.

RG Most of the time, the installation is also a trap for the audience: when you enter, it's appealing, but then you are confronted with the film, which conveys other, more painful realities.

MR In *Grotta Profunda Approfundita*, one must enter a space in order to see; the gaze is activated once inside, from within a large internal body.

RG You enter a giant organ, which resembles a placenta. We shaped the material to evoke veins and a cord, and we also worked on the colors like painters.

MR How do you work on these projects remotely from different places when they are so closely linked to the interplay of materials and have a performative dimension?

RG We share drawings, plans, and models via video calls, and even life-size materials. Most of the time, we work intensely over short periods of time. For example, the giant hand which is the entrance for *Grotta Profunda Approfondita* was sketched out in an afternoon in

Berlin when I was visiting friends and Pauline was living there. Then, of course, the actual implementation takes much longer.

MR The installations create an unsettling porosity with the films, but never use the film's sets or costumes.

PCJ For me, it's a different kind of work. It has nothing to do with presenting the film and taking over the space, but rather it is an attempt to create the best cinema for this film. It's like with mainstream movies or an amusement park, where you exaggerate the sensational aspect. Although we don't use standard movie sets, we often buy and recycle old pieces of scenery.

MR With your designs, you can often see the back of the set, the seams remain visible, fabrics and materials spill out, in a two-fold interplay that is initially a form of illusion when you enter the space, playing with lighting and color effects, then gradually deconstructs as you get closer.

RG It's true that most of the time I don't achieve perfection [laughs]: I'm a self-taught costume designer and I don't do it by the book. We blurred a lot of images in *Grotta Profunda* because the costumes were made in a hurry, and that contributed to the film's aesthetic. For *Blutbad Parade*, Pauline asked me to create a sculpture of a woman with generous curves, as was the case in certain periods of art history, and I started by putting layers of foam on my own body. In the end, I sculpted it and added a latex skin that I painted in the Fauvist style. Ultimately, it was a far cry from the glamorous woman Pauline had asked me to create. It had become a rather frightening woman that couldn't be moved around much, which gave us the idea of also using it as a landscape.

PCJ This idea of the female body as a landscape that becomes a point for observation stems from my obsession with Marcel Duchamp's *Étant donnés assemblage*, which is a veritable stage set. From a doorway, we see a horrific scene: a young naked woman with her legs spread, as if she were being raped. It's like a peep show, and this work often comes up in our conversations.

RG I truly enjoy giving accidental events a chance to bring deeper meanings to what we make.

# Notes

1 Biennial curated by Alexia Fabre. From September 21, 2024 – January 5, 2025.
2 An interview with Grace Ndiritu can be found in this volume, pp. 262–271.
3 The Paris Opera presented *The Dante Project* in May 2023.
4 Pamela Bianchi, *The Origins of Exhibition Space (1450–1750)* (Amsterdam: Amsterdam University Press, 2023).
5 Ibid., pp. 80–83.
6 Michel Foucault, "Of Other Spaces: Utopias and Heterotopias," *Architecture / Mouvement / Continuité* (March 1984), trans. Jay Miskowiec.
7 See Christian Ruby's research on this subject in his numerous publications, including *L'Archipel des spectateurs* [The Archipelago of Spectators] (Besançon: Éditions Nessy, 2012).
8 See Gaillard's conversation with Rebecca Lamarche-Vadel in *Humpty \ Dumpty*, exh. cat. Palais de Tokyo and Lafayette Anticipations (Paris, 2023), pp. 14–15.
9 Unfortunately, the management of the Centre Pompidou has decided to move the reconstitution of Brancusi's studio from the space that had been specifically designed to house it on the museum's plaza area. It should be returned to the collection spaces when the museum reopens.
10 Michael Brawne, *The New Museum: Architecture and Display* (New York: Praeger, 1965).
11 Eleanor Clayton, "The Whole Question of Plinths in Barbara Hepworth's 1968 Tate Retrospective," *Tate Papers*, no. 25, 2016. https://www.tate.org.uk/research/tate-papers/25/whole-question-of-plinths.
12 Quoted by Eleanor Clayton, ibid.
13 Translator's note: in English in the original.
14 D. H. Lawrence, *Lady Chatterley's Lover* [1928] (London: Penguin Books, 1960), p. 53.
15 Conference organized by the Paris-Malaquais School of Architecture, the Beaux-Arts de Paris and the Pavillon Bosio in Monaco as part of the "L'Entour" research program, January 10, 2024.
16 Emma Barker (ed.), *Contemporary Cultures of Display* (New Haven and London: Yale University Press, 1999), p. 14.
17 See Mathilde Roman, *Habiter l'exposition. L'artiste et la scénographie* (Paris: Manuella Éditions, 2020).
18 Excerpt from a press release for the *Machine Art* exhibition at MoMA, New York, March 5 to April 29, 1934. Press releases for the exhibition are available online at https://www.moma.org/calendar/exhibitions/1784.
19 Quoted by Sabine Folie in *unExhibit*, exh. cat. Generali Foundation (Vienna: Verlag für moderne Kunst, 2011), p. 169, based on a quotation from David Robbins (*The Independent Group: Postwar Britain and the Aesthetics of Plenty* [Cambridge, MA and London: The MIT Press, 1990], p. 161).
20 Hans Ulrich Obrist, *Interviews*, vol. 2 (Milan: Charta, 2003), interview with Richard Hamilton, p. 116.
21 Elena Crippa, "Designing Exhibitions, Exhibiting Participation," in *Exhibition, Design, Participation, 'an Exhibit' 1957 and Related Projects* (London: Afterall Books, Exhibition Histories, 2016), pp. 12–75.

22 Pamphlet for *an Exhibit*, ICA Gallery London, 1957, reproduced in ibid., pp. 114–118.
23 Reproduced in ibid., p. 134.
24 *Art Press*, no. 172, September 1992, pp. 44–46.
25 Céline Condorelli and Gavin Wade, with James Langdon, *Support Structures* (London: Sternberg Press, 2009).
26 Ibid., p. 20.
27 Ibid., p. 9: "Exhibitions of anything imaginable are made while the apparatus of exhibition-making remains largely unchallenged."
28 Magdalena Droste, "Lilly Reich: Her Career as an Artist," in *Lilly Reich: Designer and Architect*, exh. cat. The Museum of Modern Art (New York, 1996), p. 52.
29 Esther Da Costa Meyer, "Cruel Metonymies: Lilly Reich's Designs for the 1937 World's Fair," *New German Critique*, no. 76, winter 1999, special issue on Weimar Visual Culture, p. 170.
30 Ibid.
31 Matilda McQuaid, "Lilly Reich and the Art of Exhibition Design," in *Lilly Reich: Designer and Architect*, (see note 28), p. 25
32 Thus, the catalogue *Chefs-d'oeuvre? Architectures de musées, 1937–2014*, published by the Centre Pompidou-Metz in 2010, does not mention it in the presentation sheet for the German Pavilion in Barcelona (p. 15).
33 To learn more, see Laura Martínez de Guerenú, "The Sequence of Mies van der Rohe in Barcelona: The German Pavilion as Part of a much Larger Industrial Presence," *DOCoMoMo Journal*, https://docomomojournal.com/index.php/journal/article/view/285/194.
34 Cited in Federico Bucci and Augusto Rossari (eds.), *I musei e gli allestimenti di Franco Albini* (Milan: Electa, 2005), p. 6.
35 Edoardo Persico died prematurely in 1936, and the project was completed without him.
36 Peter Meyer, editor of *Das Werk*, quoted by Ross Jenner, "Ambient Atmospheres: Exhibiting the Immaterial in Works by Italian Rationalists Edoardo Persico and Franco Albini," *Interstices. Journal of Architecture and Related Arts*, no. 14, 2013, p. 16.
37 Cf. Edoardo Persico, Marcello Nizzoli and Lucio Fontana, Sala delle Medaglie d'Oro, Palazzo dell'Arte, Milan, 1934.
38 Jenner, "Ambient Atmospheres" (see note 36), referencing Raffaello Giolli, "VI Triennale di Milano: 'La Sala della Vittoria'," *Casabella*, nos. 102–103, June–July 1936, pp. 14–21.
39 Renato Luiz Sobral Anelli, "Modern Taste: Designing Exhibits and Exhibiting Design" in *Ways of Showing: The Exhibition Making of Lina Bo Bardi*, exh. cat. Museu da Casa Brasileira (São Paulo, 2014), p. 69.
40 Franca Helg, "Il problema degli allestimenti" in *Parliamo un po' di esposizioni. Le esperienze di Franco Albini, del gruppo BBPR e di Carlo Scarpa*, Barbara Pastor and Sandro Polci (eds.), (Venice: Università internazionale dell'arte, 1985), cited in Franco Albini. *La sostanza della forma*, exh. cat. Institut culturel de Paris (Paris, 2016), p. 41
41 Patricia Falguières, foreword in Philippe Duboÿ, *Carlo Scarpa. L'art d'exposer* (Paris: La Maison rouge–Fondation Antoine-de-Galbert / JRP Ringier, 2014), p. 9.
42 "In both cases, there is a desire, as with Scarpa, to bring the paintings closer to the object and make them part of the real world. When it was deemed appropriate (in the absence of convincing evidence to the contrary), they removed the frames made posthumously. Physically, this has lightened the paintings and restored their original status as paintings, rather than objects used to furnish wealthy apartments. In this sense, they have aligned the painting with the studio, but also with the museum, rather than with the private collection." – Penelope Curtis, originally published in the catalogue accompanying the exhibition *Art on Display 1949–69*, Museu Calouste Gulbenkian, Lisbon, 2019.

43 Caterina Marcenaro, "Le concept de musée et la réorganisation du Palazzo Bianco à Gênes," *Museum*, vol. 7, 1954, pp. 250–258.
44 Orietta Lanzarini, *The Living Museums: Franco Albini–BBPR–Lina Bo Bardi–Carlo Scarpa* (Rome: Nero, 2020).
45 When the Palazzo Bianco opened, she presented masterpieces that she believed she had discovered in the collection, such as Rubens and Van Eyck paintings, which turned out to merely be old copies.
46 Lanzarini, *The Living Museums* (see note 44).
47 However, these chairs are worn and fragile and need to be restored.
48 The Palazzo Bianco is not very crowded, and visitors therefore have the opportunity to discover this work in a precious contemplative isolation.
49 Kay Bea Jones, *Suspending Modernity: The Architecture of Franco Albini* (Farnham: Ashgate, 2014).
50 Quoted in Federico Bucci and Augusto Rossari (eds.), *I musei e gli allestimenti di Franco Albini*, illustrated ed. (Milan, Mondadori-Electa, 2016), pp. 24–25.
51 Edoardo Persico (attributed to), "Archi. Franco Albini, un arredamento a Milano," in *Casabella*, no. 54, June 1932. Quoted in Carlo Olmo, Giampiero Bosoni, and Marco Albini, *Franco Albini: La sostanza della forma*, exh. cat. Italian Cultural Institute, Paris, 2016, p. 31.
52 Part of the collections are exhibited in the church adjoining the building and the reserves can be visited by appointment.
53 As quoted by Lanzarini, *The Living Museums* (see note 44), p. 35.
54 A book catalogues and presents the works of Carlo Scarpa in Venice in the form of a very useful visitor's guide: Luciano Pollifrone (ed.), *Carlo Scarpa Venice* (Venice: Lineadacqua, 2023).
55 Ibid., p. 108. "Cencio di nonna," or calico, is a lightweight cotton fabric woven in plain weave.
56 Duboÿ, *Carlo Scarpa* (see note 41), p. 108.
57 Giacomo Ontano, "Dialogue between Art and Architecture, Paul Klee and Carlo Scarpa," 2012, *Zwitschermaschine. Journal on Paul Klee / Zeitschrift für Internationale Klee-Studien*, https://doi.org/10.5281/zenodo.6406531.
58 Giorgio Vigni, "New installation of the Galleria Nazionale della Sicilia, Palermo," in *Museum*, vol. X, 1956, p. 202, quoted by Duboÿ, *Carlo Scarpa* (see note 41), p. 67.
59 The project archives are now available online at: https://archiviocarloscarpa.it/il-progetto/.
60 A beautiful, voluminous book published by the Instituto Bardi allows readers to discover them: *Lina Bo Bardi* (São Paulo: Romana Guerra Editora, 2018).
61 "The captions are descriptive in order to eliminate any exaltation and allow for critical rigor." Lina Bo Bardi, "Art Museum 7 de Abril Street, São Paulo," 1947, reprinted in Marcelo Carvalho Ferraz (ed.), *Lina Bo Bardi* (São Paulo: Instituto Bardi / Romano Guerra Editora, 1993).
62 Guilherme Giufrida, "Bahia in Ibirapuera," in *Lina Bo Bardi: Habitat*, José Esparza Chong-Cuy et al. (eds.), (London: Prestel Publishing, 2020), p. 214.
63 Lina Bo Bardi, "Explicações sobre o Museu de Arte," O Estado de São Paulo, April 5, 1970, in *Concreto e cristal*, Adriano Pedrosa and Luiza Proença (eds.), (São Paulo: Cobogó/MASP, 2016), p. 136. Quoted by Adriano Pedrosa, "The Hand (and the Names) on the Brazilian People," in *Lina Bo Bardi: Habitat* (see note 62), p. 159.
64 Lina Bo Bardi and Aldo van Eyck, *Lina Bo Bardi: São Paulo Art Museum* (Lisbon: Editorial Blau, 1997).
65 I stayed in São Paulo in November 2023 and visited MASP several times to conduct these audience studies.
66 Bo Bardi, "Art Museum, 7 de Abril Street, São Paulo" (see note 61), p. 46.
67 "Lina Bo Bardi and MAM in the Park," Paulo Mendes de Almeida library, MAM São Paulo, September 5, 2023–January 28, 2024.

68 Barker, *Contemporary Cultures of Display* (see note 16).
69 Gae Aulenti, INA archives: https://fresques.ina.fr/ellescentrepompidou/fichemedia/ArtFem00167/gae-aulenti-architecte-dumusee-d-orsay.html.
70 Giovanni Agosti, *Gae Aulenti: Worlds* (Milan: Electa, 2024), p. 50.
71 See my dialogue with Thomas Demand published in: Roman, *Habiter l'exposition. L'artiste et la scénographie* (see note 17).
72 Danh Vo, https://www.pinaultcollection.com/fr/boursedecommerce/je-ne-travaille-jamaisen-decidant-de-ce-quedevrait-etre-le-resultatdanh-vo-0.
73 Fernand Deligny (1913–1996) was a French special education teacher who created a supportive environment for nonspeaking autistic children in the Cévennes region. He studied and filmed their wander lines, which result from the repetitive movements of their gestures and their movements.
74 Guillaume Leblon, quoted in the museum label for the work *The Death of Mary*.
75 Discussion with the artist, July 2024.
76 Transcript of the speech given by Franz West at the opening of the exhibition dedicated to him at Villa Arson, Nice, in 1995; quoted by Robert Fleck in *Franz West*, exh. cat. Villa Arson (Nice: Villa Arson / Le Collège / FRAC Champagne-Ardenne, 1997), p. 8.
77 I later learned that there was a museum label for the benches in the room, but I didn't spot it at the time.
78 Accompanying document produced by the Musée des Beaux-Arts in Rennes on the occasion of the first installation of the sculptures.
79 Conversation with the artist, 2023.
80 Franz West, conversation with Denys Zacharopoulos at the Palais du Tau in Reims, in *Franz West* (see note 76), p. 34.
81 See Robert Fleck's account in *Franz West* (London: Phaidon, 1999), p. 59.
82 Originally designed for the national museum of modern art when it was located in the former Palais de Tokyo; more information about the creative research by Laëtitia Badaut Haussmann can be found below.
83 Martin Szekely, *S'asseoir au Louvre*, introduction by Jean-Luc Martinez, photographs by Fabrice Gousset (Paris: B42 / MSZ in partnership with the Louvre, 2021).
84 Ibid.
85 This was the case, for example, in his installation for the exhibition *Portraits d'intérieurs* at the Nouveau Musée National de Monaco (2014, curated by Celia Bernasconi). A combination of pieces from the collection, painted installations, and design elements such as openings and curtains blended seamlessly into the Villa Sauber, where the exhibition was held. Celia Bernasconi recounts, "On the day of its installation, Marc Camille Chaimowicz noted with satisfaction that this curtain seemed to have always been there." *Portraits d'intérieurs* (Monaco: Mousse Publishing / NMNM, 2014), p. 34.
86 *Le sentiment, la pensée, l'intuition*, Musée d'Art contemporain de la Haute-Vienne, Château de Rochechouart, curated by Sébastien Faucon, 2019.
87 Text taken from the media kit published for the opening of LUMA, 2021.
88 Andreas Müller and Aaron Werbick et al. (eds.), *Re-Reading the Manual of Traveling Exhibitions*, UNESCO, 1953, (Leipzig: Spector Books, 2018).
89 Ibid., p. 19.
90 Ibid., p. 96.
91 Jermayne MacAgy, "On Installation," *California Palace of the Legion of Honor Bulletin*, vol. 11, nos. 1 and 2 (May–June 1953). Quoted in *Jermayne MacAgy: A Life Illustrated by an Exhibition* (Houston, TX: University of St. Thomas, 1968), p. 21.
92 Ibid.
93 Brooklyn Museum, 1948.

**94** *Displayer: Exhibition Design and Curatorial Practice*, Doreen Mende (ed.), HfG Karlsruhe, no. 3, 2009, p. 19.
**95** Helen Molesworth, "How to Install Art as a Feminist?" in Cornelia Butler and Alexandra Schwartz (eds.), *Women Artists at the Museum of Modern Art* (New York: MoMA, 2010), p. 507: "If we think according to the logic of the rhizome, we can see that history is filled with gaps and fissures and moments of connection and synchronicity, and that while there is loss and neglect (as there is regarding the history of art made by women), there are also alliances formed despite geographical distance and temporal incommensurability."
**96** Ibid., p. 499.
**97** *Faire, nager et s'envoler*, La Gaya Scienza, Nice, November 2023–March 2025.
**98** CAC Brétigny, from September 30 – December 9, 2017.
**99** *Valentine Schlegel: je dors, je travaille* by Hélène Bertin, Future and CAC Brétigny, 2017.
**100** Dominique Gonzalez-Foerster, *Alienarium 5* (London: Serpentine Galleries / Cologne, Buchhandlung Walther König, 2024), pp. 60–61.
**101** See also my dialogue with Dominique Gonzalez-Foerster published in *Habiter l'exposition. L'artiste et la scénographie* (see note 17).
**102** "I would say that our first concern, with Cecilia, was to develop a visitor flow. And I think it's a success. There is clarity in the route and the flow of visitors. So that was our first task. The historical sections came a little later, after the summer, when the curatorial approach became clearer," Andrea Trimarchi in "A look at the exhibition design of the Venice Art Biennale," *STIRworld*, July 5, 2022, https://www.stirworld.com/see-features-stirringdreams-a-look-at-the-exhibition-design-of-thevenice-art-biennale.
**103** *Contested Infrastructures: Art Criticism and Institutionalisation of Art*, Krakow, November 13–17, 2023.
**104** Philippe Parreno, *Voices*, Leeum Museum of Art, Seoul, February 28–July 7, 2024.
**105** Philippe Parreno is referring to Herbert Bayer's exhibition design for *Road to Victory*, Museum of Modern Art, New York, 1942.
**106** *Dancing around the Bride: Cage, Cunningham, Johns, Rauschenberg, and Duchamp*, Philadelphia Museum of Art, October 30, 2012 – January 21, 2013.
**107** Alain Robbe-Grillet, *The Erasers*, trans. Richard Howard (New York: Grove Press, 1968).
**108** *Acqua alta* refers to a tidal peak in the Venice lagoon that causes flooding in the lower parts of the city, including St. Mark's Square, where the Olivetti store is located.
**109** Katinka Bock, *Der Sonnenstich*, Fondation Pernod Ricard, Paris, February 14 – April 29, 2023.
**110** See Mélanie Bühler, "Introduction: Color Critique," in *The Art of Critique* (Milan: Lenz Press / Haarlem: Frans Hals Museum, 2022), pp. 64–71.
**111** Katinka Bock, *Silver*, CRAC Occitanie, Sète, July 1, 2023 – January 7, 2024.
**112** The Copan is an iconic building in São Paulo, built by Oscar Niemeyer between 1957 and 1966, standing 140 meters tall.
**113** Katinka Bock, *Palomar*, Jocelyn Wolff Gallery, Romainville, September 12 – October 28, 2023.
**114** Tatiana Trouvé, *Le grand atlas de la désorientation*, Centre Pompidou, Paris, 8 June – 22 August 2022.
**115** See: https://hyperallergic.com/shaking-up-the-ethnographic-museum/.
**116** *Infinite Garden: From Giverny to Amazonia*, Centre Pompidou-Metz, 18 March – 28 August 2017.
**117** Bo Bardi and van Eyck, *Lina Bo Bardi: São Paulo Art Museum* (see note 64).

**118** Ulla von Brandenburg, *Le milieu est bleu* [The Milieu is Blue], Palais de Tokyo, Paris, 21 February 2020 – 3 January 2021.
**119** *La société des spectacles* [The Society of Spectacles], Fondation Pernod Ricard, Paris, 13 February – 20 April 2024.
**120** Meris Angioletti and Ulla von Brandenburg, XNL Piacenza, 24 November 2022 – 18 June 2023.
**121** Gilles Deleuze, *Le Pli. Leibniz et le Baroque* (Paris: Éditions de Minuit, 1988). Translated as *The Fold* [1988], trans. Tom Conley (London: Continuum, 2006).
**122** Emma Goldman (1869–1940), anarchist revolutionary and activist.
**123** *Hall of Half-Life*, curated by Tessa Giblin, Steirischer Herbst, Graz, 25 September – 18 October 2015.
**124** *Bad Timing – or How to Write History Without Objects*, Den Frie, Copenhagen, 26 August – 22 October 2023.
**125** Martin Beck, *The Exhibition and the Display*, London, Whitechapel Art Gallery, 2014.
**126** The book *Support Structures* by Céline Condorelli and Gavin Wade was co-produced with James Langdon and published by Sternberg Press in 2009 (see note 25).
**127** Article republished in Jean-Claude Lebensztejn, *Annexes de l'oeuvre d'art* (Brussels: La part de l'oeil, Théorie series, 1999), pp. 181–223.
**128** See https://eastsideprojects.org.
**129** Grace Ndiritu, *Still Life: Green Textiles*, 2005/2007.
**130** See Céline Condorelli's article on this subject in *Mousse*, no. 61, 2017, "On Display."
**131** See https://www.mixdesign.online/notes-from-the-museum-bench.
**132** Johanna Burton, Lynne Cooke, and Josiah McElheny (eds.), *Interiors* (Annandale, NY: CCS Bard, 2012).
**133** Les Jardins de la sensibilité aux conditions initiales (Les jardins de Cyrus), slated to open to the public in 2027 at the Aulnay – Val Francilia station.
**134** See *Pavillon*, no. 12 (Monaco: Pavillon Bosio, 2021).
**135** *LAB #2, Hors Catégories*, curated by Marie-Claude Beaud, Nouveau Musée national de Monaco, 26 January – 18 March 2018.
**136** *Face à Arcimboldo*, Centre Pompidou-Metz, 29 May – 29 November 2021.
**137** Translator's note: in English in the original.
**138** The essay can be accessed in full at: https://wellcomecollection.org/pages/Y2zToBAAAB4AKgRn.
**139** In 1905, the Antwerp photographer Joseph Maes created this Kaiserpanorama for the Antwerp Zoo, allowing twenty-five viewers to simultaneously watch fifty stereoscopic images.
**140** "Whipping Blood and Cream" in *Fat to Ashes: Pauline Curnier Jardin* (Berlin: Nationalgalerie – Staatliche Museen zu Berlin / Cologne: Walther König, 2022).

# Photo credits

pp. 10, 41–42, 44, 52, 59, 61, 63, 69, 71, 74, 81: © Mathilde Roman
p. 16: © Timo Ohler
p. 18: © Barbara Hepworth/Bowness
p. 25: © Richard Hamilton and Victor Pasmore. DACS – Photo: Richard Hamilton Archive
p. 31: © Digital image, The Museum of Modern Art, New York/Scala, Florence
p. 35: © Triennale Milano Archivi – Photo: Crimella
p. 39: © Fondazione Franco Albini
p. 48: © Padiglione d'Arte Contemporanea della Galleria d'Arte Moderna (PAC), Milano (1947–54)
p. 54: © Fotogramma – Paolo Monti
p. 73: Archive Instituto Lina Bo e P.M. Bardi/Casa de Vidro
p. 76: Archive Instituto Lina Bo e P.M. Bardi/Casa de Vidro – Photo: Miroslav Javurek
p. 84: © Photo: Heinz Peter Knes – Tadao Ando Architect & Associates, Niney et Marca Architects, Studio Pierre-Antoine Gatier
p. 87: © Aurélien Mole
p. 90: © John Cornu
p. 95: © smarin
p. 98 © Florian Kleinefenn
p. 101: © Laëtitia Badaut Haussmann: LBH/Courtesy Galerie Allen, Ellen de Bruijne Projects, Emanuela Campoli
p. 108: © Martin Beck
p. 111: © Jean-Christophe Lett
p. 113: © ADAGP, Paris. The Estate of Jean Dupuy/Loevenbruck, Paris – Photo: Paula Court
p. 115: © Dominique Gonzalez-Foerster
p. 117: © Formafantasma
pp. 123, 125: © Andrea Rossetti
pp. 127–28: © Philippe Parreno
p. 134: © Rosa Barba/VG Bild-Kunst, Bonn, 2024 – Photo: Amélie Boulin
p. 136: © Rosa Barba
p. 141: © Rosa Barba – Photo: Agostino Osio
p. 145: © Blaise Adilon
pp. 149–50 © Katinka Bock
p. 158: © Tatiana Trouvé
p. 166: © Daniel Steegmann Mangrané
pp. 168–69: ©Andrea Rossetti
p. 178: © Ulla von Brandenburg
pp. 182, 187: © Julia Mossé
pp. 192–93: © Eastside Projects
p. 196: © Stuart Whipps
p. 199: © Bruno Lopes
pp. 205, 207: © Cabaret Voltaire and Courtesy of Zurich Art Weekend – Photo: Jessica Baumgartner
p. 210: © Markus Frietsch
pp. 212, 221, 226: © Laurent P. Berger
pp. 220, 224–25: © Berger&Berger
p. 231: © David Douard –Photo: Mathilde Roman
pp. 233, 237: © Martin Argyroglo
p. 239: © Staatliche Kunsthalle Baden-Baden – Photo: Nick Ash
p. 242: © Joep Jacobs – joepjacobs.nl
p. 245: © Diogo Passarinho Studio
p. 249: © Benoît Maire
pp. 250, 254, 257: © Arthur Pequin
pp. 263, 268: © Grace Ndiritu – Photo: We Document Art 2023
p. 270: © Grace Ndiritu – Photo: Steven Pocock, Wellcome Collection
pp. 276–77: © Pauline Curnier Jardin and Rachel Garcia

# Imprint

**Author**
Mathilde Roman

**Copy-editing**
Olivia Parkes

**Translation French into English**
Jeremy Mercer, Louise Darblay

**Project Management**
Lutz Stirl

**Graphic Design**
Neil Holt

**Typesetting**
LiteBook Prepress Services, India

**Typeface**
Arnhem

**Reproductions**
Fotimprim, Paris; DLG Graphic, Paris

**Production**
Alise Ausmane

**Paper**
Munken Print White Vol. 1.5, 90 g/m²

**Printing and Binding**
Livonia Print, Riga


Original title: *Habiter la scénographie. Quand le display fait œuvre*
First published in 2025 by Manuella Editions, Paris



Published by
Hatje Cantz Verlag GmbH
Mommsenstraße 27
10629 Berlin
Germany
contact@hatjecantz.de
www.hatjecantz.com
A Ganske Publishing Group Company



ISBN: 978-3-7757-6240-3
ISBN: 978-3-7757-6268-7 (ePDF)
ISBN: 978-3-7757-6267-0 (ePUB)

Printed in Latvia